Corporate Liberalism

Corporate Liberalism

THE ORIGINS OF MODERN AMERICAN POLITICAL THEORY, 1890–1920

R. Jeffrey Lustig

UNIVERSITY OF CALIFORNIA PRESS

BERKELEY · LOS ANGELES · LONDON

University of California Press
Berkeley and Los Angeles, California

University of California Press, Ltd.
London, England

© 1982 by
The Regents of the University of California
Printed in the United States of America
1 2 3 4 5 6 7 8 9

Library of Congress Cataloging in Publication Data

Lustig, R., Jeffrey.
   Corporate liberalism.

   Bibliography: p.
   Includes index.
   1. United States—Politics and government—1901–1953.
2. United States—Politics and government—19th century.
3. Political science—United States—History.   4. Corporations—United States—Political activity—History.
5. Liberalism—United States—History.   I. Title.
JK261.L87   320.5′1′0973   81-16376
ISBN 0-520-04387-1   AACR2

To my Mother and Father
and
to the memories of Gary Brotherton
and Steve Cherkoss,
rebels who died before their time

Contents

Preface

This inquiry grew out of a curiosity born during the 1960s about the character of modern political thought. That decade saw not only protests in the streets but retrenchments by leaders and officials who had presented themselves as spokesmen of liberalism. Political events since that time reveal that the retrenchments were of more than passing significance. Modern American liberalism has grown cautious about its historical identity. It has found itself incapable of preserving its basic programs, its political commitments, its popular constituencies, and even its fundamental purposes. Much of the opposition to liberal principles emerged, in fact, from liberalism itself, as New Deal reforms fell into "benign neglect" and prominent Democrats joined the Trilateral Commission in alleging an excess of democracy and calling for "some measure of apathy and uninvolvement" in the citizenry. By the late 1970s, Americans could no longer rely on mid-century verities. Voices thought to have been silenced for more than forty years had begun to beckon again from the grave; and, finding unexpected support from those who buried them, they had also begun to evoke a response.

Throughout this period formal American political thought has been in great confusion. As expressed in the writings of American political science, it has been unable to predict significant events, unable to explain them when they occurred, and unable to clarify important dynamics of political life. American political thought, once admired by the world, now barely interests its own citizens. Its most familiar assertion, in fact, has become the denial of its own existence.

The accepted explanation for this situation was usually that American thought had fallen behind the times. We kept thinking about individuals, it was said, while the world became organized; we still thought competitively while the world became interdependent; and we still sought equality while the world demanded expertise. The analysis was similar to the one offered by Auguste Comte in France a century ago. And its implicit lesson was also his: we kept thinking about rights when we should have been adjusting to functions. In this interpretation, our political troubles would cease if we could only adjust our ideas to reality.

This explanation, while intriguing, proved to be useless for understanding the actual texture and movement of American political ideas. I, like many others, therefore rejected it and its political lesson and began to look elsewhere to understand what was occurring in the American political mind. A close reading of American political literature has persuaded me that our political ideas have in fact been quite coherent, resilient, and even effective during this century. To understand that, however, it has been necessary to recognize that those ideas are quite different from what we normally assume. American liberalism had already ceased to be Lockean by the end of the last century. It turned on its axis early in this century and was transformed into what I describe in this book as corporate liberalism. Our prevailing confusion follows from the fitful, often unwilling, appreciation of this transformation. And the historic transition through which we are living emerges as neither a case of political backtracking nor of moral backsliding, but as a consistent development from the premises of the new outlook.

Parts of this new theoretical terrain have been marked and mapped by others in the past. Eric Goldman, in *Rendezvous with Destiny*, for example, identified the rise of a Reform Darwinism which supplanted the anti-statist teachings of Social Darwinism. Morton White, in *Social Thought in America*, anatomized the Progressive revolt against formalism in law, history, and economics. And C. Wright Mills, in *The Sociological Imagination*, identified the "illiberal practicality" which was creating a sophisticated conservatism. In the following chapters I analyze these and other shifts and present them as part of a larger transition; and I attempt to correct the false impressions created by failing to see them as parts of the broader terrain.

This book, then, examines the assumptions, the conclusions, and the social implications of the theoretical outlook which emerged in American politics during the early years of the twentieth century. I have attempted to describe the larger intellectual field within which narrower and more familiar political attitudes exist—attitudes like those which justify corporate power, or ethnic and gender privileges, or our approaches to nature and technology. And I have tried to deepen our understanding of the new orientation by interrogating it in light of questions historically posed within the tradition of political theory. These are questions about legitimacy, obligation, authority, and the grounds and character of political knowledge.

The effort is, admittedly, a risky one. Many Americans assume that a discussion of theory is necessarily opposed to an appreciation of reality. This assumption is often supported with phrases from pragmatism or Marxism. But William James and Karl Marx both knew that the relationship between ideas and social reality was more complex. Both saw theories as constitutive and not merely reflective of social facts. They saw ideas as elements *of* reality rather than as abstractions floating above them. While "the weapon of criticism cannot replace the criticism of weapons, and material force must be overthrown by material force," Marx observed, "theory also becomes a material force when it has gripped the masses." This is the concept of theory that informs this book. My concern is with a body of thought which has gripped the masses in America over the last eighty years, and which was less a rationalization for corporate society than an active force in its creation. It is with a theory which has also helped shape our collective self-identity. In that sense, finally, this book is intended as an exercise in our collective self-clarification.

I must explain at the beginning how the central concept of corporate liberalism will be used in this book. The term has been used by a number of other writers in different ways. In one current usage the term refers to an economy dominated by large monopolies. It identifies an arrangement of economic institutions. In a second usage, it identifies a particular arrangement of political institutions. "Corporatism" in this sense indicates a way of organizing representation, interest mediation, and social control, pioneered by some countries in Europe and Latin America over the last fifty years. "Liberal" characterizes one of its variants.

In a third usage, associated with the work of James Weinstein, the term identifies the political program of the most farsighted capitalists during the Progressive period and, following from that, a society in which the state is the conscious instrument of corporate capital, and capital itself has grown sober, prudent, and vaguely humanitarian. "Corporate liberalism" in this sense seemed an accurate description for periods like the early 1960s, when it appeared that the capitalism of a Robert McNamara had displaced that of a John D. Rockefeller, when welfare had supplanted scarcity, management had replaced repression, and the pink slip had given way to the food stamp.

"Corporate liberalism" will not be used in these ways, however, in this study. I employ the concept not to refer to particular arrangements of economic or political institutions, but to describe the larger cultural logic that informs them and the larger society; not to designate the outlook of a single sector of business, but to describe the broader intellectual orientation of which that outlook is an expression. My concern here is not with a particular ideological wind that grows and abates; it is with the altered theoretical climate in which we live.

I have come to believe, then, that we have not done as bad a job of keeping up with realities as we thought. The image of the cowboy may dance again in the minds of Americans. But it is an image with a difference. It emerges as a gesture of defiance rather than of affirmation. It arises in resistance to a world that fails to make room for many values Americans hold dear, and to a political outlook that fails to point them in directions they want to go. I do not believe that we can get beyond that image, that world, and the ill-fated contests between individuals and organizations that the image inspires, without first understanding our political outlook *as* a theory, without identifying its assumptions, and without getting beyond its characteristic approaches to the world.

I am greatly indebted to a number of people for the support, cajolery, and contributory insights without which this work could never have been completed. Foremost among these are my teachers of a decade and a half ago: John Schaar, who encouraged this inquiry from the beginning despite his dissent from some of its themes, and whose friendship has been a strength and support to me in far more than academics; and Sheldon Wolin, whose powerful writings and seminars have had a lasting effect on my understanding of politics and political theory. They were broad-ranging in their interests, sharp in criticism, and magnanimous in dispute—rare teachers who could instruct and inspire without demanding doctrinal uniformity.

I am also beholden to a more inchoate milieu, the men and women with whom I struggled in Berkeley, California, during the sixties. They were people who saw what was at stake and who took a stand. What has been forgotten by those who rewrite history is that the resulting struggles not only burned off the fog of the Cold War but also quickened intellectual life. By their actions, these people created not only a historical moment but the mental terrain in which it became possible to ask the questions that underlie this study. I hope that this inquiry measures up to their standards of courage and honesty.

I owe a debt of another kind to the members of the Political Science Department at Berkeley—denizens of a foremost outpost of what Mills called the institutions of hire learning. Without the clear, aggressive examples provided me as a student by these teachers, I never would have guessed the ties that bind the study to the substance of modern politics, or contemporary empiricism to traditional rationalism, or dominant methods of inquiry to a hostility for real politics. They taught me much about my world and kindled the long-lasting emotions essential to the writing of this book. For that I am grateful, though I would not wish the experience on others.

I must finally thank the close friends who have prodded, sustained, and humored me as what began as a sprint turned out to be a long-distance effort. They make up an extended family: David Wellman, Michael Sheehan, Doug Lummis, Frank Bardacke, Brian Murphy, Steve Lustig, Irwin Wall, Sahag and Elizabeth Avedesian, Gene Marine, Sheryl Lutjens, Evelyn Shapiro, the Professors David and Sharon Schuman of Deep Springs College, Richard and Mary Borevitz, and Brooks Penny. I have learned much from them and their examples. They have been my trust fund and my foundation. I also thank Michael Rogin, Charles Sellers, and William Kornhauser for reading and commenting on an earlier version of the manuscript, and especially Hanna Pitkin for her close, sensitive comments on the entirety. Eric Mills was much more than a lightning typist; I am in his debt. And one could not have wished for a more able, sensitive, and helpful editor than I have happily found in Gene Tanke.

Since the bulk of this inquiry was written a few years ago, important works on some of its themes have appeared that were unavailable to me at the time of writing. Foremost among these I would consider Wendell Berry's *The Unsettling of America*, Charles Lindblom's *Politics and Markets*, Lawrence Goodwyn's comprehensive and compassionate *Democratic Promise*, and Alan Wolfe's *Limits of Legitimacy*. The lack of reference to these books in no way indicates a lack of respect for them or their conclusions.

R. J. L.
Berkeley, California
December, 1980

1

The New Liberalism

The public interest state is the end point of a great movement of reform. But somehow the result is different from what the reformers wanted.

—CHARLES REICH, "The New Property"

Modern American political thought is usually described in terms that have acquired ritual familiarity. It is called *pragmatic* because of its flexibility and fidelity to empirical facts. It is described as *pluralistic* because it sees the main lines of social energy flowing from a variety of groups rather than from a monolithic state or polarized classes. And it is said to be *action-oriented* because of its eagerness to use the state to solve a wide range of social problems. Like many of our current political rituals, however, these terms have ceased to reassure us. Not only do they have little to do with the events we see and the speech we hear; they fail to fit together into any coherent whole.

Flexibility is a virtue only in pursuit of specific goals, but the goals of American politics are rarely defined. A commitment to the richness of group life assumes different values than those entailed in the extension of federal programs. And pragmatic adjustment to our empirically dominant "group," the corporation, introduces neither flexibility nor pluralism into our social life. We can, of course, celebrate this lack of fit and scorn ideological "fixed systems." Most Americans believe anyway that what they see is what they get. Still, an unease persists.

The argument of this book is that our political thought is more problematic than our familiar terms suggest. When the major themes of this thought are examined closely, when its assumptions are identified and traced to their theoretical conclusions, they actually limn a new political theory, one that derives from classical liberalism but that has wound up running athwart some traditional liberal commitments.

The new outlook emerged at the beginning of this century in response to the changed character and altered dynamics of American society. It attempts to justify a range of power and inequality unknown to the older liberalism. It attempts to make sense out of a world where order is administered by large organizations rather than achieved by individual consent. It has ended up, accordingly, reversing the fundamental logic of classical liberalism. Frederick Winslow Taylor caught the point early when he urged that "in the past the man has been first, in the future the system must be first."[1] It is an inability to see this modern theory clearly, to understand its implications easily, and to embrace it fully that explains the unease and confusion of current American political thought.

CLASSICAL LIBERALISM AND BEYOND

Classical liberalism approached public order from the standpoint of individual liberty. That "liberty" encompassed more than the rights of conscience implicit in the call for every believer to be his own priest and every man his own contractor. It embraced the individual's right to a material basis for that liberty, and the right to communicate with others through the market device of contract. The linkage between private liberty and the general good was thought to be provided by those market mechanisms that Edmund Burke labeled "the laws of nature and therefore the laws of God." By pursuing their self-interest members of the market world were assured that they would find the proper field for their talents, a fitting school for their character, and efficient means to the public good.

This outlook subordinated politics to economics in two important ways. First, it regarded political activity as an inferior way of spending one's life, compared to business. The liberty it offered was a liberty *from* public affairs. Freedom was a function of proprietorship; the public business was no one's business. Second and more significantly, this theory perceived political life in categories taken over from the world of economics. Important differences may have distinguished a Hobbes from a Locke, a Hamilton from a Jefferson, a Webster from a Calhoun. But despite these differences, all tended to regard the acquisitive market-man as the basic unit of society, the self-interest organization as the archetypal human association, and the contract as the paradigmatic social relationship. (Indeed the nation's founding document, the Declaration of Independence, resembled nothing so much as a suit for breach of contract.) From the perspective of classical liberalism, Aristotle had gotten it wrong: economics, not politics, held the key to living and living well.

The importation of ideas from economics into politics was not always as obvious as it was in Madison's interest-group theory or Oliver Wendell Holmes's appeal to the free marketplace of ideas.[2] But even when it was not, concerns that had been central to older traditions of political thought were absent from its commentaries. Concern for a public space was replaced by a concern for the marketplace. The idea of public action was eclipsed by that of economic activity. A furtive notion of the public good survived, but only as the sum or vector-resultant of privately reckoned wants. Attention to questions of power, finally, was discouraged in America by faith either in the natural workings of group competition (Madison) or the automatic effects of a wide diffusion of property (John Taylor). The classical liberal did not speak then, as a liberal, about such things as action, obligation, or power without casting them into the language of economics. And this often meant that he did not speak about them at all.

"In the beginning," wrote John Locke, "all the world was America." And in the beginning all America certainly seemed Lockean. The abundance of land and natural opportunities seemed to confirm the classical vision. But by the latter decades of the nineteenth century all that was changing. Combinations gave the lie to competition. Monopolies enclosed the frontier commons. And the factory system, raising the world of production into view behind that of exchange, confounded the expectations of equality, dispersed holdings, and the voluntary character of contracts. Railroads, cities, and national markets began to encircle individuals in an ever-tightening net.

All of this is familiar. What has received less attention is that while this was happening the corollary vision of politics became blurred and confounded. As the economy changed, political terms ceased to hang together in the familiar ways. The vocabulary men and women used for thinking about rights and duties failed to link dependably with reality. The immediate reaction to this disruption of a world was the widespread upheaval known as populism. The less observable long-range consequence was a profound crisis of political orientation.

It was during the Progressive era that the rudiments of a new outlook emerged in response to this crisis. The outlook has usually gone unnoticed because it lacked its synthetic theorist, its Hobbes or its Locke. It has escaped identification because its development was circuitous, and because different milieux mapped different parts of its terrain. The Progressive "ferment of ideas" has also therefore appeared to lack "echoes in the rest of the society."[3] But that ferment, in fact, revealed accurately the deeper theoretical reorientation occurring in the society. Between 1890 and the First World War a decisive shift took place in the point of view of American liberalism. It was accompanied by conceptual changes that were fundamental, wide-ranging, and irreversible.

Despite a familiar eclecticism, what appeared in the Progressive era was not the shattered fragments of the old outlook, nor the old outlook accompanied by a major anomaly ("the state" or "big business"). It was instead an altogether new way of seeing the political world and of orienting oneself within it. It is a failure to understand this new theory which has led to the current confusion about the meaning of "liberalism."

Jefferson and Paine are revered as liberals because they saw that government as best which governed least. But "liberals" have also been defined by their heavy reliance on the state.[4] The liberal hero for many is the pioneer, or the cowboy—the loner who feels easy about breaking away. But liberals have also seemed bent on "fitting in." Arthur Schlesinger, Jr., defined American liberalism as "ordinarily the movement on the part of the other sections of society to restrain the power of the business community." But Eric Goldman noted that the programs of Taft and Eisenhower, as well as those of Truman, were at the time called liberal.[5]

If we look to contemporary usage we find that "liberalism" has lost its older, substantive content, dropped to the lower case, and become a term for describing the reform (the liberal-izing) of something else. In the process it has acquired connotations of plasticity and affirmation in contrast to the stubborn, fixed qualities of "conservatism." And most textbooks identify the federal government as the agent of affirmation; it is the state that has "assumed responsibility for the direction and guidance of the economy."[6] Still, they are rarely explicit about what is being affirmed or about the direction of the government's guidance.

For some, imprecision itself is definitive of modern liberalism. The young Walter Lippmann wrote: "There is a great gap between the overthrow of authority and the creation of a substitute. That gap is called liberalism: a period of drift and doubt. We are in it today."[7] That was in 1914. Indicative of the fact the gap was still occupied at midcentury was

Richard Hofstadter's presentation of liberals as "the true conservatives of our times": "What appeals to me in the New Conservatism, insofar as anything does at all, is simply the old liberalism, chastened by adversity, tempered by time and modulated by a growing sense of reality." [8]

Since these words were written the retreat from clarity has become a rout. "How does a radical, a mild radical it is true," Nathan Glazer asked in his essays on student protest, "wind up a conservative, a mild conservative, but still closer to those who call themselves conservatives than to those who call themselves liberal in the early 1970s? I seem to have moved from a position in which I was slightly embarrassed to be considered a liberal (surely I was a degree further left than that) to a position where I was once again embarrassed, but from . . . a different perspective." [9] How indeed? And what did he mean? If language is practical consciousness, as Marx once suggested, then a confusion of such magnitude about so central a concept indicates deep uncertainty among the American people about who they are and what they are doing in the twentieth century.

The possibility of reducing this uncertainty and clarifying the situation has been blocked during the last few decades by the unwillingness of American political analysts to take political theory seriously. Inquiry into American political ideas is regarded as inevitably trivial, either because theory is said to have missed the boat to the new world or, alternately, because America is said to have always been overwhelmingly liberal. Long before Daniel Bell announced the end of ideology the American political voice, according to Louis Hartz and others, was already distinguished by a monotone. [10] Hartz did not deny that there had been momentous conflicts in American history, but he did deny that those conflicts had cut through the underlying political and ethical consensus. Our contests according to this view were over practical programs rather than fundamental ideas, over means rather than ends, and over status rather than class. This interpretation of American intellectual life is superficially plausible; it must, however, be subjected to brief scrutiny at the beginning of this study.

Hartz was undoubtedly correct in identifying liberalism as the primary political tradition in America. Liberal impulses fueled not only the Jacksonians but also their Whig opponents. They blunted the thrust of populist and labor protests; and in our own time they have ensnared much of the New Left. But this hardly means that there were no fundamental issues which divided Jefferson from Hamilton, Lincoln from Calhoun, or William Graham Sumner from Henry George. From within the artificial consensus of the Cold War it may have looked that way. But

Justice Stephen Field and Tom Watson thought that the issues that divided railroadmen from small farmers on the eve of the twentieth century were serious enough to justify wrath, demonstrations, and a resort to arms. And the audiences that heard them agreed. There are many rooms in the liberal mansion. Although the term "liberal" distinguishes American thought from what it is not (it is not communitarian like Plato's or class-oriented like Marx's), it does not define precisely what that thought *is*. Hartz's own failure to propose a consistent definition hardly clarified matters here.

Hartz and the others have failed to consider seriously that precisely because America lacked a feudal past, and a liberal vocabulary was the only vocabulary most of its citizens knew, liberal words were used to cover a multitude of meanings. But what sounds the same may not have always been the same. To see that, we need only compare Henry George's fraternal notion of association to Sumner's "antagonistic cooperation," or Jefferson's ideas of equality to Herbert Croly's. The different accent marks in this vocabulary, the different emphases and regional dialects, often signify real differences in theoretical orientation. But those orientations show up only when the ideas are viewed against their real historical backdrops. An appreciation of contexts, always important in studying political thought, therefore becomes essential for an appreciation of its American expressions.

It is true that American theory has rarely been self-conscious and seldom explicitly political. These deficiencies cannot be casually dismissed. But although they have deprived American political thought of the sort of insights and rigor we expect from a Locke or a Rousseau, they have not deprived it of its own internal logic and its effects on the world. Of someone who insisted on discussing authority in terms of incentives (as Frederick Winslow Taylor did) we could say that he was using the wrong tool for the job. We could also add that he would be unable to finish the job with the tool he was using. But that would not change the fact that a particular tool *was* being used—and that it would leave its characteristic mark on the materials. Modern American political theory may often be inchoate, but it possesses a characteristic form of social reasoning and presents a characteristic response to root questions of political life.

Over the last few decades the most familiar way of portraying American political ideas has been to see them as divided between a pro-business, anti-state conservatism and a pro-state, anti-business, regulatory liberalism. But the new theory that emerged during Progressivism constituted a third alternative that rapidly encompassed and eclipsed these two positions. It was pro-business *and* pro-state, dedicated to private profit *and* to regulatory reform. It was both corporate and liberal, and not only because it arose in defense of the corporation; it also tried to apply individualist modes of reasoning to the problems of an organized society. Its presence in our midst means that we are not the atheoretical empiricists we usually imagine. We are not simple "realists"; we bring something *to* reality.

We shall postpone for now our discussion of what this "something" is, for we must first get a sense of the world within which it emerged. The circumstances which the new liberalism arose to explain and the problems it attempted to solve were circumstances and problems of a particular world. And though no direct causal link existed between events and ideas, the informing logic of the new theory turned out to parallel the logic of social relations in that world. Let us turn now to the novelties the new theory was called upon to explain, the problems it sought to resolve, and the conceptual gaps it either bridged or was forced to deny.

ORGANIZATION AND INVERSION IN AMERICA

During the last hundred years American life has become organized, compacted, and collectivized. The process has not been limited simply to the world of business. What the president of the National Association of Manufacturers proclaimed in 1911 (when it was an association of *small* businessmen) has become true for every sector of social life: "We are living in an age of organization, an age when little can be accomplished except through organization, an age when organization must cope with organization, an age when organization alone can preserve your freedom and mine."[11]

The protests that have welled up during the long process of concentration have not been simple outcries against bigness, for most Americans accepted the tendency toward combination as inevitable (see Chapter Three). But they have also expected large organizations to reconcile private goals with the public interest; and here they have suffered a series of political reversals. What Americans have witnessed instead of reconciliation is an extension of private power within a socialized world; semi-independent empires continue to flourish in the heart of the general welfare society.

A few commentators have noted the reversals. Though A. A. Berle and others wrote that America "socialized property without a revolu-

tion," Theodore Lowi has observed that the blurring of private and public had come about "not by public expropriation of private domain, but
by private expropriation of public domain."[12] Charles Reich has noted
that the result of the struggles for a public interest state is different from
what the reformers wanted. And a leader of the Black Panthers noted a
decade ago: "This is a distorted form of collectivity. Everything's been
collected, but it is used for the interest of the ruling circle."[13]

The sense of reversal has emerged in American political culture
around a number of issues, and has been registered by writers and exploited by demagogues, even if largely ignored by political scientists.
Despite burgeoning productivity and increased federal activity, for example, most Americans are suffering from increased social *in*security.
Despite the bureaucratization of wide areas of life, officials display a new
penchant for ad hoc, informal procedures.[14] Instead of an extended "rule
of law," we therefore see an increase in personal, arbitrary powers.

A sense of inversion has even appeared in common turns of political phrase. There is growing reference to "private government" and
"private collectivism." Anthony Jay has written of "the inverted nationalism of corporations."[15] Perhaps the most profound inversion is the
one first spotted by Henry Adams when he observed (in 1905) that politics had been transformed into "a struggle not of men but of forces," and
that "all the new forces [were] condensed into corporations."[16] At the
very moment men announced their victory over nature, politics suddenly emerged as an expression not of human will, but of "forces."

The corporation, as Adams suggested, stands at the center of these
inversions. Its rise has possessed the characteristics of what Tocqueville
called a providential fact: it has been central and lasting, and all efforts
directed toward it, whether congenial or opposed, have contributed to
its progress.[17] Thorstein Veblen referred to the corporation as our "master institution." "What we look for in analyzing American society today,"
Peter Drucker added in his noted study of General Motors, "is an institution which sets the standard for the way of life of . . . our citizens; which
leads, molds and directs; which determines our perspective on our society; around which crystallize our social problems and to which we look
for their solution. What is essential is . . . not the multitude of facts, but
the symbol through which the facts are organized in a social pattern. . . .
And this in our society today is the large corporation." Drucker concluded
that labor unions and administrative agencies were "nothing but responses to the phenomenon of Big Business and the corporation."[18]

Andrew Hacker saw the corporation accomplishing for our age
what the church and armies did for ages past. And he feared that in our

mobile society it might eventually provide the only stable locus for citizenship. Robert Presthus noted that in addition to producing goods, the corporation also provided the incubation chamber for an emergent authoritarianism in American culture.[19] The corporation has altered conditions of blue-collar work, created those of white-collar work, and altered the fate of small businessmen. It has changed not only the structure of work and the quality of life in our cities, but our very ideas of ourselves. Garry Wills caught the meaning of this changed sense of self accurately when he observed that "The Natty Bumppo of free enterprise did not want community in the first place; that would have been bad enough. But this mere [technological] entanglement, this parody of community is even worse. . . . Our American frontiersman, grown of necessity flabby, feels he has betrayed a trust. . . . [He cannot rest] serene in the knowledge that his own self, at least, is made. The wires were in his way; he never got around to it somehow. And so . . . a second-rate self was foisted on him."[20]

None of this is to suggest that a corporate hand has been behind everything that has gone awry. A society is not a platoon where one element gives the orders and all others obey. There have been a number of sources of initiative in modern politics (such as labor, for example, in the thirties). There are a number of ills America shares with other societies (racism, for example). And there are problems (such as bureaucracy and technology) with their own problematics and partially autonomous lines of development. But the influence of the corporation is decisive because it (or its principles) determines the ways in which racism, or technology, or even the problems of size manifest themselves in America. What it has not directly initiated it has usually been able to blunt and shape (as, for example, the labor unions). The corporation has been at the cutting edge of change and has determined the direction of that change. It is the focal institution of social-ized existence in America—not because everything else can be reduced to it, but because nothing can be explained without it.

But what exactly *is* this pivotal institution? A rich older literature tried to answer that question. Dr. Charles O'Donnell, addressing the California constitutional convention of 1879, for example, defined a corporation as a "corrupt combination of individuals, formed for the purpose of escaping responsibility for their acts."[21] Supreme Court Justice Miller of the same era styled corporations as "persons wanting in the human affections." One of his contemporaries, a judge McCormick, explained that "these unnatural persons [were] wonderfully strong" because they "perennially recruit [their strength] from the highest ranks of the legal profession." Still, as his colleague Everett Wheeeler added in the famous United Fruit Company case of 1909, the corporate animal was swollen to such greatness as to be "absolutely regardless of law."[22]

In fact, few know exactly what the corporation is. That, for Martin Mayer, "is one of its beauties. A corporation comes into existence when it is needed and dies when its usefulness is done. It can own property and money . . . and buy and sell rather eminent men. It can make binding contracts, expand, contract, manufacture all goods, perform all services. It needs no sleep, takes no vacations. It can borrow and steal, and even beg. . . . If you prick it, it does not bleed; if you tickle it, it does not laugh. It can scream, however, if taxed or otherwise annoyed."[23]

This elusive creature also changes its aspect according to one's perspective. For the economist the corporation is a natural device for mobilizing capital, centralizing its control, and realizing economies of scale. For the organizational theorist it is the outer face of bureaucracy and the testing ground for new models of executive leadership. For the student of industrialism it is the necessary vehicle of large-scale, capital-intensive technologies. And for the lawyer it is an association granted authority to act as a legal person and enjoy privileges (like immortality) denied to real individuals. But none of these definitions really gets to the heart of the matter. Money, machines, and charters are not enough to build the corporation. Men are needed too. Corporations are ways of "condensing" human effort (to use Henry Adams's term). They are ways of structuring relations between *people*. That fact, so prominent for the nineteenth century, goes a long way toward explaining the effects of corporations on the rest of society.

With that in mind, we can see that the corporation is, politically speaking, an essential inversion. Since ancient times statesmen have attempted to create a polity that could harness private interests to the public welfare. The corporation succeeds, by contrast, in harnessing vast publics to a private interest. It subordinates plurality to singularity, the many to the few. It entrusts social production to private decision and imposes a uniformitarian logic on the various sectors of social life. Anthony Jay hinted at all of this when he explained what he meant by "inverted nationalism": "A corporation is, in fact, not something different from a state with interesting similarities. It *is* a state, with a few unimportant differences." Though Jay did not mention it, the most important of those differences is, of course, that the corporation is created for private and single-minded ends. When Jay therefore adds that "management can only be properly studied as a branch of government," it is clear that the scope of the corporation was not being broadened but that the scope of the government was being reduced.[24]

The principles of social organization that flow from corporate influence express this root inversion. The most obvious principle is its hierarchical division of labor. In condensing effort, the corporation paradoxically fragments it and then monopolizes initiative at the top. Decision and responsibility flow from above, obedience and loyalty from below.

Slightly less apparent is the promotion of the status of artificial personality over real persons. This ascendance is more than legal. The "fission" between ownership and control of property identified by Berle and Means in 1932 has proven to be only the most visible of a more extensive set of fissures that fragmented the older *persona* of ownership and divided functions that used to be performed by a single person. The result is that modern property truly is "corporate," not only in its ownership but also in its substance. The essence of productive wealth today resides *in* collectives, in patterns of social relations. The ascendance of the office over any particular man (bureau-cracy) follows from this. So too does the fact that an animal wanting in the human affections is also wanting, as Adam Smith warned, in other natural virtues.

The corporation is permitted levels of inefficiency denied to real persons. And it is permitted to commit what for them would be criminal activities. In 1907, in a chapter entitled "New Varieties of Sin," the Progressive sociologist E. A. Ross dilated on the "long-range, tentacular nature of modern homicide." In corporate society, he saw, "Our iniquity is wireless and we know not whose withers are wrung by it."[25] But even knowing would hardly help, for civil suits can rarely pierce the corporate veil. And corporations have avenues of escape not available to real individuals.

As an expression of the inversion of personality at its heart, finally, the corporation is a force for external ordering in human affairs. Rather than serving immediate human ends, it converts processes and actions into means for increasingly remote ends; they become means to other means. A "displacement of value" occurs, as both Weber and Presthus have noted, from intrinsic to extrinsic measures of the value of work and activity. This is a major cause of that "ascendance of the instrumental" which increasingly characterizes the modern world. It is also a cause, more deeply, of that expropriation of reason whereby modern rationality has ceased to be seen as rooted in individuals and come to be regarded as an emanation of large bureaucratic institutions.[26] The manifestation of this in social organization is that order arises from objective direction rather than from subjective choice. It begins to be *administered* into being. "Groups, federations, insurance companies, corporations, and government agencies share at least one common trait; they impose an administrative process on as much of their internal structures and . . . their environs as they can." [27]

The society informed by these principles of hierarchy, control, bureaucracy, and externality is not a stable domain. Instead it undergoes ceaseless change as, in obedience to the logics of both capitalism and technology, the corporation presses ever outward in its attempt to extend its methods of control over exogenous variables.

Since the end of World War II, corporate principles of social condensation have continued to penetrate further into the society. Neighborhoods, health services, leisure activities, sports, government agencies, and even small businessmen have seen their functions expropriated by business corporations or loose social "corporations." Our farms have become corporate. Our unions and federal agencies follow the latest fashions in corporate industrial relations. And the modern university, reversing the medieval notion of the corporation as a *universitas*, imagines itself a corporation. Its buildings are "plant"; its scholars are "personnel"; and its mission, according to its most prominent national spokesman, is knowledge "production and consumption." [28]

The transformation of business into big business has thus involved more than matters of size. The modern corporation is more than the old business firm writ large. It is also more than a neutral housing for technology. It is a new *form* for property, and its ascendance has altered our principles of social organization. In every sector of society, older institutions have been pulverized and new ones fashioned in their place. The process was diagnosed early in the century by the Austrian socialist Karl Renner, who complained that the microcosms of family and community were being broken up into their constituent atoms and "the atoms . . . then grouped again into modern units of possession." "The evolution of property does not stop," he lamented. "It is like a Chronos who devours—other people's children." [29]

CORPORATE CAPITALIST SOCIETY

The society that has been shaped by these inverted collectivisms can be most accurately known as corporate capitalist. Three things are intended by that term: first, the economic claim that the corporation is a capitalist device (corporate liberalism consisting initially of the attempt to graft individualist theories onto the body of the corporation); second, the cultural observation that ours is increasingly a *corporatist* society; and third, the political identification of our institutions as increasingly *corporativist*.

The term "corporatist" in what follows will be a general adjective indicating organizational characteristics of the hierarchical, bureaucratic, externalizing sort we have described. Corporatist phenomena will therefore be distinguished both from "individualist" ones and from phenomena influenced by characteristics of non-corporate forms of organization. (It will in this study also extend beyond organic groupings, like small communities, to more mechanistic arrangements, like business associations.) The term "corporat*ivist*," by contrast, will serve in a distinctively political capacity. It was first used in that way officially in the Italian Labor Code of 1927, and was immediately adopted in other countries to distinguish the political regime then emerging in Italy from the other two forms of modern political systems: liberalism and socialism. The complex linkage of state and society which is characteristic of our era is distinctive of corporativism; but the flow of power in that system is in the opposite direction from what has usually been reported.

More precisely, a fully corporativist order can be defined, in Philippe Schmitter's words, as a system of "interest intermediation in which the constituent units are organized into a limited number of singular, compulsory, noncompetitive, hierarchically ordered and functionally differentiated categories . . . licensed (if not created) by the state, and granted a deliberate representational monopoly . . . in exchange for certain controls on their . . . leaders and [on the] articulation of demands." (The term "corporate state" is also becoming familiar. Sometimes it appears to indicate an incipient corporativism, sometimes a government in which the influence of big business is too heavy-handed, and sometimes modern state-dominated society. I shall generally avoid this term.)[30]

The Capitalist Corporation: A Sustaining Presence

Readers of Berle and Means were concerned in 1932 because the 200 largest corporations in the United States had acquired 50 percent of its corporate wealth. Thirty years later half that many had acquired the same degree of control and they made two-thirds of reported after-tax profits. Two-thirds of the economically productive assets of the entire economy were owned by no more than 500 corporations, and control within these was even more concentrated because of the effects of interlocking directorships and common sources of funding. Berle admitted in 1964 that the situation produced a concentration of power over economics that made "the medieval feudal system look like a Sunday school party."[31]

This concentration of power confers on its chief holders the ability to invest or tie up capital, to build, relocate, or close plants and thus to issue birth certificates or death sentences to entire communities; to subsidize inventions and use them or prevent their use; to discover, exploit, or lock up raw materials; and to control loans for (and often production decisions of) other businesses. In addition to the familiar ability to buy the votes of lawmakers, draft laws, and limit the options of government, all this adds up to a decisive influence in the society.

The bulk of midcentury writings denied that the corporation at the heart of this concentration was still a capitalist institution. Presenting variants of Berle's and Means's old arguments, most writers argued that the "mature corporation" was a bureaucratic arrangement in which the lust for profits had yielded to staid stratagems for organizational maintenance.[32] In the "post-industrial" society, market pricing was said to have been replaced by administrative pricing, profits superseded by salaries, and the "owner" reduced to a coupon-clipper—his "share of stock . . . only a token representing a bundle of ill-protected rights and expectations . . . [and having] little influence on the instruments of production."[33]

This view of things conveyed an implicit argument that private power was ceasing to exert a force over social development. People still talked about private property, Thurman Arnold said in the thirties, but the things they talked about "were neither private, nor property, nor personally owned." Significant property today was organizational. It was incorporeal, intangible, and, because its value consisted largely of "expectation," incapable of being used independently.[34]

Drawing the sociological corollary of this point of view, other commentators urged that the importance of property ownership in society had been superseded by that of organizational status. Life-chances were said to flow not from market position but from institutional rank. In the post-proprietal society, as Paul Harbrecht put it, "property is not the organizing principle; power is." He meant the power that flowed from bureaucratic position. The same insight informed C. Wright Mills' *White Collar*, and explained his pivotal assertion that "negatively, the transformation of the middle class is a shift from property to no-property; positively, it is a shift from property to a new axis of stratification, occupation."[35]

A variant of these claims can also be traced back, interestingly enough, to the writings of Karl Marx. In *Capital* Marx also foresaw the development of a kind of property that "presupposed a social concentration of the means of production and labor-power," and reduced the capitalist to the rank of a salaried manager. Marx called this new property "social property," and like the Americans he saw it as "the abolition of capital as private property within the framework of capitalism itself." He saw this new property, however, as forcing the contradiction between social production and private appropriation to ever higher levels.[36] Berle, Arnold, and others like Galbraith (whose *New Industrial State* celebrated another fragment of the old persona of ownership, the scientist-technician) saw the new property as itself *transcending* capitalism.

What these American interpretations have correctly discerned is the demise of anything resembling a free enterprise system. That demise has not occurred because of the advent of "regulation"; Adam Smith and the other prophets of this utopia always assumed regulation of the strictest kind, competitive regulation, because they lacked faith in the unregulated sagacity of businessmen. The demise of free enterprise has occurred instead because the premises necessary for it to work and to distribute goods and talents in the public interest—namely, the freedom, equality, and independence of individual market competitors—have ceased to exist.

But that demise has not signified the demise of capitalism. Free-enterprise theory no longer explains economic realities; but it does not follow that those realities have ceased to be capitalist. If by "free-enterprise" we mean "free-market," then a system that approximated that condition existed for a scant fifty years in an economic order now three centuries old. Capitalism is defined not by free markets but by the ascendence in society of a particular device of wealth-holding and wealth production—namely, of capital. It is defined by private ownership of, and private control over rights of use to, the tools of social production. It is also therefore defined by private powers over the activities of associated producers. It is a system in which such ownership is reserved to those who can secure control over greater amounts of wealth than others. Capitalism is distinguished, in other words, by a particular pattern of ownership of producer wealth. It is a system in which production is undertaken for private profit rather than for social need—or, to put it differently, in which private profit is the effective gauge of social need.

The free-market model addressed itself primarily to the realm of exchange. But before goods can be exchanged they must be produced, and

The real story about the ascendance of the mature corporation, then, is not the divorce of ownership from control; it is the divorce of power from accountability.

The modern corporation is bureaucratic, monopolistic, administratively knit, technologically informed, and infused with political energies. It is a long way from the individual proprietor, and it is also the expropriator of his wealth, his standing, and his reason. But it is capitalist nonetheless. And the contradictions of capitalism may "operate on a higher and therefore more dangerous level," Neumann noted in 1943, "even if these antagonisms are covered up by a bureaucratic apparatus" and an ideology of consensus.[44]

One final point remains to be mentioned for it will be of central importance in the discussion that follows. This is the response to the descriptions of a new world of "position." When Mills urged that modern studies of stratification must turn to an examination of occupations, he raised an implicit question about what it was that was being "occupied." The answer, clearly, is a job within a corporation or a public institution patterned after a corporation. This is to say that the world of position has not really superseded that of possession; it has arisen *within* the world of possession. The modern world of status has arisen *within* the institution of property. It has produced what Robert Brady called a "status capitalism."[45] The new world of status has profound cultural effects, but it is not a post-capitalist phenomenon.

To acknowledge all this is to see that we have not really "socialized" property because Americans can buy an array of consumer goods and (sometimes) draw a pension in their old age. The status of ownership traditionally never indicated anything about rights to a median income or to new household gadgets. The writings of Smith, Jefferson, and John Taylor were silent about such things. What ownership did entail was a stake in productive wealth, a chance to exercise initiative, do valuable work, and earn a standing in the community.[46] Similar promises were at the heart of socialism. But modern producer wealth confers none of these things on the producers. And consumer commodities—rootless, weightless things whose values change according to distant developments—hardly even support the concept of possession. They are essentially conditional holdings; if one's income fails they can easily be "repossessed." The modern promise is really of commodity-holding, not property-holding. That means that the new world of "position," rather than signifying the emergence of a new kind of freedom (as predicted by Berle and others), actually reveals the evolution of a new kind of hierarchical dependence.[47]

The New Feudalism

This second aspect of corporate capitalism, the emergence of new relations of dependence, may be the most significant. That the medieval resonance of the adjective "corporate" should have any meaning for modern social relations seems at first surprising, for the modern era always defined itself in contrast to the medieval era. Ours is a world of contract rather than status, as Sir Henry Maine put it in the classic formulation. It is a place where obligations flow from voluntary reason rather than from custom or prescription, an open rather than a closed society, a place where politics runs in public rather than private channels. It is, in short, a liberal rather than a feudal order.

Still, even though the full ramifications of concepts like "private government" have yet to be appreciated, suspicions about a recrudescense of feudal patterns have recurred in the political commentary of the last hundred years—repressed in the main text, as it were, but cropping up in the margins. A lawyer in *The Slaughterhouse Cases* of 1873 defended his clients by charging that a state-chartered monopoly had reduced New Orleans to "enthralled ground." Henry George referred to railroad land grants as "exclusive privileges . . . such as King James might have given to Buckingham." Allusions to robber *barons*, concern in the thirties for the "return of the guild," the perception of labor as a "new estate of the realm," and Galbraith's recent tribute to the scientific-educational "estate"—all express a feeling that something alien is abroad in the land.[48]

The first explicit discussion of a "renascent feudalism" was W. J. Ghent's *Our Benevolent Feudalism*, in 1903. And he had barely finished it when he found that a Maryland lawyer had anticipated him by five years with a speech entitled "The New Feudalism." Consequent upon the movement toward large industrial combinations, Ghent explained, "The groups of captains and lieutenants of industry attain increasing power, social, industrial and political, and become the ranking order in a vast series of gradations. . . . They who desire to live . . . must make their peace with those who have the disposition of the living. The result is a renascent feudalism which, though it differs . . . from that of Edward I, is yet based upon the same status of lord, agent, and underling."[49] Ghent feared that even the holding of title deeds by these underlings would come to resemble holdings "in the nature of a fief, at the mercy of several superiors." Whereas "personal bondage to the land was the basis of villeinage in the old regime, bondage to the job" would emerge as the basis for villeinage in the new. A politics of privilege (of private law) would necessarily emerge. Indeed, the state "so strong in its relation to the propertyless citizen" was already demonstrably "weaker in relation to the man of capital." [50]

The most distinctive thing about feudal society, institutionally, was the proliferation in it of numerous "secondary" or intermediate associations standing between the individual and the state, dwarfing the former and parcelling up the prerogatives of the latter. In feudal society individuals' rights, duties, and daily tasks were defined by the churches, municipalities, guilds, universities, or domains to which they belonged. The economic historian Karl Polanyi distinguished two historical forms of feudalism. The first, a "primitive feudalism," was the product of a progressive development in which military power was being increased and a stable government established. The second, a "feudalism of decay," was a product of decomposition in which "the prerogatives of sovereignty [were] appropriated by private individuals." [51] A fragmentation of sovereignty was characteristic of both. Three other distinctive traits have followed from this: the hierarchical organization of these partial jurisdictions under a lord; the delegation of authority to those lords and the melding of social, legal, and political statuses within them; and the making of rights and protections conditional on the successful performance of particular duties within them.

To sketch this system even briefly is to see hints of present arrangements. We do not call people lord, agent, and underling as in Ghent's formula. But people's possessions do not bring them the independence, influence, or power traditionally associated with ownership, as we have seen. And people *are* bound in various ways to their jobs. Their economic situation, social status, health care, and political affiliations (or lack of affiliation) are usually determined by their positions in large secondary associations.

The transition to a status capitalism has thus created a society which, in contrast to the classic vision of the bourgeoisie, is openly hierarchical. The phenomena of subordination and dependence characterize the relations of small business to large business, employee to employer, consumer to company, and citizen to administrator. According to contract theory, social obligations were reciprocal. But in our society loyalty is expected to be tendered to the institution; the institution is not expected to be loyal to the men and women in its domain. Modern Americans have come to see the world divided into superiors and subordinates as naturally as the feudalists saw it divided into masters and men, or the American Calvinists into the elect and the fallen. In being rendered "private," furthermore, these new hierarchical relations have been cast beyond the institutions of accountability that were fought for in the republican tradition as being appropriate to any situation in which man had power over man. Mills was right to speak of "the modern hero as victim" and to characterize him as "somebody's man." [52] We have succeeded in standing Sir Henry Maine on his head.

As the capital function is imparted to more goods and services, these feudal principles become more extensive. New forms of arbitrary power invade American communities. In a modern application of the medieval principle of *nulle terre sans seigneur*, it becomes impossible to find any terrain without its lord. The corporation's ability to slough off its social burdens onto the propertyless or small property owners creates what is in essence a system of private law. And the development of a segmented economy that sorts people by race, class, and skills into fairly permanent ranks of employed, unemployed, and underemployed contributes to a society of status-orders.

Principles of deference, homage, and conditional tenure thus emerge in the society, infecting even the public institutions that were originally created to offset social inequalities, as Charles Reich explained in his article on "The New Property." "Just as the feudal system linked lord and vassal through a system of mutual dependence, obligations and loyalty," Reich wrote, "so government largess binds men to the state." And it usually binds them without the minimal liberal guarantees of due process. A decade after McCarthyism, Reich also added that loyalty or fealty was "one of the essential conditions" of continued enjoyment of the grants or licenses upon which one's very "personality" often depends. [53]

Those on the outposts of social inquiry have thus discovered a new society on the far side of the New Frontier. The imposition of semi-feudal, patronal relations in a bureaucratic milieu produces a social reflection of the internal structure of the corporation, as Brady warned. That this new society does not conform perfectly to classical feudalism is not important. [54] The comparison identifies critical features of modern American social organization and suggests a systematic rather than an accidental connection between them. A concentration of power, a scope of privilege, and a range of hierarchical dependence have emerged in this century which are unknown to liberal custom and subversive of our founding project.

The Politics of Partnership: "Buying Time and Support with Sovereignty"

A British Cabinet member explained in the 1930s that it seemed to him "to be courting failure to tell people that they have first to dress themselves in black shirts and throw their opponents downstairs in order to get the corporative state. . . . The new economic order has already developed further in England than is generally recognized." [55] And not only in England. As this statement was being written, new forms of business self-regulation in America were bringing about a "cumulative approximation to the generic conditions of the corporate or guild state." [56]

State action has always been implicated in capitalist development. It was originally invoked to defend the market (itself a "corporation") against the claims of other feudal orders. [57] It was invoked to defend the rights of property and enforce contracts, and to defend the enclosures of the commons. And state powers have always been invoked to subsidize favorites or quash opponents. What is occurring today, then, is a difference partly in degree and partly in kind. For those outside the pale of property ownership it is the former. For those within, it is the latter.

A conscious, full-scale partnership between big business and the state is now being created. Far from trying to keep politics out of business, Michael Reagan observed in 1963, the aim of modern business is to "control the direction of public policy by getting business into politics." [58] This partnership has drawn increasing comment in recent years. It has been regarded, however, as either a sectoral anomaly (as in agriculture) or a temporary deviation (as in the early oil industry). Grant McConnell called it a "blurring" of public and private jurisdictions. He saw organizations like U.S. Steel or the Farm Bureau as small associations gone wrong, groups that had sacrificed the private, voluntary status assigned them by democratic and pluralist theories.

This mix of public and private has now become so systematic and predictable that it constitutes more a fusion than a blurring; and the fusion deserves attention as a specific *form of rule*, a corporativist form of rule. The adjectival part of the term "corporate capitalism" also refers to the politics of this new jurisdiction—a jurisdiction unknown to classical liberalism. It is a politics, paradoxically, of burgeoning government activity and diminishing public authority.

If American politics are not now fully corporativistic, there are nevertheless clear tendencies in that direction. The most familiar modes of corporativist fusion are the two that McConnell and Lowi have described: the delegation to private groups of specific government powers and authority, and the infiltration of private groups into the interior of government to define "the policy agenda and the public interest . . . in terms of the organized interests."[59]

But there are two more fundamental, less visible forms of this fusion. The first is that which occurs as a daily process in industry; though modern factories are private, they "share in the distinctive functions of governance."[60] They have the power to circumscribe the enjoyment of constitutional rights, to assign duties and impose sanctions for the breach of them, and to create obligations enforceable in the courts. The modern enterprise is a social institution in which significant hierarchical power over others has been granted to private parties.

The second silent form of fusion occurs in a wide range of current policies that are truly public in substance, because of their binding effects on social life, but are made and executed by private interests. When a fictive individual kills a town and deprives real individuals of their "liberty and calling," when an industry pollutes the air over (or land under) a town, when an oil company levies private taxes on "all who pass," or a private automobile company dismantles a city's trolley system, they are all involved in the making of public policies.[61] Though we call such decisions private, and refer to their effects as "impingements" on the public realm, our common law ancestors would have known them as *political* decisions involving usurpations of the legislative power.

A corporativist jurisdiction, as McConnell has described it, is one in which people find themselves subject to "the vagaries of a power in which the compulsive force and authority of the state have been joined to the informal and social power of private groups."[62] It is an environment that lacks the guarantees that a democrat or liberal always expected to accompany significant exercises of power.

The high points on the historical road to business-state partnership are evident. They began in the private realm in the late nineteenth century, as new zones of concentration continued to appear beyond each perfected form of combination. Beyond pools came trusts, and beyond them, holding companies; then the modern corporation proper; and beyond it, new forms of "loose" combinations like the trade associations which A. J. Eddy called for (in his *New Competition* of 1912, whose frontispiece declared "Competition is war, and war is hell"). With World War I came the first explicit joining of the state to these combinations in the form of the War Industries Board, "the model, the precedent, and the inspiration for state corporate capitalism in the remainder of the twen-

tieth century." One participant later prided himself, in perfect corporativist diction, that the commodity sections of the WIB had been "business operating Government business for the public good."[63]

The twenties were the decade of trade associations, and the thirties
of the NRA, when the state again attempted openly to delegate part of
its authority to these trade associations.[64] This attempt at explicit corporativism ceased in 1935. By the late thirties, however, the partnership in
agriculture that Lowi and McConnell would later analyze had been perfected, and other sectors set out to grasp informally the power they had
briefly enjoyed before 1935. It was on the basis of his study of the emergent forms of business self-regulation at this time that Robert Brady
stated there was "nothing fundamental in history, program, structure,
organization or social outlook" that distinguished American business
associations from the cartels and Spitzenverbände that "constituted the
economic bases of fascist states."[65]

Aided by the new industry-wide Advisory Councils and Boards,
businesses succeeded so well in their post–New Deal efforts that Mc-
Connell concluded in 1961 that the "blurring" first achieved in agriculture now "constitutes the characteristic form of power in the United
States."[66] In the years since McConnell wrote, that form has been even
further perfected by means of inter-industry "complexes" and new political action committees.[67] The effect of the latter committees must inevitably be to substitute corporate groups for individuals in the very process of representation.

It would be possible to find further institutional embodiments of
corporativist principles where they have not previously been sought.
Political parties would be obvious candidates. Feared by the founders,
they have nevertheless become the exclusive agency for organizing representation, the core function of republican government. They are corporations in the familiar sense of the term: even before the advent of
political action committees they were organized like businesses and
served as conduits of business influence. (They make up the "base of
operations," Ostrogorski noted at the end of the last century, "for all the
great private interests in the efforts to bend . . . the state to their selfish
ends.") But they are also "corporations" in a more classical sense. They
hold an essential prerogative of sovereignty but are only marginally re-
sponsive to popular will.[68]

We can stop here, though, for the pattern is clear. Lowi's verdict on
the origins and subsequent character of this "interest group liberalism"
seems correct. It arose out of weakness. It was the New Deal rationalized. It was making the best of one of the worst periods of our history by

buying time and support with sovereignty.[69] The effect of this fragmentation, in contrast to the explicit premises and goals of classical liberalism, is an overt symbiosis between state and economy. Modern corporate property is as inconceivable without the daily intervention of the state as Jeffersonian property would have been without hand tools and a title deed. In 1942 Franz Neumann proposed that "in the period of monopolization, the new auxiliary guarantee of property is no longer the contract but the administrative act, the form in which the state interferes."[70] The American experience would validate the observation. In the era of monopoly capitalism, voluntary contracts no longer suffice to maintain private property, coordinate it with other properties, and provide the orderings of labor and power upon which it depends. The government therefore lends a visible hand. Politics becomes a continuation of property by other means.

Ultimately this sort of fusion transforms more than just the content of law and the process of representation. Liberal society always claimed to possess a government of laws. But modern developments are changing the *form* of law, what law fundamentally *is*. Rather than a settled framework of activity, rooted in precedent, known to citizens, and focused on the juridical individual, "law" becomes equated with changing policies and social purposes as defined by powerful groups. It also becomes oriented toward future goals. Administrative law, rather than contract law, becomes the paradigmatic form of law in the modern state. (This occurs at the same time that Neumann's "auxiliary guarantees" for property begin to be provided by administrative acts rather than contracts.) One exhaustive study already concludes, for example, that the dominant purpose of judicial review of administrative processes "is no longer the prevention of unauthorized intrusions on private autonomy, but the assurance of fair representation for all affected interests"—which means all *organized* affected interests.[71]

The historical record suggests, finally, that these corporativist arrangements, rather than being aberrations, are the ones peculiarly appropriate to advanced capitalist society. Economically, they insure that corporate capital will be able to receive more than occasional patronage, that it will gain systematized access to the bases of capital formation, and that it can socialize many of its costs (though not its profits). Politically, they assure that functional interest groups will displace individuals from the process of representation. Socially, they aid in making the adjustments, and facilitating the centralized control, necessary for rapid change and economic relocation. In fact, the European and Latin American experiences suggest that this social function—specifically, the impulse to counteract a high degree of working class organization—is decisive in the historical shift from mere corporatist tendencies to overtly corporativist arrangements.[72]

But the historical record suggests that the corporatist dream of harmony (or of total "synchronization," as Brady put it) can never really be achieved. This social-control function identifies the Achilles heel of the whole scheme, revealing why the rhetoric of harmony is always accompanied by the reality of force. As a political system, corporativism is really designed to represent only a small spectrum of interests. Others it ignores and deprives of an effective voice. It therefore does systematic violence to those other interests in the evolving definition of social reality. Bureaucratically organized institutions add to this implicit violence by choking off dissent. Thus corporativism always presents a political version of Xeno's paradox, the incidence of coercion increasing as the distance from the goal of functional interdependence seems to diminish. The system fails to do justice to the *political* (conflictual) nature of social reality in general, and to the contradictions of capitalist reality in particular.

Can a Collectivism Be Private?

Are the dominant institutions of American society still private? Many have denied it. The extension of their social domain, the advent of long-range planning, and the emergence of social claims against it have led midcentury commentators to conclude that the continued invocation of the term "private" simply reveals the hold of Thurman Arnold's "folklore of capitalism."

These commentators have unfortunately confused fundamental questions of scope and of right. The term "private" in law and politics pertains to matters of entitlement and obligation, not to matters of size or to the spontaneity of motives. Although the important property in our society is no longer "individual," as we have seen, it remains indelibly private in the rights to its control and in its principles of internal organization. As Michael Reagan explains, its private elements "lie in the insistence by business that, in return for public benefits, no limitations be placed upon resultant profits or managerial discretion, and that the public good is not to be planned but is to arise as a byproduct of private planning for private purposes."[73]

To call the dominant property "private," then, is not to be mired in the past or to indulge in folklore; it is to call a thing by its proper name. This property could never be called "public" because no institutions ex-

ist in America by which investment could be directed in the public interest, and because these collectivisms are not themselves publics (democratic organizations). Indeed, *how* these collectivisms are going to be
ordered is the most critical question before America in this century.

The corporation is the inverse of a truly public form of wealth-
holding because it subordinates its social scope to private interests. We
cannot change its character by merely changing our terms and insisting,
for example, that the corporation really *is* a public institution. "Private"
defines the dominant component in the current mix of rights and obligations; and rights and obligations are anchored to a large extent in relations of power. Corporations could not cease to be private without altering the basic relations of power in America.

Having described key aspects of the economic, cultural, and political dimensions of the society fashioned around this institution, it will
help to fix a final image of the whole by comparing it to the pluralist
vision that so enchanted midcentury political commentators. The society
shaped by private collectivisms bears a surface resemblance to this pluralist vision. Decision-making occurs not "through the summation of the
wills of individual voters, but through autonomous social organizations" (as Neumann wrote of Weimar Germany).[74] Still, there are fateful
differences between the corporatist and pluralist models. Four primary
differences are pertinent for understanding the theory discussed in this
book.

First, the element of autonomy to which Neumann alluded, which
was so important for the early European pluralists, is absent from the
corporatist model. In modern American politics, as we have seen, the
line between private and public is systematically confused.

The second point is closely related to this. Pluralism was always a
voluntarist outlook; it saw authority as constituted from below. But a
corporate society is "dominated by elites." James Petras described the
model in pre-Allende Chile as being a society in which there were "a
plurality of interest groups, each controlled from the top, and in which
individuals low in the hierarchy . . . [or outside one] have little opportunity to participate. . . . Corporatism tends to choke off conflict and to
organize society bureaucratically."[75] The difference between the two
models on this second point is captured best by their respective approaches to labor. Where pluralism would grant workers an independent voice, American politics increasingly seeks to manage workers' organizations from above and to restrain the exercise of autonomous
rights.[76] Where pluralism would favor group organization across the
whole spectrum of social interests, corporatism historically has been

skewed in favor of business organization. This, too, has been the case in America, where the government has supported that skewing by obstructing the organization of certain types of groups and by straight-forwardly denying legal standing to others.[77]

Third, in modern corporatism the commitment to direct group bargaining and social heterogeneity that distinguished classical pluralism is replaced by a fascination with administrative ordering. Though groups are expected to be many, their purposes and methods of organization are expected to be few. To put it differently, the pluralist assumption that group conflict is natural is replaced with an assumption of functional interdependence. For the pluralist, social stability was seen as the result of group interactions, cross-pressured loyalties, and overlapping memberships. For the American corporatist, it appears as the product of executive leadership and administrative engineering.

Fourth and finally, pluralism always either assumed or sought a rough equality of status among social groups. American society, on the other hand, accepts the growth of massive organizations that dwarf others in size and influence, and justifies exporting the costs of the internal contradictions of those organizations to smaller groups and to individuals.

We can see, then, that hard on the heels of the society depicted by classical liberalism there has arisen a new society which, though collective, is neither the general-welfare regime predicted by the Progressives nor the socialist society that Marxists thought would follow from the socializing of means of production. The significant thing about this society is not just that people find themselves compelled to compete as minnows with the pike, nor that they are tripped up by the "wires of technological interdependence" mentioned by Garry Wills. It is that people's status *as citizens* begins to be defined effectively by their attachment to a haphazard array of semiprivate associations. It is also that their status begins to be *pre-empted* by a kind of corporate citizenship. Already lawyers argue for the corporation's right of free speech—and win.[78] And corporations have succeeded in enclosing another piece of the commons, the essential democratic right to knowledge. "Segments of knowledge still belong to technical specialists," writes one analyst, "and pieces of knowledge to the well-educated, but only the very largest organizations are able to integrate these proliferating segments and pieces into systems of productive, effective, or more likely, profitable information."[79]

When the American liberal was forced to admit the realities of social interdependence, political power, and the social character of wealth, it was on terms defined by the capitalist corporation. *That* is the foundation fact for understanding subsequent American politics and political thought.

American political thought is therefore faced with the task of making sense out of a mix of collectivism and private interest that seemingly denies the preconditions for democracy. How is the promise of equality to be squared with social hierarchy, and the hopes for a voluntarist reason with prescriptive stratification? What is to become of the liberal's notion of unfettered freedom when our modern frontiersman hears not only his neighbor's axe on the tree but his shoes on the floor upstairs? How is modern industry to be reconciled with the liberal promise to dissolve power in the automatic workings of the market? Behind all the various political glosses and passing ideological fancies, these are the questions that have nagged at American political consciousness over the last century. It is time to explain how this book will examine the answers that have been given to these questions.

THE ORIGINS OF MODERN AMERICAN POLITICAL THEORY

The famous presidential election of 1912 demonstrated that a new political outlook was emerging in American life. This election has always fascinated American historians because it seemed to them, as it did to Woodrow Wilson, to pose the "fundamental choice" before America in the twentieth century. It marked the "parting of the ways" between Theodore Roosevelt's New Nationalism, which would accept big business and regulate it by big government, and Wilson's New Freedom, which would presumably use antitrust laws to restore room for the Jeffersonian entrepreneur.

This view of the contest fails, however, to acknowledge Wilson's real position. He did, it is true, commit himself to making room for "the man on the make." But he intended to do this with the aid of administrative commissions and a regulatory state; and he denied any intention of breaking up big business (as opposed to "trusts"). Wilson's language, if nothing else, indicated the great distance he had traveled from a truly Jeffersonian outlook. "What is liberty?" he asked of prospective voters: "Suppose that I were building a great piece of powerful machinery. . . . Liberty for the several parts would consist in the best possible assembling and adjusting of them all, would it not? . . . The piston of an engine [will] run with absolute freedom . . . not because it is left alone or isolated, but because it has been associated most skillfully and carefully with the other parts of the great structure."[80] "Association is the condition of individuality" wrote Herbert Croly, the architect of Teddy Roosevelt's program. "Only by living in integral unity can people defend freedom and democracy," asserted Eduardo Frei, a modern Latin American corporatist.[81] No, the important contrast in the election of 1912 was not between Roosevelt and Wilson, but between both of them and what had gone before.

The current ascendance of the outlook anticipated by both Roosevelt and Wilson is revealed on a day-to-day basis by an array of superficial justifications for the corporation and its influence in politics. The corporation is thus said to have emerged from voluntarist group action rather than by state aid, to have derived from a natural industrial evolution, or to have developed a "soul"; or it is defended because "the guarantee of . . . equality for functional purposes makes 'the social contract' appear as an exchange" between equal groups.[82] But underlying these surface defenses is a long-lasting and fairly stable social frame of reference. McConnell labeled it "neo-pluralism," and Lowi called it "interest-group liberalism." In McConnell's definition, its distinctive feature was an application of the Madisonian faith in competitive balance to large, semicompulsory associations. In Lowi's formulation, it was "an amalgam of capitalism, statism, and pluralism."[83] But we have seen that its pluralist element is deceptive. Because the remaining synthesis of capitalism and statism is frankly corporativistic, the new theoretical frame of reference can be accurately called "corporate liberalism."[84]

Like European and Latin American corporatism, this new theory derives partly from a well-grounded critique of classical liberal values. Its founders faulted the Lockean tradition for its egotism, its glorification of rights to the exclusion of obligations, and its invitation to social strife. They sought not merely piecemeal reform but moral regeneration. And they hoped that industrial organization would clear a new path to social solidarity. Of course, lacking the communal traditions and Catholic heritage of France, Italy, or the Latin American countries, the American idea of organization emerged looking quite different from the European or Latin American models.

In order to see this new theory, and ourselves, clearly it is first necessary to go back and look first at the rock on which nineteenth century liberalism foundered. It is also necessary to understand the range of possible answers to emergent questions that had been closed off by the dawn of the new century. Part One of this book addresses this nineteenth-century prelude by offering a re-examination of the politics of the Gilded Age as seen under the long shadow of the developing corporation.

The connection between populism and Progressivism has been recognized as having been critical in American history. But most historians have seen the movements as continuous—Progressivism flowing on from populism, as a mainstream moves on from its major tributary. Richard Hofstadter, for example, presented Progressivism as more urban, "more informed, more moderate, [and] more complex" than its rural predecessor, but as fundamentally continuous in its underlying motives.[85] The discussion in Part One (Chapters Two through Four) will present the relationship between the two movements quite differently.

Chapter Two analyzes the transformation of property during the nineteenth century, presents an overview of populism, and describes the fracturing of classical liberalism as it ran aground on the new "monopoly." Chapter Three then looks at the route the populists took away from this critical crack-up by looking closely at the thought of Henry George. Chapter Four examines the alternate path cleared by William Graham Sumner and soon traveled by the early corporatism of Andrew Carnegie and Charles Francis Adams, Jr.

Part Two (Chapters Five through Eight) then turns to the origins of corporate liberal political theory. This theory will be seen to have entailed a new vision of society, a new idea about how that society's groups and relations should be ordered, and a new sense of social purpose. It contained new ideas about the what, the how, and the why of American life. Informing this new *vision*, this new approach to *sovereignty* (and obligation), and this new idea of *authority*, was a new *epistemology*, a new idea about knowledge and its role in political affairs. These four elements came to constitute the main dimensions of American political theory and a chapter is devoted to each of them.

Chapter Five will address the group theory associated with names such as A. F. Bentley, John Dewey, Mary Parker Follett, John R. Commons, and Charles H. Cooley. In the perspective shared by these thinkers, groups were seen as having a primacy and integrity that had been denied them by classical liberalism, and self-interest ceased to be seen as a basic fact of social life. This perspective has usually been seen as a methodological innovation, a step toward "realism." But more than realistic observation, it also entailed a theoretical argument: Bentley, Dewey, and Follett were attempting to define a new theory of *industrial* democracy. We shall look closely at how they conceived of the rights of individuals within their groups, and how they characterized external relations between groups—particularly between the corporation and other groups. We shall find that the real tenor of this theory was less Tocquevillean than Comtist and functionalist.

In Chapter Six we will turn to the epistemological revolution associated with the rise of pragmatism and the emergence of a new enthusiasm for administrative reform. Like the rise of group theory, the shift in epistemological premises was more than an isolated intellectual event; it indicated a whole new way of thinking about society and the political actors within it. Everywhere writers spurned a priori assumptions, "fixed systems," and "brooding omnipresences in the sky," in the "revolt against formalism" of which Morton White has written.

As with any revolt, however, large questions remained about what would be built in the space left by the fall of old structures. Individuals, no longer conceived as bearers of natural rights—an a priori assumption to be sure, abstract and even superstitious—came to be seen as more erratic bundles of energy, buffeted by instinct, boxed in by circumstance, and driven by forces expressive of no inherent order. But how then were political rules to be conceived as anything but arbitrary? And how was pragmatism, divested of normative reference, to avoid the conclusion that whatever "is" is good? Once ceasing to judge fact by right, how would the new liberals avoid reducing right to fact? We will look at the thought of Peirce, James, Dewey, and Holmes, and then at the management proposal of Frederick Winslow Taylor to find answers to these questions.

Chapter Seven will examine the call for the activist or positive state that emerged in the early decades of this century. The seeds initially sown by Hamilton and Lincoln bore fruit during Progressivism, as America began to be considered as an integral nation. Americans began to seek state aid for the solution of their problems. Though fed by Edward Bellamy's socialist ideas and by the theories of the early political scientists, the most influential stream of new ideas was that which flowed from the New Nationalists proper: Herbert Croly, Walter Weyl, and the young Walter Lippmann.

Again, there was more at stake here than first meets the eye. Implicit in these new appeals to view politics as an "instrument rather than a prohibition" were hidden injunctions to change the prevailing views of law and sovereignty. The original attempt in America was to establish constitutional sovereignty, to create a power limited not just by checks and balances but also by broad cultural standards to which the Constitution would give legal force. But if, as the Progressive reformers urged, positive laws became king, eclipsing cultural standards, custom, and federative principles, and if "Newtonian" checks and balances were superseded by more "scientific" and efficient forms of administration, what limits on state power would remain? What would prevent the state from becoming the sole judge in its own causes?

These problems were aggravated by the effects of epistemological reformulation. After all, a nominalist view of politics joined to a nominalist view of knowledge might easily produce the Hobbesian conclusion that an absolute sovereign was of necessity also arbitrary. The basic question before the proponents of the positive state, then, was how a political order cutting its moorings from Locke was to avoid drifting back to Hobbes—and Hobbes in the service of a most unHobbesean collection of private interests.

In Chapter Eight, finally, we will turn to the corporate liberal approach to authority. Over twenty years ago Edward Mason wrote that the nineteenth century produced a social doctrine "that not only explained but justified," whereas the twentieth century has not adequately explained, or in any case has not justified the corporate system.[86] Not that there has been any lack of apologetics; but Mason was referring to a deeper kind of justification. He meant that a successful political theory must do more than rationalize whatever exists. It must explain why certain things are *worth* doing; it must help define purposes for action. In the language of political theory, it must possess a concept of authority.

"Nature" provided that principle for classical liberalism. But the belief in natural rights was failing. And the heirs of a tradition with a starved language for talking about authority could not be expected to be lucid about that lapse. Henry Adams did, however, discuss it explicitly. And William James alluded to it often, as in his observation that the American condition was "the opposite . . . from that of nightmare . . . though it produces a kindred horror. In nightmare we have motives but no power; here we have power but no motives."[87]

Progressive thought as a whole, however, did contain an *implicit* response to the loss. It was particularly evident in the literature of the period, as when the protagonist of Frank Norris's *The Octopus*, reeling under the effects of corporate rapine, suddenly turned to find solace in blind technological forces ("nature" now appearing as "a gigantic engine" running on historical tracks).[88] The essence of the response was to redirect attention from the origins of activity to its effects, from its roots to its fruits. Joined to Darwinian naturalism, this approach would install the doctrine of progress at the heart of the new political theory. Where classical liberals situated men in terms of space (the market), corporate liberals would locate them in terms of time (an evolutionary history).

Sustained by a faith in progress, corporate liberals would truly trust in time to heal all wounds.

As an intellectual maneuver, this strategy of turning from origins to ends was impressive. How well it really responded to the underlying problem was a different matter, as we shall see.

To this group vision of politics, pragmatist epistemology, national theory of sovereignty, and progressive concept of authority there was added briefly, during the twenties, a corporativist theory of representation. This was the decade when Samuel Gompers grew nostalgic with Bernard Baruch about their years on the War Production Board, when they had functioned like an economic parliament, "scarcely aware of the existence of Congress."[89] It was the decade in which many scholars, like John R. Commons, responded to the failures of the American representative system by proposing a functionalist system of industrial democracy. This theory of representation failed to develop, however, and never became a part of American corporate liberalism.

Corporatist language became explicit during the early New Deal, when the government attempted the NRA, and the technocratic ideas of Rexford Tugwell and Francis Perkins (both students of the Progressive academic Simon Patten) became popular.[90] By the time the New Deal was dismantled and explicit corporatism passed from the American scene, the basic elements of the outlook had either passed into general currency or (as with the concept of sovereignty) anticipated the ends toward which political thought would tend. These elements would define the operative frame of reference to which an apparently eclectic array of magazine writers, social scientists, and political leaders would henceforth belong.

Even New Deal and postwar reformers would join the conservative sons of Comte in accepting a corporate vision, a pragmatist epistemology, and an evolutionary view of history in thinking about modern social reality. Conservatism itself, which nineteenth-century democrats had tended to identify with a defense of social hierarchy, was redefined by these reformers as a simple reticence to move along a supposedly linear path of progress. Though stressing the adaptive capacities of thought more than the conservatives, these reformers ultimately denied to mind anything more potent than the power to streamline or adjust what was already given.[91] In matters of reform they were systematically drawn toward the administrative and redistributive rather than to the constitutive. Eventually they would prove to have more in common with the old liberals against whom they rebelled than with groups that tried sporadically to get beyond liberal assumptions altogether.

The widespread agreement on corporate liberal premises in modern American society is nowhere more evident than in the current literature on the corporation—and then it is in the questions that are *not* raised as much as in those that are. Alternatives to current industrial organization are almost universally ignored. Capitalists are called simply employers or community leaders. To refer to them as capitalists would identify the power they wield over their neighbors' lives. Arguments about the extent of stockholder democracy, the sources of investment capital, the requirements of organizational maintenance, and the modes of executive behavior take up the bulk of the literature.[92] Attention is devoted almost entirely to the society within the corporation. With few exceptions, the questions about the place of the corporation in society, which agitated discussion for fifty years, are no longer asked.[93]

In operational terms, a widespread agreement thus underlies modern political discourse. Woodrow Wilson may have disagreed with Theodore Roosevelt about how the pie should be divided. But what kind of pie it should be was not, after the early years of the century, open to dispute. Richard Nixon may have amended John F. Kennedy by telling people to go see what they could do for themselves; but it was Nixon who imposed a wage-price review board, and who, through his use of advisory councils, campaign contributions, and strategic appointments, pushed corporativist decision-making methods to unprecedented levels. The hand may have felt like the hand of Sumner, but the voice was the voice of Croly. And it has become more insistent with the years.

CORPORATE LIBERALISM OR LIBERAL CORPORATISM?

Is this peculiar synthesis of corporatism and individualism a corporate species of liberalism (with the corporation displacing the Lockean individual), or is it a liberal variety of the corporatism charted by Comte, realized by Mussolini, and celebrated today in Latin America? Is it primarily a member of the family of Jefferson and Mill, or that of which British guild socialism is a cousin on the left and fascism a cousin on the right? The answer depends upon what is judged essential and what peripheral in the liberal tradition.

What is not essential, in the view of this inquiry, is the oft-mentioned allegiance to laissez-faire principles. The central fact of historical liberalism was rather its individualism—its *propertied* individualism.[94] Classical liberalism promised autonomy, but only upon a hidden basis of uniformity. The traditional liberal aspired to individuality, but he did so in an artificial milieu of which the ground was privately enclosed wealth and the blood, as Hobbes said, was money. What was dearest to the heart of the historical, living liberal was individualism of a possessive and acquisitive sort. When the units of possession and acquisition changed, the liberal changed with them.

We shall postpone answering the question about which part of our term is primary and which conditional until Chapter Nine, our final chapter. The discussions of the intervening chapters will give us a better idea of what is at stake with the question.

Whether the theory described in this book will ever be reconciled with what Croly called "the promise of American life" remains to be seen. That it cannot be reconciled with any familiar understandings of democracy is certain. For any outlook which acknowledges social interdependence, the inescapability of political choice, and the social character of wealth, but which also attempts to build on liberal foundations—with its neglect of the public, its privatization of freedom, and its ultimate equation of order with control—is building on a base too narrow to accommodate democracy as well. The sense of betrayal that currently informs our culture may well flow from a sense of this fact. If so, the confusion of terms over the last half-century has served a functional purpose. It has hidden from the American liberal the real character of his identity and the troublesome direction of his advance.

Let us turn back now to the nineteenth century to see how America first responded to the challenge of the corporation.

PART ONE

Challenge and Response: The Fracturing of Classical American Liberalism

2

Populism and the Corporation

*There are two modes of invading private property:
the first, by which the poor plunder the rich, is
sudden and violent; the second, by which the rich
plunder the poor, slow and legal. . . . [Both] are
equally an invasion of private property, and equally
contrary to our constitutions.*

—JOHN TAYLOR

*T*he most obvious innovations in American political thought during the Progressive era were the acceptance of the concept of the positive or activist state, and the espousal of the view of society as an integral order rather than as a simple aggregate of individuals. The grounds for both of these reformulations, however, were laid in the preceding period. Dewey was late in calling for the state to be used as "an instrument rather than a prohibition," for the state had already been used instrumentally to deal with the problems of an increasingly organized society after the Civil War. When these earlier reformulations are understood, the character of the later liberalism emerges looking differently than it has usually been presented.

But how are the years between 1865 and 1895 to be understood? Historians are divided not only about the general spirit of the Gilded Age but also about the spirit of particular milieux within it. Some historians have emphasized the Darwinian temper, and seen it as revealing an evolutionary optimism. Others have pointed to the writings of Stephen

39

Crane, Frank Norris, and Theodore Dreiser as expressive of a darker sense that people were mere creatures of instinct and environment. "Man wavers," Dreiser wrote in *Sister Carrie*; "He is even as a wisp of the wind . . . acting now by his will, and now by his instincts, erring with one, only to retrieve by the other . . . a creature of incalculable variability." The young Charles Francis Adams, Jr., urged a materialist explanation for this new sense of variability by suggesting that a technical force, the railroad, "with greater force and activity than ever before [was] shaping all the social, political, and economical conditions which surround it." But Vernon Louis Parrington saw the new somberness as expressive of a changed intellectual orientation. It was an expression of the shift from a biological paradigm to one modeled on physics—"from the parts to the totality, from freedom to determinism."[1]

Another view explains the new moods politically. The most familiar of the political interpretations depicts Justice Field and his fellow judges as conservatives armed with "neat formulas of ready-made law, symmetrical in appearance and mechanical in operation," who hamstrung legal development in narrow precedents and a formalistic ideology.[2] The other side of the political spectrum is then seen as held by those who first looked to a general welfare state to right the wrongs of predatory capitalism—men such as Wilson, Simon Patten, and Richard Ely.

The era was one of tumultuous and widespread conflict. The populists were the initiators of that conflict, but their place in the cultural topology is no clearer than that of any other group. Their program was not Field's, their naturalism was not Dreiser's, and they hardly resembled the professors from Princeton and Johns Hopkins.

The populists originally appeared in American historiography as rebels and heroes, champions of "the last phase of a long and perhaps losing struggle . . . to save agricultural America from the devouring jaws of industrial America."[3] Though they lost in the short run, the major parts of their program are generally seen as having been accepted by later political reforms. The radicalism of the 1890s emerges as "the common sense" of the 1930s. In this interpretation, the populist leader appears as a latter-day Moses, forced to halt on a plateau overlooking the new century as his armies marched over to the new land.

More recently, these same populists have been presented as paranoids, nativists, and anti-Semites, people with their eyes on the past and their minds warped by crank monetary "panaceas." Worse, in America, they are said to have opposed progress. In a focal application of Progressive theory *to* populism, our present social organization is presented as the inevitable destination of Progress; past protest movements are assimilated to a scheme of transition, and those who proposed ultimately unsuccessful alternatives are accused—and convicted—of being retrograde.[4]

There are problems with all of these interpretations. Men and women do not continually risk their lives and the security of their families for the sake of crank panaceas. Nor were the populist leaders as sanguine about the way things turned out as their chroniclers suggest. Rather than feeling himself a Moses, Ignatius Donnelly inverted Bellamy's genre and gave the country its first dystopia. Eugene Debs's plateau was a prison, and he spent his time there taking up the heresy of socialism. Tom Watson underwent a painful metamorphosis that resulted in a demagoguery and racism he had previously spurned. And most ex-populists scorned Progressives like Woodrow Wilson, remembering that they had turned Gold Democrat in '96 rather than vote for even the diminished populism of Bryan.

The rank and file shared their leaders' sense of defeat. After 1896 the populist armies dispersed and the widespread participation that had characterized the Grange, the Farmers' Alliances, and the Knights of Labor ceased. Even voting in national elections dropped off dramatically after 1896, when "an increasingly large proportion of the eligible adult population either left, failed to enter, or—as was the case with the Southern Negroes . . . was systematically excluded from the American voting universe."[5] Finally, the conservative program was neither readymade nor "mechanical" in operation. It was, as we shall see, radical in the context of Anglo-American common-law traditions.

The appropriate verdict on these interpretations must be the same one Henry Adams reached on Darwinism. At first, Adams wrote, he had taken Darwin's doctrine to mean "steady, uniform, unbroken evolution from lower to higher." But he had trouble applying the doctrine to the facts. How was mutation to be explained in terms of uniformity? And if glacial ages were examples of "evolution," what then were examples of catastrophe?[6] Interpreters of populism face a similar problem. If the defeat of tradition is an example of transition, what is an example of cleavage? If the breaking of foundations is expressive of continuity, what is expressive of crisis?

The first interpretation of populism, whatever its shortcomings, was correct in sensing that much was at stake for America during this era. The conflict was not between different responses to an inevitable end, but between alternate views of what that end should be. Differences so deep as to elicit contradictory constitutional programs presented themselves for the final battle of 1896 clothed in disputes about monetary policy. Challenges to private rights of appropriation—which came closer than anything else in American history to class demands— were presented by people who saw themselves *defending* capitalism. Staunch reformers exerted themselves trying to reverse a two-century reform tradition that had struggled for liberty *against* government. By the end of the conflict, many concerns central to classical liberalism had passed from view. Those that remained were powered by a new theoretical dynamic. For populism presents an example of something rarely admitted and even more rarely accepted in America, this land of winners: it was a movement that lost. What followed was not an evolution but a new beginning.

"BETWEEN THE MIGHTY OPPOSITES"

To understand what was at stake in the populist conflict we must see what the antagonists said at the time. The largest businessmen, judges, and railroad lawyers saw the struggle as being over the rights of property, pure and simple. It turned on "liberty," which for them meant the right to use one's property as one wished, and the right to acquire more. The protesters, though more diffuse, saw the contest ultimately as pivoting on the institution of "monopoly." From the Grange to the Populist Party, the words of the early Greenback Labor Party were continually echoed: "Never before in our history have the banks, the land-grant railroads, and other monopolies been more insolent in their demands for further privilege—still more class legislation. In this emergency the dominant parties are arrayed against the people and are the abject tools of the corporate monopolies."[7]

But what was "monopoly"? Why was it associated with privilege and class legislation? In the modern view, a monopoly is simply a firm possessing a large degree of market power; the term is narrowly economic. And because largeness seems inevitable and a degree of competition re-emerged in most sectors of the American economy after 1900, most historians have discounted the validity of this anti-monopoly sentiment. Hofstadter argued that the populists, in focusing on a single issue, were actually engaging in a paranoid retreat from the complexity of the real world. They saw "history as conspiracy."[8]

Such interpretations appear to make sense only because they are based on an outlook different from that taken by the populists, an outlook which the populists in fact explicitly opposed. They are made in willful blindness to the way nineteenth-century Americans used the

term, "monopoly." In the agrarian tradition, as in the common-law tradition preceding it, a monopoly (like a corporation) was regarded as
primarily a political phenomenon. It was an association created or
chartered by the sovereign to perform some particular task (like the
founding of a colony or the building of a bridge), and granted power to
exercise certain sovereign powers. Constituting a branch of sovereignty
in the hands of a subject, a monopoly was literally a creature of privilege, of private law. Because of this and because of their great powers,
monopolies were viewed with suspicion by traditional liberals and democrats. These people understood that monopolies, as special associations, were also saddled with special obligations as set forth in their
charters. But they feared that, even when monopolies were not used
as tokens of royal favoritism, such institutions might overstep the
bounds set down in those charters and attempt to usurp the liberties of
individuals.[9]

In protesting "monopoly" the populists were not retreating from
the real world. They were actually identifying a common pattern lying
beneath superficially disparate phenomena. The pattern was of corporations gone wrong, of private companies possessing significant powers
over the commons (which for traditional liberals meant the market), yet
spurning responsibilities to it. In finance, private banks promoted federal deflationary policies and manipulated money supply according to
their own speculative designs instead of some measure of the public
need.[10] In land, large companies seized the richest parts of the public
domain.[11] The mortgage companies' and furnishing merchants' draconian loan practices bled a steady stream of the remaining settlers of their
holdings, and reduced independent farmers over the period of a few
seasons to the status of tenants.[12]

The most flagrant violation of popular expectations occurred, however, in transportation. (In fact, until 1900 to speak of "the corporation"
was largely to speak of the railroads; they made up three-quarters of the
corporations listed on the New York Stock Exchange).[13] In America most
farmers were cash-crop farmers, "cultivators of the main chance as well
as the fertile soil," as Veblen put it. For in America, unlike Europe, the
market *preceded* the farm. This meant that the railroads, monopolizing
the means of rural transportation and shipping, were able to impose arbitrary rate structures to distant markets at will. More seriously, they
were able to reduce would-be denizens of a liberal world to classic states
of dependence. The increased scope of interdependence turned out to
mean little when the *means* of interdependence were concentrated in a
few hands. The situation was made the more galling because most farm-

ers had expected the roads to be public highways. That expectation was rooted partly in English precedent regarding major roads to market towns, and partly in the practical fact that the farmers themselves had usually paid for the subsidies used to lure railroads to particular locales.[14]

The central issue that agitated the age was not "industrialization." Farmers welcomed new inventions and pioneered new forms of cooperatives to use those inventions. Nor was the issue "bigness." The call for public ownership of railroads and the telegraph arose as a conscious alternative to the demand to break up large-scale enterprise. Henry George, a pronounced individualist, acknowledged that "the most trivial businesses are being concentrated. . . . Errands are run and carpet sacks are carried by corporations." To resist successfully the tendency toward combination people would have to "throttle steam and discharge electricity from human service."[15]

Nor did the major conflicts arise over the issue of political corruption. (The election of 1896 actually found most of the early civil service reformers in McKinley's camp.) Nor, finally, could the conflict of the era be construed as having turned on arguments over state intervention. An entire wing of business had begun to urge that competition "regulates by the knife" and that unless "the weapon can be held in check, it is too dangerous an agency to be endured."[16]

The central issue was rather that monopolies were acquiring powers over market conditions, and over the political liberties seen as based in those conditions. The proximate effect of such acquisition was to tax small farmers and workers—by deflationary monetary policies, mortgage practices, and fluctuating railroad and grain rates—to pay for the capital accumulation needed for the industrialization of America. It was to tax them to support a process over which they lacked any control, a process which was, in fact, destroying their customary institutions and protections. The complaints, then, were not with industrialization but with the way industrialization was occurring. And the deeper institutional claim was that private parties were being permitted to wield a power that was illegitimate, first, because it arose from control over the *preconditions* of market activity rather than from competition within the marketplace, and second, because it threatened the market freedoms of others.

It was because of this perspective that the populists could speak as they did about conspiracy. They were not psychologically unbalanced; nor were they overly suspicious. They were voicing a verdict that followed from empirical political analysis. There had been no way, traditionally, that small bands of men could have acquired the power that bankers and railwaymen exercised freely in post–Civil War America save through force or fraud. (And this populist analysis was more accurate, Michael Rogin noted, than the conservatives' charge about anarchist conspiracies.)[17] It remains to emphasize that this verdict, rooted directly in the classical tradition, was suffused with larger moral evaluations. An account of the Farmers' Alliance explained that "A trust is a conspiracy against legitimate trade. . . . It is demoralizing in its influence, inconsistent with free institutions and dangerous to our liberties. . . . Trust is only another name for monopoly. Monopoly is wielding a greater power in the government than the people."[18]

The concerns of the conservatives, on one hand, and the agrarians, on the other, can therefore be seen to have been two sides of the same coin. One prominent judge acknowledged this straightforwardly in the wake of the watershed ruling in the *Chicago, Milwaukee Railroad* case of 1891 (discussed in Chapter Five), when he announced that "We are between the Mighty Opposites involving fundamental forces of society."[19]

What divided the opposites were antagonistic views about the political rights that should attach to newly consolidated business enterprises. Justice Field, most of his colleagues, and the larger businessmen claimed for the corporation the rights of private property. They denied its chartered and limited character. The populists, on the other hand, regarded unregulated monopolies as interlopers in market society and subverters of democracy. Tom Watson voiced this view clearly from the stump when he announced, "We have created the corporations. They are our legal off-spring," and asked whether it should ever "be said that the servant is above the master or the child above the father."[20]

It was a traditional formulation that the maverick jurist Judge Seymour Thompson of St. Louis invoked when, agreeing with Watson, he demanded to know after the *Chicago, Milwaukee* case "whether the corporation is to rule the State or the State the corporation?" A Farmers' Alliance newspaper reasoned similarly after the same ruling, when it charged that the corporation had "absorbed the liberties of the community and usurped the power of the agency that created it." Corporate activities, it wrote, had congealed "individualism" into "privilege." The task ahead was for the community to reabsorb the corporation, "to merge itself into it."[21]

The recent interpretations, in denying the integrity of this outlook and accepting the view of those who defeated it, implicitly assume that no alternatives were possible. They assume that it was somehow fated that the community had to lose its authority over the corporation.[22] The

depoliticization of "monopoly" thus grows out of a deeper depoliticization of history itself. "Nothing is any longer good or bad" in such a perspective, as Albert Camus wrote in another context, "but only either
premature or out of date." He added that while the disciples of this historicism urge others to postpone judgment to the future, "the victims
will not be there to judge. For the victim, the present is the only value,
rebellion the only action."[23] From the standpoint of the dominant outlook, the populists *must* appear to have been an irrational, backward-
looking mass. They were protesters deprived of the possibility of protest. They were rebels denied the place to take a stand.

When the populists indicted monopoly, however, they asserted the
possibility of choice and the existence of alternatives. And many of their
contemporaries agreed. The aloof Henry Adams, for example, pausing
in his search for an architectonic principle, noted that the American people had been driven for a hundred years by two forces, "the one simply
industrial," the other "capitalist, centralizing, mechanical." The trusts
and corporations "stood for the larger part of the new order and were
obnoxious because of their vigorous and unscrupulous energy. They
were revolutionary, troubling all the old conventions and values, as the
screws of the ocean steamer must trouble a school of herring." The
choice between Adams's two forces finally came to a head "on the single
gold standard," and the majority, as Adams saw it, declared for the "capitalist, centralizing, mechanical" principle.[24]

We have now identified the pivot of populist conflict. But our conclusion gives rise to a new question: why did corporate "monopoly,"
emerging as a new form of property, provoke such bitterness among a
capitalist people? To answer this we must look more deeply at the place
of the corporation in liberal culture.

PRACTICAL DEMOCRACY VS. PRACTICAL TORYISM

Corporations were long suspect in the liberal order, giving rise both
in Stuart England and a century later in the South Sea Bubble Act to
attempts at their regulation and control.[25] But the associational devices proved hardy growths, capable of adapting to the most adverse
conditions.

Despite the facts that a corporation came to America aboard the
Mayflower, that most states began their existence as corporations, and
that after the revolution those states permitted chartered bodies to de-
cisively shape "the contours of economic life," corporations continued to

be viewed askance.[26] The Constitutional Convention felt the threats of corporate *imperiums in imperio* so strongly that it denied the federal government the power to charter them. The framers also expressed the prevailing sentiment toward corporate bodies when they separated church from state, and when they repudiated political parties.[27] Madisonian aggregations they were willing to countenance; more organic, permanent groupings they were not.

That some corporate forms might protect popular liberties against the state or sustain a healthy individualism (as Tocqueville in essence argued) was considered by few.[28] Most knew only the darker face of corporatism. Acknowledging that "intermediate bodies" had obstructed sovereign power during the era of absolutism, democrats feared they might do the same once sovereignty had passed to the public. "Whatever power is granted to the corporations," they believed, "is so much abstracted from the people themselves."[29]

This animosity was rooted in the deeper logic of liberal culture. A half-century before Locke, Thomas Hobbes had already concluded that corporations were alien elements within liberal society because they emerged, unnaturally, from state favor. "Laws" (in which Hobbes included contracts) should be strictly distinguished from charters, he urged, though they were "often taken promiscuously for the same thing." But "charters are donations of the sovereign: and not laws, but *exemptions* from laws." Laws, furthermore, were "made to bind all the subjects to a commonwealth: [whereas] a liberty, or charter is only to one man, or some one part of the people." Because a corporation originated in special privilege, it therefore violated the requirement of general laws. That point was critical for Hobbes, for in upsetting the requirement of equality it confounded the conditions for general consent and obligation. In his chapter entitled "Of those things that weaken or tend to the Dissolution of the Commonwealth," Hobbes likened corporations to lesser commonwealths in the bowels of the greater—to "worms in the entrails of a natural man." They were autonomous, parasitic, and subversive of sovereignty.[30]

The classical bourgeois vision was not that of a society organically articulated into different groups, as in the medieval vision, but of a market order populated by disparate atoms. Political energy in the market order appeared to flow from such atomized wills or, marginally, from a neutral overarching state. A corporate charter could fit into such a scheme only as a temporary anomaly, a grant from the public authority. Such a grant would not constitute a title deed because the corporation was not regarded as a form of property. The grant was rather an autho-

cratic society required a wide diffusion of property. These political actors were no levelers, but they believed that social relations of a particular character were necessary if republican forms were to be imbued with any substantive meaning. When "a general and tolerably equal distribution of landed property" ceased, they predicted, "power departs, liberty expires, and a commonwealth . . . inevitably assume[s] some other form."[35] In line with this distinction between form and substance, the more radical of the Jacksonians even concluded, from the existence of the Bank and the government's funding policies, that the Revolution of 1776 had yet to be completed.[36]

Whether they accepted this political emphasis or not, however, the people for whom Locke, Smith, and Adams spoke were convinced that liberty without some material foundations amounted to very little. They accordingly asserted a man's title over the grounds and fruits of his labor. In the process wealth-holding underwent an obvious transformation, from which it emerged apparently consisting no longer of a relationship between people, and seemed instead to arise in a relationship between men and things.

The political theory and literature of the period reveal that these new concepts of individualism and liberty were far more than simple rationales for the new property. Rather, individualism, politics, and private property appeared to be parts of a conceptual whole; and the whole was reflective of a new sense of being in the world. Property lines seemed to mark out a human space in a world of chaos (as Locke's frequent resort to the metaphor of "fences" suggests). Contracts seemed to provide the possibility for communications between these separate parcels and, indeed, for the owner's very existence in the eyes of others.[37] Property was thus more than a secure basis for identity; it suggested a mode *of* identity. For the classical bourgeois, freedom appeared less as a means to property than property appeared as the embodiment of freedom.[38] What we see here is the emergence of a new existential moment in Western history. To assert private control of a piece of the world, to possess and be self-"possessed," were its insignia.[39]

The objections that radical independence is really impossible in human society, that security can be gained by means other than control, and that the new ethic obscured an unprecedented new dependence on economic conditions, would not have troubled the classical liberals. Dependence on laws, Voltaire and Rousseau explained, was no dependence at all; and that was true whether the "laws" were economic or political. The critical thing was to avoid being dependent on other people. It was in America during the Jacksonian period that this ethic witnessed its fullest flowering. The successes of the Western frontiersman and the Eastern merchant gave it the stamp of veracity. "In all my lectures I have taught one doctrine," Emerson confided in his journal, "namely, the infinitude of the private man." The conclusion followed naturally enough: in "Self-Reliance" Emerson declared, "I will have proximities but no covenants"—and this to a nation founded in Puritanism.

These were the roots of anti-corporate feeling in classical liberal culture. The resultant individualism was not without its own confusions. Classical liberalism still harbored an implicit *in*egalitarianism. This can be seen, for example, when Locke, after painting his picture of an idyllic equality, justified the existing "partage of things in an inequality of private possessions" because it improved productivity. True, the Lord had given "the world to men in common," Locke admitted; but "He gave it to the use of the industrious and the rational—and labor was to be his title to it—not the fancy and covetousness of the quarrelsome and contentious." C. B. MacPherson ties this double message to "the ambivalence of an emerging bourgeois society which demanded formal equality, but required substantive inequality" in practice.[40]

Jacksonian America also provided evidence of this ambivalence. The Jacksonians loved equality because they feared domination. But that was not the same as believing in everyone's affirmative rights. The free man could have no superiors, but that said nothing about subordinates. And liberalism not only closed its eyes to many forms of subordination, but even mandated an epochal new one. By including productive wealth within private property, it required that as a condition of labor those who owned no such wealth give up their power over the conditions and fruits of their labor. Because even small property of the capitalist kind carries the seed of aggrandizement, the affirmation of equal rights to contract also therefore affirmed the rights of some to increase their power over others. The hidden tragedy of the Jacksonian program lay in this fact. Although "opening the field for competition [might] sufficiently disarm the incorporated institutions now in being," as a contemporary held, it would not prevent new concentrations from arising in the newly opened field.[41]

Thus the Jacksonians did not carry James Harrington's insights about property and power through to their conclusions. They failed to consider that for one group of salesmen in the republic of propertyholders—the sellers of labor power—and for the Indians and blacks at its borders, the contract disguised a new form of dominion. In an era when conditions were fluid and most people felt social subordination to be a temporary rite of passage, however, such contradictions and confusions paled before common individualist antipathies to "tory" institutions and policies.

In sum, monopolies and corporations were suspect in the republic of small-property holders not only because of the power they threatened, but also because the feudal aura of status and privilege hung over them. They were seen as arising from "grants of exclusive privilege . . . wholly adverse to the genius of our institutions" and as threatening to subvert the content of formal democratic institutions until "all distinction [would] vanish . . . between practical democracy and practical toryism." [42] The first furtive expressions of laissez-faire doctrine, the first systematic protests against state activism in America, actually began as incidents of the Jacksonian anti-charter (anti-corporate) campaign. They emerged not from the ranks of big business but from classic individualists who (following Adam Smith) feared that a strong state would necessarily resuscitate "the corporation spirit" at the expense of the public. [43]

THE CORPORATION AND PRIVATE PROPERTY

Despite the deep-running currents of individualism within liberalism, associational principles began to establish a tenuous foothold again in early nineteenth-century America, this time from within the logic of liberalism itself. Corporations began to be depicted, consistent with the character of the joint-stock company, as expressions of the wills of compacting individuals. Conceived of as deriving their powers solely from the voluntary agreements of their members, they appeared to be "natural," autonomous of the state and politics, and therefore legitimate.

This view was not uncontested. The emergence of this compact view was met by a restatement of the concession theory of the corporation and the traditional view of property. That view of property would later be given clear formulation by Chief Justice Waite in the famous *Munn* cases of 1876 (which tested and then upheld the Granger regulatory laws). Waite declared that the state had the power to "regulate the conduct of its citizens one towards another and the manner in which each shall use his own property, when such regulation becomes necessary for the public good. . . . When one devotes his property to a use in which the public has an interest, he in effect grants to the public an interest in that use." [44]

The argument about the status of the corporation found its first precise expression in American political literature in the famous *Dartmouth College* case of 1819. The case appeared to reaffirm the traditional concession (or "fiction") theory. "A corporation is an artificial being," wrote Justice Marshall in what would become a widely quoted statement; it is "invisible, intangible and existing only in the contemplation of the law. Being a creature of law, it possesses only those properties which the charter of its creation confers upon it." [45]

As befits a history rich in irony and double meanings, however, Marshall's decision actually cut in the opposite direction from what was suggested by that statement. It was this decision which justified Maitland's later comment that, "contract, that greediest of legal categories, which once wanted to devour the State, resents being told that it cannot painlessly digest even a joint-stock company." [46] For the *Dartmouth* verdict declared that a corporate charter was a contract within the constitutional meaning of the term. By that decision the charter-holding of a college was given the status of a property right, and the corporation indeed began to be "devoured" by private contracts. The ultimate significance of this decision was widely appreciated by the anti-charter forces. If the many transactions of civil society were to be "engulfed in this vortex and whirled under the jurisdiction of the Supreme Court," wrote one contemporary, then "the people of the states, instead of having governments adapted to their wants, liable to be modified, altered, repealed or totally changed as was their . . . inalienable right, have in fact myriads of little perpetuities beyond the control of . . . legislation, and subject only to the will of their directors." [47]

Dartmouth began a trend, however. And the corporation began to be gradually emancipated from its traditional limitations. That emancipation was partly the work of the corporations themselves, as they sought to extricate themselves from the burdens of state oversight and taxation and as railroads began to move beyond the states in which they were chartered. [48] But it was also the unexpected fruit of the Jacksonians' own efforts. Seeking to enact General Incorporation Acts in order to abolish a major source of legislative corruption, they succeeded unwittingly in freeing the corporation from the legal bases of public obligation. With the passage of these Acts in most states between 1837 and 1850, the private status first granted to college corporations in *Dartmouth* began to be extended to all business corporations. What had been a privilege now became a right "freely available on condition it be used for business purposes." [49] Corporations would continue after this to have special powers—like limited liability for their directors, immortality, and various market powers; but they would cease to be seen in law as bearing special duties in return for those powers.

With the eclipse of their special status, corporate spokesmen began for the first time during the 1850s to appropriate the laissez-faire arguments of their opponents. It was at this time that they began to subsume their organizations to a Lockean "nature," claim a private status, and issue stern warnings to government to refrain from meddling in economic affairs.[50] Somewhat ironically, then, the philosophy of extreme economic individualism triumphed in America just as the corporations were in fact wresting the field from individuals.

Most Americans refused, however, to accept the idea that the corporation was individual property writ large because they failed to see it as property at all. It was a special association, an alienation of sovereignty to named persons for specific purposes and subject to stipulated conditions. The line between property and the corporation was observed by many entrepreneurial spokesmen as well as by the agrarians. William Graham Sumner's later idea of "plutocratic" enterprise, for example, was a precise equivalent of the Jacksonian understanding of "monopoly."[51]

By the end of the Civil War, however, pressures were building to erase this boundary and to collapse the distinctions between the corporation and property. Fueled by past victories, their need for large amounts of capital, and the mass-organizational lessons of the war, corporate directors began a systematic campaign to dispose of old restraints and to convert their institution from an occasional device to the master institution of American life. Charles Francis Adams, Jr., recorded the popular reaction to this corporate offensive in an early article in which, using explicitly political terms, he assailed the "organized lawlessness" of the railroads: "These modern potentates have declared war, negotiated peace, reduced courts, legislatures and sovereign states to obedience . . . imposed taxes, and boldly setting both law and public opinion at defiance, have freely exercised many other attributes of sovereignty."[52] The subsequent annexation of many prerogatives of sovereignty by private corporations (as by the National Banking System, private highways, company towns, company-issued scrip, and eventually, rental armies) appeared to most Americans as the natural fruit of the corporations' unnatural energies.

The ultimate problems posed by the blurring of this critical distinction were identified by Adams himself in a later volume entitled *The Railroads: Their Origin and Problems* (1878). Adams was singularly qualified to address the topic because he had helped create and had served on the Massachusetts Railway Commission, the first railroad commission in the country. Adams began his inquiry by acknowledging that the railroad problem arose from obstructions of free enterprise. The railroads were ceasing to be competitive. Worse, "the rights of use and laws of trade" were in flux because public highways were being replaced by "modern thoroughfares owned by individuals." But Adams felt that it was senseless to condemn such ownership. And it made no sense to seek analogies with King's Highways. Adams believed that the organizing abilities of profit-seekers should be rewarded. He was ceasing, then, to view the problem in his earlier political terms; it now seemed to him a physical and logistical trouble. Railroads by their very existence created "favored zones," freed from the workings of the laws of supply and demand. In this the roads were part of a larger "tendency to combination and of responsibility" that was "inevitable." Capitalism was "trying to protect itself," and Adams predicted that it would succeed.[53]

The railroad problem emerged in Adams's pages, then, as an incident in the larger pattern of capitalist development. It was in fact an early expression of the corporation problem. The railroad was only the first of numerous combinations which, through control of capital rather than geography, would also prove capable of establishing "favored zones." At the most obvious level this would produce economic imbalances, for without competition there would cease to be any assurance that rates were related to efficient services (or that roads were built in the right places). But more deeply, as Adams was vaguely aware, it would raise serious political questions—questions about the power corporate directors wielded over others, and about the legitimacy of that power, which had arisen outside the marketplace. Classical liberalism had tried to ignore such things. But by extending the scope of the means of production while at the same time trying to retain private title over them, the corporation forced back into consideration questions of legitimacy and of collective choice.

During the 1870s Oliver Wendell Holmes, Jr., delighted in deflating the claims of moralists by explaining that legal principles were "in fact and at bottom the result . . . of unconscious and inarticulate . . . views of public policy."[54] Mill's familiar formula that someone was free as long as he harmed no one else, for example, obscured the fact that societies actively choose what to consider "harmful." To view our situation in Holmesean terms, we can see that by the last quarter of the nineteenth century America faced an inarticulate policy choice about which business practices would be deemed legitimate and which harmful, which placed outside the scope of public authority and which placed within it.

Faced with such questions, classic American liberalism fractured. It was as if the railroads had criss-crossed the American mind no less than the American continent, defining regions, dividing them, and turning them against each other. The inhabitants of some of those regions argued for government limitation of property rights in order, paradoxically, to preserve a world of private property. The denizens of others, minimizing dangers to the liberal order and claiming to reject the active state, actually used the state to protect themselves from the traditional claims of the community. Let us now see how those two schools defined themselves in conflict with each other during the decades preceding Progressivism.

3

Liberalism in Protest, and the Thought of Henry George

And they shall build houses and inhabit them; and they shall plant vineyards and eat the fruits of them. They shall not build and another inhabit; they shall not plant and another eat.

—*Isaiah* 65:21–22

The diversity of interpretations about populism is matched by a diversity of judgments on the character of its thought. This is illustrated by the variety of conclusions that have been made about one of its profoundest and most representative writers, Henry George. The fact that George's eyes were fixed on matters of land tenure has meant for some that they were fixed on the distant past. Yet in proposing that the land be made "the common property of the whole people," he sounded like a contemporary socialist; and this impression is strengthened by such things as his early attempt to run guns to Juarez's revolution in Mexico, his signing of youthful letters to editors as "Proletariat," and his later vigorous championing of the Irish land struggles. His early reputation was also derived from an article in which he predicted that technical progress would exacerbate class distinctions.[1] Yet he was at pains to insist in *Progress and Poverty* that labor and capital enjoyed a harmony of interests.

George was read avidly by the populists, but he rejected the populist label. He was a self-educated intellectual, but he spurned an academic position in Political Economy created at Berkeley in the 1870s. (As a final contestant for that august position he disqualified himself by noting to assembled faculty and students that those who wanted to educate themselves needed no universities, and that political economy was invariably used to oppose the efforts of the working classes).[2] Though John Dewey considered him a philosopher of Plato's rank, more recent historians have seen him as a crank—one of those perennial sellers of snake oil who enlivened frontier existence.

Many of the recent doubts about George's thought derive from a preoccupation with his Single Tax proposal. But for his contemporaries and later reformers, his importance derived less from this proposal than from the analysis that preceded it, less from the remedy than from the diagnosis. That diagnosis anticipated many mid-twentieth-century ideas about taxation, land-use policy, and the structural roots of inflation. And although the diagnosis was ultimately anti-socialist, it also surpassed modern understandings of the class character of current technological progress. George's thinking is a clear lens to the logic of populist thought and an analysis of it will help us understand that thought. This chapter will show how populist thinking, rooted in classical liberalism, moved away from its origins under the press of circumstance and populist political organizing.

"EARNING IS MAKING"

The problem that riveted George's attention was the simultaneous advance in modern society of poverty and progress. As cities replaced settlements, he observed that workmen's wages dropped, hierarchy appeared, economic and political combines arose, and society acquired— along with the college and library—the "more hideous Huns and fiercer Vandals of whom Macauley prophecied."[3] George distinguished himself from other commentators of the times by insisting that despite phenomenal industrial progress, the heart of the American promise (opportunity, security, a rough equality, and meaningful work) would remain unfulfilled for most Americans. And he gave voice to a foreboding—not unknown to Americans of a century later—of the great costs incurred by the rapid enclosure and rapacious pillaging of the commons from which all must draw their sustenance.[4]

George's analysis of the causes of increasing poverty and misery, like the analyses of other populists, focused on monopoly. But George addressed himself to private monopolies in land. As he saw it, the right of the monopolists to siphon off, as private rent, the social wealth created by workers, capitalists, and prior community development hindered economic growth and impoverished the real producers of the nation. Landowners lived off "unearned increments." As Bellamy's Doctor Leek asked the protagonist of *Looking Backward*, "If a people eat with a spoon that leaks half of its contents between bowl and lip, are they not likely to go hungry?"[5] George assented, and identified land monopolies as the providers of the deficient tableware. Rent was the main source of contemporary injustice, demoralization, and industrial strife.

It was to correct this evil that George proposed that the state impose a Single Tax on landlords equal to the amount of the unearned increment. He believed that the tax would return to the community "for the use of the community, that value which is the creation of the community"; or that failing, that it would induce unproductive landlords to sell their unused lands to those who could make them fruitful. George considered formal expropriation unnecessary and dangerous; society could leave the shell of property with private owners as long as it took the kernel. He felt confident that with the aid of this Tax "the equality ordained by nature [would] be attained" and society would re-establish a fair field with no favors (the liberal view, again, of the public interest).[6]

George thus affirmed the Jacksonian equation of democracy and a producers' ethic. But why then did he go beyond the Jacksonians, and even Locke, and extend his attack to private property, the very basis of the Lockean order? This—and not why populists called for state intervention—is the important question to be asked about this agrarian protest. For George was only taking his contemporaries' reasoning to its logical conclusions. And in the process he revealed a road which later American liberalism might have taken. To answer our question we must understand the theories of value and politics that informed this rural American culture. The writings of Henry George gave voice to both.

The agrarian outlook saw two elements combining to create social value or wealth: land and labor. Capital was important, but it was regarded as a subspecies of labor. Primarily, "earning is making." Populist thinking on this point was identical to that of the Chartists in England who preceded and influenced Marx: capital was "stored labor."[7] And labor was regarded as the constitutive force in the transformation of natural materials into usable wealth. George's consistent effort was to emphasize the primacy of labor in the creation of value.

The introductory chapters of *Progress and Poverty* were thus devoted to lengthy proofs that capital never "advanced" wages to labor; labor advanced the value of its hourly product to capital until payday. Capital did not provide for the subsistence of the laborer, as it often seemed. In any country where there was not actual famine, food and shelter would come "not from wealth set apart for the assistance of productive capital, but from wealth set aside for subsistence."[8] Nor could productivity be attributed entirely to inherited machinery. The fifty square miles of London were the wealthiest in the world, George noted, but if productive labor there were to cease for a fortnight, people would die like sheep and "a wall of circumvallation, such as Titus drew around Jerusalem" would be drawn around each household. Wealth produced by past generations, he wrote, could no more "account for the consumption of the present than the dinner he ate last year can supply a man with present strength." And what the "rich idler" got through his inheritance was not wealth per se, but the "power of commanding wealth as others produce it."[9]

George did not deny that capital augmented labor's power to "impress upon matter the character of wealth." He even accorded capital a legitimate return when used for that purpose. But without labor and a high level of community development, no amount of capital would yield high productivity.[10] Implicit in this economic argument was a moral valuation common to agrarian culture (though no longer prevalent in America) that men and women could lead virtuous and meaningful lives without continually augmented economic productivity.

Labor required land. "Land" was defined by George as comprising "all natural materials, forces and opportunities" to which men's labor was applied in order to create usable wealth. It was only by having access to land, thus defined, that men could "come into contact with or use nature."[11] For this culture the concept of land therefore possessed a broad, metaphoric meaning that encompassed all potential productive materials lying beyond those created by men.

The just society envisioned by George and his milieu was one in which everyone had a right to labor on the land. This right, with its attendant assumptions and implications, was denoted by the concept of "opportunity." And opportunity was seen as rooted in the aboriginal and equal rights of all to "use their own faculties," to use nature and "receive and possess her reward."[12] Even Adam Smith had included within "property" one's right to use his "strength and dexterity," and considered that right "the foundation of all other property."[13] It followed, obversely, that no one had a right to wealth who did not labor for it. The fruits of labor were seen, finally, as encompassing not only material well-being but also the dignities of the mind and the pleasures of social companionship.[14]

Nowhere in American political literature was it stated more eloquently that the original promise of American life was not of great wealth nor even of equality of condition. It was the promise of "opportunity" to work, to decide how to apply one's own wit to nature, and to make one's contribution to society without being beholden to superiors. The Homestead Act was welcomed so widely because it seemed to give to natural right the blessings of positive law.

Although some of George's assertions might have been disproven by empirical facts (some mining companies *did* control housing and subsistence by this date, for example, and labor in some places *would* have ceased without capital), this did not mean for those who shared his world view that his assertions were wrong. It meant rather that the natural order of things had been denied and the functions of the public authority usurped. George claimed for his conclusions the status of science; but it was a science grounded in a particular view of human facts and institutions. It was science with a human subject. It was, paradoxically, a natural rights empiricism.[15]

George, like the populists as a whole, thus subsumed economics and politics into a larger fabric of morals. At the heart of their concerns was a fear that the physical preconditions for a particular kind of character would be destroyed. The people would then become "corrupted," in the original Roman sense of the term. The fear was that people's initiative would be undermined, their sense of their own interests deranged, and their natural instincts confused. George had already written in 1879 that "the most ominous sign in the United States is . . . that people doubt the existence of an honest man in public office, or look on him as a fool for not seizing his opportunities. That is to say that the people themselves are becoming corrupted." This was also Ignatius Donnelly's meaning, when in the dramatic preamble to the Populist Platform of 1892 he declared that "the people are demoralized." The inevitable product of such corruption, in populist eyes, would be something later called mass society.[16] With such a society, George added, it would not be difficult to turn a republican government into a despotism, without even changing its institutions. For "forms are nothing when substance is gone."[17] The sense of urgency that informed populist thinking sprang, in other words, from the fear that if the nation did not adjust its economy to fit its political goals, it would necessarily be pulled backwards, as feudal economic relations reclaimed the polity.

NEW DEPARTURES IN AGRARIAN LIBERALISM

Was this political analysis backward-looking in focusing on problems of the land? Were the agrarian liberals hopelessly fixed on an Arcadian past? Such conclusions hardly jibe with the populists' stated concern for such things as money supply, railway strikes, and new cooperative exchanges. The conclusions would be especially surprising in George's case, for he had first-hand acquaintance with the new industrial organization. As a newspaperman he had written often about the Southern Pacific, and a news service he tried to set up was crushed outright by the telegraph monopoly. But even a cursory reading of *Progress and Poverty* fails to sustain this familiar charge. An entire chapter of it was devoted to the new industrial corporations, which he styled "insidious aggregations of large masses of capital."[18] The purpose of the chapter was to distinguish legitimate profits from the "spurious" returns captured by such behemoths.

The point, however, was that industrial corporations for George and his milieu were not sui generis. The problems they posed were perceived as variations of problems that had already been posed on the land. And given their definition of "land" it is easy to see why. What the railroads, grain companies, and land monopolies were doing, in effect, was restricting the "opportunities" available, "forestalling" goods on their way to market, and pre-empting access to the "land" by setting up toll gates between man and nature.[19] They were creating a second nature.

To speak of this landed vision is to speak about populist origins. It is not, however, to say that they stayed where they began. They started like Locke "in the beginning," before the Fall. They started with a world of unlimited opportunities, where no man could "acquire to himself a property to the prejudice of his neighbor." In this world, Locke wrote, in a phrase that continues to tantalize the liberal mind, "right and convenience went together."[20] But America of the 1880s had become a world in which a person *could* acquire property to the prejudice of his neighbor and in which convenience often failed to make room for right. Ideas changed accordingly.

The most obvious signs of a flexible response were emergent concerns on the part of agrarian liberals for such things as social context and economic value, concerns that Locke had avoided by subsuming "opportunity" under a pre-existing nature. These new concerns found expression in George's theory of rent. For him the critical factor in the unjust accretion of rent was the foreclosure of alternate land available for productive settlement. Landowners claimed that high rents flowed from improvements they had made in their holdings. But to people who had seen values skyrocket or plummet because of the enclosure of land by absentee landlords, the building or rerouting of a railroad, or the discovery of a mine, a more plausible explanation suggested itself. What a person was willing to give in labor for the privilege of using a parcel of land depended not simply on his need or its presence, nor even on its productive capacity, but "upon its capacity *as compared with* that of land that can be had for nothing."[21] Where free land of good quality had ceased to exist, rents would be high and wages low.

The first premise of frontier economics was not scarcity, in other words, but plenty. Whereas subsequent economists would devote their attention to marginal utility theories of demand, the agrarians assumed an abundance of supply. The critical factor contributing to rising rents and declining wages as communities were settled, then, was the control of context, the foreclosure of other opportunities to labor. With George, rent emerged as the price which the "exclusive right to the use of natural capabilities" permitted owners to impose on others. In this Ricardean vein, rent, more bluntly, was "the price of monopoly." And its incidence came to be seen increasingly as rooted in force.[22]

From this perspective, therefore, it was an artificial scarcity that permitted landlords to impose a constantly rising tax on labor and capital "for the opportunity to use [their] powers." And it was because the context in which people labored was continually rigged and re-rigged that progress had failed "to lighten the burdens of the masses of people." Rent, then, was at the heart of the "subtle alchemy" that extracted from the masses the fruits of their labors, the primary way in which the rich, confirming John Taylor's insight, plundered the poor by legally invading their property.[23]

George also worked beyond classical liberalism in tracing the effects of land monopoly into the "stream of exchanges." There he found them altering values and adding still further to the burdens of working people. The rudiments of this analysis were already apparent in his early article on the transcontinental railroad. As he saw it, "progress" occurring in existing social arrangements actually worked to diminish the value of labor in two ways. First, by adding to population it forced wages down by increasing the competition for work. This conclusion seemed plausible given the evidence of the times, though economic development would offset its effects.

Second and more important, wages would fall relative to other production costs. With development other factors of production would become more expensive and, with concentration, corporations would begin to impose noncompetitive disadvantages on labor. As working people became less able to find independent sustenance—because arable land was already fenced off, new productive knowledge was "locked up" by patents, and individual effort had ceased to be competitive with industry—they would therefore be forced to pay a double penalty. First, their income would be diminished by the "tax" they were forced to pay to work.[24] Second, their labor would be *objectively devalued* relative to other factors of production.

Industry might develop and wages might rise for a time. But George predicted that existing social organization would ultimately thwart the promise of cheaper goods, increased security, and improved civic status for working people. Henry Demarest Lloyd made the same point in *Wealth Against Commonwealth*. Governor Lewelling of Kansas also lamented the effect of contemporary social organization on technical progress in his famous "Tramp Circular" of 1893. Lewelling saw the source of contemporary problems as consisting in the fact that the private monopoly of new labor-saving devices permitted them to be turned from social to selfish uses. Instead of technical advance working like a "lever" to raise the "whole social fabric from underneath as was . . . hoped," wrote George, such advance acted as a "wedge . . . forced through society," raising those above and crushing those below.[25]

George's primary concern was not with the clash of worker and capitalist in the factory, nor even with the conflict between the landlord and tenants who suddenly had to pay higher rents. It was with the long-term alteration of values, and the alteration of social relations that would follow from the systematic imposition of higher rents. In general form, George had identified the roots of a structurally based inflation.[26] He saw that private ownership of the grounds of common productive activity would permit owners to siphon off the value of improved common productivity for themselves. To the extent that the value of workers' labor power diminished, relative to other production and commodity values, men and women could be left in full possession of their homes, goods, and even income, but their circumstances would deteriorate and their security decline because the *value* would eventually migrate out of those holdings. ("Those steers, while they grew well, shrank . . . as fast as they grew," remarked a laconic farmer on the effect of fluctuating farm prices).[27] To put it differently, George understood that private control of "opportunity" created the institutional bases for a silent expropriation of people's wealth, status, and liberty.

In addressing himself to the fluctuations of wealth and social status following from manipulations of *value*, George succeeded in putting his finger on a primary way in which the expropriation of wealth necessary for private capital accumulation had always occurred in America. From Shays' Rebellion through the Greenback agitation of the 1870s, the rich had continually plundered the rest of the society, silently and legally, by means of taxes, tariffs, and debt and money-supply policies. George succeeded, that is, in identifying the class content of a wide range of what are normally seen as "middle-class" issues. Because so much of American history has been defined by the fortunes and culture of the old middle class, this was an accomplishment of no small significance.

ISHMAEL VS. THE BEHEMOTH

George's analysis revealed the profoundly *substantive* character of agrarian liberalism. If a private business had somehow secured control over the components of market activity, presumably set beyond the hands of man and preserved in their neutrality by government, then "monopoly" could be inferred, even in the absence of a legal charter or controlling market position.[28] It was one thing to gain power competitively in the marketplace. The populists protested the control by large capitalists of the *grounds* of market competition—the turning of the basic means of exchange, transportation, and communication into objects of private designs. Such control made presumed constants variable; it threatened to measure the world by "elastic yardsticks." The process resembled what Karl Polanyi called The Great Transformation a few centuries earlier in Europe; it can be more fully understood with that transformation in mind.

Originally, Polanyi explained, capitalist markets developed in societies in which the basic factors of market activity—land, labor, and money—were regulated by custom and religion outside the economy itself. The market arose in a context not itself governed by market principles. In the course of capitalist development, however, market principles steadily encroached on their surrounding context. In pursuit of a self-regulating market, merchants and bankers succeeded over two centuries in making land and labor alienable in the marketplace, and casting them into forms whose value could be stated quantitatively and commensurably with other commodities. At that point everything became susceptible to pricing and sale.[29]

This was The Great Transformation. Its occurrence required nothing less than "the dissolution of the body economic into its elements" so those elements could be reassembled according to the needs of capital.

In starker imagery, it required "an act of vivisection upon the body social" so that man could be reduced to "labor," nature to "property," and society itself to "an adjunct of the market." In the process labor not only was transformed into a "fictive commodity," but people were deprived of the "protective covering of social institutions" and left to experience the effect of social exposure alone. Instead of an economy embedded in social relations, social relations began to be subsumed by the economy.[30] History had already seen the transition from traditional economies containing a small market to full-scale market economies. Now it witnessed the further transformation of the market economy into a market *society*.

The populists witnessed similar transformations as the American economy became industrialized. Their ultimate fear, like Polanyi's, was that having grasped control of its own premises, the market would prove unable to preserve them. In market society, Polanyi wrote, financial speculation would periodically liquidate enterprise, unregulated land deals would despoil the countryside, and "in disposing of man's labor power, the system would incidentally dispose of the physical, psychological and moral entity 'man' attached to that tag."[31]

In response to these prospects and its own substantive orientations, populist thinking began to move in more explicitly political channels than either classical liberalism or its contemporary, Social Darwinism. The agrarian protesters rejected theories that explained their troubles by a lack of initiative or by overpopulation, just as they rejected the evolutionary "dogma" that construed their plight as the inevitable product of the fact that economic habits lagged behind developing institutions. Most populists declined Bellamy's magnanimous view that it was the capitalists' folly rather than their sins that was at issue. The large capitalists' "tyranny and rapacity," and their ability to "rob, corrupt and destroy" appeared rather, as George wrote, to be the effects of "a maladjustment in the legislative department of government."[32] They appeared to be products of will, choice, and policy.

George's novelty was that he took the political implications of the critique of monopoly to their conclusions. In this we find the answer to the question posed at the beginning of this chapter. That large corporations were rooted economically in small property-holdings was familiar. George's contribution was to see that they were also rooted *politically* in the grant to small property-holders of rights "against the world." ("From fee simple comes the modern corporation," Robert Brady later wrote, "just as surely as the oak comes from the acorn.")[33] Desirous of identifying not simply the offending institution but the historical path by which it had triumphed, George moved farther than his contemporaries; but he moved along lines they understood. His analysis led him to propose that there was "a natural distinction between property in land and property in other things," and that the former was ultimately "an usurpation, a creation of force and fraud."[34]

George argued that in the period of their growth, all peoples and nations had recognized the importance of common ownership of the land. Even the feudal system was a triumph of the idea of the common right to land, changing an absolute into a conditional tenure, and imposing special obligations in return for the privilege of receiving rent.[35] The bourgeois conjunction of personal liberty and private property in land, George urged, was a historical accident. The purposes of that conjunction had been to insure the proper use of land and to grant people security in the fruits of their labor. But private property in land now stood "in the way of its proper use" and worked to deny people the fruits of their labor. George therefore concluded that the society could no longer assure both proper uses of land and grants to exclusive ownership of it. A fundamental distinction had to be admitted between "exclusive ownership in [one's] own labor when embodied in material things" and exclusive ownership in land. It was the same distinction as Marx's between property in things and property in productive wealth; for Marx it was the latter which conferred the power to exploit others.

"There is no escape," George concluded, from the choice being forced upon the nation. That similar conclusions were being reached elsewhere was revealed on the other shore of the continent, by Robert Toombs, the old Georgia statesman and mentor of Watson, when he declared in 1877, "Better shake the pillars of property than the pillars of liberty."[36] George responded straightforwardly to the choice by concluding that "the recognition of individual proprietorship in land is the denial of the natural rights of other individuals."[37] What he asserted, in the language of an agrarian culture, was that control of "property," control of the opportunities to labor, could not be alienated from the community without undermining the political and moral foundations of democracy.

This was a radical step within liberalism and one fraught with theoretical ramifications. George was being forced by the times to destroy private property in order to save it—to impugn property in land in order to preserve the space for meaningful, dignified, and competitive economic activity.

His call for a community right to the commons was anathema to some interests, but it was not without precedent in the popular culture. The concept of wealth-holding that emerged in George's pages suited the agrarian conviction, voiced often by Jefferson and Paine, that the earth belonged in usufruct to those who worked it. The region where George lived and worked, furthermore, had known the open-handedness and easy camaraderie of unenclosed domain. George recommended the example of the California mining camps to the world because in them no one had been able to take more than he could work or to "lock" up natural resources.[38] The idea of a vast national commons in any case, had existed on the American frontier for decades. "The air, the water, and the ground are free gifts to man," Cooper's Ishmael Bush exclaimed. "And no one has the power to portion them out in parcels. Man must drink and breathe and walk, and therefore each has a right to his share of the 'arth.'"[39]

What now propelled George to his critical choice (and a number of other populists toward socialism) was the fact that the commons was being closed off and the space necessary for the fulfillment of the liberal promise forcefully pre-empted. What George sought by condemning property in "land," at the deepest level, was to somehow preserve the most important elements of liberal ethics in the midst of industrialization. In 1879 he had already voiced what would later be known as the Turner thesis. Since "our advance has reached the Pacific," he wrote, the "Republic has entered upon a new era." The "fact that has always acted and reacted in American consciousness" and given rise to a general intelligence and comfort, a generosity and independence, "this great fact which has been so potent, is ceasing to be. The public domain is almost gone."[40] His point, despite the reference to the Pacific, was political. It was that specific institutions were putting an end to a moral region, an internal frontier. "Monopoly" was foreclosing the space the Lockean individual needed in order to exist. Thus Cooper's Ishmael Bush: "Why don't the surveyors just set their compasses and run their lines over our heads as well as beneath our feet? Why do they not . . . [give to the] airholder so many rods of heaven, with the use of such a star for a boundary marker, and such a cloud to turn a mill?"[41]

And what good would Jefferson's and Webster's parcels of land be if the value of their labor was continually drained away and if their possession failed to assure the liberal virtues? In such conditions the American liberal would find himself a displaced person, a man without a country. Little wonder that the reference to Ishmael recurred through these years—in Cooper's novel, in George's and Melville's writings, and even in the young Watson's diary.[42] Ishmael meant "outcast." It was the term by which an agrarian, bible-reading culture knew what European intellectuals denoted more abstractly by the word alienation.

CLASS, MASS, OR STATUS? THE POLITICS OF POPULIST THOUGHT

What was the character of this political thought? It attempted to resuscitate liberal ethics. Its complaint was not with capitalism but with deviations from capitalism. The goal was a fair field and no favors. But its position was complex; seeking to draw the line at one point, this thought carried a dynamic that pushed beyond.

The populists initially saw society as being comprised of individuals rather than of groups. They protested such things as manipulation and "forestalling" rather than exploitation. When they did consent to use the language of class it was usually in what, for Europe, had been pre-industrial terms. They would thus draw the line between the landed strata and "the producing classes," and the latter would include both workers and capitalists. (Alternately, the mass was said to be threatened by "the class" as the democracy was threatened by the plutocracy).[43] By the mid-nineties bitter in-fighting had also developed between Populist Party members, Single Taxers, and socialists. Because of these facts, and because urban workers declined to support Bryan in 1896, most modern liberals and Marxists (following the early socialist Daniel de Leon) have characterized populism as the politics of a frustrated middle class—a petit-bourgeois, rear-guard historical action.

Hofstadter presented populism as an expression of status politics. In his view, the farmer, striving to regain his lost rank, indulged in irrational rhetoric and "ideological mass politics"; he played the "injured little yeoman," cast the world in dualistic terms, and proved incapable of engaging in healthy interest-group politics. In its underlying motives, Hofstadter saw populism as only "another episode in . . . American entrepreneurial radicalism."[44]

Such phrases fail, however, to encompass the richness and variety of the movement. Analysts have sought the embodiment of theoretical categories in the real world, and failing in their search, have charged the populists with being irrational. But the ambiguities of the populist idiom were ambiguities of the time, ambiguities rooted in the contradictions of capitalist society, then surfacing in a particular way. This is to say that populism was the expression of a political culture in transition. It may have begun as "a peculiar American device to defend the capitalism of the many against the capitalism of the few," in Theodore Draper's apt phrase.[45] But in the process of attacking the capitalism of the few it began to discern the predatory character of capitalism—of property organized *as* capital—in general. Prompted by the substantive concerns of Jacksonian liberalism, it began, as with George, to set itself against the claims of large capital for fundamentally political reasons.

The writings of George, Gronlund, and Bellamy all revealed the theoretical shifts that occurred in the twenty years which spanned the Grangers, the various Farmers' Alliances, and eventually The People's Party. This was only a "shift." In the time allotted them, the populists failed to crystallize a distinctive theoretical perspective. Still, the members of the Granges and Alliances, frustrated in a painful odyssey which led from early victories to later defeats in the counties, then state legislatures, state judiciaries, and finally the Supreme Court, and frustrated by the frequent crushing of third-party attempts by fraud and violence, began to reveal an increasing willingness to use the language of power and class.[46]

This was evident in their increasingly frequent indictments of capital and in an increasing tendency to see the world in group terms, either in terms of creditor and debtor classes, or in new terms of sectional conflict. ("The fight is upon you," Watson told Georgia farmers in 1888 after indicting "Northern capital," "not with the men who came to free your slaves, but who came to make slaves of you.")[47] Though no socialists, populist leaders also ceased to retreat before the term, and began to counterattack their accusers. "What of this cry of class legislation?" Watson asked from the stump. "What has this country ever had but class legislation? The second law Congress ever passed was aimed to build up commerce and manufactures at the expense of agriculture. . . . If we must have class legislation as we have always had it and always will have it, what class is more entitled to it than the largest class—the working class?"[48]

The shift in orientation was also apparent in an increasing willingness to regard corporate activity as "the application of force . . . [which] must be met by force" (Presidential candidate Weaver in 1892), and of "political revolution . . . [which] we hope may be accomplished by the . . . ballot, [but which] at any rate, must be accomplished" (Governor Waite of Colorado in 1894). The official history of the last Alliance convention was entitled *The Impending Revolution.* And Watson's subsequent People's Party Campaign Book of 1892 was subtitled *Not a Revolt, It's a Revolution.*[49]

The focal concern with monopoly caught the ambivalences perfectly. Monopolies seemed to provide a way of faulting errant practices without indicting capitalism. Watson later wrote (in 1910) that, "every one of the terrible conditions which Marx seeks to relieve by establishing a new order of Society grew out of the abuses of power and privilege and not out of the system itself."[50] And in the classical liberal vocabulary, as we have seen, monopoly was the incarnation of both power and privilege.

But in their attempt to put a stop to the depredations of monopoly, the populists began for the first time to consciously fix a boundary to capitalist ambition and to question capitalist rights of appropriation. They began for the first time to make an explicit distinction between "the public interest" and business interests. In an incipient way, then, their efforts pointed toward a class critique—as their enemies who were anxious about the clash of Mighty Opposites well knew. Their position always threatened to move in the direction hinted by Watson, Donnelly, and Debs.

The transitional character of the movement was manifested by a number of theoretical reformulations in the work of its most respected writers. The most dramatic expressions of these were the outbursts against capital we have already noted, and the growing acceptance of some sort of "regulation" to achieve liberty.[51] But there were also less obvious signs.

The agrarian radicals expressed an increasing concern for the plight of urban labor and a willingness to see farm and factory struggles as essentially the same. After some farmers had supported local strikes for years, the People's Party actively sought alliance with the Knights of Labor in 1891. The Populist Convention of 1892 announced itself as "the first great labor conference of the United States . . . representing all divisions of urban and rural organized industry." Its platform affirmed a labor theory of value and declared that "if any man will not work, neither shall he eat." It also identified the interests of rural and urban labor as "the same, their enemies identical."[52] This was clearly something more than "normal entrepreneurial radicalism."

Henry George himself was an apt symbol of the congeniality between the farming and laboring populations of this time. Prophet of an agrarian movement and master of the agrarian idiom, his trades were, in fact, those of seaman and printer. In *Progress and Poverty* he proudly noted his Knights of Labor affiliation. And in a society increasingly impressed with wealth, he insisted on the dignity of labor. George defined the essential crime of the modern factory as its denial to the worker of "the essential quality of . . . manhood—the godlike quality of modifying and controlling conditions."[53] He, like Marx (or anyone else who took the Lockean view seriously), felt that people who had been deprived of these "godlike" powers in their work had been crippled at a fundamental level.

The populists also began to rethink their attitudes toward race. Though a full discussion of this point would take us beyond the concerns of this volume, populist thinking regarding blacks in the South and Asians in the West proved capable of flexibility and humanitarian development. Beginning to move beyond racial vindictiveness and the anxieties of the possessive psyche, populist thought by the early 1890s had become far less racist than that of the country as a whole.[54] In 1869, for example, George had given voice to the reigning anti-Asian racism (speaking about the "swarming that is possible from this vast human hive").[55] But by the time he completed *Progress and Poverty* a decade later, he had explicitly rejected the racial doctrines of Spencer and the Darwinists. The differences between peoples, he now urged, were "not differences which inhere in the individuals, but differences which inhere in the society." The "differences" to which he referred were those in the conditions which determined how wealth was used and distributed. By 1879 he was arguing explicitly for the inherent equality of peoples.[56]

The changing character of agrarian democratic thought was registered most centrally, however, in its attitudes toward individualism. Informed by the lessons of farmers' cooperative experiments and the travails of political organizing and battle, a new emphasis on mutual aid appeared in populist writings and speeches. This was evident in the widespread acceptance of Laurence Gronlund's phrase "the cooperative commonwealth"—which until the First World War expressed the indigenous American radicals' vision of a democratic future.[57] It was also evident in George's work. He often cited Marcus Aurelius's admonition that "we are made for cooperation." The last sections of *Progress and Poverty* were a veritable ode to the arts of association. It was in part his high regard for association that led him to propose the Single Tax rather than the parcelling-up of large estates, for the latter, an agrarian analogue to trust-busting, failed to "swim . . . with the current of the times." His distance from Lockean liberalism can be measured by his straightforward assertions that "man is social in his nature" and that "association in equality is the law of progress."[58]

The point is not that George ever moved completely or consistently beyond individualism. One who praises cooperation has not necessarily adopted a communitarian ethic, any more than a farmer who helps his neighbors with harvesting and barn-raising a few times a year is a socialist. Still, their practical experience led people like George to stress the importance of cooperation *to* individualism, and to emphasize that co-operation must *underlie* a healthy individualism, in a manner unprecedented in mainstream American political writing.

Populist thinking was capable, then, of lucid insight and profound theoretical development. It was not single-issue oriented, (even in Colorado, where the silver issue was most popular).[59] It was not irrational (the Federal Reserve Act of 1913 would indicate that the theories of the Gold Bug opponents were the ones that were "superstitious").[60] And it was not in thrall to the past.

Having acquired a practical education in the limits of American democracy, George and the populists began to penetrate to a systematic critique of American political institutions and to rethink the core concepts of liberalism. They were no stand-ins for the European working class.[61] But they gave voice to the specific ways in which class contradictions were surfacing in their own milieu, and—whatever their original position—in the end they launched the broadest challenge to capitalist control over the process of industrialization that has yet been mounted on these shores.

George's power to galvanize two generations of reform thought followed from the fact that he, in particular, grasped the issues at stake in the confrontation between a would-be democratic culture and the ascendant form of industrial organization, and that he successfully articulated the concerns of a culture in motion. Faced with the fracturing of classical liberalism, that culture clung to the democratic aspects of the older promise. It moved in neither a corporatist nor a managerialist direction, and its main body never really followed Gronlund and Bellamy in their proposal to organize the country *further* into One Big Trust in order to replace competition with "planning."

Instead, they sought like George to preserve the older promises of equality, opportunity, and freedom by somehow translating them in accord with an organized world. George's central purpose was to find a way of assuring "in a more complex state of society, the same equality of rights that in a ruder state were secured by equal partitions of the soil."[62] It was ultimately to find a modern analogue of the older institution of property. His brief remarks toward the end of *Progress and Poverty* gave only hints at what this might look like. The assertions that "association in equality [was] the law of progress," "civilization is cooperation," and "union and liberty are its factors" suggested that the kind of organization he sought would be one that accorded equality to its members and that had mechanisms to assure that it was continually worthy of their voluntary "union" and commitment. Sketchy as these ideas were, they were sufficient to distinguish his associational impulse from that of Sumner and the corporate businessmen.[63]

By 1896, however, the populist movement had been defeated. And the theoretical development of indigenous American radicalism was thereafter frozen at the points of its most forward advance.[64] Men like LaFollette would continue to champion the distinctively populist program and vision well into the twentieth century, but the political base behind the program had been obliterated. One group of supporters left political life altogether. Another moved on to an American form of socialism.[65] Those remaining dug in for a defense of the smallholder that was historically intransigent and socially intolerant; from them emerged the racism, anti-Catholicism, and parochialism (though interestingly enough, pro-Bolshevism) of the later Tom Watson. Some writers have explained this response as the product of an innately regressive political theory and psychology. But a more plausible explanation is at hand.

Denied positive expression of their community's identity, the Southern poor accepted a politics of negation rather than forsake that identity altogether. Defeated in their attempts to combat their real, strongly entrenched antagonists, they turned against their weak former allies. This was not populism but populism debased. The politics that followed must be judged harshly. But so must the politics that left them no other choice *as* a community. In an instance of *political* regression, they retreated to a narrow sectionalism and broke the alliance with the West which alone had enabled populists to force fundamental questions onto the national agenda.

POPULISM AND THE TECHNIQUE OF LIBERAL REFORM

One of the more ambiguous aspects of populist political thought remained its orientation toward politics. George intended his Single Tax as a defense for the commons against private interests, and he anticipated the pragmatists in declaring the mind to be "the instrument by which man advances." But he still stopped short of fully embracing politics as the vehicle for that mind.[66] The beauty of the Single Tax for him was precisely that it was single. Its collection and disbursement would be the sole function of the reformed government. George intended not to go beyond Lockean nature, but only to shore it up.

This hesitancy to embrace an active political agency grew largely out of the older American equation of the state with a hierarchical and compulsory power, with a "punishing and restraining authority," as Gronlund put it. The agrarians saw the federal government—not entirely without cause—as an institution set apart from society and potentially dominant over it; this accounts largely for their suspicions about socialism, which they always saw as state socialism.[67]

The result was that they never achieved a consistent political perspective. On the one hand, the Alliance was supposed to be "non-political" and to avoid party activity; on the other, Ignatius Donnelly opined that creating a non-political organization was tantamount to making a gun that would do everything but shoot.[68] On the one hand, Henry George had traced the problems of the times to usurpation and a flawed structure of rights; on the other, he proposed a reform which was on the order of a legislative gimmick. Monopolists who held the power to bend legislatures and public opinion to their will would somehow be led to accept a tax that would annul their rights and expropriate their wealth. Somehow, George felt, an oblique attack would succeed where a frontal assault would fail. People would be able to enjoy by indirection what they could not claim by right. The intermediate steps of the logic were nonexistent; but the beauty of a reform engine that would move worlds at a touch would continue to seduce three generations of reform liberals.

This ambiguity about political activity traced a fault line that ran through George's work and continued to run through much of the reform liberalism of the next century. It was unclear how the imposition of his tax would actually remedy the problem he had diagnosed. There were questions about its economics.[69] But even ignoring these, it was unclear how the politics of rebate would help recreate the grounds of initiative and democracy. George proposed that the government should become "the administrator of a great cooperative society" and use its wealth to create splendid public facilities—libraries, baths, museums, lecture halls, and (this being California) waterworks. It should use its powers to beautify and enrich public life. But how would that compensate people for the loss of the "god-like qualities" of modifying and controlling circumstances? And how would that—or the alternate chance to toil on recently freed acreage in competition with established industries—recreate the ethical space for Lockean man?

It is also surprising to find an appeal to "administration" in the work of a critic of statism and a pronounced advocate of voluntaristic action. But there was a reason for this: like most populists, George gave an essentially redistributive answer for what he had diagnosed as a structural problem.

Furthermore, George failed to see, as John Chamberlain wrote in

1931, that "a land-owning class which in turn is bound up with the mortgage system is, to all intents and purposes, synonymous with the bourgeoisie itself." [70] The distinction George drew between landlord and capitalist may have made sense at an earlier date. But this was almost twentieth-century America; and in California, especially, the land was already being "mined." [71] The landowners already *were* capitalists. George did not see that ownership of the means of creating social wealth—and with it ownership of the important "opportunities"—had given large *capitalists* the power to become the primary taxers of labor and small business. Depriving pure landlords of their grasp of rent would in no way loosen the hold of business interests on the second "nature" they had created.

George's reform proposal was thus unequal to the rest of his analysis. In presenting it he inadvertently contributed to the simplistic, statist view of social reform which, fed by the evolutionary theory of Bellamy and others, would shape twentieth-century liberal thinking.

Henry George gave coherent expression to the anxiety that permeated American culture in the years after the Civil War. The malaise grew out of what he called the reaching of the Pacific—the end of Lockean America. At that point the conceptual crystal at the center of classical liberalism—the unity of liberty, equality, security, and ownership—shattered. What would happen now? Cooper's Ishmael Bush warned: "Look around you, men. What will the Yankee choppers say when they have cut their path from the eastern to the western waters. . . . They will turn on their tracks like a fox that doubles, and then the rank smell of their own footsteps will show them the madness of their waste." [72] But that terrible discovery was not, of course, inevitable. There were those who proposed a more sanguine, and dangerous, way out of the impasse. In two articles written for *The Atlantic Monthly*, Woodrow Wilson would soon suggest that the frontier simply be extended a bit, to the Philippines. [73]

But the thrust of populist thinking was different. It was to find a modern analogue for the older equality, to find a way for every member of the community to "participate in the advantages of ownership," [74] and, as George discerned, to transform the character of ownership in the process. How would such ways be found? Not without recognizing that the rights to productive wealth belonged ultimately to the community, George responded, and not without retaking those rights—and the sovereignty embedded in them—from private hands. But in what, then, would the new equivalent of property consist? How would people con-

ceive of politics and personality once those concepts were no longer subsumed into economic categories? What, finally, would "liberty" and the
power of "modifying and controlling conditions" look like *within* industrial organization? To these queries, George ultimately had no answers.
His value to his contemporaries, and to subsequent democratic thought,
lay in the fact he had asked the right questions.

4

The Corporatist Impulse: Theory and Practice

Some of you have painted a frightening picture of a sinister group plotting vast designs, exerting unseen influence upon the Government itself. . . . There are no such plottings. What . . . I would very much prefer you should say is simply that we at the House of Morgan, and others . . . are standing around in a cooperative frame of mind.

—THOMAS W. LAMONT, partner of J. P. Morgan

The growth of a corporate economy presented Americans with a Hobson's choice. Accepting Henry George's conclusions meant that one had to reject private property in land, and ultimately its corollary, freedom-as-independence. But rejecting them required a breach with liberal ethics and the inherited approach to sovereignty. The choice before American culture, then, was not a choice between radicalism and conservatism. It was a choice between equally radical departures from tradition. The theoretical foundation for the second of these departures was laid by William Graham Sumner, a man no less independent-minded than George.

Sumner's contribution, called Social Darwinism, once loomed large and still echoes in American political life. It has usually been presented as the archetype of simplistic laissez-faire conservatism. But it was not that simple. Like George's thought, it emerged from a struggle, a tension between its ethical vision and the demands of a changing world. The product of that struggle was not simply a reaffirmation of Manchester economics. It presented a new standpoint for liberal theory, and implied new doctrines of right and obligation for a culture still superficially pledged to contract theory. Behind the individualist tenets of Social Darwinism, Sumner guided a wing of American thought in corporatist directions. In doing this he also gave expression to the dominant logic of practical affairs. This logic, freed from Sumner's own hesitations, would gain powerful impetus from a number of leading capitalists, of whom we shall take Charles Francis Adams, Jr., and Andrew Carnegie as representative spokesmen.

SUMNER AND SOCIAL DARWINISM

The intellectual ascendance of Darwinism in the years after the Civil War was only partially due to the rationalizations it offered for the power of the new capitalists. Henry Adams saw a number of ways in which it suited the times. It was appropriate for a culture, he observed, that had just wasted millions of dollars and thousands of lives forcing "unity and uniformity on a people who objected to it." Then too, the "proof that one had acted wisely because of obeying the primordial habit of nature flattered one's self-esteem. Steady, uniform, unbroken evolution from lower to higher seemed easy." Finally, Adams appreciated the fact that Darwinism provided a badly disoriented culture with a "safe, conservative, practical, thoroughly Common Law deity."[1]

Sumner's feat was to assimilate Darwinism to liberal culture in such a way as to provide a rationale for the new aggregations of capital. He forged a peace between liberalism and industrial concentration; and it was a peace that lasted.

Sumner, like George, began his social ponderings with the individual, the man who applied his hands and his wit to nature. As with George, this laborer was also a capitalist, "though never a great one." He was also seen as provided by nature with a fundamental guarantee, the security "that if he employs his energies to sustain the struggle on behalf of himself and those he cares for, he shall dispose of the product exclusively as he chooses."[2] Sumner spent most of his time denouncing those who meddled with the workings of natural law, both meddlers to the left and "plutocrats" to the right—those "who erect combinations which are half political and half industrial." Unlike the populists, however, he did

not believe that these meddlers had succeeded in altering the basic character of the economy. His world remained a voluntarist world composed
of sovereign individuals. "Class" differences were still attributed to inborn talent, and a person's rewards were regarded as accurate measures
of his abilities.[3]

Sumner was therefore severely critical of attempts to improve conditions through political reforms. His hostility to state action was buttressed by a number of arguments, the subsequent popularity of which
registered the demise of the tradition of political liberalism that had
stretched from James Harrington to John Randolph to Henry George.
Central to these arguments was the Burkean assertion that social institutions were the products of long, organic developments, and could not be
legislated into being. (How, in any case, Sumner added, could "we get
bad legislators to pass a law which shall hinder bad legislators from
passing a bad law?"—a question which, as we saw from George, had to
be taken seriously).[4]

But Sumner's hostility toward political reforms was also rooted in a
lucid insight suggestive of Marx or Feuerbach in Europe and of the later
realists in America. People had a tendency, he noted, to endow states
with "conscience, power and will sublimated above human limitations."
In doing so they lost the sense of themselves as the source of their own
powers. The attempt to obtain legislative help, he added, amounted to
no more than an effort to make all-of-us do something for some-of-us.[5]

Underlying both of these arguments was a faith new to America,
which Sumner shared with a number of new industrialists. It was a faith
in what might be called a universal moral economy. Sumner could ad-
vise readers to quit complaining and "discipline themselves to the facts"
only because he first posited a belief in a natural beneficence that rewarded virtue and punished vice. This idea was nothing less than an
ontological extension of Adam Smith's free-market utopia—an assumption of natural equilibrium extending beyond Smith's market and beyond even Polanyi's "society" to the entire universe of human existence.
Not simply market competition but life's hardships themselves were presented as necessary and providential parts of the human condition. This
was a theoretical vision equal to the Great Transformation that was occurring in practical affairs.

In such a view, any attempt to enact remedial legislation or extract
political favors would simply be a sign of weakness of character. It could
be expected to shift the costs of one's failures to people who did not deserve them. According to what could be called this wage-fund theory of
evil, any conscious attempt to adjust advantages would simply destroy

natural moral harmony. The banker in his office and the drunk in the gutter had found their natural places; it would be as fruitless to help the banker as it would be to complain about the drunk. Sumner also scorned "vulgar socialists" because of their assumption that "the individual has a right to whatever he needs."[6] In short, there was a purpose to the squalor and oppression of the new factory towns and older farms.

It followed for Sumner and those who accepted this vision that "society does not need any care or supervision"—at least from politicians. About supervision by powerful business elites they were less concerned.[7]

These beliefs were not the mouthings of a simple apologist. This apostle of hardship jeopardized his teaching position at Yale three times, and became the nation's first famous academic freedom case, because he refused to trim his sail to prevailing winds. He continued to attack the railroad companies as "plutocracies." Like the populists, he distinguished these plutocrats from capitalists. He called plutocracy "the opponent" of democracy, and went so far as to say that plutocrats were extending a power over the very "formative stage of political activity"—a process he saw as posing a question of "life or death" for democracy.[8] Sumner denounced the Spanish-American War, at a time when Roosevelt and Wilson were celebrating it, because he lamented the century of militarism, imperialism, and socialism which it forecast. Viewing the results of the conflict a few years later, in fact, Sumner concluded that Spain had won the war.[9]

On the surface, then, Sumner's system was the epitome of logical consistency. Viewed against the conditions of the times, however, it held a major contradiction, and one that ran straight to its foundations. Sumner wanted to affirm the ethics of individualism and at the same time justify the natural drift of events. But the natural drift of events in his era was leading toward concentration, which threatened individualism. Faced with what could have been a crippling contradiction, Sumner hardly paused. He chose for the drift of events. This choice, like George's choice in the opposite direction, was largely determined by Sumner's implicit theory of value. For he continued to see industrial wealth as the product of the thrift and foresight of capitalists. The huge new enterprises then emerging could be attributed solely to the genius of the entrepreneurs. Sumner also accepted the view of capital as stored labor. But where George and his readers felt that the laurels should go to those who did the labor, Sumner assigned rewards to those who did the storing.

Locke had prepared the way for such reasoning by defending violations of the labor theory of value when they worked to increase productivity. He went part of the way, that is, in removing the liberal mandate from the laborer and giving it to the accumulator, the man who devoted himself (in Schumpeter's later phrase) to "creative destruction." Still, Locke's world remained a place where "individual variations in behavior" were "either cancelled out in the aggregate or suppressed by competition."[10] But Sumner went all the way. He justified the growth of centralized production and the demise of the individual laborer. And he did this because he saw the capitalist as nature's instrument for increasing productivity and advancing civilization. His goal was not to defend profits per se, but to celebrate the creative industrialist who lurked in the profit-seeker's breast.

Fundamental to such an outlook was the assumption that the capitalists and the new corporations were politically neutral. The capitalist's income was regarded simply as the reward for innovation plus "wages for superintendence." If some of these wages were too high, well, society was still the gainer by the bargain.[11] The capitalist was only an organization man. Proposals to regulate him Sumner likened to proposals to "kill off one's best generals" in a war.[12] And the capitalist's new organization, the corporation, was perceived as a neutral institution, an inevitable social response to technical progress, a device indispensable for organizing "adequate power" for the "vast undertakings" that "devolve upon society in our time." The political choices involved with its ascendance, the logic of privacy crystallized in its structure, the powers exercised by its owners over others' lives and (as George revealed) over the effects of industrial development—these had nothing to do with the matter for Sumner.

Supported by such assumptions, this champion of individual liberty was drawn to the vigorous defense of forces that made it possible "to extend efficient control, . . . [and] to keep up a close, direct and intimate action and reaction between the central control and the distributed agents." Whenever new forms of centralization and coordination became possible, Sumner added fatefully, they would also become "inevitable . . . because there is economy in it."[13]

Sumner's outlook carried an ineluctably corporatist impulse. And this impulse was in keeping with the biological outlook of the times, though the connection has usually gone unnoticed. To an era influenced by Darwin's ideas, life was not simply a tooth-and-claw struggle but a chapter in an evolutionary chronology that witnessed the creation of complex out of simpler organisms. "Evolution is the integration of matter and concomitant dissipation of motion," ran Herbert Spencer's oft-repeated formula, "during which the matter passes from an indefinite, coherent homogeneity into a definite, coherent heterogeneity."[14] If the competitive struggle *began* with individuals in the jungle, in other words, it was expected to lead to large, complex, and internally differentiated organisms in society—ultimately, to society itself as an organism. From such a perspective, "the more perfect integration of societal functions" forged by the corporation would naturally appear as "but one feature of a grand step in societal evolution."[15]

This outlook therefore provided more than a defense of the status quo. It mandated a continued corporatization of economic and social life. In doing so it removed liberal thought from a market paradigm and cast its promises into terms of time. It historicized liberalism. In Sumner's world, variation would not be canceled out, as in Locke's; it would lead through natural selection to constantly altered forms of social-life.

Such an outlook was appropriate to a society in which, for forty years, the institution of property itself had been losing the characteristics of stability in order to take on the aspect of a developmental bundle of energies.[16] It was also appropriate to a society in which the function of "entrepreneurship" was taking on a life of its own independent of the other functions of ownership, and a society in which some economists were beginning to invent an *administrative* theory of value.[17] This Social Darwinism was actually a *sociological* Darwinism. It saw the struggle for existence occurring increasingly between groups. And the real origins of such a view, to be precise in matters of intellectual pedigree, lay not with Darwin but with Auguste Comte.

Comte and the New Liberalism

Once we look beneath the surface, the influence of Comte on the era is unmistakable. Henry Adams's brother, Charles Francis, wrote that Mill's essay on Comte "revolutionized in a single morning my whole mental attitude. I emerged from the theological stage in which I had been nurtured and passed into the scientific," adding, "I had up to that time never even heard of Darwin."[18] His brother Henry, writing of himself in the third person, said: "He should have been a Marxist . . . [but] he did the next best thing; he became a Comtist within the limits of evolution. He was ready to become anything but quiet."[19] If it still helps for some purposes to see the new liberalism as a marriage of Darwin and Locke, Comte must be acknowledged as the matchmaker, and one who exercised a continuing influence over the union.

Comte had been the first to view modern society as an organic unity of industrial corporations, and the first to perceive that unity as the natural product of evolutionary history. Comte suffers the fate in America of having his name identified exclusively with his three-stage model of history. But in addition to being divided into the theological (or fictitious), the metaphysical (or abstract), and the modern scientific (or positive) epochs, history for Comte also chronicled the gradual acceptance of corporate social organization.[20] The positivism he left as a legacy to Western social thought combined his developmental schema with a scientific epistemology in a synthesis that intended to systematize history, to mark the path to the future, and to define the proper objects of human value. Industrial corporations stood at the center of this synthesis for two reasons. They appeared to be the models of future social organization, and also to embody the promise of "science."

It was Comte who, in the age when science began to be regarded as the highest mode of human cognition, explained to many Americans what that "science" was supposed to be. Comte's initial effort, like that of many before him (including Hobbes), had been to be the "Galileo of social science." From such a perspective the object of science was to chart a basic law or master principle of social life under which other laws representing the "regularities" of social activity could be grouped. The kind of "law" imagined here was the same kind as prevailed in the natural sciences. Research undertaken with the proper method was expected to produce information that would be universal in its application and unimpeachable in its certainty. The language of this effort was usually empiricist, but the underlying assumptions can be seen to have been curiously Platonic.[21]

For Henry George and many others, "science" had been a looser enterprise. It consisted simply of a regard for rigorous logic, close definition, empirical evidence, and comparative analysis when possible. The underlying goal of the scientific study of society was to discover deeply-lying patterns—the "principles"—of social development.[22] Explicit assumptions about human nature were thought essential to the formulation of such laws.

But Comte's Science of Society was different. It regarded assumptions about human nature as akin to what in the physical sciences were superstitions about hidden "stuffs" and essences. The true positivist spirit for Comte consisted "in substituting the study of the invariable laws of phenomena for that of their so-called Causes . . . in a word in studying the *How* instead of the *Why*."[23] This methodological proviso implied for Comte a political corollary: social analysts should cease discussing underlying "rights" in order to describe the functioning "laws and regularities" of society. They should proceed from what people actually do rather than from beliefs about what they are entitled to do.

Sumner followed Comte on all of these points. "A natural fact *is*, and that is the end of the matter," he insisted, "whether we give it our sovereign approval or not." He even rebuked Spencer for his allusions to natural rights. ("The thing which forever rules the world is not what is true or what is right . . . but only what is strong.")[24] Indeed, Sumner and the Americans succeeded in distilling a positivism more stringent than Comte's, for they dismissed as superstitious the thing that had animated his whole effort at social reform: a conviction about the human need for social solidarity.

The positivist dream of constructing a world-view from empirical facts alone was of course impossible. And Sumner's "science" assumed an encompassing corporate and industrial teleology. While he was a relativist in terms of moral norms, he also saw the transition between norms as marking a progressive evolution. To the extent that his Social Darwinism was conservative, then, it was a conservatism that moved— a relativist conservatism, a *progressive* conservatism.

The effects of this reformulation of the liberal project can be seen most clearly in the new attitude toward nature that emerged at the end of the nineteenth century. Contrary to the opinions of later commentators like Dewey and Commager, the legal principles enunciated at that time by Sumner and the Supreme Court and the views reflected in the novels of Dreiser and Crane were not the natural law doctrines "given authoritative utterance by the great Blackstone," but repudiations of such doctrines.[25]

Where the Nature of Locke and Jefferson was seen as informed by God's hand and possessing an inner structure, that of Sumner and the Court was viewed as formless and as yielding "laws" only over the long run. Where people were seen by the former as possessing a complement of natural rights, they were viewed by the latter as having unlimited desires. One's "right" for Sumner was simply the liberty to get and hold whatever he could. (His *duties* were exhausted by three admonitions: "Mind your own business," "take care of yourself," and as a means to this, "get capital.")[26] Where Locke and the architects of the liberal tradition presumed the existence of a clear boundary between nature and man, Sumner and Dreiser denied that boundary and argued for the universal play of biological laws, even within society. And where Enlightenment nature had endowed men with reason, Sumner's nature endowed them with only a bundle of instincts. Providence, having been constrained within Newtonian laws by the founding deists, was pulled from the skies altogether by Sumner, and said to work not through but *despite* men's consciences.

Accommodating liberalism to such a view required a reformulation of its central social values. Where classical liberalism voiced a commitment to equality, Sumner openly defended hierarchy. The important thing was the equal chance to rise to the level of one's abilities in the struggle for existence. "Industry may be republican," said Sumner, paraphrasing Comte, but "it can never be democratic." Still, he celebrated it—even as those industry-republics admittedly "drift[ed] over into oligarchies or monarchies." "We cannot go outside of this alternative," he declared: "liberty, inequality, survival of the fittest; not-liberty, equality, survival of the unfittest." [27]

"Liberty" would also undergo a change in the new society. "Why is it that man is not altogether a brute?" Sumner asked. (This was an important question for one who had dispensed with the boundary between man and nature.) Because, he answered, *some* men had the ability to create capital and thereby "to develop a great cooperation, and so to win a greater control over nature." [28] That being the case, it followed that everyone's well-being depended on the accomplishments of a few. "Liberty" emerged from this argument as a product of concentration, and Sumner concluded by justifying "a close, direct and intimate" relation "between the central control and the distributed agents."

The traditional republican fear that some people would acquire power over the grounds of others' subsistence was silenced by an argument that the economy remained "automatic and instinctive in its operation." So long as the thousands of people massed in the new economy were cooperating "without any acquaintance or conventional agreement, and without any personal interest in each other, under the play of forces which lie in human nature," one did not have to worry about power. [29] Fear of domination was thus answered by an appeal to impersonality.

The status of labor was also revalued in Sumner's scheme. Where the Lockean theory of value would spark grievances whenever people were denied title to the fruits of their labor, the new positivist approach dispensed with charges of exploitation *methodologically*—by labeling the very idea of an unfulfilled right "metaphysical."

An interesting side-effect of this outlook, finally, was its denial of the importance of action. Classical liberalism preserved a potential for judging institutions by preserving an independent standard of right. In doing so it also preserved the possibility of creative action, a possibility the rebel founders of the United States had availed themselves of. But

Sumner saw existing institutions as expressions of natural law, as immutable, and as themselves the source of standards of right. Sumner's and Comte's epistemology therefore left little room for critical judgment, save for that directed against those who failed to fall in with the dominant line of development. Their thought manifested itself in a philosophy of adjustment and acquiescence. People were as "chips in the current." [30] They might try to stay afloat, but it would be foolish to try to affect the flow.

In the midst of these major social and epistemological reformulations Sumner did, however, attempt to hold fast at one point. He planted his feet firmly in the classical liberal view of independence. Paradoxical as it seems, given his paean to "close, direct controls," he insisted on the virtues of self-reliance. Not for him was the populist drift toward association, or Comte's solidaristic "reason of the heart." For Sumner, "the free man cannot accept help from another." [31] Even when defending the quintessential importance of voluntary association for a free people and distinguishing himself by defending workers' rights to organize, Sumner insisted that such organizations were justifiable only so long as they were temporary, defensive, and held together by a spirit of "antagonistic cooperation." [32]

An impulse to impersonality has always lain at the heart of liberalism. This impulse became explicit and emphatic with Sumner. He celebrated people's working "without any acquaintance or conventional agreement, and without any personal interest in each other." But he did this at the very time he celebrated the ascendance of closely structured organizations.

Whether or not emotional distance would guarantee procedural regularity, it is hard to see how the world Sumner recommended could recreate anything like real independence. The bureaucratic capitalism that he defended could honor the liberal strategy for dignity only by boxing that dignity into the narrowest corner and denying it its supportive grounds, only by reducing it to a triumph of will over physical circumstance. The condition he recommended to America was not that of self-reliance at all, then, but the shell of self-reliance; it was the simulacrum of liberty. Sumner asked his countrymen to be in the corporate world but somehow not of it.

Lockeans in a Comtist World

Why should he have expected anyone to follow him into such conditions? Especially when, though he had admitted the necessity of "a struggle with the great corporations," he had "not any programme for it?"[33] Especially when he often feared the victory of the plutocrats?[34] This question leads us to Sumner's real theoretical achievement. Underlying his various conceptual redefinitions and moral re-evaluations was a fundamental shift in the point of view of American liberalism. To have likened the captains of industry to "our best generals" was to raise obvious questions about whether America was at war, and if so, with whom. Sumner's answer was that modern man was indeed at war, and that the enemy was nature herself. The stake in that war was nothing less than civilization, for "any high civilization must be produced and sustained by adequate force . . . [to] subjugate natural forces." Subsistence and culture could be maintained in such a view only by "a combined assault against Nature" by large organizations acting on behalf of "the whole civilized body."[35]

Classical liberalism had never assumed a harmony between man and nature in the first place; that is true. Having reduced land to property, Locke and his contemporaries felt that the proper task was "to dominate and subdue" the commons. Still, for Locke, nature was an ultimately beneficent domain. Men worked *with* it to establish the bases of civil society. For Jefferson, nature was also the realm of yeoman virtue. For Henry George, it was a primal home from which man came and to which he returned again. But with Sumner it was different. In these decades of violent social conflict, nature itself acquired a fiercer aspect. Divested of an inner structure, it began to be seen as an enemy and a threat. People came to be seen as defining themselves not by mixing their labor with nature, but by fighting *against* it to conquer it.

The intriguing thing about this new outlook was that it saw the newly hostile nature as lying not only outside society but also within it. The effect of erasing the boundary between man and nature was to invite the wilderness inside the city walls, where it would lie buried in the psyche of each individual, waiting to threaten and perhaps reclaim the fruits of collective effort. The relationship between man and external nature having been seen as one of control, the element of control was now extended to human nature itself. The answer to the ancient problem of social order, from such a perspective, could be provided only by the imposition of external rule.

In this new frame of reference we see an explanation of the origins of mass society that differs from Henry George's. The conditions that George attributed to a corruption of human nature caused by bad institutions, Sumner attributed to human nature itself. Sumner and his school conceived of social degeneration as a constant, sustained threat, held in check not by normal, self-initiating, human activity but only by the imposition of external discipline. (And this is the view which, on balance, has survived in American social science.) With this argument, capitalist industrial organization acquired a new rationale. Beyond its efficacy in the production of goods, it was credited with enforcing basic social integration and serving as the sole barrier between civilization and chaos.

By the 1880s some commentators, like Lester Ward, were already announcing an end to scarcity and to the dog-eat-dog ethics necessitated by it. But Sumner would have none of their message. Civilization could be maintained at its "unnatural level" only "by an efficient organization of the social effort and by capital." Were either the effort to be relaxed or the capital wasted, society would fall back "into the natural state of barbarism from which it arose." "We cannot stand still." [36] People could not relax for a moment. It was not for Hobbes's commodious life that Sumnerian man would spend himself, but to earn a fragile respite from the forces of decay. There was a great irony in this, though Henry Adams was the only one to catch it: the doctrine that celebrated the greatest organization and "condensation" of social life the Western world had known was also the doctrine that registered the greatest fear of entropy. In contrast to those like Ward, Sumner saw society as beset by the permanent scarcity of order itself.

Were men and women to accept this beleagured view and its underlying psychology, the intellectual contradictions of Sumner's liberalism could easily slip into insignificance, for people would accept the discipline and subordination appropriate to an army. They would accept a frame of reference in which the initial incentive to activity was no longer self-interest but the "health of the race." And they would accept a new view of their obligations, appropriate to a factory world which belied the theory of obligation implied by short-term, voluntary contracts. It is curious that when liberalism—a philosophy of toleration and compromise—was challenged to account for a greater range of social obligation than followed from contract theory, its first instinct was to invoke a war psychology.

The view of the world presented by the Social Darwinists resembled a kind of social Freudianism, in which the powerful forces of the libido posed a threat to the earnestly maintained superego of civilization. The outlook revealed an impulse to control that was independent of any direct goal of amassing profits or keeping workers in line. This impulse was rooted in a fear, which Sumner expressed, that a society organized "unnaturally" lived under constant threat of breakdown. What had been joined together by men might easily fall asunder if neglected for a moment.

Though Sumner pulled back from a full embrace of all of these implications, the concept of the individual that emerges from his pages was not, like George's, of one who was seeking new forms of equality and rational consent, but of a regimented member of an embattled race. Instead of a person seeking a scope for his own initiative, we see a subordinate subject depending on the genius of a few.

Commentators have heard the echo of Calvin in Sumner's gospel and often remarked on the somberness of his tone. His was a secular piety, Hofstadter wrote; he preached "the predestination of the social order and the salvation of the economically elect." [37] Sumner's grimness can also be explained by another aspect of this tradition. In his final doctrine, man had been condemned to live in what for the classical liberal would have been a world of sin, but he had been denied the hope for his own redemption.

THE ASCENDANCE OF THE CORPORATION
AND "THE SECOND DRED SCOTT DECISION"

At first it seemed that the older distinctions would be preserved and the lines against monopoly would hold. The traditional distinction between corporations and property was asserted in the state constitutions of the 1870s and the Granger regulatory laws; and these laws were upheld in the *Munn* cases. Entire communities, including businessmen and militia, often supported striking workers against absentee landlords and "alien" corporations. [38] During this time attacks also emerged from *within* the new imperiums, as workers organized and tried to assert ownership rights in their jobs. An article in the *Chicago Tribune* of 1874 thus reported that striking Ohio miners "felt about the same emotion on being deprived of their jobs as a homeowner would if deprived of his house"; they felt "an actual property right to their jobs." [39]

By the late eighties, however, it was clear that the struggle waged since the Jacksonian era would issue in a corporation victory. A Holmesean "policy decision" would turn the corporation from a chartered organization and a concession from the sovereign into a private association arising from the compact of its members.

The crucial steps in the corporate victory, institutionally speaking, were those fought through the due process clause of the Fourteenth Amendment. That Amendment was originally passed, legal scholars agree, to deal "with pervasive patterns of private wrongs ['to Negroes'] sheltered by state inaction" and to work "a revolution in federalism" by "nationalizing the rights of citizens."[40] By the end of the century, however, the revolution had been worked in the civil liberties of corporate persons rather than in the civil rights of blacks.

The signs of future development were plain in the first case in which the Amendment was tested before the Court. In *The Slaughterhouse Cases* (1873) a number of white workers in New Orleans attempted to use the clause prohibiting states from depriving "any person of life, liberty, or property without due process of law" to invalidate a monopoly which restricted local livestock butchering (for which a "thousand persons . . . had qualified themselves [and] framed their arrangements in life") to seventeen men. The crux of their argument lay with the claim of a property right in their jobs. Their attorney, Archibald Campbell, in a long and eloquent brief studded with citations from Locke, Smith, Thiers, and Tocqueville, argued that "the right to labor, the right to one's self physically and intellectually and to the product of one's own faculties is past doubt property" of the kind protected by the Amendment.[41] Campbell tried to create a worker's right to his calling. There was nothing in the logic of Lockeanism to fault the idea. But there was, unfortunately, something in the logic of capitalist industrialization to do so. It would be difficult to imagine the modern corporation being required to compensate working people and their families for the destruction of their occupations, or owners being forced to deal with their workers as fellow property-holders. The Court rejected Campbell's argument.

It also denied that a revolution in federalism had occurred. This holding was reaffirmed in *The Civil Rights Cases* (1883), when the Court denied to the government the power to protect civil rights that had been violated by "private action" alone, without "color of state laws." The case did not directly involve corporate rights. But the Court's decision to deal with inns and public conveyances as private businesses—rather than traditionally, as semi-public enterprises or businesses clothed with a public interest—revealed the tendency of the times. Private interests were enclosing large portions of what previously had been the public domain.[42] The scope of private property was being enlarged.

Then in 1886, ten years after Chief Justice Waite's affirmation of a state's right to regulate property when it was devoted to a "use in which the public had an interest," the *Munn* ruling was undermined by three legal events. First, the creation of the Interstate Commerce Commission removed railroads engaged in interstate commerce from the state regulatory provisions enacted by the Grangers. Second, the Court handed industrialists a major victory in a Southern Pacific case when it declared, in an unprecedented *obiter dictum*, that the corporation was a "person" within the meaning of the Fourteenth Amendment. In a single stroke, and without explanation, the Court raised the corporation "to the protective eminence of a person."[43] Third, the Court began to reveal confusion about the status of regulatory provisions. Waite himself began to speak of regulation as a "taking of private property for public use," indicating that he was beginning to subsume it under the law of eminent domain, a field where the courts had a larger jurisdiction than they did with the review of regulatory procedures.[44]

Justice Field's dissents to the *Slaughterhouse* and *Munn* rulings anticipated the doctrines eventually adopted by the Court. Field argued that there could be no public claims on corporations, whether established by legal charter or not. ("Laws cannot in common honesty be used so as to destroy or essentially impair the value" of obligations incurred under the authority of the states.)[45] Field then inverted the logic of Campbell's earlier argument: rather than workers acquiring a right to their callings against monopolies, he proposed a corporation's right to its calling against state regulation!

Capping a stormy history written largely in state courts, Field's approach emerged victorious in the *Chicago, Milwaukee and St. Paul Railway Co. v. Minnesota* case of 1890, in which the Court invalidated a Minnesota rate schedule on substantive as well as procedural grounds. The Court ruled that the road had a right to judicial investigation before it could be subjected to the state's traditional police powers.

This was the watershed case, and it was recognized as such by both businessmen and populists. Supreme Court Justice Brewer, Field's nephew, rejoiced to have been able to "put one stone . . . into the strong and unconquerable fortress . . . standing between individual rights and the public good." Judge Thompson, in the other camp, asked whether "the corporation [was] to rule the State or the State the corporation." And Farmer's Alliance newspapers expressed their outrage by referring to the holding as a "second Dred Scott decision."[46] The corporation, already declared to be an individual, was now declared to have the status of individual property as well. And in shielding corporations like this and protecting their often fraudulent activities, the federal government also denied the states power to protect real individuals from having to subsidize private development.[47]

Having won property status for the corporation, railroad lawyers then steadily augmented the rights attaching to property. In 1893 the Court held that franchises, once granted, were vested rights that could be retaken for public use "only as other private property," upon the "payment of just compensation." A year later, it in effect created a right to receive compensation for the use of property.[48] Then in *Allgeyer v. Louisiana* the "liberty" protected by the Fourteenth Amendment was defined as including not only the right to acquire and use property but also "to make all proper contracts pertaining thereto." Roscoe Pound noted that this liberty of contract was a construct unknown to the Anglo-American tradition. Its effect was to shift legal protection from "the natural force of promises once made . . . to an unrestricted right to make promises."[49]

In *Smythe v. Ames* (1898), finally, the Court held that "earning power" was an essential part of the "value" to which public utilities (railroads) were entitled. The "just return" it thenceforth sought in regulatory cases turned out to be the 6 percent that corporate businessmen had been seeking since the 1840s (though even that amount would at times be judged "confiscatory").[50]

During these years many state courts, aided by the formalistic doctrine of equal rights of contract between corporate and real persons, had already begun to strike down protective labor legislation. At a time when a labor contract was tantamount to a command in the guise of an agreement, courts struck down, for example, a statute outlawing the payment of miners in company scrip as "an insulting attempt to put the laborer under legislative tutelage, which is not only degrading of his manhood, but subversive of his rights as a citizen."[51] Having failed to win a property right in their jobs, these workers, like the farmers, saw their position steadily deteriorating. These were the years, for example, when business was able to get the courts to annul job-tenure traditions and establish the modern doctrine of employment at will.[52]

The corporations, finally, were also able to win a number of victories outside the Fourteenth Amendment cases. Individual states began to annul traditional limits on corporate organization (like those limiting their activities and prohibiting intercorporate holdings). And railroad directors, seeking a more dependable force against strikers than local militia and private armies, began to count on federal support, provided first via the Interstate Commerce Clause, then through the practice of federal receivership.[53] Finally, this support was provided more systematically through the new vehicle of the anti-strike injunction. This injunction was first used to crush the radical American Railway Union (numbering 150,000 in its second year) and the Pullman Strike. Compounded of the traditional law of criminal conspiracy and the equity power of the courts, it was in effect a means of administering criminal law without jury trial.[54]

Federal troops were deployed against striking workers in both Illinois and Colorado not only without requests but over the explicit objections of their governors. The separate states, which appeared so strong when it came to federal protection against private injuries to blacks, thus found themselves weak in matters of corporate labor policy. (Thomas Cooley, the author of a book that early influenced Field, and by the 1890s a judge and receiver for the Wabash Railroad, branded Governor Altgeld's states' rights position in the Pullman Strike "revolutionary.")[55] The Madisonian strategy for dealing with "domestic faction" thus surfaced in the American polity, and over precisely the issues Madison had anticipated in the Tenth *Federalist*.

What have usually been seen as populist successes at the federal level were in fact unavailing against the ascendant monopolies. President Cleveland's Attorney General, Richard Olney, the same man who had developed the government strategy for silencing the American Railway Union and jailing its president, Eugene Debs, had earlier mollified business worried about the ICC by explaining that the Commission as it had been shaped "is, or can be made, of great use to the railroads. It satisfies the public clamor for a government supervision . . . at the same time that such supervision is almost entirely nominal. Further, the older such a commission gets to be, the more inclined it will be to take the business and railroad view of things. It thus becomes a sort of barrier between the railroad corporations and the people. . . . The part of wisdom is not to destroy the Commission, but to utilize it."[56]

The ubiquitous Olney also explained why the Sherman Anti-Trust Act was invoked only once during this period of rapid combination. "You will have noted that the government has been defeated on the Trust question," he wrote to a friend after the famous sugar monopoly case of 1895. "I always supposed that it would be and have taken the responsibility of not prosecuting a law I believe to be no good."[57]

It is necessary to understand these manifold events and the legal and social artifact created by them in order to place the political thinking of the times in its proper light. Roscoe Pound described the product of these efforts as a liberty of contract. Others have spoken of the "triumph of conservatism"; and still others of an "entrepreneurial liberty" fashioned by private governments.[58] But none of these terms are adequate to the new institution. The term "liberty" is questionable in this context. "Entrepreneurship" suggests individual activity, whereas this development marked the demise of the individual capitalist. Nor was what occurred really "conservative," in the sense of conserving traditions.

In the liberal tradition "liberty" has always implied an immunity, a getting away. In the eyes of Thomas Hobbes, "to say that all people . . . have a liberty . . . is to say that in such a case, there hath been no law made." [59] But what was abundantly clear during these years—with land grants, receivership practices, labor policies, and the remolding of the Fourteenth Amendment—was that the modern corporation did not emerge from a process of exemption. It arose from the farming-out of powers previously considered part of a neutral public domain. These included the oversight of nature's "opportunities," supervision of economic units of great size and special consequence, and a number of more particular tasks such as that of overseeing the commons, coining currency, regulating common carriers, and raising armies. Put differently, what was involved in the corporation's grasping of power over the context and the direction of industrial development was a *taking* of various powers over peoples' common existence.

The fashioning of this new institution raised questions of constitutional status. When the Supreme Court made itself into a supra-legislature in matters of regulation, it simultaneously removed those matters from the jurisdiction of the real legislature, and thus from the range of legitimate public debate. That is to say that in regard to basic economic issues and their social consequences, it redrew the fundamental law of the nation. Little wonder farmers and rural workers branded the *Chicago, Milwaukee and St. Paul Railway* case a second Dred Scott decision, indicating that it was worthy of a second Civil War.

The capitalists of the Gilded Age succeeded, then, not in securing an exemption, and not in gaining protection for a pre-existing private right, but in fashioning a new privacy out of the stuff of public affairs. And the proper legal term for this status is not liberty or right, but privilege—a private legal status restricted to one class of subjects and giving it significant powers over others. The product of the Civil War Amendments was a system of *corporate privilege* within an altered body politic. And for half a century it was their only product.

The essential characteristics of the institution at the heart of this new system have already been discussed, so we may summarize them here. First, the corporation was largely unregulated. By creating "favored zones" similar to those Charles Francis Adams, Jr., described, the corporation was increasingly able to protect itself from what businessmen saw as "ruinous competition." At the same time it dispensed with the political limits incident both to chartered institutions and to property clothed with a public interest. The business corporation emerged at the end of the nineteenth century as Professor Abram Chayes has described it: "the first successful institutional claimant of significant unregulated power since the nation-state established its title in the sixteenth and seventeenth centuries." [60]

Second and more profoundly, this institution represented a further extension of The Great Transformation Polanyi described. It signified the successful enclosure by private interests of the context, the *preconditions*, of market activity, a realm which liberals had previously regarded as part of a neutral nature and as guarded by the public sovereign. The *function* of capital was altered in the process of this concentration. Instead of remaining one factor of many in the process of production, it achieved the status that Henry George feared. Capital became the critical factor of production. The men who centralized it were given a power of command over the economy and the working lives of others. Simultaneously, the majority of working people also ceased to possess "capital," properly speaking, at all. In the crucial inversion that Marx had already noted, the system that was supposed to grant "the exclusive title of every laborer to the product of his labor" wound up systematically separating property *from* labor. [61]

Third, the lapse of external political identity was accompanied by an internal lapse in the corporation. From its origins as an association of persons sharing a common purpose and engaged in matters of internal governance, the corporation became in the eyes of the law a device for the exclusive management of concentrated capital for private profit. This is to say that the associative elements were refined out of the society's dominant organization. (With the emergence of modern stockholding, even ownership itself would eventually become a transitory condition in which an owner would rarely know his partners and would be able to join or leave the collective according to private calculations of his own advantage.) At precisely the moment its social domain was being extended, the corporation became in fact and at law a simple framework for administration.

Finally, the change in the function of capital was accompanied by a change in its *form*. From being a simple holding, property was transformed into a social organization and informed with energies of growth and aggrandizement. Rights of property were thus extended even to the contractual relations into which such organizations might enter, as we have seen. "This shift in the meaning of property," John R. Commons explained in the twenties, was "a shift from the common law . . . meaning of physical things held exclusively for one's use, to the business-law meaning of property as . . . the exchange value . . . in one's business. It is the difference between . . . *things owned*, and the *powers of acquisition* residing in the ownership of things . . . [from] property in things to both property and liberty in the expected acquiring, holding, enlarging and selling of those things." [62] This new property embraced rights of use and disposition not only in things but in "powers of acquisition," and it covered a wide range of social transactions involved with those things. (During the nineties, to take one example, railroad strikes—a collective decision to stop work—were made into a crime). [63]

The concept of "social property" accurately describes this new institution, but not merely because it exercised great social influence and not simply because some capitalists began to think of themselves as a class. [64] The new property was quintessentially social because both the "subject" and the object of ownership were becoming incorporate. The greatest irony, in an era rich in ironies, was that the rights of a single, unitary form of ownership were accentuated at the very moment that the personality doing the owning was becoming increasingly artificial.

The new system of corporate privilege not only gave business an unprecedented position vis-à-vis the rest of the society; it also began to unleash the social energies that would become so palpable a half-century later. Communities, political parties, trade unions, and even the national government began to adopt corporate methods of organization. [65] And a wide range of conflicts became increasingly subject to adjudication by the dictates of a single social interest. The overt violence of the federal troops called into Illinois and Colorado over the objections of local communities and state officials stands as a palpable symbol of the deeper violence worked by this on community expectations and customary social relations.

THE LOGIC OF CORPORATISM: ADAMS AND CARNEGIE

Given the triumph of the corporation, it would be surprising if the era's theoretical legacy took either of the two forms that have usually been assumed. Solon Buck presented the regulatory interpretation in his early account of the Grangers. "In spite of later developments," he wrote, "the fundamental principle of the Granger cases still stands, and no one today questions the existence of a right on the part of the state to regulate . . . railroads and other businesses of a public nature." [66] On the other hand, the era is often viewed as having established the dominance of a laissez-faire outlook. However, neither of these theoretical strains was as prominent as often supposed.

The populists wanted to reaffirm common authority over the bases of freedom. And to thus revive the classical commitment to public authority over public matters would have been a pivotal contribution to modern political thought. But their thinking about politics was ambiguous, and this ambiguity informed the regulatory theory afterwards identified with them. Moreover, the populists ignored the question of how the authority they wanted to create was to be created. Tom Watson declared, "The issue is national; the danger national; the disease national," and he concluded, "the remedy must be national." [67] But the flowing rhetoric disguised a logical disjunction. Because the remedy should be national in scope it did not follow that *any* national government was capable of applying it. Nor did it necessarily follow that a central national agency was the best means for providing it. Everything hung on a discussion of the kind of power that was needed, and on an explanation of how a *public* authority, properly speaking, would be constituted. Those discussions never occurred.

Still largely committed to the liberal idea of freedom-as-independence, the populists equivocated between the recognition of a need for power sufficient to control monopoly and the fear of coercive government. Ultimately they failed to think about freedom, initiative, and political authority in new ways. Unused to thinking about power, they called for strengthened sovereignty without thinking about the substantive social forces that would have the ability to control that sovereignty. Having shifted their focus from economy to polity, they fell back on the idea of natural harmony to guarantee that the new state would represent the interests of all. Later American reform thinking followed where they led.

Sumner and Justice Field, for their part, were trying to occupy an illusory terrain. Practically, they tried to discourage pools and trusts (and Sumner, plutocracy) without blocking the structural tendencies toward combination. Theoretically, they disdained explanation where explanation was most needed. For the strongest is never "strong enough to always be master," as Rousseau observed, "unless he transforms his strength into right and obedience into duty." [68] Unanswered behind Sumner's theory were precisely such questions of right and obligation— the right of the new corporatists to command and the obligation of others to obey and to exert themselves in the new domains.

Unanswered, too, were questions about politics per se, questions about the means and purposes of collective choice. Such questions had not arisen in classical market theory because of its faith in natural harmonies. But once people begin to see society as critically affected by decision, as Michael Reagan has put it, "some essentially political questions come to the fore. Who will do the managing? For whose benefit?

What will be the goals? . . . These are political questions in the best sense because they are concerned with power and purpose." [69]

But Sumner and Field ignored such questions. Failing to address politics and to transform strength into right, their efforts came down to stop-gap measures, attempts to wall-off the anomalous. (This was clear in their language. Justice Brewer welcomed the "fortress" between individual rights and "the public good." Olney presented the ICC as a "barrier" between the corporations and the people.) These approaches were more like formulas for class war than prescriptions for cultural hegemony. Sumner probably meant to console readers when he told them that the Constitution guaranteed the right only to *pursue* happiness, and said nothing about actually catching it. [70] But more than consolation was necessary if Americans were to come to grips with emergent social conditions.

The vital intellectual germ was contained in a third strain of thought, that of the new capitalists. Expressing at first only a practical impulse, then gaining strength with an infusion from Comte, corporatism grew in strength until it diverged from Field's position in the late 1890s and began to exert a flank attack against it. The corporate spokesmen were the ones who took the crucial step of working to convert their strength into right and the obedience of others into duty. So persuasive were their arguments, in conjunction with the force of events, that most later analysts have accepted without question their major assumptions: that social progress depends on the rare gifts of a few businessmen, that industrial initiative must be centralized, and that hierarchy and bureaucratic rationality are inevitable in the modern world.

Spokesmen for this third view accepted the lapse of the competitive market and its accompanying ethics without Sumner's misgivings; they looked to the new corporations themselves to fill the resultant gaps. The drift in the ideas of Charles Francis Adams, Jr., demonstrates clearly how the new view evolved out of the old.

Adams had begun by seeking a way to protect the public authority from corporate usurpation, and he had helped create the Massachusetts Railway Commission. But he eventually wound up condemning Sumner as an "extremist" for his critique of plutocracy and his refusal to bow "to the inevitable trend of events." [71] The direction of Adams's development was clearly suggested in his early volume *The Railroads: Their Origin and Problems* (1878).

Having concluded that the railroad problem resulted from the creation of favored zones, Adams turned to solutions. The possibility of reviving competition in railroad transportation he considered negli-

gible. He also rejected the idea of converting the roads into public highways, either through close supervision as some reformers suggested or
through outright government ownership—the "German" or bureaucratic solution, as he called it. By the late seventies he had also forsaken
the political vocabulary of his earlier analysis, showing the waning concern in his milieu for the political character of monopolies. The solution
he now proposed was to grant the corporations the greater power they
demanded. He urged that combinations had only seemed an evil because they were "unrecognized." The proper way to deal with them was
"through regulation and not through prohibition." With "some healthy
control" railroad directors would "have due regard to the general advantage of the public." Adams concluded that "a properly regulated combination of railroad companies for the avowed purpose of *controlling
competition* might be a most useful public agency."[72]

It was a sophisticated argument. Adams never denied the massive
corruption, the overcapitalization of stock, the manipulated rates, and
the vastly overexpanded facilities that were familiar. But he explained
such things as products of the attempt to get around the influence of
obsolete ideas and institutions. Here Comte's teachings had indeed
struck fertile ground. Adams attributed the problem of the railroads not
to the corporations but to those who failed to adjust themselves to a corporate economy. (He actually attributed the crises in transportation to
the *small* roads). Competitive attrition should be accepted, he advised,
and price-setting should be sought under the eyes of a public commission in order to permit the remaining roads to forestall ruinous competition. These proposals for "regulation rather than prohibition," and for
letting corporations attain responsibilities equal to their powers, would
become standard themes during the Progressive era.

Adams's scheme revealed two further reformulations being worked
in American political thinking. The first regarded the way in which the
economy was seen as providing for efficiency and "due regard for the
public." Adams suggested that the industrialists themselves would handle these tasks and that they would be made accountable by "the mill of
competition," through which "the great principle of the survival of the
fittest is worked out."[73] Such a suggestion would have startled not only
Henry George but Adam Smith as well.[74] Competition, instead of functioning as a continuous regulator, would be expected to act as a "mill"
for selecting individuals who, once selected, would themselves be entrusted with supervisory powers over production and distribution. The
job of the "regulatory" commission, blessing the whole arrangement
with the state's authority, would be merely to require standardized man-

agement and bookkeeping practices, and to act as "a sort of a lens by . . . which otherwise scattered rays of public opinion could be . . . brought to bear upon a given point."[75]

The underlying purpose of such regulation would be to enlist government help in creating "certainty"—which he defined as a "stable economy in transportation." Government help was needed because the business community had become so "thoroughly accustomed to the extreme instabilities of railroad competition [that] it has wholly lost sight of what its own interest requires."[76] This was a proposal that businessmen, who were already expressing their willingness to accept the "direct supervision of the National Government" in return for a 6 percent return, could easily live with.

By 1878, in other words, Adams's brand of liberalism saw the remedy for industrial ills as lying not in a free market and a neutral state, but in further economic concentration and government support for it. The melding of business and state so feared by laissez-faire spokesmen was here straightforwardly embraced. And most of the new corporate capitalists favored Adams's approach. (By the 1870s, as Kolko notes, over half of the railroad presidents had either held or were holding public office).[77]

Adams's ingeniousness did not stop with the problem of guaranteeing efficient production and fair rates. His second contribution derived from his recognition of the need for a new attitude toward work and security. As temporary president of Gould's Union Pacific in the eighties, he proposed an essentially corporatist scheme of labor relations. The plan, eventually published in *Scribner's Magazine*, envisioned a kind of corporate citizenship in which workers would enjoy "permanent service" in the railroad companies, due process rights in the corporation, minimal insurance for death, disability, and old age, and schooling for their children, "the best of whom would at the proper age be sent out upon the road to take their place in the shops, on the track, or at the break." This approach anticipated a number of programs actually adopted by some roads, as well as Henry Ford's "welfare capitalism" and Elton Mayo's industrial psychology of the twenties.[78]

It was with such plans in mind that Ghent had coined the term "benevolent feudalism." The young Richard Ely had also noted, in the course of using the same term to describe the model company town of Pullman, Illinois, that despite the amenities of such arrangements, the powers held by Pullman's directors made Bismarck's powers seem "utterly insignificant" and produced a "benevolent, well-wishing feudalism" and a politics fundamentally at odds with the American ideal. Considering the paternalism of such plans and their attempt to create a job-based villeinage in order to undermine union organizing, Ely's charge of "enlightened despotism" was also well taken.[79]

In his provision for labor as well as for capital, then, Adams's thinking registered the imminent drive within liberalism away from principles of competitive individualism and, ultimately, away from democracy as well. Like Henry George he admitted that market mechanisms had been impaired; but instead of seeking a new structure of authority for the commons, he proposed simply that larger tasks be entrusted to the captains of the private domains. The hands that inflicted the wound would be trusted to heal it.

The problem of *legitimating* this new power and of converting obedience into duty was addressed more directly by Andrew Carnegie. Carnegie brought to this endeavor a candor that is at first startling. He admitted that industrial conditions were massifying labor, creating class distinctions, depressing wages, and making a sham of the free labor contract. They were also, he frankly acknowledged, producing "surplus wealth." But having admitted such things, Carnegie broke with liberal precedent by urging that these new conditions be cheerfully embraced. Extracting the Comtist nut from Sumner's shell, he argued that although the new conditions were "sometimes hard on the individual, they [were] beneficial to the race."[80]

The essence of Carnegie's argument was that the new powers of the corporatists were legitimated because it was the corporatists who knew best how to distribute the society's surplus wealth. "The problem of our age," he announced in his article "The Gospel of Wealth," is "the proper administration of wealth so that the ties of brotherhood may still bind together the rich and poor in harmonious relations." If C. F. Adams had admitted the failure of market laws in the realms of production and labor relations, Carnegie now admitted them in the realm of distribution.[81] The capitalist appeared to him as "a mere agent and trustee of his poorer brethren, bringing to their service his superior wisdom, experience and ability, . . . and doing for them better than they could do for themselves." The capitalist's virtue was that he was able to administer social wealth in nothing less than "the spirit of Jesus."

This gospel captured the inverted socialism at the heart of future corporatism: through proper philanthropic administration "the surplus wealth of the few will become in the best sense the property of the many."[82] The private and the social were mixed not to subordinate the private to the social, but to justify the private interest's grasp of a larger share of the social product than would be permitted by classical liberalism. Carnegie's idea of trusteeship, already hinted at in Sumner, also revealed the peculiar twist being given to the American idea of consent. For while trustees do embody consent, it is not the consent of those for whom they exercise their power. A trustee has responsibilities *for* the beneficiaries, not directly to them. Toward them his relationship is paternal.

In Carnegie's theory, finally, the administering character of this paternalism took the place of a concern for labor and for the producer ethic—topics of central importance for George and, to a lesser degree, for Sumner. The reason for Carnegie's silence on these topics is obvious. Like Adams, he was defending a social organization that denied values central to the tradition that ran from Locke through Jefferson to the populists. Carnegie's was really the first of a new species of liberalism that would entirely divorce questions of personal fulfillment from matters of work. In the new view, people would be fulfilled by what they received and not what they made, by their mouths rather than their hands, by their supplicance rather than their autonomous action. They would fulfill themselves, that is, as subjects rather than as citizens.

Carnegie's scheme stood to Sumner's as the New Testament to the Old, the Gospel to the Law. In place of Sumner's severity it generously promised redemption from sin, and redemption through freely given grace rather than the exclusive efforts of the sufferer. But in conceiving of man as a recipient rather than an actor and acquiescing in the devaluation of work, Carnegie demeaned the very mode of activity through which Americans had traditionally expected to surmount existential trials and achieve personal worth. He degraded liberal man and deflated the liberal project. This Sumner had refused to do. But if those who shared Sumner's basic theory of value wanted to hold fast to it while the society changed, they would have to follow where Adams and Carnegie led. They would ultimately have to give up the personal ethics, the political values, and the epistemology of classical liberalism. They would have to follow Comte toward an organically defined individualism, a greatly diminished liberty, and a paternalism that was distinguished from domination only by the fact that workers in the new order would never be permitted to voice their own interests in the first place.

THE PROMISE OF "FEDERATED DEMOCRACY"

The late nineteenth century witnessed the development of a variant of liberal thought in America which openly defended economic combination, recast the premises of the older outlook, and straightforwardly welcomed state aid. Though this variant was originally viewed with suspicion by most Americans, that did not deter the corporatists. Accused of "sinister plottings," Thomas W. Lamont of the Morgan interests responded that he and his colleagues were merely "standing around in a cooperative frame of mind." Accused more pointedly of being "communistic," one of the organizers of the Southern California Fruit Grower's Exchange (later Sunkist) blandly replied that his program was simply one of "federated democracy."[83] The question that was actually being posed during these years was not whether such federation should occur or whether the state should intervene, but *how* that federation and that intervention should occur.

The essentials of the struggle around these questions can be seen in the conflict that surrounded the ICC, the cornerstone of the future regulatory state. Historians, beginning with Solon Buck, have usually seen the commission as a first step toward building a regulatory apparatus that would work in the public interest. No matter what the limitations of the original commission, they have urged, it represented a foot in the door. They have not, however, looked closely enough to see whose foot it was.

In fact, by 1886 three different approaches to government regulation vied with each other for acceptance. The first and most familiar was the agrarian approach, spelled out most clearly by the Illinois and Wisconsin Granges; it sought strict rate regulation by legislatively appointed commissions.[84] Adams's approach, a more conciliatory proposal for bookkeeping oversight and publicity, was the second. The third approach sought like the populist proposal to create strict federal powers, but it would use such powers to enforce corporate self-regulation, as represented by the pooling arrangements. This proposal was put forth by the railroadmen themselves in response to overexpansion and their own cutthroat practices; its purpose was "not to control the roads," as President Walker of the Pennsylvania Railroad put it, "but to protect them . . . against themselves and each other." It was also put forth to undercut the appeal of the populists. "The public will regulate us," Charles E. Perkins of the Baltimore and Ohio (and later a spokesman of the Morgan interests) wrote to a friend; at least with the bill being considered (a variant of the one which was eventually passed), "we can go to sleep and rest assured that their report will *not be communistic.*"[85]

The partisans of this third approach were the ones who were ultimately successful.[86] And the subsequent vulnerability of government commissions to being controlled by the interests they are supposed to regulate can be understood not as the product of a natural degenerative process (as Marver Bernstein suggested in his noted study), but as the expression of a congenital defect built into the model from the beginning.[87]

It is not surprising, then, that Senator Cullom, one of the major architects of the bill actually adopted, later wrote that "the Act of 1887 was conservative legislation, but in Congress and among the people generally it was considered radical." What is surprising is that Charles Francis Adams, Jr., whom one historian has called "the founder of modern state commissions," and who had now been propelled beyond his second attitude toward business combinations to a third one, played a role in the drafting of this bill and regarded the ICC as the means of "self-preservation for the company I represent."[88]

"What is desired if I understand it," he had written to a member of the House Committee on Commerce, based on his experience in Massachusetts, "is something having a good sound, but quite harmless which will impress the popular mind with the idea that a great deal is being done, when in reality very little is intended to be done." From his previous experience he knew that "everything depends upon the men who, so to speak, are inside of [the Commission] and who are to make it work. In the hands of the right men, any bill would produce the desired results."[89]

The advice was not wholly disingenuous. The evolution of Adams's thought about these matters was expressive of the implicit logic of a corporate liberalism. His early criticism of the "organized lawlessness" of the railroads could not have come easily. American liberals were not accustomed to pitting economic against political power. But as the immediate interests of capital continued to move away from inherited ideas of the public interest, a choice between the two became necessary. At this point Comte's influence became decisive. Armed with faith in a developmental progress and in the virtue of a few private businessmen, Adams and men like him renounced their criticisms of the corporations and chose without remorse a new, though belated, synthesis of private and public. In this new outlook the public welfare would be implemented by magnates themselves rather than by market mechanisms, and in a historical rather than an immediate time-frame.

With each decade Adams traveled farther along this line of thought. After serving on the Massachusetts Commission, in the early 1870s he became the officer of a large trunk-line association. He moved on from there to the presidency of the Union Pacific. When Jay Gould resumed that office in 1893, Adams became an investor and a director of other trusts. His odyssey was accompanied by a growing hostility toward political reform and toward attempts to reassert the sovereignty of the public over business. His earlier conciliatory approach to regulation, he now admitted, had come to naught. By the 1890s, this reform Republican of 1872 was openly justifying trusts, complaining of the depredations of government, and even lending his name to legislative bribes. He now called for a "Bismarck of the railways" and thought that Morgan might be the answer to the call.[90] No more than his brothers Henry or Brooks had Charles Francis, Jr.,—initially protesting a Grant—intended to wind up with a Morgan. But his conclusions were contained in his assumptions; the fruit was in the seed. And as the times forced hard choices, Adams moved to those conclusions. What complicated the matter was that he did not see himself, like Brewer and Field, as acting *against* the masses. He saw the people's interests as eventually identical to his own. It was simply necessary, he probably thought as he wrote the drafters of the Interstate Commerce Act, to deceive the people in order to save them.

PART TWO

The Emergence of Corporate Liberalism

5

The United States Incorporated: The Group Vision

When the rugged individual totters, at last, into some recognition of human interdependence, there is nothing to do but smother him with cotton candy. There has been no structure of human need and textured life with others in the past.

—GARRY WILLS

Questions about the character of organized social conditions lay at the center of the struggles that made up Progressivism. The increasing numbers and size of organizations forced "the fact of association" into social consciousness. But how would associations fit into liberal society? What would the rights of individuals be within organizations, and the rights of organizations against each other? What would democracy look like in organized conditions? Different answers to these questions produced the different approaches to industrial democracy that distinguished the scientific management movement from the Wobblies, the municipal commission movement from the AFL, and the state Progressive parties from the New Nationalists. The corporation had been accepted into American life, but the terms on which it would stay remained to be worked out.

Roosevelt's attempt to draw a line between good and bad trusts, the

Taft Court's attempt to distinguish reasonable from unreasonable restraints of trade, and Wilson's distinction between trusts and "big business" all responded to these questions in different ways. So too did the unions—and the offensives *against* the unions epitomized by the attempt of the National Association of Manufacturers (NAM) to make them subject to the terms of the Sherman Anti-Trust Act.[1]

Even stubborn individualists acknowledged that the context of individualism was changing. President Kirby's admission to the NAM that "we are living in an age of organization," an age "when organization alone can preserve your freedom and mine," attested to that.[2] But many thinkers departed from the classical liberal vision altogether and began to see groups rather than individuals as the constituent elements of society. The older individualism was judged by Arthur F. Bentley to be methodologically misleading; by Mary Parker Follet, Thorstein Veblen, and Charles Horton Cooley to be psychologically false; by Herbert Croly to be ethically unworthy; and by John Dewey to be socially disruptive. Bentley explained that "the whole of social life in all its phases can be stated in . . . [terms of] groups of active men." "When the groups are adequately stated, everything is stated." And in case anyone missed the point: "When I say everything, I mean everything."[3] Mary Parker Follett agreed that "association is the law of life." And Oliver Wendell Holmes, Jr., cast the idea in an evolutionary perspective when he declared in a Massachusetts labor case of 1896 that it was "plain from the slightest consideration of practical affairs . . . that free competition means combination, and that the organization of the world now going on so fast, means an ever-increasing might and scope of combination."[4] Associations, for these thinkers, were the real and meaningful bases of social life.

The group thinkers were diverse in their purposes, sentiments, and styles, and any composite portrait does an injustice to the richness and precise character of their individual contributions. But there were strong similarities between them. In this chapter we shall identify those similarities and describe the common social vision that emerged during the Progressive era, as well as the theoretical logic it bequeathed to the future.

BACKGROUNDS

As a beginning, it will be useful to take a look at the traditions from which the group thinkers took their bearings. The most obvious of these was the tradition of European pluralism. Though associated more recently with the legacy of Tocqueville, group ideas during the Progressive era were often buttressed by references to Otto Gierke. Gierke's basic argument in his widely read *Political Theories of the Middle Age* (1900) was that the real character of social associations had been misunderstood by the modern world. Since the late Middle Ages associations had been seen as fictitious personalities, instead of as real, organic wholes. They had been seen as falling within the categories of private law (the law of partnership, analogous to the Roman *societas*) rather than of public law (analogous to the German "fellowship" or the Roman *universitas*). The effect of this misperception, as Gierke saw it, was to deprive associational life of a social form capable of expressing its real character. The historical product was a society in which an all-absorptive, compulsory state came to rule over a multitude of atomized individuals bound together by mechanical contracts rather than by real voluntarist ties.[5]

The pluralists of the various European schools sought to go back, in effect, and correct this wrong turn that Gierke identified in Western development. The monistic structure of the modern state was to be destroyed and the "harmoniously articulated community" of medieval times revived. This was seen as a step toward "realism," for as Harold Laski wrote, "we are all hyphens in our loyalties."[6] Instead of concentrating political authority at a single point, authority was to be pluralized among secondary and intermediate groups—churches, schools, clubs, and unions. These were to be acknowledged in public law as the natural, necessary, and autonomous bases of social life.

Other proposals accompanied the pluralist critique of the liberal order. New concepts of representation were put forth. New theories of constitutionalism were presented. And the prevailing Austinian notion of law as command was faulted in favor of a more democratic and vitalistic view of law as the "objective manifestation of the totality of social purposes."[7] Central to all the other proposals, however, was the emphasis on social groups—larger than the individual, fundamental in their claims, and binding because of the primacy of their norms even without the compulsory authority of the state. The political implications of this attack on monism were obviously decentralist. The economic implications, as between groups, were egalitarian.

The second intellectual current that flowed into the work of the group thinkers has usually been ignored. This current, hinted at in Holmes's remark about the increasing "might and scope of combination," was the evolutionary naturalism of Sumner and Spencer—and behind them, the positivism of Auguste Comte. The paradigm here was biological rather than historical. Groups were seen, as Sumner saw them, as increasingly complex and internally differentiated products of an organic historical development. The evolutionists joined the Gierkeans in regarding groups as natural and real, and in rejecting the theory that they originated as concessions from the sovereign. But evolutionists parted from pluralists in holding, with Comte, that the primary modern "groups" were economic and technical—that is, that they were occupational groups.

While such a view was congenial to people like Charles Francis Adams and Andrew Carnegie, it was also capable of fueling deep critiques of the existing industrial order. Comte's and Durkheim's positivism had been inextricably bound up with an appeal for solidarist institutions. For them, the beauty of the group approach was that it provided a remedy for liberal atomization, a cure for the anomie engendered by a society that guided itself by the anarchic movement of commodities and contracts. This search for social wholeness also manifested itself during Progressivism, particularly with Follett's "new psychology," Croly's proposed reforms, and Elton Mayo's later industrial psychology. All of these programs welcomed industrial organization for primarily moral and cultural rather than economic reasons. It was seen as providing a different and better foundation for society than bourgeois egotism. Less quiescent than the positivist label normally suggests, these thinkers criticized modern capitalism for its assault on natural communities and on customary solidarist relations.

Progressive thinkers drew on both the Gierkean and Comtist lines of thought in their attempts to find a way out of the impasse created by America having reached "the Pacific," the political and psychological limit to the older approach. Their response bore some resemblance to Marx's class theory. Like the European socialists, the Progressives hoped to chart a path toward a cooperative society and a positive mode of freedom. But these Americans considered themselves more realistic than the Marxists. They looked to group interaction rather than to polarization, to the grievances of many groups rather than simply to labor, and to evolution rather than to revolution.

In this chapter we shall consider thinkers who focused on group theory per se. The work of another set of organizational thinkers, those concerned with administrative theory, will be examined in Chapter Six.

We shall find that although this new approach enriched American political thought and nurtured an appreciation for the benefits of association, it failed in the end to achieve the high goals it set for itself. This was a failure of great importance, for it lives on in American thought.

Though it sprang in part from a Jamesean concern for vital individualism, group theory failed finally to provide a clear place for independent will. Though it offered a critique of capitalism, it failed to focus that critique sharply enough to avoid being annexed itself by the emergent capitalism. Arising in attack, it ended in accommodation.

The liberal tradition had never, as Garry Wills put it, acknowledged a "structure of human need and textured life with others." And the group thinkers inherited its difficulty with "texture"—with thinking about social structure, differential social patterns, and interdependent relations. Though themselves respecters of persons, they therefore adopted theoretical assumptions which, in ceasing to exalt the rugged individual, threatened instead to bury him beneath the imperatives of objective order.

We shall begin our analysis by looking at a superficial but quite influential form of group theory, that propounded by the corporate businessmen. Then we shall turn to the group thought embedded in the jurisprudence of Justice Holmes, for it constitutes a conceptual bridge between the business outlook and that of the group thinkers proper.

GROUP THEORY AND BUSINESS: THE GROWTH OF CAPITALIST CORPORATISM

During the early years of this century, those who engineered the "morganization" of business which occurred between 1897 and 1903 began to develop a common self-consciousness and a defense for their power over the opportunities and choices of others.[8] The organizational vehicle they created for their purposes was the National Civic Federation (NCF), founded in 1901. Members of the NCF proceeded to lay down lines of communication to the White House, to promote trade associations, call conferences, draft model legislation, and generally fashion the formal lineaments of what Gabriel Kolko has called "political capitalism."[9]

Projecting outward the rationalizing methods that had worked so well within their own precincts, businessmen began to accept the necessity for conscious planning and regulation over broad areas of social life. They even tried to legalize unions in order to promote in-house cooperation between labor and capital. They seated Samuel Gompers on their executive board along with John Mitchell, the President of the United Mine Workers, who had gained a national reputation as the leader of the long and bitter coal strike of 1902.[10] And they soon startled the nation by announcing business support for government regulation. Seth Low, then president of the NCF, reported to Senator Newlands' Committee in 1911 that a large survey had found that American business supported federal incorporation laws by a majority of four to one, a licensing law nearly two to one, and a trade commission modeled after the ICC by nearly three to one.[11]

We have already encountered the philosophy behind the corporate businessman's approach to regulation. The purpose of the Bureau of Corporations, which formalized relations created between capital (as represented in the House of Morgan) and the Executive Branch, its first chairman explained, was "not to enforce the trust laws," but "to obtain . . . hearty cooperation. . . . Its purpose [is] to avoid ill-considered attacks upon corporations charged with unfair and dishonest practices."[12] The Bureau, that is, was an Executive (and corporativist) device to circumvent the Sherman Act. Part of the motive behind business's proposed reforms was also to subvert more radical regulation. Charles Mellen of the New Haven Railroad repeated Adams's and Perkins's sentiments of thirty years before when he explained (in 1904) that "a public must be led, but not driven, and I prefer to go with it and shape or modify, in a measure, its opinion, rather than be swept from my bearings with loss to myself and the interests in my charge."[13]

Our concern here is not with the Federation's proposals, nor with its history as an organization, however, but with the outlook that came to be identified with it. This outlook was a rough synthesis of the historical vision of Sumner and the paternalism of Carnegie and C. F. Adams. Corporations appeared in this perspective as the only organizations capable of undertaking the vast projects which devolved upon modern society. They were no longer simply tools of production or means for amassing profits. They were charged with maintaining social health and cohesion, and said to be responsible for "that habitual sense of solidarity which is the foundation stone of democracy." They had become "vital institutions" of social life.[14]

Corporate leaders themselves obviously underwent a transformation in such a world. They ceased to be simply owners and profiteers. Their positions at the "commanding heights" of industry permitted them, it was said, to move beyond self-interest and see matters from "the point of view of an intelligent, well-posted and fair arbiter." As early as 1910, George W. Perkins of the Morgan interests was claiming that "the officers of the great corporations instinctively lose sight of the interest of any one individual, and work for what is the broadest, most enduring interest of the many."[15] Businessmen, then, were becoming "public officials" and "industrial statesmen." Possessed of such sovereign virtues, they saw no reason why they should be denied the extensive power they were beginning to wield in national life.

The NCF's approach to "business self-regulation" set the stage for what one participant later called the super-corporation of the War Industries Board, and for the trade-association politics that would follow.[16] But the long-term significance of that approach had less to do with its practical victories than with its theoretical assimilation of association to the capitalist outlook. Theodore Roosevelt's belief that his goal was to save capitalism from its more irresponsible (laissez-faire) spokesmen revealed the Federation's influence—as did his failure to deliver on his bombastic promises of anti-trust action.[17]

The social impulses to which the NCF gave expression surfaced in many places. A *Banker's Magazine* article of 1901 thus instructed people to anticipate the day when every professional man, legislator, and executive would find himself "affiliated by the strongest ties to one or the other of the consolidated industries." Independence of action would remain, the writer assured readers, because "the degree of independence which each individual would sacrifice to the good of the whole" would be no greater than what he currently "sacrifices to existing law and custom." This would obviously be independence with a difference. It would consist in the fact that everyone "according to his merit" could "attain higher prizes in life."[18] It would be independence, that is, within a highly structured milieu.

By 1898 Richard Olney, the man who had engineered the defeat of the American Railway Union at Pullman, was also helping draft the nation's first labor arbitration act. The Erdman Act provided grievance and arbitration procedures for the railroad brotherhoods; it went so far as to outlaw the use by railroad companies of yellow-dog contracts.[19] So committed was Olney to the anti-yellow-dog provision that when the Court struck it down, in the *Adair* case of 1908, he wrote an angry letter to the *Harvard Law Review*. Had he undergone a change of heart since the 1890's? Not really. He was not an anti-union official who had suddenly become pro-union; he was an opponent of independent unionism who had decided to seek ways to encourage compliant unionism. To him and many others, the interdependence of the new economy and the need for a stable labor force made it necessary to "cease treating workers as individuals," and to use the Executive branch to mediate strikes. It is significant that the first federal labor act in America embodied Olney's later outlook, just as the first regulatory act had embodied the later views of Charles Francis Adams.

HOLMES AND THE GROWTH OF OBJECTIVIST JURISPRUDENCE

The shift in outlook manifested by the NCF and Olney was elucidated clearly in the work of Oliver Wendell Holmes, Jr., a Justice of the Supreme Court for thirty years after 1902, and a man celebrated as a modern liberal because of his willingness to suit legal doctrines to the times, his defense of labor's right to organize, and his defense of free speech.

Holmes gave voice to the new outlook while still a Justice on the Supreme Judicial Court of Massachusetts. Faced in 1896 with the question of the legality of an anti-strike injunction, he shocked fellow-Bostonians in *Vegelahn v. Guntner* by upholding, in dissent, workers' rights to organize and strike. The fact of dissent, however, was not the only significant thing about his opinion. Had the workers studied Holmes's argument, they might have been as surprised as his colleagues.

Vegelahn was the case in which Holmes gave voice to the idea that industrial affairs demonstrated that free competition was leading to an "ever-increasing might and scope of combination." Workers, he therefore concluded, were entitled to the same rights of combination as capitalists. Such organization was necessary for the economic battle to be carried on "in a fair and equal way." Just as "society, disguised under the name of capital," sought to get the efforts of every man as cheaply as possible, so workers should have the power to get as high a price as they could. And once organized they should have the "same liberty . . . to support their interest by argument, persuasion and the bestowal or refusal" of their labor that they had as individuals. (He added, in a subsequent case, that he had "no illusions as to the meaning and effect of strikes." Holding personally to a wage-fund theory, he believed that one worker's gain was another's loss.)

The fact that the object of a strike might be to injure an opponent of the strikers, Holmes explained, did "not necessarily make it unlawful." For there were, again, implicit questions of policy at issue. The law permitted many kinds of harm when it was deemed in society's interest—as when "a great house" lowered the price of goods to drive "a smaller antagonist from the business."[20]

Holmes's assumption, then, was that history was the chronicle of increasing combination and that people should be permitted to adjust accordingly. Just as surely as this belief led him to defend union organizing, it led him later to argue *against* anti-trust prosecution (and to anger Theodore Roosevelt) in the famous *Northern Securities* case. It also led him a few years later to raise the sole dissenting voice in a decision that ruled against the legality of price-maintenance contracts. The logic used in this dissent should have been an embarrassment for a true realist, for Holmes argued that the competition of suppliers had little to do with production and distribution decisions, and that what fixed fair prices was "the competition of conflicting desire." Thus the company knew "better than we" what would give it the highest returns, and "the public will . . . be served" by giving the company its head.[21] This was in 1911, the year of the Standard Oil and International Harvester anti-trust prosecutions.

A decade later found Holmes still defending the course of combination in the form of collusive "open-price reporting," arguing again in dissent that the Sherman Act had never intended to "set itself against knowledge." Such price-fixing should be protected by the First Amendment. Anyway, a combination to "get and distribute . . . knowledge" about pricing was "very far from a combination in unreasonable restraint of trade." However much competition was diminished, he affirmed faithfully, it would be "for the purposes of industrial order."[22]

Holmes, then, was a group theorist with a vengeance. His outlook implied no necessary antagonism toward capital, however, as most of his interpreters have concluded. It is true that in *Lochner v. New York* he issued a famous attack on the liberty of contract doctrine ("the Fourteenth Amendment does not enact Herbert Spencer's *Social Statics*"). It is also true that as early as 1881, in *The Common Law*, he declared that "the absolute protection of property . . . is hardly consistent with the requirements of modern business."[23] And forty years later he again brought his realist's perspective to bear, emphasizing that property was not a "thing," but a set of relations: "You cannot give an established business definiteness of contour by calling it a thing. It is a course of conduct and like any other conduct is subject to substantial modification according to time and circumstances."[24] The corollary, which he also propounded vigorously, was that property was a creature of civil policy rather than of natural right.

Holmes was an antagonist, then, of the concept of property held by Field and Brewer; he was a patient, pithy, and sometimes mordant critic of exclusive and particularized holdings. But that did not mean what it is often assumed. His *Lochner* opinion was based on a substantive point, not on procedural considerations. The point was that the Court majority had enacted "an economic theory which a large part of this country does not entertain." What theory did the country entertain? The one Holmes himself held. His opposition to "the absolute protection of private property" in *The Common Law* had followed from a belief that such protection was inconsistent with the requirements of "*modern* business"—meaning the business undertaken by large combinations. In fact, Holmes actually took heart from the course of capitalist development. He believed (with the young Walter Lippmann) that "the great body of property is socially administered now, and the function of private ownership is to divine in advance the equilibrium of social desires. . . . The hated capitalist is simply the mediator." [25]

Holmes's break with the Lockeans, and his early criticism of Spencer for failing to acknowledge conflicts between interests, did not, then, indicate that he was a champion of the underdog. He assumed that domination was a fact of life. He often ridiculed workers' demands, scorned strikes and argued that all talk about exploitation was meaningless moralizing. [26] His point, like Olney's, was simply that it no longer made sense to treat workers as particularized individuals, or to treat property as a fixed "thing." He was not pro-labor; he was pro-combination. And he was content that modern society was dominated by capitalist combinations. (When labor's rights were judged antagonistic to corporate organization, as when the Court held in *Loewe v. Lawlor* that unions should not be exempt from the provisions of the Sherman Act, Holmes could be found with the Court majority.) [27]

This group outlook also manifested itself, interestingly enough, in Holmes's free-speech doctrine, a doctrine which one assumes would have protected individuals against the claims of larger "groups." His famous "clear and present danger" test proposed that speech should not be punished unless words had been "used in such circumstances . . . as to create a clear and present danger that they will bring about a substantive evil that Congress has a right to prevent." In *Schenck v. U.S.*, however—the case in which the test was first formulated—it was actually used to justify the conviction of a man whose only crime had been the distribution of anti-war leaflets. [28]

The fact was that the clear and present danger test was not a libertarian test, in either its origins or its effects. It proposed to ignore both the intent of a speaker and whether a crime had actually been committed by him, so that a judge could determine guilt by an assessment of the effects of words used in particular "circumstances." [29] The plaudits of legal writers notwithstanding, what Holmes wrote was that if the words were judged to have a direct relation to an immediate evil, and if the dangers posed were of a specific type, then "we perceive no ground for saying that success alone warrants the making of the act a crime." Consistent with this reasoning, Holmes voted for conviction in most of the free-speech cases that came before the Court at the time.

His famous *Abrams* opinion might seem to contradict this conclusion, both because Holmes voted for acquittal and because he put forth his famous free-market view of free speech.[30] But this opinion was consistent with his others, and its surface brilliance was, in fact, dimmed by two points. The first is that the free-market theory of truth, no matter how congenial it sounds to a business society, is not a democratic theory. In fact, it is not even a theory of truth. What "lasts" or "wins" in the market bears no necessary relation to the truth. Even if it were not the case that intellectual markets are rigged no less than commodity markets, "the power of thought to get itself accepted in the competition of the marketplace" is not a test of veracity. Holmes's formula simply translated Sumner's vision of the survival of the fittest into the realm of ideas. It proposed not that the truth would survive, but that whatever survived would, operationally, be regarded as "true."

The second point, which should have given pause to Holmes scholars, was the great man's actual intolerance, his explicit disdain for the defendant. Holmes ridiculed Abrams's anti-war leaflets as "poor and puny anonymities." He scorned them as the "surreptitious publishings of a silly leaflet by an unknown man." Such statements were not what we would expect from a humanitarian and friend of the common man. But there was method in his meanness.

Under the test Holmes had fashioned in *Schenck*, Abrams's efforts *had* to be puny and silly in order to escape punishment. Had they posed the danger of a "substantive evil" such as Congress had a right to prevent, Abrams would have lost his protection. To state the obverse, Holmes's test provided no real protection for powerful and contentious dissent that might stimulate effective action.[31] His test gave the paternalistic power to judges to decide when "circumstances" could afford the exercise of rights, just as his economic theory gave a paternalistic power over work and production to the directors of corporations.

This test and its implications were consistent with the larger vision of law and social institutions that Holmes first expressed in *The Common Law*. It was the view of law as an external force: "For the most part the purpose of the criminal law is only to induce external conformity to rule. . . . The law is equally satisfied whatever the motive."[32] Carried to its conclusions, such a view implied that people could be prosecuted simply for failing to conform to popular or official standards. We shall come back to this outlook in the next chapter. Here it is sufficient to note that in an age when associations were increasingly defining the opportunities and actions of individuals, Holmes's preoccupation with the logic of the whole ultimately provided little protection for the integrity of the parts. He may truly have been a friend of the common man, but only to the extent that such men and women would benefit by life in a society where order flowed from the needs of objective institutions rather than from subjective rights.

Brooks Adams, the brother of Henry and Charles Francis, Jr., chided American capitalists during the Progressive years for their refusal to accept the obligations of a ruling class. They ruled, he charged, but they would not govern. His indictment was reminiscent of Tocqueville's warning that the manufacturing aristocracy in America aimed "not to govern the population but to use it."[33] But men like Holmes or Perkins or Olney did not deserve Brooks Adams's censure. They were quite willing to assume leadership over the organized means of existence. Left to their own devices, they would gladly have used *and* have governed the population.

GROUP THEORY

Most notable among the exponents of formal group theory were A. F. Bentley, John Dewey, and Herbert Croly. They were joined by a number of less eminent but no less profound commentators of whom the most important was Mary Parker Follett. Though sharing much of the corporate capitalists' outlook, these social thinkers usually opposed the capitalists' claims to social trusteeship.

Vision and Critique

Bentley's approach was the narrowest of the new group theorists because his goals and concerns were primarily methodological. Grafted onto the foundations laid by Madison, and later refined by David Truman, his approach would later issue in the analytic pluralism of mid-twentieth-century political science.

For Bentley, as for his contemporaries, the first step of any scientific method was to dispense with a priori assumptions in order to observe "what was actually occurring." It was to substitute inductive for deductive method. Bentley, apparently following Comte, concluded that this meant that the search for causal motives and intentions had to be expunged from political inquiry. As he explained in *The Process of Government*, "the scientific question" was not "*why* are these men doing these things and not others?" but "*how* are these masses and groups of men doing these things in these ways?" (or "how are these processes of men working?").[34] Once people understood this, they would get over the prevailing "metaphysical preoccupation with the individual in social thought. To posit individuals prior to investigation, Bentley declared, was to interject false entities or "spooks" into the real flow of events. In most cases, what the inquirer actually saw when he looked at society was not separate men or women but processes, relations, and "streams."

Like his contemporaries, Bentley also saw a commitment to mathematical measurement as an essential part of the scientific enterprise. Science required not only verifiable statements, but also that those statements be cast in a quantitative form. That the quantitative measurement and comparison of different phenomena would first require the abstraction of partial aspects from those phenomena posed no special problem. He assumed that "the quantities are present in every bit of political life." "Measurement," he explained with unexpected grandeur, "conquers chaos."[35]

The job of the scientific student of politics, then, was to study the empirical political process, shunning a fixation on such things as the formal executive or the legislature in order to focus on the groups whose interests were being mediated by those men and institutions. In addition to producing more certain political knowledge, Bentley believed that this approach would dispense with the false dualisms that had dogged political thought in the past—the dualisms of subject and object, mind and matter, public and private. (Bentley distinguished the private from the public simply by size, intensity of member commitment, and organizational technique—matters conveniently susceptible to quantitative measurement rather than qualitative distinction.)

More fundamentally, this approach would reveal that social life was made up of stable, measurable configurations. To these Bentley gave the name "groups." The word for him emphasized their multiplicity and the conflictual interaction between them.[36] More deeply, *The Process of Government* reveals that this term expressed Bentley's belief that political reality was constituted basically of *interests*. An appreciation of "groups" would wean political thought from its static, "mechanistic" orientation and direct it toward the observable signs of flowing, changing interests. Bentley's purpose in all of this, he explained, was not to dispense with underlying values and "meanings," but to see how those values and meanings were actually manifested in practice.[37]

Finally, Bentley's theory evidenced the faith, shared by subsequent American pluralists, in an equilibrating dynamic underlying this group conflict. Whether revealed in his example of a town's taxpayers rising up against drayage interests or his reflections about national politics, Bentley expressed a faith in political homeostasis: "When the struggle proceeds too harshly at any point there will always become insistent in the society a group more powerful than either of those involved which tends to suppress the extreme . . . methods of the groups in the primary struggle." When he wrote that "there is no group without its interest," Bentley therefore seems to have assumed the reverse: that there was no interest without its group.[38]

American society's commitment to individualism emerged from this account as the fruit of a long-lived methodological error. Bentley's general purpose in all of this was descriptive rather than prescriptive; it was to prove that people lived in the midst of a group process, not to recommend a particular kind of group life. But it is nevertheless clear from his pages that under cover of an attack on metaphysical "spooks," he was actually attempting an epistemological solution to the social crisis of American individualism.

His contemporaries were more explicitly hortatory. Where Bentley joined Holmes in avoiding concern with subjective purpose and intentionality, Dewey, Follett, and Croly invoked group theory in order to expand the scope of personal efficacy in social life. Where Bentley simply declared that people lived in groups, his contemporaries condemned contemporary groups and recommended others.[39] These thinkers also invoked the authority of science. Mary Parker Follett even expected her "new psychology" to accomplish for politics what "the law of gravitation [had] in the physical world."[40] And Dewey, like Bentley, felt that progress in social thought would follow, as in physics, from "abandoning the search for causes and forces, and turning to the analysis of what is going on and how it goes on." But unlike Bentley, these thinkers concluded from scientific analysis that "the great society created by steam and electricity may be a society, but it is no community."[41]

For such thinkers, a fully realized life was life in common with others. This was stated clearest by Follett, who contraposed a group-based vitalism to the Benthamite image of man as a lone, calculating animal. The language of Jamesean and Bergsonian "surges" and "forces" welled up in her pages, underscoring her conviction that people were healthiest, most creative and enthusiastic, not when they were alone or competing with others but when they were acting as members of a group, infused with group energies.

The kind of group she sought was not a simple aggregation of individuals (a "crowd"). Nor, she explained, was it the kind Ernest Barker suggested when he remarked that "if we are individualists now, we are corporate individualists."[42] Follett thought Barker's approach to the ego-writ-large would produce a group solipsism. The proper group for realizing man's potential, she wrote, was one guided by "the law of interpenetration" and synthesis rather than by the law of the crowd; it would be a group that achieved unity out of conflict and diversity not out of mere aggregation.

Dewey reasoned similarly. As early as 1894, in an analysis of the Austinian theory of sovereignty, he had written that real social organization was the embodiment not of simple aggregation but of shared will and purpose.[43] His subsequent work in semantics and logic led him to conceive of such will and purpose as the product of shared meanings, the product of a common use of signs and symbols. Such meanings did not arise automatically from the world but were projected, instrumentally, *into* the world. They were projected, as he came to see it, as expressions of underlying, primarily occupational, purposes: "Roughly speaking, tools and implements determine occupations, and occupations determine the consequence of associated activity. In determining consequences, they institute different interests."[44] Dewey's was a Durkheimean social vision buttressed by a phenomenological epistemology (rather than Durkheim's objectivism).

The problem with contemporary social organization for Dewey was that it was basically mechanical and external. People had been forced together from the outside; their unity expressed no voluntary choice, no common purpose. At best their groups were false unities; at worst, mere sand-heaps. In neither case were they real cooperatives. And it was the "balked demand for genuine cooperation and reciprocal solidarity in daily life" that produced such contemporary disorders as industrial strikes, the false "belonging" of nationalism, and the superficial and "excessive sociability" of Americans.[45]

Most Progressives explained the rise of these standardizing, mechanical organizations in economic terms. For Dewey, they reflected the influence of an "economic oligarchy" and the values of a pecuniary culture which restricted "corporateness . . . to the cash level," permitted individuals to siphon off the fruits of collective development, and hindered technological progress.[46] For Herbert Croly, industrial development had eroded the "promise of American life," which had once unified the American people and made possible a real camaraderie. Such development produced new cleavages in "class standards, point of view, and wealth," and prevented the easy familiarity which he, like the Jacksonians, saw as necessary for a democratic way of life. The new capital-

ists had not only "conquered" but had gone on to "occupy all the strategic points on the economic battlefield." "Power exercised in the hands of
a few" was beginning to deny power and the promise of American life to
the rest of the population.[47]

But Croly was no socialist. In the hands of the group thinkers, as of
Progressives in general, such analysis revealed a belief not in the existence of class conflict but in the occurrence of historical lag. Dewey denied that there had been any "criminal conspiracy or . . . sinister intent"
on the part of businessmen. Attitudes learned through "eons of separate
individual effort" and habits of privatism which had prevailed "since the
dawn of civilization" had simply continued to hold sway after they had
become obsolete.[48] This view of social history was clearly a long way not
only from the socialists', but from the populists' as well.

The group thinkers' basic response to the problems they discerned
was revealed in Dewey's *The Public and Its Problems*. It was an adaptive
and technically oriented response. In Dewey's eyes, two things were
necessary to turn groups into expressions of voluntary choice and into
vehicles of shared meanings: improved means of cooperation and improved means of communication. Though he sometimes suggested cooperative control of industry as a path to the former, his emphasis normally fell on the latter, on improving means of communication. New
"political instruments" were necessary to facilitate person-to-person
communication in an age of associated and scientific intelligence. New
instruments were also necessary simply to inform people about the
long-range consequences of their actions, and Dewey saw the ability to
guide present actions by a knowledge of future "consequences" as the
distinctive characteristic of human intelligence. The particular group
that used such instruments, that came to recognize itself as a group, and
that defined its own interests, Dewey called a "public." And Dewey thus
gave to the term a qualitative connotation that Bentley had denied.

The status of technical arrangements in this was revealed in the
opening pages of *The Public and Its Problems*. Dewey there distinguished
"facts" from "the *meaning* of facts," and then went on to observe that
"bare phenomena" lacked the power to command anyone's belief. What
held that power was not—as the reader expects him to say, on the basis
of his prior distinction—"their meaning," but rather "method, the technique of research and calculation."[49] Not fact and meaning, but fact and
method constituted the Progressives' epistemological world. Meaning
was expected to follow from the correct application of method. And
shared meanings—along with an "integrated" personality in an inte-

grated society—were therefore expected to emerge automatically from the creation of a "public," a group which had adopted modern methods of communication. New technological breakthroughs seemed to Dewey the most promising for breaking down "devotion to external standardization and the mass-quantity ideal." [50]

Follett also saw the path to democracy as lying in the direction of new "method." She called it "a scientific technique for evolving the will of the people." But as this sentence suggests, Follett emphasized more than Dewey the importance of creating a new substance for the formal technique, a "will to will the common will." To be a democrat, as she defined it, "is not to decide on a certain form of human association; it is to learn to live with other men. . . . I have used [the term] group . . . with the meaning of men associated under the law of interpenetration as opposed to the law of the crowd." [51]

This emphasis on solidarism also played a central role, finally, in the work of Herbert Croly, the son of an early translator of Comte. Croly saw the increasingly organized character of American life as presenting a golden opportunity to develop the fraternal and creative aspects of social life long frustrated by liberal individualism and by naive Jeffersonian optimism and "drift." Croly, like Follett, identified real democracy with a quality of life rather than with a set of institutions. Democracy was not a matter of negative liberties and formal equality, he wrote, but of liberty and equality as they made for human brotherhood. It consisted essentially in the "comprehensive and unmitigable . . . responsibility and loyalty" of each citizen to the others. [52]

For Croly, however, there were problems with contemporary associations beyond their inability to develop a common will. One was that they were increasingly bereft of common purposes because the old authoritative ideal was dying and a new one had not yet arisen. Another was that an abnormal amount of strife was being provoked by "the disregard by the official American political system of the necessity and the consequences of specialized leadership and associated action." [53] Croly's approach thus added to the concerns of the others a desire for authoritative ideals and for public recognition of the importance of leadership and cooperation.

The Remedy

The move toward group theory thus occurred on a number of levels. Dewey, Follett, and Croly turned toward groups for empirical reasons because they believed, like Gierke, that the group perspective acknowledged real interests and natural associations that classical liberalism had denied. They also embraced it on normative grounds because group theory implied a critique of bourgeois egotism and the defense of a "positive" concept of freedom. They recommended a group perspective, finally, on historical grounds because they believed, like Comte, that it was the perspective appropriate to an era in which organizations would provide the rights and securities previously provided by private property.

The result was a deeply social vision of the individual and of politics. Holmes identified legal principles as the expressions of social policy. Holmes and Croly defined property as a social rather than a natural construct. And Dewey presented knowledge itself as "a function of association and communication."[54] The purpose of such claims was not to deny or to quash the individual. It was, the group thinkers explained, to use the benefits of organized society to emancipate and strengthen him. The individual was the end and the group the method, as Follett put it. Dewey urged, with an echo of George, that the point was to use "the realities of corporate civilization" to create "a new individualism as significant for modern conditions as the old individualism at its best." It was to produce arrangements which would preserve "the distinctive moral element in . . . American individualism: Equality and freedom expressed not merely externally and politically but through personal participation in the development of a shared culture."[55]

The "group" that could provide this for Dewey was a public, as we have seen. He looked to participation in a real public to convert simple "conjoint behavior" into a "community of interest and endeavor" by nurturing shared meanings and symbols. In this way the physical stage of associated behavior would be superseded by "a community of action saturated and regulated by mutual interest." Lacking a public, Dewey doubted that democracy could survive in modern conditions.[56]

Mary Parker Follett proposed a similar program. Indeed Dewey's argument, appearing a decade after hers, may well have derived from her program. Follett looked to neighborhood organization as the proper context for modern group life. She saw local community councils flanked by a multitude of improvement leagues, social clubs, church societies, and workers' committees as capable, together, of solving their common problems and, in the process, recreating organic social wholes. In the realm of industry, she proposed workshop committees and joint control of industry (rather than collective bargaining) as the means to promote real social syntheses and avoid the clash of "group particular-isms." By these means individual consciences could be "incorporated" into a larger national consciousness rather than simply being "absorbed" into it.[57]

For Follett, neighborhood organization could also provide a remedy for what she saw as a crisis of political representation. History had dem-onstrated (by 1918) that "representative democracy has failed." Like the European pluralists, she therefore rejected the electoral approach to democracy. The guild socialist G. D. H. Cole had already urged, for example, that it was "nonsense" to talk of one man representing another. "There is no such thing as representation of one person by another, because . . . a man is such a being that he cannot be repre-sented." All true representation, he wrote, was "representation of com-mon purposes, or . . . functional representation." Cole proposed that from a merging of "medieval functionalism with . . . Victorian democ-racy, the real functional democracy of the future" would issue.[58]

Follett accepted Cole's kind of diagnosis; but she refused his rem-edy. She charged that this attempt to classify people by function would deny their real versatility and obscure the opportunities modern society provided for their all-around development. Cole's approach threatened to supersede the individual with "the purpose." Rather than replacing numbers with interests, she argued, the proper thing to do was to make "mere numbers" into real collectives. Her thinking was identical to Toc-queville's a century earlier. The real task was to "educate democracy." Such a claim broke with the traditional thrust of American political thought. This, as Madison put it, had been to provide institutional bal-ances for "the defect of better motives." Follett proposed to *correct* that defect. She would use neighborhood groups to develop a higher kind of social motive. The point was not to find better means for people to influ-ence politics, but to find means to enable them to *be* politics. The critical question, she had already concluded by the end of the First World War, was whether America could make direct democracy work.[59]

Croly, for his part, felt that the corporation itself should become the basic building block of the new society. He would find the answer to his larger search for leadership in a special concept of "the nation," as we shall see in Chapter Seven; but he identified the corporation as the immediate context for group participation. He valued the corporation not only because it brought people together and not only because its productivity would eliminate scarcity, thus making class conflict unnec-essary as he saw it, but also because it would give people room for "distinction" within an organized world. Rather than simply "adding individual imperfections" together, the corporation, as he saw it, would give to "each a sufficient sphere of exercise." [60]

It was true, he admitted, that the corporation had destroyed many older solidarist groupings and that its directors had sabotaged production, mistreated workers, and appropriated too great a share of the social product. But Croly, like most Progressives (and like Sumner), saw the corporation as a natural response to "a real and permanent need." [61] The real problem was not the corporation but the fact that America was hamstringing itself with Jeffersonian illusions and mechanistic institutions. The system's checks and balances blocked effective action and threw the real control of public life to trusts and bosses. These agencies, though illegal, could "get things done."

Like Holmes, Croly argued that seeking reform by making the government impartial was not a real possibility. Every government action discriminated in one direction or another. In "a legal system that holds private property sacred," for example, the normal course of activity would produce results "substantially equivalent to the exercise of privilege." Emphatically embracing a civil law approach, Croly therefore concluded that the society should straightforwardly adopt priorities that would permit "the process of industrial organization . . . [to] work itself out," and by so doing promote "selective individualism." [62] It should adopt Hamiltonian means for Jeffersonian ends—the ends of camaraderie and opportunity.

Croly's program was to legalize trusts and to create a national agency for their regulation. "Recognition tempered by regulation" was the proper course. By "regulation," however, Croly meant publicity, the promotion of common standards, and the provision of information (the regulatory approach of the early C. F. Adams). He did not think that the new agency should have the power to "promulgate rates" or "control the service granted to the public." That would involve it in management and prevent the concentrated authority he felt necessary for efficiency and accountability. [63] Rather, the existing corporate leadership should continue to run the roads in the regulated system.

Thinly veiled in this proposal was a fundamental disagreement with the intent of the Sherman Anti-Trust Act, and with the strategy of "mutilation and destruction" that Croly and other Progressives assumed the Act represented. Condemning the populists as ignorant and superstitious, Walter Lippmann, for example, was lecturing readers that the way to deal with "drives" was not to obstruct them but to give them "guidance." This recommendation for social sublimation revealed that

Lippmann, too, had imbibed something of a new psychology. If the corporations had gone on a "joy ride," the job for reformers was not to "set up fences, Sherman Acts and injunctions . . . but to take the wheel and to steer." [64] Roosevelt voiced the same view in his famous Osawatomie speech of 1910, when he said that prohibition had failed and that "the way out lies . . . in completely controlling [combinations] in the public welfare." [65]

Though this approach was not far from Carnegie's or Gary's, Croly denied any affection for capitalist arrangements per se. He was simply seeking the goals of industrial efficiency and Comtist moral regeneration. But such efforts were not easy. His range of concerns lay outside the normal American consensus: social bonds, obligation, loyalty, affection, leadership. Such things would sound strange to American ears. It was probably for this reason that Croly invoked the name of Hamilton and consciously called for a mercantilist mantle in the cold dawn of the corporatist era. Hamilton represented a wing of American politics that had always favored conscious direction rather than drift, and national goals rather than individual liberties. By using Hamilton's name Croly hoped to legitimate concentration and evoke a sense of shared purpose as well.

Theoretical Reformulations

The group thinkers clearly cut into the liberal grain more deeply than has been supposed. They grasped the significance of the transformations being worked in American life, and sought to rephrase the liberal promise in terms of group membership rather than private property-holding. The theoretical reformulations worked as they sought organizational equivalents for the older benefits of ownership—indeed, as they sought to present organizational status as the modern *form* of property—are clear from this account.

In place of negative liberty, the group thinkers emphasized participation, and participation as Dewey put it, in "the development of a shared culture." This emphasis grew partly from an appreciation of the fact that if freedom were civilly constituted, its enjoyment depended on the quality of civic relations rather than on a deceptive privacy. The emphasis grew partly, too, from the lessons of contemporary labor and free-speech struggles about the limits of merely formal rights. The resulting revolt against legal formalism resuscitated the Jacksonian and populist concerns for substantive freedom. The revolt might be dated as beginning a year before Roscoe Pound's important "Liberty of Contract" article, when Dewey and James Tufts introduced the concept of "effective freedom." In their *Ethics* (1908) Dewey and Tufts explained that such "effective freedom" involved more than formal immunities. It also entailed "*positive* control of resources" and—an important addition—the "trained powers of initiative and reflection" necessary for weighing and choosing between long-range alternatives.[66] And Follett argued similarly that if democracy did not exist in local communities, workplaces, and schools as a quality of peoples' social relations, it would not exist at all.

This emphasis on positive freedom also derived more deeply from the partial perception on the group thinkers' part of an ethical standpoint different from the liberal one, from the partial perception of a different normative outlook. The group thinkers began to think of freedom as something realized not in the absence of others but along with others, in commitment to specific principles. This was a concept of freedom with a *content*. What the classical liberals called freedom appeared from this new view not to be freedom at all but isolation and anomie. It was a condition Dewey saw actually producing the weakness that expressed itself in superficial conformism. Real freedom arose from a particular quality of activity with others, a quality that strengthened individual will and powers of action. What this quality was, however, was never fully explained by the group thinkers. They therefore left this alternative ethic largely undeveloped.

"Equality" also underwent a redefinition by the group thinkers. Dewey was at pains to explain that the kind of equality people should enjoy was not an exact physical or mathematical equivalence, not an equality that "deprived some in order to give to others"; it was an assurance that each would have his own "need for care and development attended to." What sort of development? With Follett, people were to be granted equal rights to political participation in neighborhood groups. But with Croly (often joined by Dewey), "equality" acquired the accent marks it thenceforth enjoyed in American corporate liberalism—it became equality of opportunity. The kind of equality a person should seek in modern conditions was the equal chance to rise to his or her level in a hierarchical social structure. This was the old bourgeois concern for "careers open to talent" with a meritocratic twist, a twist identical to Sumner's. The country should really be interested not in equality, but in the promotion of specialization and "distinction."

How would "individualism" fare in the new conditions? The group theorists, we remember, were attempting a difficult passage. They were trying to move beyond classical individualism without losing the individual altogether. For "in the real world, groups do not 'claim,' 'wish,' or have 'interests'; only individuals do." [67] The new society, for Follett, was supposed to provide the individual with a "liberty" from chaotic egotism, a liberty from "particularism." The new individualism would be one that was somehow not motivated by self-interest. It was not accidental that the Progressives in fact began to praise the virtues of "complete *dis*interestedness." [68] Croly saw such disinterest as the mark of distinction for both the craftsman and the political leader.

On balance it is clear that the older liberal concern for independence was really replaced in the pages of the group thinkers by the neglected member of the bourgeois trinity: the concept of fraternity. Armed with his faith in solidarism, the normally dispassionate Croly vied with the NCF in hurling invective against "anarchists" in the economy; he called non-union workers "industrial derelicts," and grandly offered the small businessman the right "when unable to keep his head above water . . . to drown." [69]

There was, finally, one new element in this group outlook. This was a concern for political education. Classical liberals, having taken "the individual" and a natural complement of rights for granted, had been able to ignore several questions central to the older tradition of political theory—questions about how people came to be citizens and how a polity learned to recognize its proper goals. In repudiating the assumption of natural rights, however, the group thinkers were forced to confront such questions directly. And they appeared at first to accept the challenge. They acknowledged that some form of education was necessary to convert natural men into citizens; that it was necessary, in fact, to "learn to be human" in the first place. [70] Freedom was not inborn. Special experiences were necessary in order to teach people their obligations toward each other and toward the larger society.

Dewey built this idea of education into his very concept of democracy. Adopting Charles Peirce's vision of the scientific community as a self-correcting community of inquirers, he defined the democratic polity as an experimental polity capable of continually judging the results of its experimentation. Democracy for him became the uniquely self-correcting polity. And Follett rejected the representative form of democracy precisely because it failed at the task of political education. She insisted that the skills necessary for a democratic life could not be exercised by representatives, could not be conferred, or even "taken"; they had to be learned. All three thinkers employed the metaphor of the school, as Tocqueville had, to talk about the capabilities of the group-oriented society they envisioned.

"GROUP PARTICULARISM" AND THE LOGIC
OF FUNCTIONALISM

Grant McConnell observed that "Most of the pluralists of earlier times combined a deep respect for individual rights with a concern for the corporate personality of the association. If there is irony in their position, it has become apparent only in recent years." [71] What are the bases of that irony? If a plan had to be devised to make the individual the end and the group the method, as Follett said, what sort of plan had the group thinkers devised?

Unfortunately, the basic logic of group thought was flawed by a critical vagueness and a failure of rigor. Croly's devotion to "fulfillment," "amelioration," and "distinction" was admirable. But he did not specify exactly what sort of distinction was to be sought. He did mention capacities for fraternity and technical skill, but these, taken by themselves in a corporate society, could be capable of quashing individuality altogether. Nor did Dewey's appeals for "all-around growth," and "the release of capacity from whatever hems it in" make things clearer. [72] One can respect his intentions, but it has been clear at least since Plato that human desires are not all harmonious with each other. The fulfillment of some easily leads to the tyranny of others. Some more precise value judgments were in order, some sharper qualitative distinctions.

This vagueness does not indicate, however, that group theory failed. It indicates rather that it succeeded in doing something different than is normally supposed. The group thinkers saw themselves and have been seen as pluralists. But the theory they produced is more accurately viewed as a nascent corporatism. This is clear from a consideration of what may roughly be grouped as four of its major characteristics. First, the concept of community it put forth was not really a concept of political community, and it was not democratic in its implications. Second, as a result of a submerged faith in natural harmony, group theory's revolt against formalism remained largely formalistic. Third, the group thinkers' legal thinking revealed a distinctively functionalist cast of mind. Finally, they failed in one of their major goals: to improve the ability of Americans to think about power.

Community and Politics

That individuality is shaped by larger social conditions, as the group thinkers argued, is now generally agreed. That the sharing of values can make these inert "conditions" into real communities is also clear.

But sharing in itself does not suffice for *political* community, nor for democracy. Aristotle made the classic distinctions here when he stressed that political societies differed from families, clans, and armies because they embraced a plurality of interests. They drew their purposes from no single source, and were therefore marked quintessentially by controversy, conflict, and the possibility of choice.

Tocqueville, with whom the group thinkers are usually compared, expanded upon the point. The associational life that impressed him when he came to America in the 1830s was not that of the business corporation. Nor was it really that of the ubiquitous single-issue reform groups. What most impressed him were the town councils by which the New England townships governed themselves. The councils suggested to him a way that democratic "secondary powers" or "intermediate agencies" might be created to stand between the centralized state and an atomized citizenry, and prevent tendencies toward further centralization and atomization.[73] The township suggested to him that new *political* corporations could be created to "divide" sovereignty and provide an ongoing political education for the citizenry. Indeed, for Tocqueville, such participation provided the only possible way modern democrats could learn about their common interests and acquire clear ideas "on the nature of [their] duties and the extent of [their] rights." He saw such participation "rubbing off the rust" of self-interest, breeding an affection for community, and eliciting people's confidence for action. "The art of association" was "the mother of action"; and Tocqueville saw the townships as the "large free schools" in which that art was taught.[74]

The township's importance derived for Tocqueville from a number of things. First there was autonomy; it was "sovereign in all that concerns it alone." ("The native of New England is attached to his township because it is independent and free.") Second was its voluntarism; it was constituted from below. (The townships "did not receive their powers from the central authority," but "gave up a portion of their independence to the state.") This voluntarism permitted the free "alliance of human will" which Tocqueville felt was necessary for any real power among men.

Genuine group life for Tocqueville, thirdly, was necessarily political. This meant that it embraced plurality and conflict, and that it also invited participation. Though Tocqueville was intrigued by civil associations, the political township was central because of this element of plurality. The township was the realm, finally, in which people exercised real power over their collective affairs. This fourth element of power underlay and enlivened the rest. Tocqueville was a realist. He understood the difficulties involved in persuading men "to busy themselves about their own affairs." Unless they were given real power he knew these difficulties would be insurmountable, because participation would be meaningless. The genius of the New England approach, as he saw it, was that it achieved liberty *in* public affairs. Without such "power and independence a town may have good subjects," he concluded with a distinction that was subsequently lost to American political thought, "but it can contain no active citizens." [75]

These concerns for autonomy, voluntarism, participation, and power—or industrial analogues for them—were generally absent from American group theory. Mary Parker Follett came closest to a truly democratic vision with her emphasis on neighborhood participation. But it is doubtful that she intended this to be political in Tocqueville's sense. Though she called for "interpenetration" in contrast to "absorption," she never clarified exactly what that distinction meant. And her chapter on "The Unity of the Social Process" in *The New State* revealed that it was the unity that really concerned her, not the conflictual process by which it was to be attained. She eventually went so far as to declare that, "the individual alone cannot decide what is right and wrong." And she branded "the identification of free will with free choice . . . the most superficial of all views." Any impulse "not capable of relation" was mere eccentricity. [76]

Dewey, too, failed to make real provision for diversity and conflict in his concept of a public. His emphasis fell on technical reforms, and he assumed that fluid communication and shared symbols would automatically produce ethical and political agreement. Democracy he actually equated as "the idea of community itself." [77] And though Herbert Croly knew that association was "the condition of individuality," he also tended to assume that it was a sufficient condition. In the end he subordinated the individual *to* the association—indeed, to a specific, functional niche within it. ("The individual becomes a nation in miniature. . . . The nation becomes an enlargened individual . . . in whose life every individual should find some particular but essential function.") [78]

The problem with these ideas from a democratic point of view was a product of a fundamental assumption that seems to have rested beneath their reasoning. They began with the proposition that individuals possessed rights only as members of groups; they then seemed to have assumed that the interests of individuals were the same as the interests of their groups; and they concluded that for people to claim rights against the group would be to involve themselves in a contradiction. The middle term of the syllogism was obviously false. But the group theorists accepted it. And they were aided in this by a failure of empirical investigation into the actual character of contemporary group life. (Rogin notes that it was at this precise time that Michels in Germany was concluding that the interests of group elites always diverged from the interests of the rank and file.) The group thinkers thus treated groups as false unities and embraced the group solipsism that Follett had warned against. They drifted toward that belief in "the corporate personality of the association" about which McConnell has written.[79]

In arguing that membership in a neighborhood group or business corporation should become an acknowledged and primary fact of modern life, the group thinkers also in effect converted voluntary into compulsory associations. They did this, however, contrary to the requirements of a democratic theory, without specifying the political rights that members would enjoy in these groups in order to guarantee a democratic group process.[80] By writing off the interior of group life like this, the group thinkers compromised their commitment to the educational features of associational life.[81]

Thus, although Dewey, Follett, and Croly intended to avoid the simplistic features of Bentley's positivism, their conclusions dovetailed with his. For Bentley's attempt to resolve the subject-object dichotomy had not been as persuasive as he thought. To have succeeded in his attempt he would at least have needed a coherent concept of subjectivity. But his process-oriented positivism prevented that. It reduced subjectivity to the presumed substratum of successful, objective facts. Though Bentley appeared to scorn conservatism, his writings therefore presented an epistemological corollary to Sumner's ethics: it was not by their values or projects that you should know men, he proposed, but by the fitness of their values to survive.

It is true that "tendencies that are suppressed, checked, inhibited, postponed are the most difficult to illustrate," as Bentley wrote.[82] But that would be no reason to exclude them from study—unless a prior decision has been made to equate knowledge with operationally verifiable certainty. Bentley, imitating the natural scientists, made that equation. And the others, anxious to find certainty in social analysis, followed. Any aspects of subjectivity that were defeated, obscured, or deflected by social events ("group" activities) were thereby denied. And an independent standpoint on the corporate condition, along with the possibility of dissent—indeed of politics itself—was also denied. Truly, when the rugged individual reached "some recognition of human interdependence," there turned out to be "nothing to do but to smother him." Having dismissed the natural rights concept of the individual, the group thinkers failed to produce a new concept of individuality to take its place. Their theory could eventually be used to justify the denials of diversity, meaningful choice, and power imposed by the primary groups of American society.

From Legal Formalism to Social Formalism

Bereft of any real view of politics, the only way the group thinkers could have promised justice and harmony at the end of the group process was by assuming it from the beginning. And, despite their frequent listings of diverse associations—churches, clubs, unions, lodges, schools, and neighborhoods—they did believe, like Comte, in the essential harmony between industrial groups. They gave priority to occupationally based "interests" and saw occupations as functional parts of an integral industrial structure.[83]

Central to these faiths in harmony and equilibrium was a basic indifference to the actual power embedded in the corporate form, a willingness to perceive the corporation as the product of a natural social evolution. Dewey asked: "What are the modern forces of production save those of scientific technology? And what is scientific technology save a large-scale demonstration of organized intelligence in action?"[84] With social choice thus denied in the realm of production, the group thinkers confined their protests (and the very concept of capitalism) to the world of distribution.

There is a profound irony in this. "Realists" who scorned doctrines about the personality of the state accepted doctrines that defended the burgeoning claims of corporate "persons." In contrast to genuine pluralists, they never questioned the grant of powers to a business regime that was creating a monist system beside which the fumbling activity of the emergent state was mere child's play.[85]

We have noted Bentley's faith in an underlying competitive equilibrium. That a whole range of social groups were, as a matter of historical fact, being destroyed during his time gave this empiricist no pause. Aware that many interests remained unorganized, he simply introduced late in his volume the idea of a "latent group" (an afterthought that fulfilled for him the same function as "tacit consent" for Locke). But this concept failed to meet even his own standards, for he never explained how to *measure* a latent group.

Toward the end of his volume, Bentley improvised even further by justifying the study of "forms of wealth" and industrial organization as special "groups" which were important in determining "underlying conditions." [86] But this gesture of flexibility only confused the enterprise. Bentley had announced on his first page, "This book is an Attempt to Fashion a Tool." But a concept that referred simultaneously to organized groups, latent communities-of-interest, and "lower-lying" forms of wealth was a tool too blunt to be used for scientific purposes.

What appears at first to have been an interest-group theory thus produced no appreciation for real social conflict. In spite of the unparalleled degree of industrial violence in America during their era, the group thinkers posited a belief in society's basically integral character. Follett's corporatist proposal that "if we want harmony . . . we must make labor and capital into one group" revealed no appreciation of the fact that one of these groups might have dominated the other. [87] The neglect of the empirical character of contemporary interests prevented these thinkers from acknowledging that U.S. Steel, Debs's American Railway Union, and the proposed neighborhoods were "groups" of far different weight and specific gravity. It prevented them from seeing, as Schattschneider later put it, that "the range of organized, identifiable, known groups is amazingly narrow. . . . The flaw in the pluralist heaven is that the heavenly chorus sings with a strong upper-class accent. Probably about 90 per cent of the people cannot get into the pressure system." [88]

It was this lack of appreciation for the real quality of the group life around them that made it possible for the group thinkers to wax eloquent about participation at the precise moment when the few realms of participation left to Americans were being expropriated. It is what made it possible for them to pin their hopes for solidarity and a new social substance on technical and logistical procedures. It is what permitted Dewey to sustain his faith in technology depite the fact that there was nothing in the history or method of technology—even if it were as free of capitalist influence as he imagined—to suggest it could do anything but *augment* the "devotion to external standardization and the mass-quantity ideal" he so much regretted. The group thinkers never seriously asked whether the "groups" coming into prominence in American life had been created to express mutual purposes and whether it was remotely possible for them to give rise to shared meanings.

The "society" that the group thinkers conceived of as underlying formal laws and political institutions was therefore a false unity, an over-integrated whole. And their revolt against formalism turns out to have been a false revolt, a balked revolt. The faith in natural harmony that they threw out the front door they invited in at the back—but with two changes. The implicit balance in which they now believed existed be-

tween groups rather than between individuals; and they saw that balance emerging in the course of history rather than already existing. By
historicizing conflict and attributing it to lagging values, they implied
that all current interests were consensual and mutually consistent.

The group thinkers were aided in this new formalism by their view
of science. They expected that science would be able to guarantee the
social unity no longer assured by pre-existing moral values. Scientific
method for them would provide the major check against the radical subjectivism threatened by the collapse of old standards. "The discipline of
science," Lippmann wrote in his influential *Drift and Mastery*, "is the
only one which gives any assurance that from the same set of facts men
will come to approximately the same conclusions." [89] The formalism lay
in Lippmann's assumption that science could deliver on its promise only
if people first started "from the same set of facts." The scientific impulse
with these Progressives, in other words, carried a hidden injunction: it
was necessary in order to reach the same conclusions to begin by denying the legitimacy of *qualitative* differences, fundamental differences, differences (such as most of those between employers and workers) not
susceptible to quantitative adjudication.

The resultant complacency was evident, among other places, in the
Americans' attitude toward the monist state, the focus of the pluralist
critique in Europe. Regarding the increasingly powerful nation-state,
the Americans remained vague and unengaged. Their frequent denial of
qualitative differences between the state-group and other groups obscured an appreciation of the real dangers posed by the former. If, as
they often said, "the 'state' . . . [was only] a temporary parallelogram of
forces," then the task for reform would be to dispose of any obstacles
that kept it from registering the balance of social forces accurately (a proposal hardly democratic in its implications). Alternately, Dewey had several proposals: first, that the state was one organization among others;
next, that it was an "instrumentality for promoting . . . more voluntary
forms of association"; and finally that it was a "regulator and adjustor"
of other groups. [90] Bentley's *Process of Government*, similarly, was all about
process and said little about government.

Absent from the American approach were concrete proposals for
how the state should deal with conflict between specific groups, how
intermediate groups might be strengthened against the state, or why
downtrodden groups might want to rebel against the entrenched. Absent also was a sense that anything was at stake in these issues.

Ultimately this faith in the underlying harmony of industrial groups
bled the force from the group thinkers' critique of capitalism. Their eco-

nomic complaints would be resolved if corporate activities became more regular and more scientific, and if the social product were distributed a bit more equally. Though criticizing the capitalists' grasp of "strategic positions," Croly never attempted, like Henry George, to trace the structural effects of that grasp. And while everyone acknowledged the emergence of meritocratic institutions, no one traced their potential implications for democracy. (Or *almost* no one. Fremont Older in California did inquire why those who had been lucky enough to be born with brains should be paid great fortunes. One might as well return to feudalism, he wrote, for there was "no more intrinsic merit in having talent than in having noble lineage." But he earned the scorn of other Progressives for these insights).[91]

European pluralism, guild socialism, and syndicalism had all put forth programs for decentralizing production and for decentralizing control within productive units. But such challenges found only faint echoes in American group thought. Outside of the IWW, sections of the Social Gospel movement, and stray proposals for co-management from Follett and Commons, worker participation in industry was not a concern of the American thinkers. Working people were said to be fighting for higher wages; and that goal could be provided by "more efficient" corporate directors—that is, by vesting even greater powers with the managers.

Notable in the new perspective was the lapse of older liberal fears about social hierarchy, about the political effects of economic dependence, and about the private pre-emption of public functions. One would never guess from reading Bentley that control of government *by* special interests was one of the burning issues of his day. He did admit that "we have a government which tends to favor class dominance." But he felt confident that "the class tendency can only advance to a certain degree before being overwhelmed," and that that degree was probably short of the need for violence.[92] Dewey was confident that the power of an "economic class" could be checked by "the method of intelligence." And even Louis Brandeis, who sometimes appears to be a latter-day populist, "cursed" bigness not from the perspective of the agrarian democrats but (as befit a member of the Connecticut Civic Federation) out of a concern for productive efficiency.[93] On balance, the Progressives were distraught about disorganization and outmoded individualism, not about exploitation. E. H. Carr noted that "even more than natural law, the harmony of interests was essentially a conservative doctrine."[94] It is not surprising, then, that the assumption of a latent harmony of interests should eventually provide a powerful rationalization for the impersonal, objectified (group-ified) forms of domination then emerging in American society.

In sum, when the group thinkers moved away from classical liberal-ism with its formalistic conception of rights, they did not really move toward a conception of effective rights (of labor, for example, or free speech), and toward a strategy for creating a voluntarist group life in America. They moved instead, in a critical inversion, toward the celebra-tion of *functions*.

The path from right to function was usually implicit in their argu-ments, but sometimes it became quite explicit. Follett described the "chief end of education" as being to "fit the child into the life of the com-munity." Croly inverted the meaning of Tocqueville's metaphor of the school by arguing that "master, teachers, pupils and janitors" should feel "an indestructible loyalty to each other"—such loyalty being "merely the subjective aspect of their inevitable mutual association." Right, in other words, became seen as the internalized expression of duty. And Dewey also appealed to people to "internalize" the existing "corporate-ness." He ended *Individualism, Old and New*, with this announcement: "By accepting the corporate and industrial world in which we live, and by thus fulfilling the precondition for interaction with it, we . . . create ourselves as we create an unknown future." [95] The definition of healthy individualism that emerged from such ideas was that of "adjusted" indi-vidualism—the individual adjusted to external functions. [96] That was the real thrust of Dewey's formalistic emphasis on "integration."

Group Theory and the Law

The most dramatic evidence of group theory's failure to achieve its own goals was provided by its legal theory. What looked at first like a move toward humanistic jurisprudence turned out once again to be a move in functionalist directions. That was the deeper significance of Holmes's theory of law as an externality.

European pluralism drew much of its sense of mission from legal concerns. Central to its social outlook was a critique of the concept of law as the command of the sovereign (Austin) and of law as a codifica-tion of the consent of atomized individuals (Locke). It proposed instead, as we saw, that law was the expression of the community purposes which stood behind the formal political sovereign and behind palpable institutions.

The Americans followed the Europeans in rejecting the command

and consent theories of the law. But instead of then looking to "will" as the fulcrum of the legal system and turning to questions about how the wills of individuals-in-groups might be created and democratically expressed, the group thinkers shifted their attention to "habits."

Follett wrote that legal principles were simply the "outcome of our daily life." They were not even "formal expressions of social habits," Bentley argued. "They are the social habits themselves as mediated by government"; "law matches government every inch of its course." Dewey defined laws as "structures which canalize action." They were useful because they made social action predictable; they gave it "method." Did that mean that one canal was ultimately as good as another? That judging between legal principles was an arbitrary activity? Dewey sometimes responded in the affirmative: "within limits" it made no difference "what results are fixed. . . . What is important is that the consequences themselves be certain enough to be predictable."[97] At points like these Follett and Dewey gave up any attempt at qualitative distinctions and slipped back again into Bentley's non-purposive world of process.

The pluralist revolt in the law was not a revolt in favor of seeing law as the embodiment of standards of right, nor even as a tool for resolving conflicts between such standards. When the group thinkers proposed to suit legal doctrines to "the needs of the hour" or to "social purposes," they conceived of those needs and purposes as embodied in objective, unconscious norms. Theirs was a revolt, to put it differently, in the direction of an external and behavioralist jurisprudence. Rather than assaulting mechanistic institutions and expanding the scope for will, as they claimed was their goal, the thrust of their attack on natural rights was ultimately to dispense with any intentional content in the law whatsoever, and to reduce law to the reflex of unconscious habits of interaction.

Such an attempt might have the benefit of making the law easier to understand for the positivistically inclined. But its conclusions were of questionable veracity. By treating all laws as essentially arbitrary and by lumping together constitutions, laws, statutes, and policies, it obscured the precise character of what societies call "law." And in stating that law matched government "every inch of the way," they failed to explain what should take precedence in case of dispute. Should it be fundamental law or immediate policy? Habit or statute? And if habit, *which* habit? How were appeals to be made from short-run to long-range community interests? The group thinkers' jurisprudence failed even to acknowledge these questions.

The ultimate implications of this approach are sobering. If the ethical and voluntarist elements were to be removed from the concept of law, if law and morality were really to be divorced, as Follett and Bentley implied, and Holmes explicitly proposed in "The Path of the Law" (to be discussed in the next chapter), then the juridical individual of liberal doctrine would not simply be transformed or reconceived; ultimately he would be eliminated. This is precisely what one modern legal scholar sees as happening in Anglo-American law: "Once legal order comes to be seen as an expression of 'shared social purposes' . . . the concept of individual rights must also be understood in terms of social purposes. Rights become sociohistorical rather than ontological phenomena. In fact, many legal scholars [already] reject the concept of 'rights.'" Carried to its conclusion, such a doctrine would produce a legal system in which citizens would derive their status not from underlying rights but from "the purposive, instrumental attempt to coordinate a community of functional interest groups." [98]

Holmes's judicial realism must be seen, then, as an incident in the larger process of objectification of the legal order—itself part of the objectification of social relations appropriate to the regime of social capital. Where the Europeans used group thinking as a tool for criticism, the Americans (following Darwin?) used it for adaptation. They sought to wean Americans from an individualist past and prepare them for a collective future. The new century would reveal that more than one kind of collectivism was possible.

Group Theory and Power

The flawed appreciation of politics, the social formalism, and the externalist legal theory finally frustrated the group theorists' attempt to introduce new ways of thinking about political power.

Part of Bentley's, Dewey's, and Follett's claim to realism derived initially from their refusal to accept the consent theory of law, and their refusal of an easy faith in free-market harmony. They intended to take people beyond laissez-faire ideology and toward an appreciation of the structural conditions of market life, beyond an exclusive concern with private competitors and toward an appreciation of social institutions (an attempt subsequently sustained by the Institutionalist school of American economics). More deeply, they challenged the "Newtonian" and mechanistic approach to power, which they saw as being shared by both American liberals (with their devotion to checks and balances) and

Marxists (with their view of classes as fixed, block entities).[99] They believed that both approaches reified power, contributed to narrow, instrumentalist ideas of social causation, and provoked unnecessary conflict.

Bentley proposed that government should be conceived of as "the process of adjustment of a set of interest groups." It was not a certain number of people, but "a certain network of activities." He felt, proudly, that in proposing such a reformulation he was performing the same feat for political theory that Einstein had worked for physics. He was opening political study to relativity, activity, process, and "the standpoint of the actor."[100] And indeed, if he and his colleagues had used their concept of "group" to describe those broad institutional patterns which simultaneously shape activity, frame social options, and stimulate action in society, Bentley's confidence would have been justified.

But it is clear that their assumptions and oversights bled their initial insights of their potential. Having pointed to "interests," they failed to analyze empirically how those interests were structured in particular configurations. In the end, they returned to a variant of the old Madisonian faith in latent harmony. So long as vigorous tugging and hauling could be observed, a healthy competition and the success of democracy was assumed; they did not look to see whether the competitive process was rigged to the advantage of some groups, and whether the ability to organize was restricted to some areas of the society. Indeed, in certain ways they fell short of the older approach. For though they claimed to be concerned with the effectuating substratum of formal rights, they retreated altogether from the older concerns about hierarchy and dependence.

After the sound and fury of their assault, the American view of power remained roughly where it had been before, divided between an instrumentalist view which was mechanical and schematic, and no view at all—an absence which set the observer adrift on a relativist, equilibrating sea, from which depths the public interest was expected to emerge.[101] To the extent that their perspective eliminated attention to the subjective intentions, values, and uncertainties that always lie behind the objective facts, it also hobbled social thought by preventing an understanding of the "standpoint of the actor," a standpoint always rooted in such considerations.

"JUNIOR PARTNERSHIP"—A NOTE ON
AMERICAN LABOR

Group theory has long been recognized as having had close affinities with the trade-union movement. Labor's struggles are credited with instructing the group thinkers in the limits of purely formal liberties and in the importance of group action. The rise of the American Federation of Labor has been seen in turn as ratifying the pluralist thesis about American politics. As Frank Tannenbaum wrote in the 1920s: "The labor movement has been . . . one of the chief factors in shaping society away from individual self-sufficiency, individual responsibility, and towards functional group solidarity. . . . The organic unit rather than the individual, one might say, is today . . . the basis of government function." [102]

The affinities between theory and practice were certainly there. Their character tended more, however, toward the functionalism suggested by Tannenbaum than toward Tocquevillean pluralism. The eventual thrust of Samuel Gompers's ideas revealed the conclusions toward which American group theory could easily lead.

By the turn of the century the AFL had emerged as the dominant group in American labor. It had also, in response to capitalists' growing power over national markets and ability to focus bargaining power over large areas at a single point, adopted a strategy aimed at acquiring national monopolies over the skilled crafts. Influenced by the carrot (of NCF sponsorship) and the stick (of heavy reprisals), the AFL finally submitted to a view of labor not as an autonomous force but as a subordinate factor in the existing arrangements of production. Its policies over the next few decades followed from this fundamental view. [103]

Despite the federative character of its formal structure and the voluntarism of its theory, the AFL engaged in a long process of forcing union amalgamations and of creating new unions from the top, out of whole cloth. [104] The products of such efforts enjoyed unity in a mechanical, business sense, but they obviously lacked common roots and the bases of a natural solidarity. The organizations created in this way, for example, were indifferent to traditional benevolent and cooperative union functions. "Stripped of universal and appealing ideals," John R. Commons wrote in his massive study of American labor, "without establishing a single labor paper to carry an appeal to the country, the skilled trades settled down to the cold business of getting more pay for themselves by means of permanent and exclusive organization." [105]

Despite attributions of diversity, the AFL was also quite successful in weakening and undermining alternative forms of working class organization outside its ranks, and in muzzling dissent within them. Its officials opposed city centrals and mixed locals, which were natural groupings and natural schools of solidarity, because of their innate radicalism. Such groupings frustrated Gompers's strategy of insuring a contractually responsible labor force in the separate trades. Gompers began as early as 1895 to institute procedural reforms that muzzled the voices of the city centrals and the socialists within the Federation. The doctrine of voluntarism, as Michael Rogin has shown, eventually disguised the growing internal domination of the AFL by the Executive Council, and the growing external oligarchy of the craft unions over the rest of the labor movement.[106] Commons concluded that the Federation had actually been organized to "keep out disunion" and had, "like the American political parties, [become] a 'machine.'"[107]

The IWW, to take a contrasting example, was committed to direct action in pursuit of a voluntarist syndicalism (though also, interestingly, of a functionalist rather than a political variety).[108] But though their acts trailed behind their words, it was for their words that the IWW eventually paid. The AFL avoided this fate by trimming their words to their acts, and their acts to the needs of the prevailing order, in a near perfect application of Dewey's occupationally based instrumentalism. The concept of exploitation, even the Lockean idea that a worker had the right to the product of his or her labor, passed out of the vocabulary of organized labor. Just as Bentley's and Dewey's rejection of "metaphysics" left them without an independent perspective on their society, so this intellectual retrenchment deprived the AFL of an autonomous view of the economy. The intellectual result was not an "unideological" practicality, but a replacement of qualitative goals with the quantitative pursuit of whatever the dominant system had to offer. Gompers was eloquent on the point. "I want more, more, more for labor" he responded in a famous cross-examination by the socialist Morris Hillquit. And at another time: "I ask that the trade union movement . . . may be an instrumentality to secure better and better and constantly better conditions for the workers of our country."[109]

Contrary to the goal of autonomous power, in other words, Gompers and the Executive Council had by the First World War decided to become a "junior partner" of business. George Bernard Shaw in England questioned whether the resulting organization was unionism at all and called it the capitalism of the working class.[110]

With the re-emergence of anti-labor business tactics after the war and brief internal challenges by the Seattle, Chicago, and Detroit labor centrals, Gompers followed out the ultimate implications of his prior decisions. The experience of the War Labor Board fresh in his mind, he despaired of the current "disorganized . . . aggregation of conflicting groups" and proposed the corporatist goal of an economic parliament for America.[111] This repudiation of competition was suggestive of Mussolini's ideas. Gompers himself was aware of the similarity. In a review of one of Mussolini's books for a 1923 issue of *The Federationist* he spoke glowingly of Italy's "new functional democracy" and of its attempt to create "an industrial state to replace the political state" and parliamentary democracy. He agreed that a concern about class struggle should be rejected in order to "recognize producers and production, and [to] throw open the state not to classes but to functions." He even justified the fascist coup in Italy as a necessary response to the threat of Bolshevism.[112] Gompers thus gave expression to the corporativist implications of American group thought.

That the sector of American society normally credited with restraining the power of business, and normally credited with creating a functioning pluralism, was organized according to the principles we have enumerated is important for understanding the character of modern American society. It is not surprising that the real achievement of this "group" was not to preserve autonomous values, to nurture independent action, or to promote pluralist conflict in American society; it was instead to extend corporate methods of organization over, and disseminate corporate liberal values within, the organized sector of the American working class.

MODERN TIMES:
FROM THE PARTS TO THE WHOLE

"After changing location several times Henry Edgar finally made his home in . . . Modern Times, a community founded in 1851 by Josiah Warren and Stephen Pearl Andrews and dedicated to the principle of 'the sovereignty of the individual.' . . . Edgar [then] passed from Warren's anarchism to Comte's religion [of Humanity] and carried on an extensive correspondence with the philosopher."[113] So wrote Ralph Gabriel of an early American disciple of Comte.

Henry Edgar was ahead of his time. But the course he traveled from the sovereignty of the individual to the Religion of Humanity was one over which the dominant sectors of American society would move in half a century. For there was an underlying logic to the drift. The indi-

vidualism promised by classical liberalism had been largely a false individualism; it had always existed within a context of uniformity—that of
the marketplace. That was why it had been able to dispense with real
politics, with means for resolving deep conflicts and for making conscious public choices. Now, as that underlying context was disrupted,
the concern for order became explicit; and the idea of "order" that
appeared was all the more simplistic and monolithic for having been so
long ignored. The resultant liberalism, still lacking a sense of social texture and an appreciation for conflict, still lacking an understanding of
organic social association—still mired, that is, in the classical liberal perception of social reality as constituted of atomized subjects in an objective order and still endowing the economy with a primary reality—this
liberalism was propelled paradoxically but easily from Lockean atomism
to Comtist corporatism, from the vision of society held together by
rights to a vision of one cemented by function. The process was identical
to the one that led Sumner from the sovereign individual to the regimented army. Strange and surprising as such a line of reasoning may at
first appear, it was the natural way for the American mind to move so
long as it refused to recast its fundamental perceptions of the world.

Group theory has usually been viewed as a bold challenge to
acknowledge the real bases of social life. Holmes, Dewey, and Croly
seemed to dare their readers to cast off a moribund past in order to
embrace a radical future. But social life was already being consolidated
when the group theorists took up their cudgels. What was novel in their
approach was not the call for America to move from individuals to
groups, but the call for the groups that were then emerging to be made
schools for democratic solidarity and the public interest.

Viewed in this light, group thought takes on a more defensive cast.
Its propositions were not so much demands as appeals. The group
thinkers were attempting to influence the locomotive of history after
it had already picked up a head of steam. It was weakness and not
strength that caused Croly to draft Alexander Hamilton into Progressive
service. For though Hamilton lay outside the tradition of laissez-faire
conservatism, he lay outside it not because he shared Croly's concern for
social bonds or for binding and healing the body politic. Hamiltonian
means were precisely what had brought America to the pass Croly
lamented.

In the end, group theory came down to a statement and a plea: a
statement about the group bases of individual life and a plea for belonging. The statement we have discussed. It remains to note that the plea,

despite its sound, was not really democratic. Bentley, Follett, and Croly failed to acknowledge the importance of rights of dissent and participation within associations, of rights against compulsory group membership, and of standards by which exploited groups might justify their claims against dominant interests. Moreover, these thinkers divorced the abstract fact of "belonging" from its concrete character as determined by a group's specific purposes.

In practical terms, their plea came down to a proposal to suit ideas more closely to realities. Dewey traced the real cause of contemporary conflicts to the "separation" of morality from real social relations. "Low" morality emerged as the product of "defective interaction of the individual with the social environment." [114] The prescription that followed naturally from such diagnosis was "integration," at the social and personal levels. And because the external or social world was accepted largely as given, the new field of action, the new frontier for national effort that opened up during the Progressive era, turns out to have been the minds of the nation's citizens. Within a half-century's time, that frontier would also be teeming with explorers.

In redefining political ideas, the group theorists rejected not only individualism but also the classical liberal strategy for achieving freedom. Recognizing that the unity at the heart of the older vision had been broken, they dismissed independence, individual ownership, and equality as abstract concepts inconsistent with the facts of social life. Philosophically, moreover, they attacked the classical approach to liberty for its negativity, its emphasis on mere lack of restraint. They identified freedom with positive commitment and sought a social content for that commitment.

It is a matter of profound historical importance, however, that in the process of rejecting the bourgeois approach to freedom, these new liberals also rejected a good deal of what was being approached. They moved from self-interest to dis-interest, obscuring the freedom to do anything more than throw oneself into the pre-defined flow of events.

What was noteworthy about the resulting theory was not its emphasis on duty, obligation, or respect for existing norms; the importance of these has been acknowledged by every political philosophy worth the name. But where a democratic theory would have to stress the importance of freely given commitments, of external norms that embodied chosen standards, and of a dialectic between unrealized values and given facts, the thrust of American group thought was to present social order as the simple product of internalized rules. Instead of dialectic and mutual conflict it presented a one-way flow. The question of how to evoke a new commitment was answered in terms of habit and socialization. Having attempted to augment individual freedom, group theory ultimately failed to provide for the voluntary and free aspects of human association.

6

Pragmatism, Science, and the Politics of Administration

*[Locke's] natural state is a curious affair, peopled
with the Indians of North America and run by the
scientific principles of his friend Sir Isaac Newton.
But in time the savages were banished and the
Newtonian norms grew and possessed social inquiry.*

—WALTON HAMILTON

*I*n May of 1902 one emergent group
in the national arena, the United Mine Workers, declared hostilities
against another, the anthracite coal operators led by the Pennsylvania
Railroad interests, in a strike notable for its length, bitterness, and potential seriousness, for it threatened the public's winter heating supplies. The strike is worth remembering not because of its length or costs,
however, but because of the manner in which it was resolved. For the
first time in American history, a President intervened energetically in a
major strike to secure arbitration. The private efforts of the house of
Morgan having failed, Theodore Roosevelt succeeded, through the vehicle of an investigatory committee, in restoring order, securing a wage
increase for the miners, and guaranteeing warmth to the families of the
eastern seaboard.

Many of the themes of Progressive politics were apparent in this event: the attempt to engineer a solution to conflict from beyond the field of battle; the direct collaboration of business and the White House; and the illusory quality of the labor victory.[1] But two things were especially symbolic of the era then beginning. First, an independent commission was presented as the proper mechanism for resolving an industrial dispute.[2] Second, the executive branch of government appeared as the neutral steward of the public's welfare, standing above it and protecting it from special interests. The strike's "real winner was the President," one commentator concludes. "Without calling on Congress for support he . . . expanded his own authority and hence that of the federal government to protect the public interest."[3]

A fascination with administrative solutions became a hallmark of the Progressive Era. Whether in state commission movements like those of Wisconsin or California, the nationwide municipal reform movement, or the rise of managerial engineers, whether evidenced by pragmatist thinkers, educational reformers, or politicians like Woodrow Wilson, American culture in the early twentieth century displayed a faith in the virtues of expert intelligence and efficient organization that distinguished it from the populist past. Administrative principles were the means by which Americans would organize the groups emerging in their society.

This administrative impulse found many expressions. One of the most rigorous was Frederick Winslow Taylor's scientific management scheme, to which we will return. A less weighty and more accessible manifestation was Lincoln Steffens' muckraking report, *The Shame of the Cities*, in which the urban reformer first appeared as the modern hero. Steffens presented this reformer as the only sort of man capable of dealing with the complexities of modern industrial society because he was a doer, a respecter of facts, and the possessor of method. Shunning any political base or constituency, maneuvering his way through a maze of special interests, this reformer sliced through obsolete customs and institutional red tape (such as legal warrants and provisions for safe-deposit box secrecy) to locate records, discover graft, promote reforms, and turn the citizenry into an "effective force." This new hero rose to the occasion because he was a "first class executive mind and a natural manager of men." He understood that "municipal government is business not politics." He was, Steffens felt (speaking of Seth Low, the mayor of New York and soon president of the NCF), "what the whole country has been looking for . . . the non-political ruler."[4]

Indeed, this was the era in which the call for the non-political professional first reverberated through American society. Richard T. Ely

called for a new "class of office holders," E. A. Ross for a new "manda-
rinate," and Woodrow Wilson for augmenting the role of administrators
in politics. The typical Progressive leader, registering the lapsed authority of self-interest, began to shun the Madisonian role of interest-group
spokesman and to present himself as a representative of national interests. Whatever else divided the serried ranks of reformers, they were
unified by the idea that the way to get things done was to remove them
from the play of factions, insulate them from politicking, and assign
them to the leadership of the competent. The ultimate thrust of this approach was to free the country not only from petty politicking but, more
fundamentally, from politics itself. That was the significance of Steffens's
"non-political ruler" and of the plethora of new scientific commissions.
It was also the point of Roosevelt's Bull Moose Progressives, an organization intended to be less a third party than an *anti*-party, a means of transcending the party system. It is not so much that politics recognized the
importance of administration during these years, as that the political
was eclipsed by the administrative way of confronting the world.

This emergence of an administrative outlook was attributable to a
number of things. In part, it derived from the growth of the national
government. In part, it reflected the new market strategies of the corporation. But more deeply, it revealed the growing authority of science.
First expressed by intellectuals like Bentley and Dewey and engineers
from the science-based industries, scientific assumptions about evidence, method, and reason rapidly coursed through the entire society.[5]
The idea of efficiency captured the urban imagination. People praised
the efficient leader, trained the efficient student, and sought the efficient
citizen. They even called for the efficient housewife, telling her to quit
"soldiering" (wasting time) and to free her home from the grip of custom because it was "part of the great factory for the production of citizens."[6] Indeed, the concepts of efficiency and democracy became nearly
synonymous during these years. Henry Jones Ford took it to be the "law
of political progress that sound developments are the result of "administrative initiative guided by scientific knowledge."[7] Just as technology
appeared to be the simple product of science applied to industry, so administration appeared to be the simple product of science applied to social relations.

At first glance, of course, people's ideas about science seem little
related to the stuff of politics. Epistemology is a rarified topic, uncon-
nected with interest groups, bosses, or trusts. What people think about
their thinking seems to bear little relationship to their acting in pursuit
of their interests. But assumptions about what people know and can

know, and about the character of reliable conclusions, are involved at the bases of social action. They are embedded in popular assumptions about what an "interest" is, appeals for the legitimacy of one's goals, and verdicts on the adequacy of solutions. This close connection of epistemology and politics was especially evident in the liberal tradition, where a concept of reason provided the basis for both stable individualism and social order. That connection became even closer during the Progressive era.

If the ascendance of the administrative outlook can be attributed in part to the growing authority of science, to what then was the scientific authority due? First, to the impact of Darwinism. Darwin's work in biology, along with Maxwell's in magnetism and Boyle's in gases, not only presented powerful findings about the world, but also demonstrated a powerful new method of inquiry. This was one that avoided the "rationalist" analysis of individual phenomena and sought patterns and probabilities among large numbers of events.[8]

Second, the harnessing of new forms of energy to production and the adoption of new technologies in industry redounded to the authority of science. Vast increases in productivity seemed to prove that the scientific approach was not only useful but in some deeper way correct. "For a generation in which . . . true and good often seemed indistinguishable, science, which was a more certain form of the true, could also appear as a more rigorous form of the good."[9] The science-based industries spawned a new species of engineer, who stood at the matrix of corporate capitalism and scientific technology ("the twin forces that shaped modern America") and identified his future with the further advent of science.[10]

There was, thirdly, a political element in the new fascination. Science was seen as the vehicle of political as well as of economic and laboratory hopes. Not that the Progressives still believed, as the Social Science Association declared in 1865, that it was for science to ascertain "the laws of Education—of Public Health and Social Economics," so that when they were fully ascertained, "the laws of the land should recognize and define them all."[11] The Progressives did not expect science to validate morals, but they did look to it to provide means for the peaceful and orderly resolution of disputes. Scientists would constitute a neutral bar before whom people of differing outlooks could bring their conflicts, and by whose verdicts they would willingly be bound. Professionals armed with scientific method would thus make it possible to dispense with the conflict and uncertainty that had always characterized the political realm.

Comte hoped that his science would provide for the same sort of willing assent to the laws of "social physics" that mathematicians and astronomers brought to laws in their fields. His hope was that science would facilitate the voluntary subordination necessary for a real social regime, and that in so doing it would solve the essential problem of the modern era—that of achieving order without either God or King.[12] The Progressive turn to neutral commissions and to detached reformers followed from the same epistemological promise about the possibility of independent and objective social knowledge.

It must also be remembered, finally, that this science answered the cultural needs of a people no longer sure of their moral footing. Both the Lockean tradition and its heir, Scottish Common Sense Realism, had ceased to make much sense in a world where individuals were no longer in command, events were not tractable to reason, and the standards of common sense were themselves unclear. Locke expressed the optimism of an earlier era when he wrote that "the candle that is set up in us shines bright enough for all our needs."[13] But Americans were no longer sure. And if those candles went out, the effects could be serious for a culture given to a sensationalist theory of mind and an individualist approach to politics.

Locke had, however, also suggested a path of transition. He had tried to prove that "morality [was] among the sciences capable of demonstration." Though ethical matters required "reasoning and discourse and some exercise of the mind," whereas mathematics did not, the two kinds of knowledge were "equally true, though not equally evident."[14] What the Progressives attempted to do was to redefine the sort of "exercise of mind" that was required. The belief in empiricism remained a constant, but they transferred it from a natural-rights basis to a scientific foundation. Having dispensed with natural right and "banished the savage," in Walton Hamilton's phrase, they would turn for their "laws" to the world of the laboratory. The result would be a distinctively utilitarian and formalistic view of "science," in contrast to the qualitative, moral approach of the past.

This intellectual revolution and its political ramifications are the subject of this chapter. For whatever its own political and material causes, that revolution produced ideas that soon acquired an internal coherence and soon began to exercise an independent influence on American politics and society. It produced the epistemology of corporate liberalism.

The intriguing thing about this epistemology, despite the Progressives' desires for consistency and certainty, were its own internal ambiguities. Those ambiguities were related to larger political contradictions of the era. Here was an empiricism which claimed to vindicate common sense and the common man, employed by an elitist middle class bent on making the submerged masses more like itself.[15] Here was a movement for emancipation that produced a social psychology preoccupied with control and adjustment. On the one hand, pragmatism, with its spirit of "cosmic republicanism," was, in K. C. Hsiao's words, an attempt to "extend the libertarian idea of self-government into the realm . . . of metaphysics"; it was an assertion of men's "natural right to take the government of the universe into their hands."[16] But on the other hand, the economist E. A. Ross (in *Social Control*) defined "the goal of social development," more passively, as lying in "better adaptation."[17]

From one perspective, the new empiricism constituted a declaration of intellectual independence. From another, it mandated factory schemes and commission reforms that expropriated people's effective political intelligence. Here was an intellectual orientation, finally, that often failed to express the humility and skepticism one expects with empiricism, and instead revealed a sweep and severity of which the stoutest rationalists would have been proud.

We shall begin our study of this epistemology and its ambivalences with the pragmatists. They most clearly expressed its range of motives and its tensions; and we will want to see how they resolved those tensions. We will then turn to the work of the administrative reformers to trace the political implications of that resolution. This is not to suggest that the two movements were identical. They were in many ways opposed. John Dewey was of a different breed from Frederick Winslow Taylor. But Dewey's epistemological conclusions dovetailed with Taylor's assumptions; and both men expressed similar confusions about the character of reason at a time when the development of social capital was "rationalizing" broad sectors of American life. Working together both movements also unleashed a current that by the 1930s would carry new professionals, managers, behaviorists, social scientists, and industrial psychologists toward a world view in which human conflicts appeared as problems fit for engineering solutions.

How a mode of thinking initially antagonistic to simple materialism wound up pulling in a positivist direction, and how an attempt to assert the primacy of experience *over* reason led to plans for enclosing experience *within* new rationalist schemes, are puzzles that must be unravelled in order to understand modern American politics.

THE PRAGMATIST PROJECT

The normal starting point for the Progressive thinker was an attack on rationalists' "fixed systems" and an assertion of the value of experience and action. As Charles Sanders Peirce put it: "The elements of every concept enter into logical thought at the gate of perception and make their exit at the gate of purposive action; and whatever cannot show its passports at both those two gates is to be arrested as unauthorized by reason." [18]

Rare was the book or lecture that failed to devote its opening paragraph to an assault on the determinism of Spencer, the mechanistic outlook of the founders, or the "block-universes" of Newton and Hegel. William James announced the need for a shift in "the center of gravity" and for something on the order of a new Protestant Reformation. [19] Oliver Wendell Holmes, Jr., emphasized that even "the life of the law has not been logic; it has been experience." The men who administered the law were too able and experienced "to sacrifice good sense to syllogism." [20] The claims of particulars were upheld against universals, and declarations of mental independence issued against the tyranny of absolutes.

Science and Action

This attack on "a priori reasons, fixed principles, and closed systems" was the first step of the pragmatist method. If people could only conceive of the practical effects of their ideas, Charles S. Peirce explained in the first formulation of the pragmatist rule, then their "conception of those effects [would be] the *whole* of [their] conception of the objects" of their ideas. [21] Ideas thus liberated from abstractions would prove themselves useful to people's real, practical problems. An early application of the approach was provided by Roscoe Pound's "Liberty of Contract" essay, the first shot in the campaign for a sociological jurisprudence. The essay launched a sustained critique of the doctrines of the Field Court. Pound charged that the Court's obeisance to natural rights, deductive logic, and "an individualist conception of justice" caused it to adopt property and contract doctrines that contradicted the facts of social life. The Court, he charged, was embracing a mechanical instead of a "scientific" jurisprudence. [22]

This charge, and Peirce's statement, displayed the mix of sensationalist epistemology and utilitarian morality that was distinctive of American pragmatism. First came the call for liberation from abstract, "block universes"; then came the auxiliary, second call to discipline ideas to the lessons of concrete experience as revealed by conceivable "effects."

Now at first glance this mix of instructions might seem strange. Movements of intellectual liberation have not usually remanded mind to the authority of material facts. But the pragmatists were aware of the dangers lurking in naive positivism and meant to avoid them. In different ways they all recognized the inadequacies of a simple scientism for social thought. Holmes denied that the story of societies could ever be "reduced to the axioms and corollaries of a book of mathematics," and criticized Spencer's assumption of the harmony of social interests.[23] William James urged that the physical scientists' assumption of uniformity was ill-suited to social matters. Dewey labeled the attempt to find a psychological science similar to physics absurd. And the attempt to implement such a science, he added, would only reduce "human beings to the plane of inanimate things mechanically manipulated from without."[24] Animating these criticisms, at some level, was an awareness of what David W. Noble called the Paradox of Progressivism—the fact that at the same time science promised certainty, it also threatened to release an unhinged relativism.[25] But central to all of the pragmatist concerns, as Peirce's remark about "the gate of purposive action" made clear, was the commitment to action. This was the element that linked their critique of Social Darwinism with that of the populists.

Henry George's arguments against genetic determinism and evolutionary "fatalism," for example, had been based on the epistemological premise that "mind is the instrument by which man advances." That was the primary fact ignored by all those "who seek to account for all phenomena under terms of matter and force."[26] And Lester Ward, "the forgotten prophet of the New Deal" and a self-trained statistician, scientist, and geologist, had also criticized the Darwinists' attempts to deny the boundaries between man and the rest of nature.

Striking to the heart of Sumner's teaching, Ward declared that "nature has no economy." It was only through foresight and planning that anything could be done "economically."[27] The briefest glance at human history revealed that men advanced not when they ran from floods but when they built dams, not when they escaped the wind but when they built windmills, not when they were passively transformed by environment but when they actively transformed the environment. The real lesson to be gleaned from biology was "the survival of the *plastic*." Ward argued that Comte and others had neglected the "psychic" or "telic" factor. An adequate human science, a "sociology" (Comte's word), had to rest on an appreciation of psychology, and psychology in turn had to rest on "a philosophy of action."[28] Society would only enter a truly human era, Ward wrote, when sociology was perfected, when "nature comes to be regarded as passive and men as active, rather than as now . . . and when the power of the intellect over vital psychic and social phenomena is practically conceded."[29]

Implicit in both George's and Ward's arguments was a common-sense rejoinder to Social Darwinism, which Eric Goldman has called Reform Darwinism, and which would later inform the ranks of Progressivism.[30] If history really told a story of evolution, and if evolution were really the result of an adaptation of organism to environment, ran the implicit argument, then the process could be made more efficient and humane if the adaptation were conscious and if each stage of environmental development were organized consistently.

The pragmatists moved toward a similar emphasis early and quite personally in the context of an informal discussion group that met at Harvard during the 1870s. Self-mockingly called The Metaphysical Club, the group included James, Holmes, and Peirce among its members. These three cut their philosophic teeth in affectionate rebellion against "our boxing master," Chauncey Wright. Wright, a logician and formidable student of scientific method, believed, like many thinkers of the day, that scientific reasoning was the highest form of human cognition. As a strict and severe nominalist, he advised that inquiry in all fields should imitate mathematics and physics by addressing itself to the "eyes with which nature is seen, [rather] than the elements and constituents of the objects discovered."[31] In an essay which drew Darwin's praise he explained the origins of human consciousness as lying in an extension of animal powers of memory and response, an extension brought about by the struggle for existence between mental "signs." Wright anticipated the pragmatists in holding that the meaning of a concept or proposition was defined by its sensible, verifiable, effects.[32]

Wright's younger colleagues shared his commitment to empirical method. But they were concerned with empirical method as a means for resolving central problems of life, like those of belief—"and not merely scientific belief, which is always provisional [Peirce wrote], but also a living, practical belief, logically justified in crossing the Rubicon with all the freightage of eternity."[33]

James's writings reveal that he initially considered dilemmas to be an irreducible part of human existence. Central among these was the "dilemma of determinism." Evolutionary philosophy might be condemned because it called "good" whatever survived. But "if what prevails and survives does so by my help . . . how can I possibly now, conscious of alternative courses of action before me . . . decide which course to take?" Choice, for James, as for the other pragmatists, was the essential part of that intentional moment which separated incoming sensations from outgoing "desires." "To put an extinguisher" to choice would "violate our general wish to lead and not to follow." [34]

The dilemma was that without the security and direction provided by older metaphysical systems, men would find it difficult to act. But the all-embracing explanations provided by such systems would leave them little room to act. They could hold onto the rationalist's ideal and deny free will, on the one hand, or they could live in an empiricist's world and deny ideals, on the other. James had no doubt on which of these horns modern man would be impaled. Our condition, he wrote, is "the opposite condition from that of nightmare . . . [though] it produces a kindred horror. In nightmare we have motives but no power; here we have power, but no motives." [35]

James did not think it was possible to avoid these problems by sticking to the facts, because the light of material facts was usually too dim to inspire real action. In fact, it was inadequate to itself. For belief was "an indispensable condition" of even the material world. James explained what he meant by this in "The Will to Believe." He offered the example of a man who failed to ask for a woman's hand in marriage because he lacked evidence about her probable response. He also offered the example of a man who isolated himself because he "asked a warrant for every concession and believed no one's word without proof." [36] Both examples were of events which failed to occur because of an absence of belief. And both suggested that it was particularly in the world of interpersonal relations that the positivist, fact-enclosed approach would prove crippling.

The problem of positivism for James, then, was not so much that its explanations denied the role of action in past history as that it discouraged action in the present. The scientist's habit of waiting until all the data was in was simply inadequate to the real, empirical world. For the positivist, action was always premature. (James even suggested that Chauncey Wright's personal inability to order his career and his personal affairs followed from Wright's narrow scientism; he had let the habit of waiting for factual warrant "creep into the region of conduct.") [37]

The pragmatists also noted other problems with the prevailing scientism. Peirce observed dryly that the positivist program was internally inconsistent because "what is and is not direct observation" is not itself "a question capable of being decided by direct observation." [38] And James noted that there were a number of important philosophic issues that the prevailing approach ignored. Lurking behind the daily newspaper reports of gratuitous violence, for example, was the ancient problem of evil. How could one regret such violence unless life were part of a larger whole? Yet what sort of world would permit such violence to occur?[39] And James also worried about what it meant that men bore the signs of "partness." For modern mortals (anticipating Pirandello), it was as if "the characters in a novel were to get up from the pages and . . . transact business . . . outside the author's story."[40] The issue was one of authorship, or in the traditional vocabulary of political theory, of authority. But positivist thought refused to acknowledge these problems. James was therefore troubled by Wright's unflinching declaration that "behind the bare phenomenal facts" was only "weather." With positivism, he remarked, "I can't make out what has become of the universe."[41]

Central to all of these considerations, however, was the pragmatists' concern about action and belief. Thirty years after Peirce's and James's comments, Dewey would still urge that it was a failure to distinguish between "facts which are what they are independent of human desire and endeavor" and facts which are "to some extent what they are because of human interest and purpose," that produced the "pseudoscience" which degraded people to the status of mechanical objects.[42] The sum and substance of the early critiques of scientism was that it failed to recognize that the objects of a *social* science were subjects—acting beings. Matter in the social world was shot through with mind. The pragmatists insisted that society had to be understood not as an opaque objectivity, but as the complex product of purposive, problem-solving animals.

The Pragmatist Program

Pragmatism, William James tells us, was intended as both a method and a theory of truth. The method, as we have seen, was to determine the meaning of a concept, proposition, or belief by "looking away from first things, principles, . . . supposed necessities . . . towards last things, fruits, consequences, facts." It was to gauge meaning by sensible consequences. The theory of truth followed directly from this. The true was "whatever proved itself good in the way of belief" as judged by that cash value—and, James added, "good, too, for definite, assignable reasons."[43]

Peirce's early writings reveal why the pragmatists attached such great importance to these definitions. "How to Make Our Ideas Clear" urged that modern intellectual confusions originated primarily from vagueness of ideas and poor logic and could be eliminated by applying greater conceptual and logical precision. "The Fixation of Belief" urged that ideas could prove more useful if experimental methods were used to "fix" underlying beliefs rather than the methods of "tenacity," a priori reason, or "authority." Indeed, the basic logic of the whole approach was experimentalist. Peirce went so far as to argue that a proposition had to be understood as meaning that "if a given prescription . . . for an experiment . . . can be carried out," certain experiences would result; if it could not be thus understood, it meant nothing at all.[44] Peirce had been educated initially as a Kantian. And though he broke with his early training because he could not accept Kant's transcendental categories, the rules of experimental inquiry can be seen as having served him in the way those categories had served Kant. They provided a means of organizing sense data and arriving at a reliable knowledge of "universals," apparently without embracing a priori facts. Little wonder Peirce and the others were so proud of their approach. They felt they had answered nominalism and established a basis for action within the limits of empiricism alone.

Underlying this methodological advice and adding to its importance were serious epistemological arguments with the older liberal theories of knowledge. Peirce again gave sharpest expression to these arguments, and in his response to Wright. While Peirce agreed with Wright that consciousness revolved around signs, he saw signification and hence language and experience, unlike Wright, as being "general," "social," and "purposive." By "general" he meant that signification embodied "whole" concepts which defied breakdown (analysis) into Cartesian elements. The existence of these wholes also defied associationist attempts at psychological explanation. By "social" he meant that signs and symbols, indeed intelligence itself, were collective and not private in origin. What enabled scientists to seek truth, Peirce held, was not a privately perceived, pre-existing order, but prior rules and a common vocabulary that had been posited *by* the scientific community. It was never "'my' experience but 'our' experience" which was at issue. "Truth is public." It originated intersubjectively and had to be warranted intersubjectively. Indeed, "truth" *was* but "the opinion which is fated to be ultimately agreed to by all who investigate."[45]

Finally, in contrast to those who saw mind as a passive register of external signals, Peirce saw people ordering their impressions—and their world—purposefully. Perception was intentional. People observed what they were "adjusted for interpreting." There was therefore "an inseparable connection between rational cognition and human purpose." Even positivism functioned, despite itself, as a purposive activity, for it projected a definition of the objects of possible knowledge into the world. Though experiential facts might be the basis of knowledge, Peirce therefore argued, "the knowledge of things can only be attained by the knowledge of ideas."[46] In stating this, he gave lucid formulation to that thread of idealism, that emphasis on intentionality, which was distinctive of American pragmatism and which would also be apparent in James's voluntarism and Dewey's instrumentalism. Knowledge, Dewey wrote, always "implies judgment."

Where the pragmatists disagreed with each other was in the way they defined "purpose." Peirce addressed himself rather narrowly to scientific purposes and the scientific community, even though he saw that community as the model and the germ of future social organization. This was because Peirce, despite himself and like most of his contemporaries, retained a teleological faith that people's activities were charting "a process of evolution whereby the existent comes . . . to embody the generals which . . . are reasonable."[47]

James's "purposes" were more personal. He might imply that social "facts" were informed by intentionality, but like most Americans, he continued to see institutions and social structures as vague obstacles in the field of individual motion.[48] The pragmatist method recommended itself to him because he thought it would provide "solid warrant for our emotional ends." His diverse musings on part and whole, fact and faith, freedom and determinism, revealed that the purposes he was concerned about were primarily ethical rather than technical or utilitarian. It was apparently out of his concern for the ethical problems of free will that he undertook his exotic researches into extrasensory perception, uncaused ("tychistic") states of mind, and religious conversions.[49]

Dewey criticized this subjectivism and the ahistoricism of James's trait psychology, and moved in a more utilitarian direction. Thought was not primarily a means to sensation, he argued, but to problem-solving, and problem-solving of a practical sort. An idea's validity was not determined by subjective satisfaction but by an organism's ability to master a problematic situation and thereby restore a habitual pattern to existence. Intelligent human activity was defined as activity guided by an understanding of "meanings" and meanings were said to be determined by "consequences." Cast into the language of experimentalism, knowledge was distinguished from mere opinion by the fact it was "the product of competent inquiries." Dewey's own pragmatist definition of truth followed from this: "If ideas, meanings, conceptions, notions, theories, systems are instrumental to an active organization of the given environment, to a removal of some specific trouble and perplexity, . . . they are reliable, sound, valid, good, true. If they fail to clear up confusion . . . they are false. . . . The hypothesis that works is the *true* one."[50] It followed, for Dewey as for Peirce, that truth and intelligence were also social: "Knowledge is a function of communication and association."[51]

Although they differed in their ideas of appropriate purposes, the pragmatists agreed on the third and last step of their approach. This step, less apparent than the other two, was in fact distinctive of the whole pragmatist enterprise. Having shown that ideas were purposive and instrumental, the pragmatists then urged people to engage in practical activity—but activity guided by the lessons (or for Peirce, the *conceivable* lessons) of sensible experience. In other words, pragmatism, usually seen as a counsel of worldly practice, contained a reflexive impulse; it cut back into the mind of the knower, the knower as potential actor. The point of Peirce's "pragmaticism," as of Holmes's legal realism and Dewey's instrumentalism, was to get people to "purport" only concepts that could be demonstrated to be "realistic."

James was confident that this approach would point toward a solution to the problems of human existence. It would reveal that people were justified both in breaking the rules of the formal idealists *and* in preserving their own beliefs—if those beliefs had proven themselves experientially. *"Believe what is in the line of your needs,"* he concluded; believe what makes you strong. Granted, people had different beliefs, rooted in different temperaments (tough or tender-minded, nervous or robust); still, if they admitted the limits of their experience, remained open to tychistic events, and would "live and let live in speculative as well as practical things," they could bring about the "intellectual republic." James concluded by advising people to avoid all-or-nothing terms. The world might defy the idealists in being a plastic, loose-jointed "pluraverse," but it also defied the Cartesian assumption that it was strewn with atomized data. For the radical empiricist, reality flowed in "streams." It was like a "joint-stock society . . . in which the sharers have both limited liabilities and limited powers."[52]

Dewey, for his part, urged a socialized version of the pragmatist approach. If the method of "cooperative, experimental intelligence" could be established at the heart of the social process and citizens, in addition, could be trained in "the experimental habit of mind," then a heightened respect for "consequences" would elicit shared social purposiveness.[53] Such innovations would require the industrial reforms we noted in the last chapter. They would also require that Americans break with liberal epistemology and a privatistic business psychology and acknowledge the true social character of intelligence.

The pragmatist rejection of a spectator theory of knowledge and its experimentalism led Dewey more than the others to an explicit program of social reform. If the world did not exist independently of the knowing subject, if knowledge was intentional, then people should exercise some control over the context in which their intentionality arose. Dewey accordingly became a vigorous participant in labor and free speech struggles, and in debates about educational reform. He trusted that the method of intelligence would produce a "renascent liberalism" and realize a third way between obsolete Jeffersonianism on one hand and fascism or communism on the other (or, alternately, between "drift" and "resort to violence").[54]

Thus with Dewey, the close connection between epistemology and politics at the heart of modern liberalism became explicit. "The method of intelligence" was equated *with* "the method of democracy."[55] For all its novelty this approach was, interestingly, continuous with the main line of American political thought. For, like Madison's approach, it sought to achieve political order in a highly differentiated, fractionated society through formal procedures rather than by addressing the substance of different interests and purposes.

In sum, we can see that the collapse of the older natural-rights tradition left large questions looming in American culture, questions about the external world and about people's ability to know that world. It was with the latter that the pragmatists expected to make their contribution—although through it they hoped to address the former. If people would adopt the pragmatist method they could know reality more dependably. Action based on that knowledge would then *make* reality more orderly and rational.

The Temptations of Science

Throughout their lives James and Dewey had to defend their work against charges of narrowness and triviality. They presented less a philosophy, it was said, than a way of doing without one; they justified any belief as long as it was held strongly enough. James tried to respond that he was concerned with cash value and usefulness "in the long run" and "on the whole." He was interested in "the collectivity of experience's demands, nothing being omitted." But the man in the street continued to see pragmatism more narrowly, as a counsel of expedience, a means for privatizing moral decisions, a justification for ignoring the larger contexts of meaning.

There was a reason why this issue kept arising. It had to do with the pragmatists' fundamental commitment to technical validation, and more deeply with a confusion about the form of "reason" they embraced. The effect of this commitment was to undermine their repeated call for the fullness of experience and to flaw their system at its heart.

The initial pragmatist assertion, that men know only what they learn from experience (that "the ends of life are within the sphere of life," as Wright put it), would be a plausible one if the boundaries of experience were drawn broadly.[56] That conception of experience would have to embrace many aspects of life in addition to its recordable or measurable events—the inchoate "experience" of traditions, the spirit of an age, the vague experience of as-yet unverbalized desires, and the partial promptings of ethical impulses. It is from the entire range of such "facts" that people learn about themselves and their world.[57] But the pragmatists—and the "realists" and administrative reformers who followed—drew their boundaries narrowly. And they did so because of their pre-eminent desires to find "definite, assignable reasons" (James's words) for accepting one idea rather than another, because of their desire to find science-like precision and objectivity in social knowledge.

The concern for validation varied. It was not particularly evident in James's *Varieties of Religious Experience*. And James never emphasized the mechanics of verification as much as Peirce or Dewey did. Still, James's commitment to sensible consequences and direct experience could hardly equip him or others to deal with "the whole setting" and "the long run." Nor could Dewey's experimentalism, in itself, equip people to handle the diverse sorts of information generated by history and society. That welter of information regularly imposes the necessity of weighing different *sorts* of values, balancing conflicting obligations, and even choosing different variables at different times. And the standards for making such choices lie outside the domain of immediate experiment. Personal and historical decisions require a more sophisticated calculus and a subtler discussion of the relationship of short-run pain to long-range pleasure than is provided by direct experience—especially by an experience refracted through technical lenses. The advice to look away from first things and toward "last things, fruits, facts" fails to help one compare fruit from different experiential trees. It also fails to help one choose between facts that contradict each other. It was the assumption that such advice *was* sufficient, however, that the weighing of "consequences" was not itself problematic, that gave to pragmatism its aura of expedience.

Why did the pragmatists cast their concern for experience in this form? Why did they establish techniques of verification at the center of their program?[58] It was because, despite their sophisticated critique of naive scientism, they continued to be influenced by scientific assumptions. They were fascinated by science. They borrowed its terms. They invoked its authority. They paralleled Ward, who had actually defined his chief purposes as emphasizing that "sociology is a science" and teaching that man could govern social forces "precisely as he has taken advantage of the physical forces of nature."[59] Holmes announced that "the next century belongs to the man of economics and statistics." And Dewey equated science with "the method of intelligence in action." He also spent his last years lamenting that America had still failed to develop a "political technology."[60]

Such views were not unprecedented. They had found their classic statement in the work of Auguste Comte, as we have seen. Comte's science of society also embraced a method and a program. Indeed its method *was* its program. Comte assumed that once people adopted the positivist method and agreed to "regulate their ideas and actions" by positive facts—those that were "real, useful, precise, certain," and historically relative—the modern insurrection of the heart against the head, that legacy of the metaphysical era, could be ended. The extension of scientific methods would then lead not just to personal but also to social harmony. It would make voluntary subordination possible again as in medieval times, and contribute to the comprehensive organization of society. (Corporations, for example, would be transformed from private businesses into social trusts.) The fulfillment of the promise of modern science, in Comte's eyes, would permit men to move finally "from the dominion of Will to the dominion of Laws."[61] And it was to the discovery of such laws—or, he hoped, a single Law—that Comte devoted himself. He announced in *The Positive Philosophy* that it was time to complete the "vast intellectual operation begun by Bacon, Descartes and Galileo, by "constructing the system of general ideas which must henceforth prevail among the human race. . . . The ultimate perfection of the Positive System would be . . . to represent all phenomena as particular aspects of a single general fact—such as Gravitation, for instance."[62]

The pragmatists meant to reject Comte's approach. But if they declined his and Spencer's architectonic pretensions, they nevertheless accepted the assumptions about the primacy of scientific cognition. If they felt that the content of social science was unique, they nevertheless believed that its form, and the kind of certainty it made possible, were not.

Thus Ward, too, defined his goal as the presentation of social phenomena under the aspect of a single fact or law. The "action" he had defended so strongly turned out to have been that which was rooted in "multiplied and ever-increasing wants." It turned out, that is, to be a utilitarian rather than a truly ethical or political—a constitutive—action. His inquiry also taught him, he wrote, that "evil" was "merely friction" and that the way to overcome it and realize "true morality" was not "by exhortation . . . [but] by perfecting the social mechanism." From this angle, not merely liberal morality but moral discourse itself was convicted of being unscientific, and therefore "anti-progressive."[63]

Peirce too believed that science was the paradigmatic form of reason. He even asserted that "the exact logic of Boole and DeMorgan" was the only lasting contribution of the century, beside which the schools of Hegel and Mill were but "coteries of philodoxers." It is true, as many have written, that Peirce's was a non-determinist science. His work on probability, his concepts of fallibilism and "tychisms," and his germinal insight that only "retroduction" (inference from imperfect analogy) *advanced* knowledge, all revealed an open view of the world. Peirce also distinguished himself from most later social scientists by refusing to accept contemporaneous operational testing as a full warrantor of truth. Nevertheless, the lessons to which he felt scientists should remain open for the future were still those that would be taught by manipulators of the experimental method.

Peirce still defined the goal of inquiry as being the discovery of a "single definite meaning, universally accepted among students of the subject."[64] He still equated understanding with the ability to specify how evidence for or against an assertion could be intentionally produced. His approach was empiricist, in other words, only insofar as sensible experience provided the raw material for his testing. Verifying operations for him were the real pegs upon which reality was hung.

Dewey also saw science as the animating spirit, the "genuinely active force" in modern society. (It was a force not provided, for example, by class struggle, "whose spirit and method are opposed to science.")[65] The corporation appeared to him to be the embodiment of science, not of capital. In fact, he saw pragmatism itself as much more than a discrete method for solving problems; it emerges in his pages as the operational handle on a larger "collective art of technology," a "socially organized intelligence," a corpus of scientific institutions and activities that constituted something on the order of a new, collective, human instinct. This scientism exercised a steady undertow in his pages. It pulled, for example, in the direction of an ethical naturalism. The reason Dewey felt it was "absurd" to model a social science on physics turns out to have been because new knowledge always altered human activity, not because of "anything called free will." And the reason a positivist science might reduce people to the status of objects was that "we are . . . but at the beginning of the possibilities of control of the physical conditions of mental and moral life."[66] The implication was that the threat would subside when the possibilities of control were more fully developed. The fact that beyond a certain point even differences in degree would impose qualitative difference in perception, in action, in modes of inference (as Aristotle saw), and in "science" itself was not appreciated by Dewey.[67]

Though the pragmatists were more sophisticated philosophically and more sensitive than the administrative managers who would follow, their basic idea about the appropriate tests for reason was similar to the one adopted by the managers. They never developed an idea of a distinctively *social* reason, or a democratic reason, that would serve as an alternative to the objectivist epistemology Comte had identified as peculiarly appropriate to the corporate world. The move from Lockean reason to scientific rationality on one hand (with Peirce and Dewey), and to subjectivist "desires" on the other (with James), was well-suited to a world in which institutional property was swallowing up the outer face of individuality and consigning ethical and critical consciousness to a purely private realm.

Having originated in a critique of positivism, American pragmatism was therefore weakened by unacknowledged positivist elements that remained within it. Admittedly, the pragmatist's world was more dynamic than the positivist's. People were seen as involved in real-life projects, as participating in a process rather than being mired in completed, objectified facts; and the validity of ideas was said to be proven by practice rather than by mere intellectual analysis. But the pragmatists resembled the positivists in their central commitment to method, in their preoccupation with one step in the process of inquiry and confusion of it with the whole. This commitment eventually manifested itself in their substantive philosophy. It revealed itself in the assumption—sometimes explicit, sometimes hinted, but always there—that the important questions of life were really questions of technique and method.[68]

Peirce was explicit about this. After first declaring an ontological neutrality and recognizing separate jurisdictions between science and morals, he later revealed the underlying impulse to expand his territory by proposing to "make morals more scientific," by declaring that metaphysics was "more curious than useful," and by announcing that those questions about which "the pendulum of opinion . . . never cease[s] to oscillate . . . are *ipso facto* not real questions."[69] Such a conclusion (like Ward's about morality) followed not from a study of the empirical, historical record, but from Peirce's own a priori assumption about the necessary character of knowledge. Like the positivists, the pragmatists proposed to let scientific criteria determine even "the admissibility of hypotheses"—to let them decide which questions people might legitimately ask.

The approach here was pre-eminently Baconian. Knowledge was power. What could be verified intersubjectively could be known. But the implication, conversely, was that what did not contain empirical, demonstrative power, what could not be verified operationally, could *not* be "known." It would not count as knowledge. Ideas that failed, as Dewey defined them, were "false." These assumptions, though logically impeccable, led Peirce and the others to most unempirical conclusions. For there are obvious "understandings" that yield no contemporaneous potential for control (as Henry Adams's understanding of the technological character of the era, or Debs's understanding of its class character). And there are obvious exercises of power that betray an "understanding" (such as the Court's imposition of the liberty of contract doctrine).

The theory of knowledge put forth by the post-Lockean philosophers in America was therefore more troublesome than it first appeared. What has always looked, from one angle, like a program for enriching experience, turns out, when viewed from another, to have projected a plan for the operationalization of consciousness. What looks like a program of emancipation turns out to have been emancipatory only insofar as individuals would agree to regulate their ideas to realities, and to trim purporting wills so as to make "the existent" rational. "By a surgical procedure," John Schaar writes of a later application of the approach, older concepts were to be "trimmed of [their] cumbersome 'normative' . . . parts," in order to make them fit for scientific duty. It might turn out, however, adds Schaar, that "Occam's razor has cut off a part or two that will be missed later on." [70] An approach that is usually celebrated for admitting that social matter was informed by mind turns out to have actually provided a rationale for applying *to* mind a set of techniques proven useful in dealing with matter.

Though the pragmatists echoed the Enlightenment prophecy that the real would be made rational, it was not, then, because they shared the Enlightenment concept of reason. Their "reason" was formal, not substantive. It was raised not on human facts, which are synthetic, historical, and dialectical, but on positive facts, which are measurable, precise, and cumulable. Whereas history for Rousseau, Kant, and Hegel was a field for practical-critical reason, for the Americans it was a field for adjustment. In the pragmatists' world it would not be experience that determined consciousness (to paraphrase both James and Marx); it would be method that determined both experience *and* consciousness. But the hubris of assuming that rational technique could control the human mind (and even the race, for eugenics was a recurrent theme of the period) never struck these thinkers as manipulative or objectionable. For with the elimination of traditional normative elements from social thought, the belief in a human nature capable of being manipulated was ceasing to inform the culture.

The Politics of Pragmatism

In his study of modern science, E. A. Burtt observed that scientific inquirers are usually under a strong temptation "to make a metaphysics out of [their] method, that is, to suppose the universe ultimately of such a sort that [their] method must be appropriate and successful."[71] When the pragmatists raised scientific technique to central status, they similarly assumed that the social world was a place for which their method was appropriate. This primary commitment to method was therefore of decisive significance in shaping the politics of pragmatism. Behind any particular reform proposal or opinion, the supposition that social processes were capable of laboratory discovery and control required a prior supposition that the world was lawful and continuous in its basic processes. It also required the assumption that their society was willing to make use of the lessons of science. And to put the mechanics of verification at the center of consciousness assumed, finally, that mind would yield its secrets to such operational tests.

The first thing that strikes the modern reader about these assumptions was their faith in underlying harmony and consensus. To propose that all questions were susceptible to quantitative or technical adjudication required the prior assumption that the world was not divided over *qualitative* issues. The hidden message of Peirce's "How to Make Our Ideas Clear" was, to put it differently, that social problems originated not in experience itself but in the imprecise use of language. Ward and Dewey explicated the underlying faith. Where James noted that scientists presumed a uniformity of physical nature, Ward proposed the uniformity of *human* nature. ("Upon nearly all important questions . . . all citizens are agreed.")[72] And Dewey, a half century later, reaffirmed that "serious minds are pretty well agreed as to both evils and ideals." He did admit that there were deep "conflicting interests," but insisted that "the method of democracy—inasmuch as it is that of organized intelligence," could resolve those differences simply by putting them out in the open where "a more inclusive social interest" could be discovered.[73] Dewey could present social strife as the product simply of clashes between new and old, between biased and "serious minds," and between "the social" and "the private," only because he first assumed that current realities were not riven by real conflicts.

This approach to society was fundamentally apolitical, even antipolitical. If people were "pretty well agreed" in their definitions of social problems and if the method of intelligence could dispose of the confusions that remained, then, as Ward had seen, there was "no need of . . . partisan strains upon the public energies"—no need for political participation nor for the institutions created over many generations for dealing with political issues. Benthamite elites informed by Baconian facts could easily substitute "scientific lawmaking" for the older activities of juries, legislatures, and political parties.[74] Peirce's vision of the scientific community as the model of future society expressed this depoliticized orientation perfectly. For the scientific community is pre-eminently a collegial body, unified in its underlying goals and its methods.[75]

The confusions in political theory following from this basic outlook were most apparent in Dewey's work. On one hand, Dewey sounded eminently democratic. He emphasized the importance of "personal participation" in a "shared culture," of democracy as an end and not only as a means, and of creating not only a planned but a plann*ing* society.[76] On the other hand, he criticized "discussion and dialectics" as "weak reeds to depend upon for systematic origination of comprehensive plans." He judged the additive process of voting and the divisive process of party conflict as having "nothing in common with the procedure of cooperative, organized inquiry." According to his social version of pragmatism, real knowledge would prove itself by its enabling "the controlled transformation of an indeterminate solution" into one so determinate that the elements of the original situation were converted "into a unified whole."[77]

But such knowledge would only be a small part of the product of the motley, sometimes inefficient participation praised in *The Public and Its Problems*. Nor did his concern for "comprehensive plans" and for a "method of experimentation based on insight into social desires and actual conditions" admit the presence of some inherently political questions: Who would undertake the experiments? Which experiments would be attempted? How would conflicting evaluations of results be weighted?[78]

In terms of his personal intentions, Dewey occupied a position on the grassroots wing of Progressivism. But his philosophy failed to explain this position. It failed to justify his own principled championing of the disadvantaged. It tended instead toward a counsel of "control of the physical conditions of mental and moral life," a control that might easily pre-empt the space for moral discourse and political action.[79] The pragmatist approach ultimately led away from the "methods" that would be necessary to *teach* people about politics practically. It led away from the sort of activity necessary to create a democratic "reason" in society in the first place. The task of *attaining* agreement out of conflict, of *building* a more orderly society through the self-directed activity of its members, was never mapped out. The pragmatists stopped, ironically, exactly where many of the scorned "idealists" began.

From Dewey it also became clear that the ultimate cost of putting all of one's eggs in the methodological basket was the sacrifice of realism itself. In an era when corporate organization was rapidly changing the face of America and corporate directors were revealing an occasional willingness to gun down striking workers and their families (as in Ludlow, Colorado, in 1914), the pragmatists argued as if power lay in the leading-strings of ideas. They proposed that knowledge, indeed, *was* power. The error of such an idea would not keep it from enjoying a half-century's popularity in America.

Eric Goldman was right to call this outlook Reform Darwinism. Although the Progressives rejected Sumner's historical quietism, they failed in important ways to transcend the vision of the conservative Darwinists. Their view of society remained organic. Their view of intelligence remained adaptive. Their notion of historical change remained evolutionary. And their writings even suggested a danger absent from the ideas of the conservatives—the possibility of society as a totally administered organism. That was what Ward's proposal to concede "the power of the intellect over vital psychic and social phenomena" might easily come down to.[80]

The pragmatists' original concern had been for action. But if we understand "action" as entailing elements of innovation, unpredictability, and risk in a world of incomplete information, and as requiring choice between ambiguous facts and between complex relations of means and ends, then the pragmatists did *not* produce a theory of action. Their preoccupation with precision and predictability revealed instead the epistemology of scientific observation. And when the scientific observer becomes practical, it is not as a political actor but as a social engineer. The world most conducive to his engineering, furthermore, is one from which the space for real action has been eliminated as much as possible. This is to say that pragmatist epistemology was ultimately hostile not only to the modes of reason entailed in moral judgment and political action; it was hostile also to the world in which such judgment and action could occur.

The pragmatist theory of knowledge thus shaped Peirce's and Dewey's ideas about society. But at the same time it struck forward to influence ideas about the world known, this theory also struck backward to shape ideas about the knower. Once knowledge had been equated with the product of institutionalized inquiry, once it had been subsumed to a bureaucratic epistemology, the "knower" began to be seen as a person guided in his or her judgments by the verdicts of institutional processes.[81] And because disagreements about the purposes behind experimental procedures, and about meanings excluded from dominant categories, could not be adjudicated in the terms of such procedures, "knowledgeable" persons would be men and women who agreed to trim off their normative concerns and banish disagreements to the realm of the eccentric, the subjective, the rationally unclarifiable. That is what it would mean, practically speaking, for people to "incorporate" the era's "dominant energies" into their minds. It was not for nothing that in his private writings Peirce referred to people, like insects in a colony, as "mere cells in a social organism."[82] The new view of knowledge implied that modern individuals should seek corporate validation for their reason and identity.

The pragmatists admitted contradiction into the world with one hand, then, only to deny it with the other. They affirmed plurality at the start only to smuggle unity back into the picture through the requirements of their technique. We have concentrated on the political implications of this sleight-of-hand, but there was also a philosophic cost. This was evident in James's work, for example; for the philosophic answers he proposed were not answers to the questions he had originally asked. His question in "The Will to Believe" had not been about the permissibility of belief but about its possibility, about whether there were grounds for it in the modern world. In advising us to determine the cash value of beliefs, he forgot that the original dilemma had been caused by a devaluation of the currency. And his conclusions failed to preserve his original sense of the radical discontinuity of existence.[83]

James's failure to consider that a person's feelings are often contradictory, and that his actions invariably wash over the borders of others' projects, revealed a politics of personality identical to Ward's and Dewey's politics of society. James may have called it a joint-stock world; but he assumed that its shareholders shared a common charter. His belief in the sufficiency of immediate experience and in the advisability of choosing "the concrete" over the abstract revealed a complacent assumption that the concrete itself was never fundamentally problematic. His outlook gave no warrant for the temporarily unsuccessful idea or the unacknowledged claim—or indeed for his own vocation of critical thought.

This refusal to acknowledge qualitative differences in the world, and to make their own qualitative judgments, kept both Dewey and James from developing pragmatism's insights about human intentionality. It led Dewey to root consciousness simply in technical function, as we have seen. And it led James to lodge consciousness in very close quarters, between inborn temperament on one side and sensory desires on the other.[84] It also led him to that curious mix of moral pain and ethical Babbitry which characterized his work.[85] The refusal to state moral ideals ultimately reduced his counsel (and that of the human potential philosophies which, following him, came to occupy one corner of corporate America) to the merely therapeutic. Act confidently in pursuit of desires that can be satisfied by direct experience, it advised, and the larger problems will either take care of themselves or prove not to have been real problems. Such was the solace of letting one's method determine the admissibility of hypotheses. Such advice was not only simpleminded; its methodological inhibitions would prevent the very kind of action that James himself admired.[86]

The pragmatist program was fated to forever fall short of its intended goals. Its zeal to equate meaning with sensible consequences, and its aversion to any mode of inference besides the scientific, prevented it from acknowledging the larger historical and theoretical contexts in which facts and ideas are always embedded, and from which they take their bearings. It militated against action appropriate to those contexts and to the larger issues at stake in them. The attempt to encompass ideas and politics by experimental method led the pragmatists not to clarity but to obfuscation. It led them to the "subordination of values to technique" that Randolph Bourne deplored in Dewey's students. These were people, Bourne said, who had "no clear philosophy of life except that of intelligent service, the admirable adaptation of means to ends."[87]

The pragmatist revolt sometimes appears to have been similar to the epistemological revolts against a reified Reason waged by the Marxists or the existentialists in Europe. But where Marx called for *praxis* and Nietzsche for self-overcoming, the Americans moved toward a counsel of simple activity or "doing." This was not an innovative or reconstructive activity; it was the doing of practical sorts of things. For having liberated the purporting will, the pragmatists turned around and grounded purposiveness (intentionality) in given facts, given ends. The sources of political conflict or of intellectual uncertainty emerged from such a perspective not as real conflicts of interests and wills, requiring bold, transcending action. The sources of conflict appeared instead as "gaps" or lags, as we saw, between people's ideas and the factual situation. And the remedial activity prescribed by such analysis was hardly conducive to the creation of democratic social relations.

What would be lost, Dewey asked—hinting at that remedy—by closing the gap altogether, dropping "the conception of Right" and being "left face to face with actual fact?" It was a question the ultimate implications of which Rousseau had traced a century and a half before. "It was Grotius's invariable mode of reasoning to establish right from fact," he wrote. "There may have been juster methods, but none more favorable to tyrants."[88]

While the full significance of their method remained muted and unstated with the pragmatists, others were anxious to take things to their conclusions. The ideas of these others are important to our story. For the epistemology of corporate liberalism consisted not only of the pragmatist theory of knowledge but also of an impulse to act in the world and to re-form that world *on the basis of that knowledge*. This is to say, that for all of its piecemeal, fragmented appearance, this reform approach embodied a comprehensive and transformative impulse. There were many who, taking up the pragmatists' program, would seize on the new, narrowed idea of knowledge and act aggressively to reshape key sectors of social activity. The confusion about different modes of reason turned out at this point to be critical. The failure to establish a post-Lockean approach to individual consciousness, and to acknowledge the distinctive properties of an intersubjective "reason," left the new liberals with only objectified conditions as the basis for human consciousness. It left them with the possibility only of grounding "right" in "fact." It projected them toward a rationalism which would, paradoxically, end by assaulting the empirical richness and texture of social life.

In the remainder of this chapter we will turn to two critical efforts to extend this approach into new social domains. We will look first at Oliver Wendell Holmes's application of the doctrine to the field of law, and then at Frederick Winslow Taylor's lucid expression of the new epistemology in his classic formulation of American administrative theory.

JUDICIAL REALISM

Sociological jurisprudence and judicial realism carried the pragmatist revolt into the field of law. Holmes was associated with both movements, the former by proximity, the latter by parental influence. And the intellectual drama of pragmatism found complete expression—from optimistic origins to grim conclusions, from Bergsonian enthusiasm to Comtist functionalism—in his work.

Holmes's early book, *The Common Law*, already struck the themes that would be characteristic of pragmatism. It faulted arid logic in favor of experience. It argued that legal doctrines were the changing artifacts of history rather than fixed emanations of abstract reason, that they were "in fact and at bottom" expressions of public policy.[89] The book thus also gave voice to the pragmatist recognition of a "purporting will" behind the seemingly objective facts. Finally, it attacked abstract system-building in its critique of the Kantian jurists' explanation of legal evolution in terms of the unfolding of human free will. Holmes argued on the basis of historical research that legal doctrines (of property, contract, or torts, for example) were actually survivals of codes that had originated in primitive instinct. ("The criminal law stands to the passion for revenge in much the same relation as marriage to the sexual appetite.")[90] The theory of law as an externality originated here. Holmes saw history as a process in which instinctual practices had slowly crystallized into moral codes, and those codes into "external or objective [standards] from which the actual [intent or] guilt of the party is wholly eliminated."[91]

Holmes was celebrated during his day for his famous "prediction theory" of law, delivered in 1897 in the essay "The Path of the Law." Law, he urged in that formula, was nothing more than "the prediction of the incidence of the public force through the instrumentality of the courts." That was the way "the bad man," the potential law-breaker, saw it, Holmes wrote. And bad men were more concerned than others to acquire a precise definition of legality. "Just so far as the aid of the public force is given a man, he has a legal right."[92] The corollary of that definition of law was that legal concepts should be washed in "cynical acid" in order to "expel everything except . . . the operations of the law." Holmes urged that it would probably be a gain in fact "if every word of moral significance could be banished from the law altogether."[93]

Holmes recommended in *The Common Law* "a more conscious recognition of the legislative function of the courts" in order to facilitate the adaptation of old rules to new needs, and to organize the legal world by formulating the "fixed and uniform standards of external conduct" then evolving. Because people were punished only for external conduct, it was necessary to chart only the "known tendencies" of their acts—a set of tendencies for which the concept of "intent" was now a vague and obsolete referent.[94] Anticipating his later recommendation that legal and moral discourse be divorced, he therefore proposed that a concept of "the ideal average, prudent man" (whom the jury would be taken to represent) be employed as the intellectual device to facilitate the systematization of external rules. That man, happily, was a "constant."[95]

Finally, in this and in Holmes's prediction theory of law we see the characteristic pragmatist concerns to establish operational tests for the precise definition of the phenomena under consideration, and then to recommend action based on that definition. ("When we are studying law, we are not studying a mystery but a well-known profession.")[96]

Holmes has usually been praised in the same terms as pragmatism as a whole. He has been lauded for his "skepticism and humility" and for his judicial restraint (Felix Frankfurter); for his rejection of "fixed programs" and panaceas; and because of his belief that intelligence was "the supreme force in the settlement of social issues" (Dewey). He was celebrated for being "the completely adult lawyer," a man who had overcome the need for an authority figure and retained the patience and courage, in the face of larger uncertainties, that were necessary in a democracy (Jerome Frank).[97]

And yet there was another side to Holmes, a side we have seen in Chapter Five. This was the side that produced opinions which even his admiring student Max Lerner admitted were "draconian."[98] Thus Holmes justified the state's right to sterilize the insane because "three generations of imbeciles is enough"; and he justified the state's invasion of individual rights, because "all societies are founded on the death of men."[99] Holmes's presumed restraint did not prevent him from overruling state laws in 131 of the 174 cases that were brought under the Fourteenth Amendment while he sat on the Supreme Court. And Holmes also generally upheld arbitrary administrative actions against the rights of particular categories of claimants—non-whites, aliens, and radical labor organizers.[100]

This side of the Holmes story has been ignored by most scholars because it is hard to fit into the normal scheme of interpretation; but it is nevertheless consistent with his familiar views. His draconian statements only expressed the legal implications of the approach analyzed in this chapter. They were the statements of a pragmatism grown articulate in its major premises and rigorous in its conclusions. The fact is that Holmes's prediction theory, and his technique of verification, had brought him to a most eccentric view of the law.

In any stable society the heart of the law is its normative content. Unless people believe that the basic principles and procedures of a legal system are just, they will not agree to entrust their disputes to it, nor will they consent to obey it. A juridical law, unlike a natural law (such as the law of gravity), is not merely descriptive, an explanation of how things do occur. It is also prescriptive. To some extent it says how things *should* occur.[101] Moreover, laws which are in fact obeyed—in contrast to manipulative policies—embody standards and point toward goals that seem *worth* pursuing. The leaders of the American Revolution acknowledged this moral content when they spoke of law as being founded in consent.

But Holmes's view of law excluded this ethical element—and not only from his strategy of research but also from his fundamental concept of what was being studied. He cut behavior loose from conscience. Law was seen as an external form, devoid of moral content. It was equated with whatever courts did (just as "truth" in *Abrams* was defined as whatever survived in the marketplace of ideas). Holmes failed to appreciate, as Yosal Rogat writes, "the extent to which general commitments to fairness, generality and neutrality are built into the idea of legality and constitute part of its meaning."[102]

Such view of law might suffice for "the bad man," for whom law certainly was an externality. But it would be inadequate for any of the normal members of a community who expect legal provisions to make ethical sense. It is inadequate for judges who, faced with a choice between precedents, seek a rule to guide their decisions.[103] It is inadequate for anyone concerned with the educative functions of the law.[104] And it is inadequate for the consistent behavioralist himself, for it avoids underlying questions of legitimacy and therefore fails to help predict when and for what reasons people's behavior will change.

Holmes adopted this notion of law, however, because he accepted the bundle of epistemological and political assumptions identified in this chapter. He proposed that all words with moral connotations be banished from legal discourse because he thought we would "gain very much in the clearness of our thoughts."[105] He proposed it, that is, not because that was what law empirically was, but because he first accepted the positivist metaphysics about the necessary properties of knowledge. Though he had once written that the laws of society could never be reduced to a book of mathematics, he more normally saw human progress as consisting of "an increase in the knowledge of measure"—meaning "a substitution of quantitative for qualitative judgements." Occasionally he even looked to science to "determine as much as it can the relative worth of our different social ends." When we consider his claim that the law takes morals into account "only for the purpose of drawing a line between such bodily motions and rests as it permits, and such as it does not," we in fact encounter a materialist scientism not far from Hobbes's.[106] Despite the rich historicism of *The Common Law*, often associated with his name, Holmes actually wrote that "the true science of the law" consisted in the establishment of its postulates "from within, upon accurately measured social desires instead of tradition."[107] Holmes, in short, was not the Burke of American law; he was its Darwin.

No matter if Holmes would argue, with James, that he meant "the incidence of force" over the long run, and "prediction" for the whole. His experimental test made no provision for the long run or the whole. His attempt to understand legal phenomena consisted simply of calculating "the material consequences" of court activity for the bad man. Subtle or longer-range effects that could not be verified by such a person were to be ignored. For him, as for the legal technician whom Jacques Ellul describes, "there is no law but in its application."[108]

The effects of this approach on the particulars of legal theory were predictable. Like Ward and Dewey, Holmes expressed little concern for traditional political institutions. If the social world were capable of being ordered scientifically, then there was little need for customary rules or even for the circuitous methods of debate. The jury—an institution considered central to the Anglo-Americal legal system because of its role in the articulation of standards of reasonableness, and central to people like Tocqueville because of its capacities for civic education—was said by Holmes, because of its dependence on the services of "twelve random men," to be inferior to the contributions of "a sensible and well-trained judge."[109]

Holmes's similar aloofness toward many of the events of his day has been noted by many commentators. Despite the fact he was celebrated along with Pound for the concern with "consequences," he actually maintained a proud ignorance of a large range of social phenomena, refused Brandeis's invitations to visit scenes of social conflict, and possessed only a haphazard knowledge of economics.[110]

In light of our analysis we can see that this aloofness was a product of more than his temperament. Indeed, we can discover in it something essential about this epistemology as a whole. The hidden secret of the new approach was that its informing spirit was not really empiricist at all. It was rationalist. It trusted not in the facts of experience but only in those facts that could be filtered through the sieve of verifying techniques. Its methods had indeed given rise to a metaphysics. What might have remained simply a decision to adopt a particular form of inquiry became instead a belief that only the phenomena examined were real. What might have remained simply a decision to study how laws worked as external standards became a decision that laws *were* external standards. From behavioralism as a method of inquiry, Holmes moved to behavioralism as a theory of social order. All of this was particularly disappointing in Holmes's case because he was a gifted craftsman of the common law, the most impressive monument to a truly empirical method in the Western tradition.

With Holmes, the different political effects of the underlying technicism became more explicit than with the others. First, the fact that the "prudent man" at the center of his jurisprudence was conceived of as being a constant meant that his legal system would embody a tyranny of existing norms. It would be blind to the qualitative differences that distinguish, for example, culture from subculture, or class from class. Second, the fact the law would be concerned with only "known tendencies" and a person would be expected to "find out at his own peril . . . [what] a reasonable and prudent man would have inferred" threw the burden of proof in his proposed system on the accused.[111]

Third, the revolt against the atomistic ontology of classical liberalism yielded an approach that focused on functions. In this it anticipated the actual movement of American law away from conceptual formalism and toward an appreciation of social substance. This substantive approach is now familiar in administrative law (with its concern for public policies), labor law (in its concern for conditions necessary for fair contract), and contract law (with its shift from a doctrine of strict conditions to one of material breach). But Holmes's sensitivity was not for social substance as interpreted by individuals or publics; it was for substance as defined by corporate realities and scientifically trained judges. Thus the new sensitivity to social substance, in other words, like Peircean pragmatism, was accompanied by a bias against the individual.

Finally, Holmes gave voice to a concern for force which had remained muted with the others. He defined law, we have seen, in terms of the incidence of a particular kind of force. And he wrote that the "*ultima ratio* not only of *regnum*, but of private persons is force." Though Holmes never believed, with Ward and Dewey, in a latent social harmony and though he admitted there were "*de facto* supreme powers in the community," he arrived at the equivalent of Ward's and Dewey's assumptions by assuming that individuals and laws would eventually accept the dominant powers. Whether obedience to rule was induced "by the use of force" or whether it was brought about "mediately through men's fears" was all the same from Holmes's standpoint.[112]

This preoccupation with force and the desire to present social relations as ultimately resting on force also expressed more than personal eccentricity. It was the expression of Holmes's basic philosophic stance. This was the stance of the nominalist, one who believes that facts are ultimately unknowable and that people take their cues from names and assigned labels. The nominalist, to state the obverse, is one who assumes that facts lack order or ordering principles, and that they achieve their shape and coherence only from without.

The classic exponent of such view was, of course, Thomas Hobbes. Hobbes explained that "words of good and evil" are always "used with relation to the person that useth them; there being nothing . . . absolutely so, nor any common rule . . . to be taken from the nature of the objects themselves, but from . . . any man, where there is no commonwealth; or in a commonwealth, from the person that representeth it or from an arbitrator or judge.[113]

Hobbes's nominalism has been frequently discussed, as has his authoritarian social theory. But the organic connection between the two has usually been ignored. If, however, as Hobbes said, there is "nothing absolutely so, nor any common rule to be taken from the nature of the objects," then any common rule that exists must be imposed *upon* those objects. The political implications follow straightforwardly. Where social order is not conceived as a product of participation or shared intentionality, external rules must emerge as the only source of social cohesion. Once the mind of the individual has been ignored for operational purposes, the next step must be to see social order as the achievement of manipulation and force, as the result of managing objects externally, rather than of dealing with subjects rationally. The question of rights becomes irrelevant from such a perspective because nominalist particulars lack any deep structure of legitimacy. Paradoxically, the philosophic nominalism which at first appears to mandate great respect for particulars comes out, with regard to politics, supporting a doctrine that easily denies the integrity of those particulars. That is the way it worked for Hobbes; and that is the way it wound up working for Holmes.

Holmes was propelled toward this theory of order by his underlying scientistic assumption that the lack of absolute certainty in moral matters deprived morality of a binding role in the world. It was this assumption that also fueled his personal cynicism and his impatience with allegations of such things as exploitation. The philosopher Max

Otto, and Holmes's friend Sir Frederick Pollack, pointed out to him more than once that lack of absolute certitude in no way deprived moral standards of their significance or authority in social life. But their words fell on deaf ears. For Holmes there was no midpoint between absolute morality and trivial moralizing. Having no use for either, he answered Pollack and Otto in terms of basic arbitrariness; "truth" was simply what he "can't help" believing.[114]

Strict adherence to external standards as enforced by the courts therefore became as important for Holmes as the strict use of language had been for Hobbes, and for the same reason—not essentially to achieve justice, but to avoid disorder.[115] The element of force in the scheme derived from two things. The first was the assumption of underlying arbitrariness ("I believe that the claim of our special code to respect is simply that it exists").[116] The second was the nominalist's vague appreciation of the fact that he lacked the means for adjudicating claims voiced outside the stipulated categories. Science can clarify concepts and determine efficient means for given ends; but it lacks mechanisms for deliberating *about* given categories and different ends. The theory of law as command, which many thought Holmes had rejected in his youthful criticisms of Austin and Hobbes, therefore turns out to have been alive and well in the body of his work—though the sovereign voice was not the state's now but the standards of the "supreme powers in the community" as articulated by the court.

The larger, juridical thrust of Holmes's proposals was to orient people away from conceiving of the law as embodying *ratio* in addition to *voluntas*, as Franz Neumann has defined those concepts in his study of German jurisprudence. It was to wean people away from seeing law as an expression of both sovereign will and ethical content.[117] Neumann argued that this reorientation is appropriate historically to the needs of an administrative society and a decisionist state. The necessary results, however, are that "law" is reduced to "a technical instrument for the execution of certain political objectives"—an instrument of command; and that not only the mask of the juridical individual, but many protections for the real individuals behind that mask, are repudiated. (A contemporary scholar follows Neumann's drift when he warns that "fascism in America [will be] the form of law without its content.")[118]

This elimination of *ratio* had been Holmes's drift from the beginning. His attack on Kantian jurisprudence in *The Common Law* actually assaulted more than abstract system-building. It challenged the point of view that would make law *into* an expression of individual free will. In its place Holmes proposed the point of view which saw society as a corporate whole and regarded law not as a guide toward reason, nor as a vehicle of consent, nor as an expression of community will, but as a tool for the top-down maintenance of order. Holmesean realism was not, then, a modern method that "wants to find out what the law is [rather than] what it ought to be"; to the contrary, it neglected a major part of what law *was* and went on to equate it with positive decree. Holmes as much as admitted this when he remarked that he made a "rough equation between isness and oughtness."[119]

With Holmes we see that the Progressive campaign against metaphysical absolutes did not indicate humility, restraint, or a new Humean skepticism. Holmes might have spoken of "unimaginable wholes" but he never ceased to imagine that such wholes existed, that a "general" was in charge, and that the role for citizens was intelligent service in the ranks.[120]

As with subsequent liberalism as a whole, initial assertions of skepticism led ultimately to unconditioned conclusions and to an illiberal willingness to rely on force. The individual was freed from tradition and the prohibitions of absolutist metaphysics only to be subordinated to the tacit, but no less absolute, requirements of an administered order.

THE HIDDEN POLITICS OF ADMINISTRATION

Jacques Ellul writes: "Once the pure technical mentality . . . has penetrated the legal world, legal technique, which no longer has its roots in law but in the physical sciences or perhaps even in biology, brings about certain decisive upheavals in social life."[121] What the new human engineers of Progressivism contemplated would produce just such upheavals.

We have seen that the central commitment to verification, scientifically conceived, narrowed the pragmatist perspective and actually devalued the multi-faceted experience of individuals. The underlying logic of the whole approach was given stark expression by a number of lesser-known thinkers of the day. The sociologist Luther Lee Bernard of the University of Chicago was one of these. In "The Transition to an Objective Standard of Social Control" (1911), Bernard attributed the majority of contemporary problems to the continuing influence of subjectivist social thought. The object of his animosity was clearly classical liberalism, which he styled "an introspective mental discipline based on the solipsistic assumption of independent psychical causation." Bernard then called for the "elimination of the standpoint of the subject." Sociologists had discovered that society was a functional whole, "self-existent, organic and self-perpetuating," and were therefore in a position to record the norms that could serve as objective standards of "control." Such standards would be used to promote "adjustment," facilitate efficiency, and ease social development.[122]

In such a program, the laboratory notion of control was inextricably linked to the political. (This link was also apparent in E. A. Ross's *Social Control*, a book read by Theodore Roosevelt on Holmes's recommendation). Social control, Bernard explained, "cannot be individually determined, but must proceed from a controlled environment which provides the individual with a uniform and constant source of stimuli."[123] Emile Durkheim had asked the obvious question about such an approach: how was the observer supposed to know when the norm (the standard that provided the basis for control) was itself pathological? But Bernard sidestepped the query (as had Durkheim) and justified the reigning standards simply because they were the reigning standards. In the process society was again cast as a continuous, integrated whole. The "is" once again acquired the authority of an "ought."

Bernard moved to his conclusions with the sureness of a scientist who had proven his case. He embraced an underlying element of force, he said, because society should be frankly admitted to be "a compulsory unity." He struck a note of paternalism when he proposed that society should aid its members by helping them choose for themselves or by enabling elites to guide their activities when they "are incapable of choosing them in a social way either because of defectiveness or delinquency." The idea that individuals would have rights against a controlled environment was as inconceivable as the idea that they should have rights against the law of gravity or the effects of poor sanitation.[124] Bernard equated morality with the product of conditioning, and consciousness with a reflection of the "facts"; and like the group theorists, he replaced the emphasis on rights with an emphasis on duties ("the ideal of social service in place of . . . hedonism"). From a preoccupation with objective certainty, Bernard and his ilk moved toward programs for treating people *as* objects.

Though Bernard was of a narrower cast of mind than Dewey or Peirce, or even Holmes, he shared in the culture's confusion about reason and sought direction from the same quarters: the laboratory and the factory. Both pragmatists and administrative rationalists sought to give to social knowledge the reliability and cumulative character of the physical sciences. Both conceived of society as a realm fit for the experimenter, one that could be apprehended in uniform and quantifiable categories. The pragmatists also joined the administrators in perceiving social relations, ultimately, in administrative rather than in political terms.

The "knowledge" these men sought to impart to social affairs was not the knowledge appropriate to "action," to the initiation of new events or new lines of effort in the world. They sought a scientific kind of knowledge in which operations would be strictly controlled, or a ret-rospective historicist's knowledge, in which effects are clear, relevant variables are fairly apparent, and a degree of objectivity is possible. But "action" is prospective, and looks to the future. It requires not only mas-tery of data but skills of inference about the world *beyond* the data. It therefore requires training not only in the acquisition of information but, as the Greeks stressed, in matters of character—in patience, per-severence, and the ability to reflect on one's ends. The primary virtue for action, as Aristotle defined it, was *prudence*. The primary virtue of scien-tific activity Hobbes defined, by contrast, as *sapience*. The marks of sa-pience were regular method and "infallible" results. Hobbes was also the first modern to dream that true sapience was possible in broad-scale social affairs.[125]

The lapse of a concern for the knowledge appropriate to action dur-ing the Progressive era was more than a matter of neglect. It expressed an underlying inarticulate "purpose," as the pragmatists might have put it. That purpose was to realize a world of true sapience, a world where the rough, inferential knowledge peculiar to action—indeed action itself—would be unnecessary. To realize that end they proposed human engineering.[126] This proposal was clearest in the work of the administra-tive reformer Frederick Winslow Taylor. Though he has been celebrated as the architect of scientific management, Taylor's real significance for American intellectual history was that he articulated the informing pur-pose of the major wing of Progressive reform.

Taylor's work has been treated elsewhere and a full discussion of it is unnecessary here.[127] What he proposed, in essence, was to rationalize shop-floor production by reorganizing work processes around the One Best Way of doing separate segments of each job. His plan constituted an operationalization of the scientific method. First, the larger work pro-cess was to be dis-integrated into its separate components (analysis), and then those components were to be reintegrated into a coherent system consistent with the realization of a single, clearly defined goal. Over the reorganized terrain a shop manager would be assigned to set tasks, retrain workers, and coordinate further research. Taylor also acknowledged that full implementation of the plan would require a "mental revolution" on the part of the workers to secure their loyalty to the scientifically coordinated plant.[128]

Taylor thus proposed a Baconian program of classification, followed by a mathematico-deductive strategy to reorganize the world so it would yield the classified categories and nothing more. He sought to create a social whole that would never become more than the sum of its parts, an association that would never become a community. In doing so he revealed the tacit assumption and projective impulse of the whole approach as far back as Ward: *in order to realize the benefits of exact knowledge in society, the society first had to be comprehensively reorganized.* In order to realize such benefits, furthermore, men's minds also had to be disciplined to scientific terms.[129] Taylor's aggressive rationality derived from these facts. He had first subsumed social conflict and the workers themselves to "nature," and then sought to redeem nature with scientific rationality.[130] But in the process his rationality found itself besieged on all sides—on one side by capitalists' "rules of thumb," on another by work-group solidarity, and overall by a "dangerous empiricism."

Taylor's approach revealed the essentially manipulative thrust of the new epistemology. It also revealed that this thrust was not confined to a local setting. In order to implement the One Best Way of doing each job, it would be necessary to bring the entire factory under control; but in order to do this it would be necessary, in turn, to extend factory control over ever-wider ranges of external variables. The expansionary logic of Taylorism complemented that of American capitalism.

The appeal to neutrality characteristic of American Progressivism was explicit in Taylor's writing. Seeing himself standing above all partial factions, he proposed the adoption of exact knowledge "equally binding upon employers and workmen," and the elimination of waste (primarily in the form of workers' "soldiering"). The result would be higher profits for business, higher wages for labor, and more goods for consumers. Workers would also be freed from "isolation" and from having to work without guidance.[131] They would achieve Woodrow Wilson's freedom of the well-adjusted piston.

Despite his intentions, however, Taylor's scheme was not neutral; and it could never have been implemented in the interests of the whole. As one student of planning has written: "Apolitical planning is a fiction. . . . The One Best Way approach that [sought to] . . . 'Keep Planning out of Politics' was political planning; it kept planning out of one kind of politics and confined it to another."[132] The hopes of the era first raised by Roosevelt's strike intervention and Steffens's reform proposals were based on some basic illusions. And Americans who accepted them were bound at some future date to become profoundly disillusioned.

Three types of politics underlay Taylor's scheme and, by implication, the main body of Progressive reform: a politics of administration, a contemporary class politics, and the politics of the technological project. The course of the middle-class reformer who eschewed a political base in order to guide himself by neutral facts and proper method was not a course toward objectivity, but toward obfuscation of these politics and their effects. A case of the pragmatist fallacy made flesh, he would end by purchasing certainty at the price of understanding. Let us look at each of these types of politics.

The Politics of Administration

Scientific management proposed to implement the logic of uniformity that lay at the heart of pragmatism. This first step—the critical proposition which Ward and Dewey assumed and which Holmes consigned to force—management engineers hoped to implement by a reorganization of "conditions."

Their reorganized terrain would be structured hierarchically. It would centralize initiative and invite paternalistic social relations. It would embody only the dominant norms, atypical types and rates of work having been factored out of effective reality. These three things would be central to its politics.

What is of critical significance here, however, is that these politics would be a hidden politics, a suppressed politics, a politics worked out in the original design and denied recognition in subsequent operations. For conflict was regarded as wasteful, and compromise as out of place, in a world of exact information.[133]

The questions about how people were to be moved into this world, how they were to be induced to work within it, and how they were to be punished for their refusal to work, were all essentially political questions. But Taylor dealt with them only in passing, consigning them simply to managerial discretion. The new idea, the critical voice, and the innovation would be suppressed in the scientifically managed factory— not through argument or deliberation, and not because they had been proven wrong, but because they *had to be* excluded in the first place in order for the artificial system to work. For a society that lacks methods for making conflict fruitful and cannot afford to create them, bureaucratic ordering provides the only means of associated activity.

Science, admittedly, may be said to have a politics of its own. This politics is contained in the prescriptive parts of its formulas: *if* specific laboratory steps are followed, and *if* proper attitudes are maintained, certain results can be expected to follow. The "ifs" are all-important, for they indicate the choices that are being made. They can usually remain unstated, however, because the community of scientists, as Peirce saw, has adopted them as a precondition of its own activity. These preliminary choices take up but a small part of normal science. But the reverse is true of normal politics. There, it is precisely the procedures and the definition of facts that command the bulk of attention.

The plans advanced by Taylor and the administrative reformers stinted where a real political theory would have spent itself generously—in the attempt to *create* factory unity and to *elicit* agreement on shared goals. Having turned away from these tasks, their vision of the future amounted to a new utopia—a systems utopia, and one that harbored a potential for real harshness. Taylor's own account of his "friendly war" with the workers, in which he discharged or reduced the pay of "the stubborn men," revealed that this approach, having suppressed politics, left no way for dealing with real differences except through force. Taylor did not hesitate to say that it was "only through *enforced* standardization . . . and *enforced* cooperation that faster work can be assured," and to add that "the duty of enforcing rests with *management* alone."[134] This same tropism toward force that we saw in Holmes and Bernard points to a profound paradox about the entire approach: the imposition of a decisive, unappealable force was mandated by reformers whose stated goals were the elimination of coercion and conflict from social life.

Taylor's plan was but one expression of the Progressive impulse to subsume politics to administration. We have encountered another expression in Steffens's call for the "non-political ruler" who understood that "municipal government is business." The impulse found sharpest expression in the broad range of Progressive proposals that replaced legislative with executive bodies—and executive bodies fashioned after the model of business. The Progressive reformers apparently never considered the critical differences between legislative and executive functions, and never imagined the serious consequences that would follow from their confusion.

A legislative body is the public body par excellence, the place where different interests and the conflicts between them gain a hearing, and where a synthesis of goals becomes possible. Executive institutions have no way of accomplishing these things; they lack means for acknowledging and airing deep differences (just as Peirce's "techniques" lacked ways of acknowledging disagreements about the ends for which they were used). This means that the expert who functioned so prominently in Progressive reform plans—as shop manager, city manager, or state commissioner—would really find himself engaged as part of his tasks in the making of important political decisions. But he would engage in these politics obliquely and under the guise of simply implementing the policies of others.[135] Politics would have been relegated to backrooms and corridors, rather than seated in the formal offices of power. And the new administrators would be insulated from larger political forces, rather than made responsible to them. Following the example of business leaders, they would operate under the constant temptation to become private legislators. The thrust of this reform program, then, was neither to cleanse nor to eliminate politics, but to render politics invisible, haphazard, and unaccountable.

Scientific Management and American Politics

Taylorism also failed in its efforts at neutrality for a second reason: it arose in the service of particular social interests. The "facts" it proposed to reorganize were facts already possessed of a political content: the facts that economic elites knew what was in the best interests of workers, for instance, or that "soldiering" was an improper response to new working conditions, or that capitalist hierarchy should be preserved and some people granted the power to control "experience." These facts were politically weighted, but Taylor took them to be objective data. Taylor's very approach in fact *presumed* a structure of domination. It presumed that both the liberal principles of consent and the newer "ideologies of work performance" were out of place in the modern factory.[136] The bureaucratic hierarchy he promoted was to be laid atop the existing capitalist hierarchy.

The emergence of scientific management was in itself a significant political event, though Taylor was unaware of it at the time. It arose at a particular moment and was eagerly accepted (in its less rigorous forms) because it promised to make recently amalgamated industries profitable, and to combat resistance by workers to new working conditions. Its popularity, recent studies demonstrate, was due largely to the new sorts of control it facilitated rather than to any proven ability to increase production.[137] Management science proposed to solve factory problems not simply by reorganizing existing factors of production, but by extending the logic of the corporation over each element of the job process, by abolishing worker autonomy, and by reducing the worker to the status of a factor of production.

This was another reason for the furtive concern with force. The concentration of work authority Taylor proposed required more than a simple reassignment of tasks; it required the active *taking* of initiative away from work groups that had previously exercised it. By showing capitalists a way of enclosing the last aberrant factor, the "human factor," within the logic of the corporation, Taylor actually propounded a politics of expropriation. American industry had already taken from working people control over the means of production. Scientific management now helped it usurp the workers' authority over their crafts and, eventually, over productive intelligence itself.[138]

Put in more historical terms, Taylor proposed to capitalists a new way of negotiating class conflict. He set the course for technological corporatism, the highest stage of capitalism. He proposed to remold the context in which class conflict occurred. The goal was to suppress conflict by *reconstituting* the world as the mechanical embodiment of the corporate director's own categories. It was to rationalize domination by rendering it part of an impersonal, objective whole, and by justifying it according to new standards of technical reason. Under the guise of "the power of facts," as Marcuse has put it, the power of man over man would then appear as "an objective and rational condition."[139] Once the corporate capitalist had understood this idea he would cease to be content with dominating the world fitfully, by buying an occasional judge or Pinkerton army, and would adopt a more comprehensive design. He would also cease to see the worker as a serious human opponent, and would come to see him as a recalcitrant bit of matter that demanded ever-subtler and more effective forms of manipulation.

Taylor's approach thus implied a symbiosis between the new administrators and the world of business. The administrators might sound disdainful of businessmen for their outmoded rules of thumb and their selfish (subjectivist) outlook; but as a practical matter the administrators needed the capitalists, both for patronage and for the industrial concentration they effected.[140] The administrators, given their vested interest in predictability and formal order, also shared with the capitalists a bias in favor of fixed capital and against dependence on human labor and worker autonomy. Though science might at some point part ways with profit-making, as Veblen and Brandeis both argued, there had actually been a standardizing, systematizing impulse in capitalism from the beginning.[141] The administrative engineers, without knowing it, now refined that impulse and fashioned a standard of commensurability that corporate capitalists could use for coordinating a disparate world beyond the marketplace. In a classic and long-lived confusion about who was serving whom, the new spokesmen of the administrative ethos imagined that the capitalists, by extending the corporate order, were doing their job for them.

The Technological Project

The intellectual approach traced in this chapter can be seen, thirdly, as the expression of an attempt to employ technical reason to solve serious social problems by suppressing qualitative distinctions and masking fundamental incommensurabilities. The effort arose at a specific historical juncture. It emerged as corporate forces began to exacerbate the contradiction, basic to bourgeois society, between formal rationality and substantive irrationality—between the original promise of an order rooted in reason and procedural regularity and the realities of unstable markets, ineffective rights, and muted force (or as Marx put it, between the radical form of bourgeois political ideas and "its conservative form of life").[142] The response to the heightened sense of contradiction, in the form of a desire for unity and consistency, was apparent in all the theories we have studied. It was evident, for example, in Bentley's and James's assertion that all "dualisms" were false, and in Dewey's later statement that he had retained Hegel's teaching that the "hard and fast dividing walls" separating subject and object, matter and spirit, form and content could be transcended through some form of "lived unity."[143]

Such a will to unity was not peculiar to American reformers. Marx, for example, also set out to transcend the antinomies of classical liberalism. He proposed to do this by creating a world in which the false walls dividing subject and object (and labor and capital) would be dissolved, and people would cease to have to treat others as objects, because social institutions would have been reappropriated by the whole community. Marx, like the pragmatists, criticized previous materialisms for having seen the world in wholly objectivist terms. Society had to be understood, instead, as the product of "human sensuous activity." But that activity was currently crippled because of the "self-cleavage and self-contradictoriness" of the world in which it occurred.[144] Marx's goal therefore was to transcend that world historically, and establish the bases for a different form of world-creating activity.

But the pragmatists disdained all this talk about alienation, reappropriation, and transcendence. And they disdained it not simply because the words smacked of abstract system-building. They spurned it because their views of human consciousness and social order were fundamentally different from those of Marx or Hegel, or even of their own predecessors. Having taken their bearings from the physical sciences and capitalist industries, they proposed to resolve the contradictions of their era by enlisting technical reason in the re-formation of mind and society.

At this point the rationalist thread in their thought became decisive. It was a thread which had, in fact, run through Western scientific culture from its beginnings during the Renaissance. The task of science, Galileo admitted at the time, was not primarily to validate empirical reality or common experience at all. Its purpose instead was to "violate" common expectations, "to commit . . . a rape on the senses," as he put it bluntly, in order to upset sense impressions (such as the impression that the sun moved around the earth). Science would reveal the hidden, fixed, and for Galileo, mathematical structure of the universe.[145] The "purport" behind the scientific project, to put it differently, had *not* actually been to do justice to the richness of experience, but to find laws by which that experience could be reduced and ordered.

This is to say that one of the guiding threads of Western scientism, the thread which positivism picked up to the exclusion of all others, was not merely non-qualitative; it was *anti*-qualitative. It sought a kind of knowledge directly opposed to the sort that ponders qualitative differences and incommensurabilities, and attempts to make correct judgments in the absence of certain proofs.[146]

The critical point about the new epistemology, then, is not simply that the kind of knowledge it defined was narrow, nor that it could be influenced by business interests, but that it was supposed to fuel a transformative technical thrust *against* existing realities. The impulse that became explicit in Taylor was to intervene in the world in order to transform it into a place fit for positivist cognition—a place bereft of qualitative differences, incommensurable phenomena, and conflicting wills.

Carried to fruition, such a strategy would attempt to reconcile a world of rational forms and irrational substance by reshaping them both to the requirements of technical reason. The dream of an objective social order had appeared before in Western culture. Now, for the first time, because of industrial advances, it seemed capable of practical fulfillment.

CONCLUSION: "THE AMERICAN WAY" OF SOCIAL CONTROL

Pragmatist epistemology embodied an aborted dialectic. An approach which initially attempted to liberate human consciousness from brute facticity wound up remanding mind to the factual world for the resolution of its problems. The ethical was returned to the positive fact, the Why to the How. And with this turning-back, the possibility of a truly reconstructive form of action was lost.

The new notion of reason diverged from, and was in many ways antagonistic to, classical liberal reason. But it was appropriate to an era in which the logic of privatism had unexpectedly survived into a world of organization. For from the view of such logic, the basic requisite of freedom and security must still be control. The classical bourgeois had placed primary emphasis on control of terrain, self-control, and interpersonal control, in the sense that one's property was held against the world. The new liberal, too, would emphasize control as the test of real knowledge, scientific "controls," and ultimately, social control. The continuity of the concept is not accidental. The new liberalism sustained the old liberalism's preoccupation with ownership, fixed boundaries, and "holdings," but transposed them into the realm of knowledge. For without any vital institutions for sharing and for mutual cooperation, scientific "controls" appear to offer the only possibility for reliability in social intelligence. The new epistemology is appropriate, then, to a world which has become collective without being cooperative, and closely structured without offering security. It is appropriate to a world that remains private in its power, its opportunities, and its basic strategies for dignity.

In urging the view of knowledge-as-control, and in losing touch with any view of human possibility (Lockean, Marxian, or whatever) that went beyond the given situation, the Progressives acquiesced, finally, in seeing man as a conditioned animal. Their thinking ran not only against an intersubjective form of reason but also against a voluntarist idea of reason. The idea of knowledge at the heart of the new political culture could not easily be appropriated for democratic attempts at *self*-control.[147]

The epistemological premises thus returned in the conclusions. An administrative outlook erected on facts that excluded will and intentionality at the start could not make provision for consent and intentionality at the end. Men were not like rocks or trees. They had, as Ward knew, a psychic factor. They moved, as Dewey noted, via symbols and meanings. Having admitted these things, however, Progressive respect for human nature came down to a decision to resolve social conflicts by controlling the conditions in which psyches developed and symbols emerged. In the fullness of a half-century, this would come to be known as "channeling"—what a government document from the Vietnam era would call the "American or indirect way" of achieving what is done by compulsion in "foreign countries where choice is not allowed." In the channeled world individuals would not be subjects of activity, but objects of planning by elites in the "national interest." Italy called it "guided democracy." The American document called it a "system of pressurized guidance." Whether participants accept their alternatives gladly or with reluctance, it added in a Holmesean vein, "the consequences are approximately the same."[148]

7

The New Nationalism: Lineaments of Corporate Liberalism

A people which becomes more of a nation has a tendency to become for that reason more of a democracy.

—HERBERT CROLY (1909)

I loathe the nation-state. It's a kind of secular church in an age without religion. But it's the only political community we have these days. It holds things together. . . . The damned thing is necessary.
—ROBERT HEILBRONER (1975)

*T*wentieth-century liberalism takes the nation for granted. Textbooks no longer have to justify a focus on the federal government. The public has learned there is a National Interest, and even reformers cast their eyes up to the national legislature. It is easily forgotten that the ascendance of the national paradigm for thinking about American politics is barely as old as the century.

Many of the avenues by which America traveled to this new paradigm have been discussed in other contexts: the Darwinists' habit of thinking about society as an organism; the corporation's search for uniform interstate regulations and for a policing agent for business "self-regulation"; the Progressive tendency to see the national executive as the agent of administrative reform; and labor's increasingly functionalist perspective with the nation as the function-defining unit. When Wilson spoke of the Anglo-American duty in the Philippines, it was the national government that he saw as the vehicle of the race. And when Holmes wrote that legal principles were rooted in social policy, he meant *national* policy.[1] God was becoming historicized; and it was the nation that voiced His will for the lives of men.

Though some Progressives were organicists and some mechanists, and some wished to give social power to neutral administrators and others to farsighted businessmen, all but a few syndicalists on the left and localists on the right shared the faith expressed by Herbert Croly that "the American democracy can . . . safely entrust its genuine interests to the keeping of those who represent the national interest." As Croly explained: "No voluntary association of individuals is competent to assume the responsibility of fulfilling the Promise of American Life. The Problem belongs to the American national democracy, and its solution must be attempted chiefly by means of official national action."[2]

Though the growth of the federal government was due to a number of practical causes, our interest here is in the explanations by which that growth became legitimate and the "nation" secured a conscious claim on the future. Necessity may be the mother of invention; but people usually shape their inventions according to ideas in their minds. Though America had been founded as a federal republic, indeed as an empire with semi-autonomous provinces, it had after the Civil War increasingly come to resemble a unified nation. Still, a new intellectual outlook, a new structure of political intentionality, had yet to be developed. That deficiency was corrected during Progressivism, in the course of articulating a call for a positive state.

THE POSITIVE STATE AND THE NATIONAL SYSTEM

Three principal tributaries led into the new intellectual outlook. The first was the socialist nationalism of Edward Bellamy. The second was the new political science and economics of the American social scientists who returned from Germany in the eighties and nineties. Sidney Fine attributes to such people as Richard Ely, Simon Patten, and John Bates Clark the basic theory of the "general welfare state," an idea whose time would come in the middle of the next century. Finally, and most important, was the program of the New Nationalists proper—the editors of *The New Republic*. These men forged the most complete synthesis of group theory, realist epistemology, and new politics; they presented the country with the first statement of a general theory to replace classical liberalism.

This was no small achievement. Men like Wilson, Croly, and Lippmann were addressing themselves to the political ideas of a country which had not only tried to create a minimalist state but had also tried to establish a special sort of sovereignty—constitutional sovereignty. Political power in America was supposed to have been "diffused by a written constitution, and the holders of power held in check by the rule of law." In more classical language, force was supposed to have been transmuted into power by being exercised according to law.[3] Two faces of constitutionalism can in turn be distinguished. The most apparent was the external face, consisting of Madison's checks and balances and Marshall's judicial review. But behind this there was an internal sense in which sovereignty was supposed to be constitutional: it was supposed to be *infused* with moral principles. The common law defined those principles by immemorial custom. Stoic and natural law traditions defined them by "right reason." All of these perspectives conceived of law as an ethical vehicle, and power as residing "in the leading strings of moral principles."[4] Law was not just *voluntas*; it was also *ratio*.

Thomas Paine alluded to both aspects of constitutionalism when he remarked that written constitutions were "to liberty what grammar is to language"; they not only constrained speech but also made speech possible in the first place. Paine also caught the constructive, voluntarist side of constitutionalism when he explained that a constitution was "not an act of a government, but of a people constituting a government."[5] It was not simply a fact but a continuous *act*. Tocqueville alluded to this inner face of constitutionalism when he recognized the possibility of a "lawful" tyranny: "Tyranny may be exercised by means of the law itself; and in that case it is not arbitrary; arbitrary power may be exercised in the public good, in which case it is not tyrannical."[6]

Constitutionalism, then, is more than a commitment to procedure and form; it is concerned with the *content* of power. The test of its mechanical aspect might be said to be legality; that of its voluntarist side, legitimacy. New Nationalist theory was faced with finding new formulations for both.

The rise of judicial activism during the 1890s had indicated a crisis in the original approach to sovereignty. In America, both legality *and* legitimacy had been rooted in the natural rights tradition.[7] But in a few short years—between the *Munn* and *Lochner* decisions of 1886 and 1905—the meaning of this tradition had been transformed. From being conceived of as a determinant of the common weal, natural rights came to be seen as protection for private interests *against* the common weal. And from being seen as a charter of public law, the Constitution began to be viewed by the authorities charged with enforcing it as "the final breakwater *against* the haste and passions of the people—against the tumultuous ocean of democracy."[8]

Progressive jurisprudence never identified this issue explicitly. When Oliver Wendell Holmes, Jr., took up the cudgel against Justice Field, he did not argue, as Waite had in *Munn*, that law was framed in some larger form of the public interest and that Field's doctrines violated that interest. In cases like *Tyson Brothers v. Banton* (1927) he argued instead that the very notion "that a business is clothed with a public interest [when it] has been devoted to the public use" was little more than a "fiction intended to beautify what is disagreeable to the sufferers." "The public interest" was a myth, and "rights" were simply what the dominant force in the community said they were. (State legislature could do "whatever [they saw] fit to do unless . . . restrainted by some express prohibition.")[9] For Holmes, Field was in error because he was out of step with "the force of public opinion."

What was at stake in the three-cornered dispute between Waite, Field, and Holmes was nothing less than the internal, substantive side of constitutionalism—and with it the broader basis for political obligation. It was nothing less than the distinction between a sovereignty which carried an inherent set of purposes and limits and one that did not. In the heat of the argument, this point was missed. But the contest of the era was not between those who would embalm the Supreme Court in mechanistic doctrines and those who would liberate it for serving "life"; it was a contest between opposing ideas about the basis of law in the liberal state.

None of this seemed troublesome at first. Most reformers felt that the federal government was more capable than state or local governments of dealing with political problems. And they may have been correct. Still, the classical liberal had been wary of the state. For him, to speak of the "negative" state had been to speak of the subordination of positive law to natural law. But once liberals rejected natural law, what would keep positive law from expanding until the state appeared to be an authority *over* society—the *source* of rights and the ethical context of all human activity? What was to keep the new call for absolute sovereignty from spilling over into a mandate for *arbitrary* sovereignty as well? What would prevent the authorities, in the words of Albert Camus, from substituting for the divinity of God the divinity of the nation? Let us see how the new thinkers conceived of democracy in a world of functional groups and positivist rights.

THE NATIONALISM OF EDWARD BELLAMY

Edward Bellamy, like Henry George, was read widely by the populists. Like George, he sought economic reorganization primarily for purposes of moral regeneration. But though Bellamy was a member of the populist family, he was an errant son—a wanderer who had seen other lands and accepted other gods. The new lands he saw were bounded by the nation, not by nature. And the state he sought would be used to replace nature, not to guarantee its harmonies. Where George affirmed collective property in land in order to preserve the space for individual liberty, Bellamy asserted the social character of all wealth in order to create a collective existence. Where George drew the line at the associational, Bellamy moved on to the organic.

Bellamy regarded nationalism as the form in which socialism would come to America. He was joined in this belief by increasing numbers of people who read *Looking Backward* and eagerly formed the numerous Nationalist Clubs of the nineties.[10] He justified the advent of nationalism partly on technical grounds (it provided more efficient and comprehensive planning). And he also justified it on ethical grounds. Like Follett and Croly, he saw classical liberalism as a mandate for anarchic egotism. In *Looking Backward*, Dr. Leek explained to Julian West that the increased productivity of the future, made possible by industrial efficiency, would not be used to fatten individuals but would be spent "on the social side, that which we share with our fellows." Bellamy grounded his nationalist outlook in the sociological insight that individual development was shaped by "conditions," and the novel though valid recognition that "the men and women with whom we mingle . . . are as much conditions of our lives as the air we breathe." Wise social policy would therefore take special care for those people's education and health.[11]

Bellamy saw the path from the waste and "leakage" of the present to the efficiency of the future as being blazed by the corporations themselves. As he saw it, the nation was being consolidated into "one great business corporation in which all the other corporations [would be] absorbed." When the nation had become One Big Trust, industry would be "entrusted to a single syndicate representing the people." The nationalist society would turn out to be a state socialism mediated by industrial corporations—at once the highest stage of capitalist corporatism and a step beyond. Its government would be staffed by a graduated corps of industrial statesmen, ranked and differentiated as in Plato's Republic—though qualified by industrial ability rather than transcendental knowledge. In the new society the title to one's "allotment" would no longer be decided by industrial status but by his or her humanity. "The basis of his claim is that he is a man," not his wealth or birth.[12]

As a social allegory or morality play, *Looking Backward* was impressive. But as a political theory it had a number of problems. One of these was that it failed to make clear what the tasks of democratic citizenship would be. Bellamy's neglect on this point paralleled that of the group theorists. The benefits people would derive as members of this close-order world were obvious: solidarity, industrial peace, equality of opportunity, and bountiful public facilities. But their *rights* were not so clear. Bellamy made no appeal to Tocquevillean participation; the heads of national trusts would handle political affairs. Nor was there any appeal to Jeffersonian free conscience or free speech; Bellamy mentioned neither. Nor, importantly, was there any discussion of the quality of work— no appeal to the "god-like power" of fashioning circumstances, the frontier goal of versatility, or the promise of a title to the fruits of one's labor. What remained a threat for Henry George thus became a desirable reality for Bellamy. The development of a person's character was separated entirely from the quality of his workday life.[13] Like Carnegie on the right, Bellamy on the left shifted the emphasis from work as the definitive human activity to consumption, from the citizen as producer to the citizen as recipient.

Bellamy's underlying social vision, like Taylor's, was administrative. As such, it was essentially a-constitutionalist. For once a society is equated with "a national family," complicated constitutionalist considerations become irrelevant, because politics themselves have become irrelevant.[14] External and internal checks become unnecessary where basic conflict is nonexistent. In Bellamy's scheme, like Ward's, political parties, lawyers, and juries would disappear, and crime itself would become an "atavism."[15]

Another major problem of Bellamy's approach was a confusion between nationalism and socialism. His evolutionary assumption—that the corporate hand which inflicted the wound would also be the hand that healed it—had the effect of subsuming national development into a providential historical flow and identifying any form of collectivism with socialism.

A nationalist perspective can be defined as one which seeks to centralize government over the jurisdiction of a nation-state, and to promote intervention by that government in large areas of social life. Aside from the fact that statism would expropriate authority from local communities, its politics are not exclusive to any point on the familiar political spectrum. One could promote administrative reforms like Wilson, capitalist privileges like C. F. Adams, or farmer-labor measures like the early Watson, and still be a "nationalist."

The socialist, by contrast, is committed to implementing the interests of the community—or the public—and, in America, of protecting the social conditions of individual development against pre-emption by private interests. The connection between federal means and socialist ends is not a necessary one. But Bellamy believed it was. He presumed that a national government, simply by virtue of being national, would also be publicly oriented. Because it was Highest and Most Unified, it would also express the interests of the whole. But this link was symbolic rather than real, the fruit of hope rather than analysis; and the hope masked the capitalist character of the new collectivisms. In placing society on a military footing against waste, inefficiency, and ignorance, Bellamy clearly thought he had found the social equivalent of war. But no one previously had thought to call a society like Plato's Republic a democracy, nor "Von Moltke's fighting machine" an egalitarian institution.[16]

Through these aspects of his thought, Bellamy bequeathed to the future an easy faith that social justice would emerge as a function of corporate rationalization, as well as a flawed appreciation for the potential role of capitalist interests in national government. History was expected to alchemize a public interest out of private trusts. In such a perspective the role of political action was nonexistent.

SPOKESMEN OF THE GENERAL-WELFARE
STATE AND WOODROW WILSON

Bellamy's inclusive nationalism was anathema to the new political economists and their students. The purpose of a positive state, wrote Woodrow Wilson, was only "to create conditions, not to mold individuals." J. R. Commons explained that state action should set the stage for "a higher individualism."[17] These new political economists were, then, neither socialists nor full-fledged statists. They were institutional reformers who proposed to use the state instrumentally to deal with specific irrationalities and injustices of entrepreneurial capitalism. Many of them were motivated by ethical and religious convictions, Ely and Commons in particular having been influenced by the Social Gospel movement.[18] It was the language of objective fact and inductive method, however, that dominated their work, clothing and eventually hiding the religious element.

The new economists and political scientists first aimed their artillery at the Lockean and Social Darwinist ideas of natural law. They insisted that social laws were historically derived, and therefore laden with specific political and ethical decisions. Having captured this important stronghold, they then went on to challenge prevailing ideas about individualism and the sanctity of market laws, and then finally to attack their main target, the negative, minimalist state. The railroads provided them with good examples in these efforts. They provided abundant evidence, for example, that there was no necessary connection between unrestricted liberty and the public good. "Individualism" there had produced waste, injustice, and the misallocation of resources. Clearly, to reap the fruits of competition in railway transport *required* regulation. The government, then, should "interfere in all instances when its interference will tell for the better education, better morals, greater comfort for the community."[19]

The goal was a "positive liberalism." This entailed, more than the elimination of restraint, "the presence of conditions which make possible the unfolding of our faculties."[20] These scholars called for a wide range of ameliorative measures regarding business, labor, education, the courts, and urban organization. The regulation of monopolies, however, was central to their concerns. Some, like Simon Patten, proposed outright government ownership of the largest; others, like Richard Ely and Henry Carter Adams, proposed government control of "natural monopolies" and the strict regulation of competition to raise its moral level; and still others, like John Bates Clark, trusted to the enforcement of competitive conditions to rekindle initiative.[21] Woodrow Wilson himself traveled a course from a Charles Francis Adams-like equation of regulation with "publicity" about corporate activities, to a later approval of control of "natural monopolies" and a concern to enforce the Sherman Act against corporations that had originated in artificial merger rather than organic growth.[22] The unifying assumption of these "positive" liberals was that politics should oversee economics rather than vice versa.

Central to this approach were also proposals for the reform of national institutions. If the state were to assume its appropriate func-

tions, it would have to be streamlined and granted "powers commensu-
rate with its responsibilities." Once these things were accomplished,
they believed, scientifically informed leaders and investigators would be
attracted to public office, and professionals would replace politicians.

The early proponents of the general welfare state thus reached the
federal camp by a number of routes. They looked to the national government to arbitrate industrial conflict (transferring the myth of neutrality,
interestingly, from the older to the modern paradigm). They also looked
to the federal government as the fulcrum for social change. They rejected the standpoint of the individual utilitarian calculator and looked
to the state, additionally, to institutionalize the objective standpoint of
"society." Finally, looking to historical habit and custom as the source of
social order rather than to contract, they saw in the federal government
an agency which could define authoritative customs and consciously
nurture new national "habits."

In all of this the political economists, like the administrative reformers, saw themselves as politically neutral. They cast their eyes beyond
"the greed of the capitalists" and the "short-sightedness of labor." Still,
having accepted the larger social landscape as shaped by private capital,
and having accepted what the populists regarded as the gerrymander-
ing of the public domain implicit in the corporation form, their approach
was subject to the same confusions that beset the pragmatists and administrative reformers. Their concept of the positive state, moreover,
was not really adequate to the crisis of constitutionality shaping up in
American politics. For illustration of both of these points we can turn to
the writings of Woodrow Wilson, a student of Ely's and eventually the
most famous of the new institutionalists.

Wilson's early political science revealed the influence of diverse
strains of thought. From classical economics he retained a belief in natural law and in the moral primacy of the individual. From Burke and
Bagehot he took a view of social institutions as the product of historic
and organic evolution. And on these foundations he placed the scientific, inductive attitudes of the new social scientists.[23] The product of it all
was a new Whiggery, the view of an organic society properly led by a
governing elite. But in place of the old Whig guides of reason and tradition, Wilson looked to the modern guides of science and natural
evolution.

The differences between Wilson's liberalism and the classical approach were already evident in his pre-Presidential writings. His book
The State and his articles on the Philippines revealed that he, too, took
his bearings not from contract but from the growth of and competition

between "races" (a competition in which the better always "of course" prevailed).[24] From such origins he moved to the modern condition via instinct, utility, force, and "national development." ("The obedience of the subject to the sovereign has its roots not in contract but in force, the force of the sovereign to punish disobedience; but that force must be backed by general habit.")[25] The role of enlightened leadership in the resultant scheme was to make rational adjustments to the historically evolving context—to "adjust your laws to the facts." In this lucid formulation of the Reform Darwinist outlook, Wilson revealed the Progressive tendency to bow to the authority of given facts. If laws were not adjusted to facts, he explained, "so much the worse for the laws, not for the facts, because law trails after the facts." Indeed, "the law, unless I have studied amiss, is the expression of the facts in legal relationships."[26] Part of Wilson's program to eliminate the lag between law and evolving "facts" was to adjust law and government to the fact that "business [is] done by great combinations." There was a conservative tenor to these remarks, as there was to Wilson's ideas about leadership. The latter were conservative not because Wilson felt leaders should act as the conservators of tradition (he did not), but because he accepted the basic, hierarchical facts of corporate capitalist society, and saw leaders as the tutors to a more inert citizenry.

What is to be made, then, of his oft-celebrated reformism and his attempts as President to enforce the Sherman Anti-Trust Act against some of the largest corporations of the day? This question takes us to central aspects of Progressivism and of corporate liberalism as a whole.

To answer this question we must detach ourselves from isolated remarks and get a sense of Wilson's larger political theory. Wilson made a multitude of statements over a long career and in a number of genres (institutional analyses, textbook descriptions, magazine articles, speeches, executive memos, and personal letters). When we attempt to get a picture of the whole, however, the first thing that strikes us is his fundamentally biological cast of mind. "Government is not a machine," Wilson wrote, "but a living thing. It falls not under the theory of the universe, but under the theory of organic life. . . . It is accountable to Darwin not to Newton."[27] This biologism underlay his institutional analysis and his use of German historical method.

Specific political institutions appeared to him, as to Sumner, as complex, gradually defined and internally differentiated organs, which were in turn specialized parts of an evolving body social. There were two differences between his view and Sumner's. The first was that Wilson and the political economists provided for a directive intelligence within the

organism. Atop the corporate body they would place an active state—
and at its head, an active Presidency: "Government is merely the executive organ of society." Wilson's articles on the Philippines revealed that
the imagery was also applicable beyond domestic borders. He described
America's role as being that of teaching the Filipinos, still in the child-
hood of the race, "the drill and habit and obedience we long ago got out
of the strenuous process of English history." By submitting to such
tutelage, the Filipinos would be prepared for self-rule.[28]

Secondly, the new social scientists did not share Sumner's belief that
the society was already an organism. They saw it *becoming* more organic.
And they saw leaders and reformers as having a role to play in guiding and coordinating this evolutionary process. Further centralization
through executive and administrative action was the intelligent course
of action.[29] Part of the lesson of this outlook was also that such reform
should be limited. The main lines of evolution having already been set,
nothing qualitatively new should be attempted. Reform was in order;
but it should be meliorist reform.

These assumptions permitted Wilson to fit apparently contradictory
ideas together neatly. He accepted the corporations as "indispensable to
modern business enterprise," accepted organized social conditions, and
felt that people should adjust to both.[30] But he also saw the need of anti-
trust and regulatory policies. He justified these reforms partly because
he felt that many corporations were not the product of "natural growth"
(a distinction he got from Brandeis and which both men thought,
wrongly, would help them identify combinations that failed to promote
real economies of scale). In part he justified reform by the older, Sumnerian distinction between "real" corporations and plutocracies. And
overall he justified reform because he felt it was time for leaders to find
the "common interest" in the country in order to consciously promote
the development of a truly national life.[31]

It is wrong, then, to see Wilson as having been fundamentally
opposed to the evolution of the corporate capitalist world. It would be
wrong, that is, to see him as a modern Jeffersonian. Certainly the tenor
of his career prior to the campaign of 1912 had always been closer to
Hamilton's thinking than to Jefferson's—and to the Hamiltonianism of a
Lodge rather than of a Croly. His view of liberty as the freedom of the
piston, his continuing concern for improving the administrative aspects
of *national* government, his solicitousness to the needs for leadership
(often spilling over into outright paternalism)—not to mention his practical concessions to corporate capitalism in the form of commission
appointments, unwillingness to lobby Congress for stronger Federal

Reserve and Clayton Acts, and delegations of great power to business during the war—all revealed a spirit far distant from that of a voluntarist free-enterpriser.[32] Though Wilson was no business apologist, his was a class-bound point of view.[33] And the executive state he helped found was an organization of sovereignty appropriate to the economic and political needs of advanced capitalism.

The underlying biological point of view of society he shared with the political scientists Henry Jones Ford and A. Lawrence Lowell, and with other promoters of the positive state, could yield powerful analytic tools.[34] But it also had effects on the substance of their political thought.

First, the organic frame of reference conveyed an implicit message that social change was natural and not the product of political choice, that evolving facts were possessed of an innate direction and order. (Explaining why he did not oppose "big business" as well as trusts, Wilson explained that "no one indicts natural history.") The rise of the federal political structure was accompanied, that is, by the rise of an apolitical theory of its functions.

In the second place, as we saw, the outlook predisposed politics and reform toward further centralization. In its view successful government required the close, instinctive coordination of the different organs of national life. Wilson's criticism of government by standing committee in Congress had been provoked by its basic "scheme of distributed power and disintegrated rule." "Its powers are divided. [It] lacks promptness because its authorities are multiplied, lacks wieldiness because its processes are roundabout, lacks efficiency because responsibility is indistinct."[35] The obvious solution was to integrate, unify, streamline, and provide efficient direction. (It should be noted in passing that Wilson's political science, like Bentley's, provided little information about the vested interests which, as an empirical fact, controlled congressional committees during those years.)

Third, the organic outlook implied a unitary principle of political ordering. It supported an administrative and executive logic. From his proposals for a reformed Congress to his proposals for a strengthened Presidency was therefore only a short step for Wilson. *The State*, written twelve years after the work on Congress, identified the degree of integration of executive and legislative functions as "an important criterion of the grade and character . . . of political institutions."[36] By *Constitutional Government*, a decade later, he was looking to the Presidency to fulfill the functions he had earlier located within a reformed Congress. He still gave isolated support to the principles of public debate, as he had in his earlier work. But the drift of his theory was to subordinate them to the requirements of efficient leadership.

Most impressive in all this, as in Bellamy's thought, was the eclipse of the Madisonian tone which had previously distinguished American political thought. It was more intriguing even than the epistemological shift from natural right to natural fact. Gone not only was a respect for "Newtonian" checks and balances, but also a respect for the problems that led Madison to defend them. In the work of the new political economists, the desire for institutional balance, the fear of majority faction, and the concern about the impingement of private powers on the political process were all subordinated to the controlling desire to unify, coordinate, and "get things done."

What theory of constitutionalism was implicit in all of this? The internal face of sovereignty, the *content* of law, was identifed as residing in "habit." It was seen as defined by evolving social customs and needs. But "habit" is a concept without any normative content. It provides no standards for choice in cases of conflicting needs (and American "habits" were in any case undergoing profound change during this time), and no appreciation of the fact that "habit" for some, as Tocqueville noted, might be tyranny for others.

And although their concern for procedural regularity led Wilson and others to acknowledge the need for external checks, their assumption of an integral, harmonious character of social interests bled that rule-orientation of real importance. The Wilson of 1908 wrote that "a constitution is only as good as its courts." But a few years later he was complaining that politicians talked about interests "as if all interests were not linked together provided we understand them." Wilson believed that they *were* linked together, and that he understood them. That is why he proposed that "the way to purify our politics is to simplify them, and . . . the way to simplify them is to establish responsible leadership." [37] With this assumption he anticipated the curious development of American politics by which a growing commitment to administration would be combined with an increasing casualness about procedures and forms. The constitutional element in this proposal to centralize sovereignty was largely superficial.

Not even the prospect of a new leadership elite was seen as posing real constitutional problems. [38] For if society possessed the latent unity of an organic body, its leaders must necessarily be in touch with the people as closely as a mind is in touch with its body. In such a situation the way to improve activity is to *dispose* of checks, balances, and all other impediments to action. Sidney Fine caught the essential steps of this reasoning in his paraphrase of Ely's position: "In a democratic state the government is not something apart from the people. It *is* the people. In fact it is the only institution that stands for all the people. . . . When the people therefore use the democratic state to promote their own interests, they are not subjecting themselves to paternalism, but are merely helping themselves."[39]

This argument, like that of the group theorists, could easily degenerate into an apology for the sovereignty of the whole. That, too, reveals the essentially conservative cast of this theory of the positive state. Indeed, it is a paradox of American historical commentary, as one analyst notes, that where "the dominant economic ideas and policies of 'welfare statism' of late nineteenth century Germany are almost unanimously regarded as profoundly conservative, highly similar ideas and policies . . . which were directly influenced by those . . . [have been] often treated as progressive or even radical."[40] Though Wilson and the others paid homage to the *idea* of constitutional government, the principles behind the parchment were on the wane.

One final point about this approach to the positive state must be noted. Despite their desire to put politics in command, the new social scientists' assumptions about underlying social harmony prevented them from recognizing the real power of the new monopolies. They assigned to the state an independence from organized institutions and forces. But in doing so they only assumed, like Bellamy, what it was their task to achieve.[41] It is often said that the Keynesian policies of the 1930s enabled spokesmen of the positive state to finally subordinate private interests to their plan. Given these theoretical oversights, however, it is not surprising that the influence in fact ran in the opposite direction.

THE NEW NATIONALISM: A MIGHTY
FORTRESS IS OUR GOD

Combining Bellamy's concerns for a new normative ethic and for comprehensive planning, the political economists' practicality and administrative orientation, and the Social Gospelers' quest for spiritual renewal, the New Nationalists fashioned a program in which the national state emerged as the vehicle of modern democracy. Similar to Comte in their vision and cultural emphasis, the editors of *The New Republic* nevertheless founded their church on the rock of the nation rather than on science. They can be said, in fact, to have tried to fulfill Comte's ends with Machiavelli's means, for like Machiavelli they presented the contemporary strife of jurisdictions as a prelude to unification and secular redemption, and presented a national myth to inspire their fellow citizens. The distance between their efficient leader and Machiavelli's prince measured the distance they had traveled from truly political concerns.

The Nationalist Program

The New Nationalists' primary concern was for the social bonds that lie deeper than economic interests and formal law. Like Bellamy or Follett, they defined true citizenship and healthy individualism as functions of solidarity and of one's trust in neighbors and co-workers. Contemporary strikes, conflict, and general distrust they attributed to the failure of such bonds and responsibilities. They admitted that class arrangements were partially to blame for this failure. But their primary critique was of the failed social cohesion, not of exploitation or industrial domination per se. The course of social reform, Walter Weyl prophesied, would "constitute less a class struggle than a national adjustment." Progress would occur by "expansion" of existing opportunities, not by "rebound." [42] (A long unfinished book of Weyl's underwent a change in title by the twenties, from *The Class Struggle* to *The Social Concert*.)

The New Nationalists saw the agency of social change, appropriately, as being the middle class. The editors of *The New Republic* saw themselves and Progressivism in general as the vanguard of a middle-class movement that would promote the binding and healing necessary for the emergence of a "single, broad, intelligent, socialized and victorious democracy." Walter Lippmann asserted in 1914: "The middle class has put the 'Money Power' on the defensive. Big Business is losing its control of the government. . . . There is a growth of that abused thing, the public spirit, and the growth is so powerful that it may be able to ride the mere clashing of self-interest." [43]

The course of middle class ascendance would be aided in the New Nationalist perspective by fundamental changes occurring in corporate organization. Lippmann voiced the idea we have encountered with Holmes, soon to be made popular by Berle and Means: "The real government is passing into a hierarchy of managers and deputies who, by what would look like a miracle to Adam Smith, are able to cooperate pretty well toward a common end. . . . The real news about business . . . is that it is being administered by men who are not profiteers. The managers are on salary divorced from ownership." [44] This view, which mistook the appearance of a new stage of capitalism for its demise, was attractive to the ranks of new urban professionals and industrial managers. But they could only adopt it by ignoring certain salient facts—such as the fact that at this time 65 percent of the workers for U.S. Steel, who worked seventy-two hours a week, were still earning less than the minimum cost of living while the corporation was averaging a 40 percent profit on every pound of steel.[45]

The positive state appeared in the Nationalist program as both the means and the end of necessary reforms. As the means, it was supposed to implement real "social democracy" by increasing productivity and partially equalizing distribution.[46] As the end, it was supposed to inspire society with a new ideal and a new sense of common purpose.

Because improved distribution was seen as following automatically from increased productivity, "equality" boiled down in practice to an emphasis on improved social and corporate organization. Croly proposed (in what seems a direct paraphrase of Henry George) that the strengthened federal government appropriate the excess profits of the monopolies in order "to secure for the whole community those elements in value which are made by the community." Weyl coined the term "social surplus" to denote the socialized form of Marx's surplus value, which he saw now available to the whole society. Lippmann christened the surplus a Fund for Progress. Applying the lessons of psychology once again, he urged that the best course was not to expropriate (or curb) capital but to build up that fund and channel it in the public interest by "cutting out . . . sinecures, consolidating jobs, substituting competent for incompetent officials."[47] As with Progressivism in general, the problem was not seen as having to do with structures of power but with disorganization and waste.

Once waste was eliminated, these reformers believed, "the submerged" would "emerge" above the poverty line, and the society could move from the ethics of scarcity to the ethics of freedom. Admitting that Americans were divided by geography, background, and productive role, the New Nationalists yet trusted that they could be united by a common interest in rising levels of consumption. The consuming "mass" would thus oppose the pretensions of a "class."[48]

Inspiring devotion to common ideals was more difficult. The New Nationalists understood that in itself the collapse of old values did not guarantee the emergence of new ones, that it did not assure spiritual *re*generation. The age had "lost authority but retained need of it," Lippmann wrote in a Jamesean vein; "all of us are immigrants spiritually. We are all of us immigrants in the industrial world and we have no authority to lean on." This led him to propose an interesting definition: "There is a great gap between the overthrow of authority and the creation of a substitute. That gap is called liberalism: a period of drift and doubt; we are in it today."[49]

What would bring that period to a close? Lippmann's ideas varied over the years, but in *Drift and Mastery* (1914) he looked to science to remedy the problem. By science he meant "mastery rather than drift," "the substitution of conscious intention for unconscious striving," and, as we have seen, the unification of diverse groups through common use of laboratory methods. His familiarity with James and Sorel led him to question the normative grounds of contemporary science. But he answered the question simply, by proposing a Baconian "sense of mastery in a winning battle against the conditions of our life [as] the social myth that will inspire our reconstruction."[50]

Herbert Croly was more rigorous. He respected science because of its craftsmanlike and dispassionate methods of work.[51] But he insisted that an end was required for its means. Like many Progressives he saw this end as being provided by national leadership and by the nation itself. In this view "the nation" became not only the context for loyalty (because it was the context for civil law), but also the primary *object* for that loyalty. This view of the positive state, to put it differently, was grounded in a nationalist *ethic*.

As opposed to the European historicist approach, these men seemed to be attracted to the nation because of its physical comprehensiveness. Lippmann thus ridiculed the "anarchy of retail business" and "the village view of life." He celebrated new department stores because they focused the buyer's attention: "He could not focus on a congery of little shops. But where there is centralization, he has something of which to take hold."[52] The editors of *The New Republic* also celebrated the centralization of the national government, because they also believed it would automatically counteract the forces of fragmentation. Having begun by rooting healthy individualism in solidarity, and solidarity in a closeness to one's "nation," these men located the effective seat of nationality with the federal government. Similar ideas had been put forth by Machiavelli in regard to the *patria* and by Rousseau in regard to the general will. But a "nation" spread over many different regions and half a continent, with half its population made up of immigrants and children of immigrants, was a social unit unknown to previous political thought.

The ultimate vision of the New Nationalists was that of a strong state in a corporate society. In pursuit of their goals they proposed, like Wilson, that the federal government be simplified in its organization,

augmented in its powers, and adorned by a presidency capable of joining together what the Newtonian founders had put asunder. They, too,
took business as their model. Lippmann argued that private enterprise—with its "autocratic" management, highly paid administrators,
and "power adequate to . . . responsibility"—need have no advantage
over public administration. The advantage could be eliminated, however, only by government's imitation of private enterprise. What then
would become of democracy? Lippmann gave a partial answer in his
early statement that "the real problem of collectivism is the difficulty of
combining popular control with administrative power." [53] But lest the
modern reader get the wrong idea of what he meant by popular control,
it is important to remember that he presented the construction of the
Panama Canal as a "classic example of what government can do if it is
ready to centralize power and let it work without democratic interrup-
tion." (The example was more telling than Lippmann intended, considering the project's actual record of deceit, force, and usurpation.) From
his perspective, the new state should look primarily to "the infusion of
scientific method, the careful application of administrative technique,
the organization of the consumer for control, [and] the discipline of
labor for an increasing share of the management." [54]

The place of business in this new vision was clear. Croly, Lippmann,
and Weyl all believed that the magnates who had overseen the corporate
revolution should retain managerial control of the economy in the new
society. Close government supervision would create confusion. Croly referred to the capitalists simply as "specialists," and though he admitted
that the corporations threatened "the ideas, institutions and practices
out of which they issued," he sought only the reforms we mentioned in
Chapter Five. [55] Though Weyl was usually considered more of a socialist
than his colleagues, he also praised corporate capitalists as the syn-
thesizers of others' talents, the planners who now, avoiding "foolish,
short-sighted actions," could afford a "broader ethical view," the friends
of workers who could pass the cost of pension and benefit plans on to
consumers. Businessmen, as he saw them, had been seized by "an ana-
lytical and objective spirit" and transformed into something like a neutral, Taylorite elite. [56]

The place of labor in the Nationalist scheme was more ambiguous,
as the proposal to "discipline labor" revealed. The editors of *The New Republic* felt that workers should be encouraged in their industrial education by "participating in the control of industry." But although they were
at first enamored of the IWW and of syndicalist unionism, they even-

tually turned to the conservative railroad brotherhoods as the models for such education. Croly urged the compulsory organization of workers, arbitration, and the denial of the right to strike. He proposed that union recognition be conditioned on the unions' "conformity to . . . conditions" other than those formulated by their members, so that labor could be fitted "into a nationalized economic system." Unions that refused, he thought, should be replaced by federally created unions. This New Nationalist denial of an autonomous role to labor organizations was also revealed in Lippmann's suggestion that "you have to find ways of making the worker an integral part of industry." [57] They did not propose first to make industry worthy of workers' voluntary commitment.

The essentially elitist character of these reformers' approach was evident not only with labor. Croly stated that "the average American individual is morally and intellectually inadequate to a serious conception of his responsibilities as a democrat." [58] And Lippmann opined that most men "will do almost anything but govern themselves. They don't want the responsibility. In the main, they are looking for some benevolent guardian." More startlingly: "You can't build a modern nation of Georgia crackers, poverty-stricken negroes, the homeless and helpless of the great cities. They make a governing class essential." [59] Consumers, in other words, might become a unifying and powerful force, but only *after* a centralizing elite had organized their choices for them. Leaders were first needed to inspire and "leaven the inert mass." [60]

But exactly what sort of sovereignty is consumer sovereignty? It was to Herbert Croly's credit that he saw the importance of this question and addressed himself outspokenly to it. His argument is worth following closely; it traces the logic of an era.

Sovereignty in the New Liberalism

Democracy meant popular sovereignty. That was the starting point. [61] But what sovereignty meant, Croly admitted in *The Promise of American Life*, was far from clear. It did not simply mean majority rule, for a majority could oppress minority rights. It did not only mean protection of individual rights and liberties, as liberals and constitutionalists held, for those people failed to explain where the protection derived its authority. And the appeal to natural rights or to equality was in itself inadequate because Americans held different ideas about the meaning of rights and of equality. [62] Furthermore, in a country "which holds private property sacred there may be equal rights, but there cannot possi-

bly be any equal opportunities for exercising such rights."[63] Croly therefore concluded that the accepted approaches were dodges and evasions.

Because "ultimate responsibility for the government of a community must reside somewhere," he argued, there was "no logical escape"
from the need to acknowledge some form of absolute sovereignty. The
only rules that could be imposed on a sovereign power were those it imposed upon itself—as America had done when it adopted its Constitution. And it followed that "a power which is theoretically absolute is under no obligation to respect the rights of individuals or minorities."
While it was generally true "that the efficient use of force is contingent
. . . upon its responsible use," it was nevertheless also the case that a
national polity remained "an organization based upon force." Lippmann
agreed. He argued in *A Preface to Morals* that the idea of absolute power
was at the heart of the very idea of a state: "There is no theoretical limit
upon the power of ultimate majorities which create civil government.
There are only practical limits."[64]

The precise problem, then, was making sure that the state reflected
the will of the people, of "combining popular control with administrative power."[65] Croly took this to mean that all obstacles preventing people from expressing their changing will had to be removed. The point
was a tricky one, however, because for Croly these obstacles included
not only Madisonian checks but also obstacles the people themselves
might create through ignorance or inexperience. ("There can be no democracy where the people do not rule; but government by the people is
not necessarily democratic.") The real "sovereign," then, was neither individual liberty nor majority will, but the will which expressed democracy's true interest; this was defined as a will which would not "contradict and destroy the continuous existence of its own Sovereign power."

At this critical juncture in his initial discussion of the topic, however, Croly wandered off. He moved from definition to loose description. Beyond clarifying that majority rule and universal suffrage were
only means to an end, he failed to specify exactly what sort of activities
would create the sovereign will he had defined.

Returning to the topic later in the volume, Croly rephrased the
question. If the people in a democracy were sovereign, who were "the
people"? They were not, again, a chance majority. They were those who
were bearers of the "collective will."[66] Croly distinguished them from
members of a "semi-democratic nation," people who remained separated from and suspicious of each other despite democratic legal institutions. Citizens of a "nationalized democracy or a democratic nation"

would feel common bonds of trust, loyalty, and affection. This criticism of a semi-democratic nation was identical to Hegel's criticism of civil society. Both were places where the pursuit of happiness was a private affair and relations with fellow citizens were as those between strangers.[67]

Croly then moved to the conclusion implicit in his whole volume: if the key to realizing popular sovereignty was creating a collective will in modern society, then the way of accomplishing this was to seek fullness and consistency in "national life." This was the fundamental argument for the New Nationalist position: "The phrase popular Sovereignty is . . . for us Americans equal to the phrase 'national Sovereignty.' The people are not Sovereign as individuals. They are not Sovereign in reason and morals even when united into a majority. They become Sovereign in so far as they succeed in reaching and expressing a collective purpose."

But this formulation still left a major question unanswered. Was *any* collective purpose sovereign? Was *ratio* required, or was *voluntas* alone sufficient? At this point Croly seemed to veer off again in other directions: he explained that schemes of Tolstoyan democracy were premature, that "in this world faith cannot dispense with power and organization." He attributed the ascendance of political over religious organizations in the West to the former's use of force. He presented the nation as a "school" and emphasized the disciplinary—indeed coercive—aspects of that schooling. ("Men being as unregenerate as they are, the policeman and the soldier will continue for an indefinite period to be the guardian of the nation's schools.")[68]

Croly was not, however, despite appearances, wandering at all. He was giving a discursive answer to the question he had left unstated. The underlying message of this answer was not, as he wrote, that "faith cannot dispense with power and organization"; it was that faith would *result from* power and organization. External order, external unity in itself would give rise to the sentiment of community. Croly could continue to talk about the need for friendship and fellow-feeling without first discussing the *content* of that friendship, as he could talk about the need for a common will without first identifying the *content* of that will, because beyond a few formal characteristics (provisions for fairness and equal distribution), he considered questions about content as being beside the point. Morality, as for Wilson, was basically dissolved into habit.

This reasoning found precise parallel in Lippmann's thoughts about psychology, where order was seen as flowing from external discipline and "mastery," from an act of imposition upon amorphous materials (as

Sumner had seen the industrial superego laid atop a libidinous nature). The reasoning found an additional statement in Wilson's identification of "the drill and habit of law" as the basic training for Filipino "order and self-control."

The New Nationalists' insight into the need for community in democracy, their valid criticism of classical liberalism, and their recognition of the necessity of political action to create order, in other words, were accompanied by no ideas of a principle or process that could *evoke* community voluntarily. The New Nationalists doubted that individuals could initiate community from below; and their discomfort with the vocabulary of morality dissuaded them from proposing substantive moral principles themselves. As a result, their preliminary insight turned in on itself. Their recognition that political democracy required particular social relations led them to seek the outer pattern of those relations and to hope that the spirit would follow—to assume the pose and wait for the feeling, to call for Paul and anticipate Jesus. From Aristotle's or Rousseau's or even Hegel's perspective, such a program would have seemed curiously foreshortened. It stopped short of the ethical appeal which alone could *create* social unity by giving expression to people's sense of right and eliciting their voluntary obedience.[69] But this theoretical gap corresponded perfectly to the practical gap in American society between the collectivism called a corporation and the one called a community.

Croly, like Hegel, criticized the bourgeois emphasis of individualist rights. But where Hegel moved from natural to "rational" rights, Croly moved from natural to *national* rights. In the process the concept of democracy was hollowed out. Democracy was reduced to a *function* of "national purpose": "All rights under the law are functions in a democratic political organism, and must be justified by their actual or presumable functional adequacy." Lippmann added: "There is no question of inalienable rights. It is a question of good use and bad use, wise and foolish use."[70] Where the emphasis on rights had been exaggerated by the classical liberals, it was now subordinated to a concern for function and use. Popular sovereignty was equated, operationally, with the national will as articulated by federal institutions. Any other sources of authority and any substantive theory of reason were denied political standing. The struggle for democracy was equated with attempts to promote efficiency, encourage solidarity, and create a national government for corporate society.

THE CORPORATE LIBERAL THEORY OF SOVEREIGNTY

A national theory of sovereignty remains the closest approximation to a modern theory of political order in America. The distinctive thing about it from a democratic point of view is its neglect of the internal, active side of constitutionalism, its decision that "absolute" sovereignty must also necessarily be "arbitrary." To understand more about these terms and locate the positive statists in our larger concerns, we must return for another brief look at the European pluralists.

We saw that European pluralism began in protest against the rise, out of the motley system of medieval power, of what Gierke called an "antique-modern" politics. It was "antique" because, like Roman law, it viewed the state as sovereign (that is, as the supreme coercive organ of society and the exclusive agent of the good life); it was "modern" because it saw that state as composed of atomized individuals possessing aboriginal rights. The early pluralists argued that the ascendance of the state over all other social relations and the concentration of authority at a single point betrayed proper historical development and was profoundly dangerous. Gierke acknowledged that "political thought when . . . genuinely *medieval* start[ed] from the Whole." But he pointed out that its idea was of a composite whole—a body articulated into different ranks, professions, and estates rather than into arithmetically equal units.[71] The state in such a system was "sovereign" in neither an external nor an internal sense.

Externally, it was seen as bounded by a higher law, the standards of Christendom. Medieval doctrine "never surrendered the thought that the Law [was] by its origin of equal rank with the State and [did] not depend upon the State for its existence."[72] More practically, feudal rulers, though uninterested in institutional checks and balances, were nevertheless checked by different systems of law—municipal, religious, mercantile, and manorial. All of these limited their authority.[73] Finally, the personal character of feudal bonds gave to political relations an implicitly reciprocal quality. The terms of that reciprocity were sometimes violated by the lords in a social order where subjects lacked power. But the unilateral abrogation of obligations was regarded during the Middle Ages as an injustice and a usurpation. "Lordship was never . . . mere right; primarily it was duty. . . . Rulers [were] instituted for the sake of Peoples, not Peoples for the sake of Rulers."[74] As a result of these three conditions, authority was constantly checked and broken in its flow.

Internally, the power of the medieval state was limited by the fact that these different relations were not merely checks against power but sources *of* it. Kings could not ignore such sources because they underlay the substance of kingly power, as Henry IV, for example, discovered to his surprise when he attempted to override the papal excommunication of 1076 and found his vassals absolved of their oaths. "Those who repeat . . . that the prince is above the law," Bertrand de Jouvenal cites a sixteenth-century pamphleteer as explaining, "say what is true but in a wrong sense. For what they mean . . . is that he can break and abolish the law at will; whereas its true meaning is that he is above the law as a building is above its foundation—tamper with the foundation and the building collapses." Varying the metaphor for a situation that later liberals would find paradoxical: "His majesty is the fountain of justice; and though all justice which is done within the realm flows from this fountain, yet it must run in certain and known channels." [75]

Sovereignty for the medievalist, in other words, did not confer on the sovereign the right to do whatever he wanted, but only "the obligation to command what should be commanded." This view persisted. When sovereignty became increasingly unitary, began to be focused at a single point and made "absolute" at the close of the Middle Ages, it was not seen for that reason as becoming "arbitrary." [76] A single will was endowed with supremacy. But principles and procedures were seen as *informing* that will and bringing it into consonance with reason and custom.

The artillery of the early pluralists was aimed, however, against both absolute and arbitrary sovereignty. They opposed absoluteness, which they associated with monopolization of initiative and political standardization, because by the mid-nineteenth century they thought it amply proven that such centralization necessarily led to arbitrariness— the quality they saw, with Tocqueville, as the essence of tyranny. The ultimate effect of setting up a liberal state over atomized, apolitical individuals, and of conceiving of power as lying at some point, they argued, must be a view of state-protected rights not as residing *within* other rights but as the source *of* them. The pluralists doubted that the limits set by natural law or written statute would halt this development. [77]

The pluralists proposed to "destroy sovereignty," by which they meant the monist state. They argued that real "sovereignty [was] not merely government, merely law as promulgated by the government, not even merely the will of the people as political beings, but . . . the harmony of the articulated [social] wills . . . projected into a functional system." [78]

Though our main concern here is not with the pluralists, it should be noted in passing that their solution was inadequate to the problem they had articulately defined. The functional system they proposed was hardly more pluralistic than a monist state. It simply substituted a concept of *social* harmony for legal monism. Indeed, none of the familiar pluralist proposals (for functional representation, administrative decentralization, guild socialism, interest-group pluralism, or federalism) was necessarily anti-monist in its ultimate conception of power. The pluralists dissolved Austinian legal sovereignty into its presumed social roots, but then imbued those roots with the consistency, legitimacy, and a priori reasonableness they had just denied to law. They attempted to destroy sovereignty, but inadvertently restored it; and when it came back, Hsiao wrote, it "came back with a vengeance."[79]

The New Nationalist project in many ways paralleled this effort of the pluralists. Its concern was with the nation rather than with plural groups. But it, too, entailed an implicit effort to prevent the slide of absolute sovereignty into arbitrariness. Political sovereignty, in their view (as in Bellamy's and Wilson's), was to be checked and guided by the social purposes lying behind it—the "higher" law in this case emanating from society and being conceived of as following from the requirements of "welfare."[80] Law for them would be distinguished from Austin's or Hobbes's concept of law as an external command by its embodiment of the inner commitment to welfare.

The original proponents of the positive state in America, then, were not full-blown statists. The cohering element in society, for them, was not political force. The state was seen as serving group needs and the goal of economic abundance. The new thinkers, like the group thinkers, argued that when real political relations were not misrepresented by a Hobbes (emphasizing force) or a Locke (abstract rights), they turned out to be nothing more than the natural expressions of shared customs and habits. This is to say that the New Nationalists, like Wilson and Dewey, subsumed political relations into natural history. On balance, they saw politics and political membership as functions of accident and habituation.[81] Order was seen as provided by custom and, increasingly, by consciously managed "habits."

Valid though its criticisms of liberal politics were, this approach obviously had problems of its own. How could appeal be made to custom-as-habit in a country with a multitude of customs, and in an era when habits were changing rapidly? The problem here was not with simple matters of policy, but with the underlying standards by which policies would be judged. Strictly speaking, one could not resort to legal guidance for answers, for law itself (as we saw in Chapter Five) was being transformed from a body of neutral rules governing the activity of juridical persons to an ends-oriented administrative process intended to coordinate functional groups.[82]

One task of an adequate theory of sovereignty, as Croly and Lippmann knew, is to supply a principle of obligation, an explanation of why people should bind themselves voluntarily to the policies of a state. But reducing political society to customary community, and law to habit, would fail to provide such a principle. The New Nationalists therefore argued that the abundance of commodities and the promise of eventual equality of opportunity indicated that society was fulfilling its part of the "promise of American life," that it was fulfilling its part of a collective contract, and that citizens were therefore obliged to accept the new social arrangements. This new argument to obligation consisted of two steps. First, the Progressives changed the unit of consent; they altered the terms of the original market contract from the individual contractor to the societal (or racial) body. Next, they made a retrospective imputation of consent: people had at some point joined a purposive organization that was now delivering on its promises. By these arguments, subordinate status in an industrial world could be justified in a way that would have been impossible with the myth of individual, short-term contracts. More importantly, a basis was also laid for transcending the normal quid pro quo of individual consent theory, and for providing some members of the association with tasks of leadership and education that went beyond the strict terms of their authorizations. A basis was laid for achieving what Croly called a "higher level of association."

This was, however, a peculiar theory of consent. Even if the argument were superficially successful—even if people could be persuaded that the "promise of American life" consisted only of a full dinner table, and that "a fair field and no favors" meant a fair run at the competitive ladder—it reversed the normal democratic order of consent and obligation.[83] It made the fulfillment of obligation *precede* the conditions necessary to justify consent. People were expected to acknowledge claims on their efforts and loyalties not on the basis of prior agreement, but on the basis of an unsecured promise of future rewards. The theorists of the welfare state thus proposed to the American public something on the order of an open contract. By its terms it would be impossible to tell at any particular moment whether the conditions of one's obligation had been fulfilled or not.

Perhaps it was in tacit appreciation of this critical shortcoming that the new political thinkers often sidestepped the problem of obligation, and relied instead on the management of "conditions" (as we saw in Chapter Six). They turned, in other words, to manipulation, the counterfeit of consent.

The New Nationalists failed, in short, to produce a democratic theory of obligation. Their ultimate appeal was not really to obligation but to simple *obedience*, without much clarification of its grounds and limits. "Obligation [was] simply what is done." [84] Though they went beyond previous American political thought in seeing that democracy required democratic *social* relations, and that an ongoing association required political functions that could not be explained by consent theory, their real commitment was to the *idea* of solidarity. They never succeeded in articulating a substantive principle or set of values that would *evoke* popular loyalty. They failed to consider that in a democracy, any dominant social principle must be capable of earning the voluntary commitment of the people.

Political thinkers must consider not only "when people obey and how to get them to obey, but also why, in some fundamental sense, they must obey." "The sovereign must be concerned," Hsiao wrote in analyzing Hobbes, "not only with giving commands, but [with] so giving them that they will actually be obeyed; it must not only know that it possesses legal power but [must] constitute power in such a way that it may be exercised in the most competent fashion." [85] In terms of our previous discussion, this means that sovereignty must be informed by legitimate principles—constituted *of* them—if it is to be constitutional. Because they ignored such principles, and because, like the pluralists, they conceived of social "will" as essentially harmonious, the Progressive proponents of the positive state enunciated a theory which was not only absolute but which also pointed toward arbitrariness.

The idea of the state as manager of industrial abundance did not, then, take them very far. They may have alleged a right to welfare, but they never explained what obligations the citizen assumed in return for that right, nor what rights of dissent and deliberation he or she would have in the provision of that abundance. If the danger of classical liberalism was that there would be no public interest apart from private interests, the danger of this new liberalism was that there would be no private interests apart from the national interest. In the world projected by the New Nationalists, the citizen would be told to ask not what the whole could do for him, but what he could do for the functional whole.

But there is no need to belabor the point. The New Nationalists were explicit about it. They assumed that arbitrary power was a necessary function of absolute sovereignty. The idea of imposing conditions on a centralized power seemed to them—and to subsequent liberals—a contradiction in terms. "A power which is theoretically absolute is under no obligation," wrote Croly. The situation in which a sovereign was bound to rule "on established foundations" was quite inconceivable to them. Nor could they have understood Tocqueville's claim that to say a people can "never outstep the boundaries of reason and justice" in its own affairs was to use "the language of a slave." [86]

The flawed theory of sovereignty was the central problem of the Progressive approach to the positive state. But it was not the only problem. To have created a state like the one they proposed would have required, negatively, the clearing away of obstacles to cooperation and fraternity, and positively, the creation of agencies of democratic political education. Either of these tasks would have required a confrontation with the substantive power of the capitalist corporation.

But the New Nationalists joined Ely, Patten, and Wilson in a leap of faith at this point. Rather than acknowledge the substance of the capitalist corporation, they tried to draft it into service. They called it a school for industrial habits, ignoring the facts that this school taught only top-down discipline and hierarchical dependence, and that these are hardly the "habits" of a sovereign populace. [87] Even were corporate capitalists somehow to be deprived of their control of distribution, the New Nationalists were still asking people to feel solidarity toward each other within mechanical institutions, organized to extract private wealth from a cooperative work process. They were entrusting the creation of democratic social relations to an institution whose private and hierarchical qualities they refused to challenge.

Though most Progressives were willing to speak informally of the educational functions of corporations, they never proposed to make them formal sub-national agencies of democratic education and democratic participation (as Follett or even Hegel had proposed). [88] Again, they ignored the active, constitutive side of sovereignty. This is why they were drawn toward manipulation and externally imposed "discipline" as the only means to political order. "The nation" was seen as coming into existence independently of its constituents' consent. The universal would not derive from the particulars, but would be laid atop them.

By the 1920s the New Nationalists were aware of the shortcomings of their theory. Croly lamented that prewar liberals like himself never saw how much their ideas actually served to keep "economic and social power predominantly in the hands of one class." Weyl had also concluded by 1919 that the issue was "not one of political forms but of class supremacy within a nation."[89] But though aware of the problems, they still lacked a theoretical framework to take them beyond the theory we have analyzed in this chapter. Failing to rework their premises, they proceeded to meet continued failures of prediction by recommending an ever-greater expansion and centralization of federal power.[90]

CONCLUSION: THE STATIST IMPLICATIONS OF PROGRESSIVE THOUGHT

Though the New Nationalists were not overt statists, there was a patently statist thrust to their thought. They proposed to guide the government by an antecedent social will, but they said nothing about the content of that will. They were even satisfied, operationally, to let the state be the articulator of that will. Indeed, they impugned the legitimacy of all other candidates for that job—whether custom, common law, Higher Law, or the separate states of the union. They also ignored the existence of any partial obligations independent of the duties owed to the national government—whether they were those of an independent-minded citizen to the society, of a doctor to the ill, of a labor leader to his union members, of a teacher to his students, or of a lawyer to the aggrieved in search of redress. Paradoxically, an initial desire to assert the rights of society against the state wound up justifying the state's right to define the terms of social membership.

Ultimately, then, these new ideas were in many ways similar to the older theories of Hobbes, Bentham, and Austin. Although Croly and Wilson rooted law in social norm, they also rooted norm in habit, and felt that because habits originated ultimately in accident, they were finally buttressed by force. ("The obedience of the subject . . . has its roots not in contract but in force.")[91] Their theory was an inversion of Rousseau's. The idea that national law should express the "sovereign will" meant for them that national will was sovereign, not that a particular sort of "will" should be deemed sovereign, and the state bound by it.

The essence of the approach was again caught by Holmes; it was what produced his draconian decisions. For Holmes, sovereignty was identified straightforwardly with power, "force," "strength." This meant that there were no "rights created by law as against the sovereign who makes the law by which right is to be created."[92] The reason, for exam-

ple, that it was not a tort to persuade a sovereign to do something otherwise illegal was that "it is a contradiction in terms to say that within its
jurisdiction it is unlawful to persuade a sovereign power to bring about a
result that it declares . . . to be desirable and proper. . . . It makes the
persuasion lawful by its own act. The very meaning of sovereignty is
that the decree of the sovereign makes law." This language is what
Tocqueville had characterized as the language of a slave. But for Holmes
sovereignty was "pure fact." [93]

Holmes's characteristic mode of reasoning reflected the movement
of New Nationalist thought. This movement was from the whole back to
the parts—from the most basic requirements of sovereignty, the most
arbitrary acts permitted a government, back to the case at hand. Thus
the insane could be sterilized, because if the "public welfare may call
upon the best citizens for their lives," then "it would be strange . . . if it
could not call upon those who already sap the strength of the state for
these lesser sacrifices." [94]

"Society," "the predominant power in the community," the "state"—
these were the points from which Holmes *began*. In *Moyer v. Peabody* (a
case that involved the jailing of IWW leaders for four months despite
writs of habeas corpus), Holmes reasoned that if a governor could in the
course of restoring civil order "kill people who resist," he could "of
course . . . use the milder measure of seizing the bodies of those whom
he considers to stand in the way of restoring peace." "So long as arrests
are made in good faith and in the honest belief that they were needed
. . . the governor is the final judge." [95]

Max Lerner inadvertently identified the problem with this approach
when he praised Holmes for bringing to civil liberties "a solicitude for
individual experience and a thoroughness of mind which saw the survival of the state as a condition precedent to the creativeness of the individuals within it." [96] Lerner was right to pose the problem in terms of
individual liberty, on the one hand, and the survival of the state on the
other. He was also right in seeing that this approach subordinated the
enjoyment of the former to the survival of the latter. Because once the
issue is defined in that way (as the balancing tests of the 1950s would
again reveal) no other conclusion is possible. That is not the only way of
framing the alternatives; but it has been the dominant one within liberalism since Hobbes. This approach does not consider several points:
(a) that rights might be defined by something other than a nation-state;
(b) that different kinds of rights are appropriate to different kinds of
states; or (c) that the survival of a democratic state presumes the mainte-

nance of certain rights rather than vice versa. Brandeis gave fleeting recognition to these points.[97] But Holmes simply contrasted the threat of anarchy to the need for order and let it go at that. As a school, the Progressives dissolved obligation into mere obedience and legitimacy into legality.

The founders who urged that American constitutionalism could never depend on mere parchment were correct.[98] Constitutionalism required the existence of popular standards and norms beyond the positive law. Locke had recognized such a standard when he grounded civil government in natural rights. The abolitionists preserved the idea when they appealed to Higher Law. And Tocqueville invoked such a standard when he defined the task of a "nation" as being "to represent society and to apply justice, which is its [society's] law."[99] Even Comte approximated this constitutionalist idea (and violated his otherwise unitary vision) when he provided for a moral priesthood to stand over the patriciate, as the spiritual power had stood over the temporal in medieval times.

But the Progressives, by denying any ethical standard beyond the nation, by making the nation itself the object of ethical commitment, deprived constitutionalism of its basic meaning. Appeals to the division of powers and "a written framework of laws" might continue to occur. But the promotion of an administrative paradigm, the failure to address intrinsic standards of legitimacy, and the failure to acknowledge real structures of power, bled such appeals of any real force.

By the early twentieth century the ancient struggles between right reason and the Prince, between natural law and political will, had been reduced to a narrow battle between property rights and legislative policy (with the legislature itself often reduced to an arena of private interests). It was a battle from which a real notion of *public* interest had departed. The most advanced liberals talked simply of making the Constitution expressive of "the needs of the hour" as against those who wanted to preserve its traditional character. But they said nothing about how the needs of the hour were to be determined in the public interest, nor how they were to be reconciled with the needs of the society over time. In all of this, the reformers only contributed to a political decisionism which, undesirable in itself, would be made even less desirable by its susceptibility to control by private corporations.

The product of this theory was not something "more than popular sovereignty," as Croly sought, but something less. Lippmann's consumer imagery caught it best. In the society proposed by the new political thinkers, citizens would stand passively before a bazaar of retailed options produced and organized by unaccountable elites. E. E. Schattschneider would write by the 1940s that "the sovereignty of the voter consists in his freedom of choice, just as the sovereignty of the consumer . . . consists in his freedom to trade." He then suggested the hollowness of the idea when he added, "the people are a sovereign whose vocabulary is limited to two words, Yes and No. This sovereign, moreover, can speak only when spoken to."[100] With a sovereign like this, one hardly needs subjects.

8

"Here We Have Power, but No Motives"

A nation that had a great social revolution and was
untroubled by it would baffle the social Freudian, but
a nation 'born equal' does not, save of course for the
fact that it poses the unusual problem
of a fatherless tribe.

—LOUIS HARTZ

The acceptance of the positive state, like the acceptance of group theory and of a positivistically inclined epistemology, was a double-edged event. On the one hand it revealed flexibility and a real sense of practicality; on the other it required cutting loose from past moorings and departing from known navigational points. The freeing of thought from the constraints of natural law was an important event in American political culture.

But liberation was only one side of the story. As the young Walter Lippmann observed, there was something else beneath the surface: "The outstanding fact is the decay of *authority*. . . . This does not mean . . . that we are [now] able to command ourselves. In fact, if a man dare sum up the spiritual condition of his time, he might say of ours that it has lost authority, but retained the need of it."[1] Herbert Croly referred to that loss when he wrote about the end of the older "promise of American life" and the need of a new, conscious ideal. William James also referred to it when he characterized the modern era, with its abundance of power and lack of "motives," as inverting the sense of nightmare. His image of a novel's characters escaping their author's intent also registered the larger implications of this.[2] The point was that the demise of a source of common inspiration "freed" people not only from obstacles to action but also from purposes *for* action in the first place.[3] The resultant condition might easily be mistaken for either aimlessness or paralysis.

The problem was not with authority of the "punishing and restraining" sort—the sort that normally monopolizes American attention. It was with the collapse of a principle capable of inspiring shared projects and of eliciting what Comte called "spiritual order."

Vernon Louis Parrington noted signs of the collapse in the literature of the 1890s and attributed it to the rise of a physical and mechanical view of the universe. Displacing the older Enlightenment optimism of the biological paradigm, this mechanical outlook suddenly suggested that life occurred without "purpose or plan in a changing universe of matter." It was this which had evoked the "unconscious return to the dark spirit" of Calvinism which Parrington saw in the new writers.[4] Henry Adams concurred. After reflecting on the dynamo, he concluded that "modern politics is, at bottom, a struggle not of men but of forces," and the struggle produced only greater and more mechanical consolidations of force.[5]

But there were hints of the loss even before the 1890s, during the era that Parrington saw as so optimistic. The spirit of Calvinism was surely present in Sumner's biologism. Despite his denial of pessimism, he and others who had grown up in a culture that glorified the will must have been deeply affected by a doctrine that dispensed with voluntary powers, reduced history to matter, and attributed progress to the unconscious evolution of the race.

Henry George called it a "hopeful fatalism" and attributed it to the more general decay of religious sentiment in the West. "Christianity is dying at the roots. And nothing arises to take its place."[6] Because human will for George was "the great factor" in social life, this spiritual loss exacerbated the corrupting effect of monopolies, at the same time that the monopolies prevented the forms of association and activity necessary to develop new values. "He would have been a rash man," George noted, "who, when Augustus was changing the Rome of brick into the Rome of marble, when wealth was augmenting and magnificence increasing, when victorious legions were extending the frontier . . . then would have said Rome was entering her decline. Yet such was the case."[7] With the terms of his analysis in mind, it is clear that George himself was the rash man of whom he spoke—surveying the new Rome of Carnegie, Morgan, and Rockefeller. For he saw the capacity for common inspiration as failing in America.

The collapse these thinkers chronicled was not something that could have been remedied simply—as by a minor factory reform or a temporary federal program. What was required was not a feat of social engineering, not a channeling of people's efforts, but the discovery of a principle that could elicit purpose and order within an atomized and increasingly disoriented population. It was not an instrumental problem, to put it differently, but a problem about the *ends* for which instruments would be used. It was the epochal problem Comte had described, of creating social order without appeal to God or king. But an adequate response to it was hindered by a number of things: the narrow vocabulary inherited from the past, the new form of social organization, and the epistemological sensibility that denied rational, willing capacities to the average citizen.

Improvisations were made. But ultimately the new liberalism failed to deal adequately with this crisis of authority. That failure would deprive it of the long-term power of its Lockean predecessor. It explains why a half-century later, in John Schaar's lucid words, "What we mainly see are the eroded forms of once authoritative institutions and ideas. What we mainly hear are the hollow winds of once compelling ideologies. . . . What we mainly feel in our hearts is the granite consolidation of the technological and bureaucratic order, which may bring physical comfort and great collective power, or sterility, but not political liberty or moral authority."[8]

Schaar's last sentence suggests the significance of the problem in the world of politics. But before following that lead we must look more closely at what it was that was departing from American culture. William James's comment locates the proper starting point, for his references to nightmare, motive, and power take us directly to considerations of will and action.

THE PROBLEM OF AUTHORITY

"Authority," from the Latin *auctoritas*, as Hannah Arendt has explained, derived originally from the verb *augere*, to augment. The concept was first articulated by the Romans, and what they saw being augmented, according to Arendt, were the foundations of the political order. The "authors," then, were not necessarily contemporary leaders

or those who built on the old foundations, but were those who preserved the original spirit of the founding and communicated it to new
leaders.[9] John Schaar also traces the origins of the concept to the notion
of an *auctor* or originator, and adds the important point that it implies
the idea of "originator by right."[10] For Schaar, what is augmented by
authority is an actor's capability and his or her confidence, his or her
will. This concept is fleshed out in Schaar's discussion of a personal
authority as one who counsels, whose "deeds we strive to imitate and
enlarge" and who increases the confidence and ability of his fellows. An
authority "starts lines of action" and is therefore "metaphorically the
father of [others'] actions."

These root meanings help to clarify the concept. "Authority" was of
central significance to Roman society not because its traditions were
heavy burdens for Roman men and women but because those traditions inspired them to new and creative deeds. Similarly, natural law for
nineteenth-century Americans was not a "brooding omnipresence"
hanging *over* people, Holmes's remark notwithstanding; it was a generative principle acting *in* them, both to stimulate action and to provide a
standard by which those acts could be judged. Without such a principle
how would a person ever attain the confidence to make the leap James
identified at the heart of real action? And without a *common* principle,
what would induce a person to hold out his hand to a stranger?

Passing to a political context, authority has been seen since classical
times as necessary to enduring rule because it alone was regarded as
capable of converting power into right and force into legitimate power.[11]
It alone was seen as capable of establishing the kind of "obedience in
which [men] can retain their freedom."[12] Unless they believe a rule to be
legitimate, men will not acknowledge obedience to it as an obligation.
They may submit, but they will not choose freely to obey. Science
seemed *politically* authoritative for Comte, for example, precisely because it seemed to possess this capacity to elicit general assent, to "reconcile independence and social union."[13] The importance of this sort of
authority has been acknowledged by such widely divergent writers as
the socialist Laski and the conservative Tocqueville.

"Men will obey when their allegiance is grounded in an ability to
revere," Laski wrote; he added that such reverence was "also a basis of
self-respect."[14] Tocqueville urged (in implicit response to Hobbes) that it
was faith, not fear or self-interest, that created a great people; and that
the man who "submits to that right of authority" was elevated just as
surely as one who submitted through violence or fear was debased.[15]

The difference between the two forms of obedience measured the difference between citizens and subjects.

The perception at the heart of these various statements is that a society which would enlarge people's capacities of action, would provide for an obedience in which people remained free, and would enable people to renew their allegiance to each other, must embody a principle of authority. Without such principle power will be obeyed first through trust, then through dull habit, then finally with resignation, so that when it is finally challenged, it must turn to force as the only guarantor of order. As willing assent fails, the space for freely assumed obligations is filled first by strategies of manipulation and then by the logistics of coercion.

Most Progressives were less than articulate about these matters. Henry Adams, however, was an exception. His account of his personal struggle and eventual disenchantment with Darwinism provided an oblique discourse on the problem of authority at the end of the nineteenth century. "By rights he should have been a Marxist," Adams wrote of himself, "but . . . he tried in vain to make himself a convert. He did the next best thing; he became a Comtist within the limits of evolution. He was ready to become anything but quiet."[16] Comte in America meant Darwin; but after an initial romance with Darwinism he had been forced to conclude that the evidence failed to sustain its claims. Natural history demonstrated only an evolution that did not evolve, a uniformity that was not uniform, and a selection that did not select. He could find no real *evolution* in the naturalists' story, no purpose: "All he could prove was change."

Adams's words were important. He could not get excited over the recently discovered ganoid fish, saying that while he was willing to accept the *pterapsis* as a cousin, a great-uncle, or a grandfather, he was not willing to accept it as a father. "To an American in search of a father, it mattered nothing whether the father breathed through his lungs, or walked on fins or on feet," so long as he bequeathed some sense of purpose. The concept of fatherhood is one of the main ways in which the Western tradition has apprehended authority (as revealed in the words *patria*, patriarch, Pope). Adams had been seeking a key to the mystery of the "evolution of mind."[17] The *pterapsis* gave him no help because it conveyed no idea of an initiating principle, no inspiration. It gave no hint about what men should do—nor indeed, why they should do anything.

Darwinism, in other words, presented a view of history without paternity, of tradition without authority. Comte and Dewey asked peo-

ple to concentrate on the How rather than the Why. But Adams, like
James, wondered what difference it made *how* people did things if there
was no reason for doing them in the first place.

How would their question be answered? No one familiar with
American culture would expect God to be returned to his heaven or a
king invited to Washington. (Henry George even discounted the possibility of a constructive socialism because of the decline of religion.)
Bereft of even the deist God, liberal man was by the latter decades of the
nineteenth century free—but in the double-edged sense we mentioned.
How would Americans find a new principle of authority? Where, beyond their own changing desires, might they find a grounds for legitimacy and an object of shared allegiance?

PROGRESS IS OUR MOST IMPORTANT PRODUCT

Progressive thought possessed a number of superficial strategies for
handling these questions, and underlying them, one master strategy
which it bequeathed to corporate liberalism. The first of the superficial
responses, as Theodore Lowi noted in his analysis of interest-group liberalism, "sought to solve the problems of public authority by defining
them away." Instead of articulating an authoritative goal for politics it
pretended that the definition of that goal would emerge from the tugging and hauling of interest groups. "A most maladaptive political formula," Lowi called it: "it will inevitably exacerbate rather than end the
crisis, even though its short-run effects seem to be those of consensus
and stabilization."[18] And, it can be added, high productivity.

A second response urged that this productivity itself would dispose
of the problems. Holmes was only one of many who believed that modern society, by making life "more complex and intense" would also make
it "fuller and richer." "Life is an end in itself."[19] Quantity, in other words,
would dispose of questions about quality. "More complex," "intense,"
"more." These were the words of a Comtist or Darwinian—of a positivist—trying to explain to someone who had trouble following biology that far, why a more highly developed organism was *better*. (The attempt was the same as Gompers's in construing the goal of the AFL as
"more.")[20]

A third response trusted to a combination of exemplary leadership
and administrative methods. The hope was for new "authorities" and
"authoritative" rules. Yet most Americans of the era did not yearn for a
man on horseback; nor, as we have seen, were they really legalists.[21]

Underlying these other responses and giving substance to them, however, was a deeper response to the problem of authority. Its logic was captured most succinctly by the pragmatist proposal to judge actions and ideas by their consequences rather than their causes, by their fruits rather than their roots. The basic strategy of this response was to reverse the direction of the quest for meaning, to look to *effects* rather than to origins to legitimize activity. This strategy appeared justified by pragmatist epistemology. Chauncey Wright, for example, had always defined scientific formulas as "finders" rather than summaries of truth; and James and Dewey defined "truth" as something that happened to an idea in the world.

Dewey carried the reasoning in social directions. Though community life was threatened with "invasion . . . by new and relatively impersonal and mechanical modes of combined human behavior," improved means of communication and a knowledge of consequences could reestablish social purposes and meet the threat. " 'We' exist," he proposed in a technical variant of Descartes's *cogito*, "only when the consequences of combined action are perceived and become an object of desire and effort." [22]

Lippmann started at the same place, as we have seen, though he moved to an unexpected conclusion. Having observed that people retained the need for authority, Lippmann proposed that they get over that need—at least as it had been traditionally conceived. That is where science and "mastery" came in. For "when we speak of the modern intellect we mean this habit of judging rules by their results instead of their sources." People should "act for results *instead of* in response to authority." At this stage in his development, he thought "scientific discipline" would provide the "substitute for authority." [23]

Croly was the most lucid of the Progressives in calling for a new "authoritative and edifying . . . social ideal." [24] And yet, as we have seen, once he identified the problem, his thought followed its characteristic drift from large ends down to small means. The first step in meeting the problem, he explained, would be to perfect the instrument of regeneration: the working citizen. (Whatever the new standard turned out to be, its "instrument must . . . be thoroughly well-made, and in the beginning it is necessary to insist upon merely instrumental excellence.") [25] Once the individual citizen had been educated to his proper role, he was to be given "the nation" as his ideal. The legitimacy of the nation's rule would then be judged not by its origins, its members' consent or lack thereof, but by the abundance it provided.

The essence of this approach was Comtist, though the Progressives gave to Comte a peculiarly American cast. Comte, too, had abjured a concern with "causes." He proposed his Religion of Humanity as the forward-looking ethic people could adopt in order to be "saved."[26] Positive science would point the way through which men and women could be incorporated into this new *corpus mysticum*. Corporations, as the schools of science and solidarity, would be the de facto churches of the new religion.

The Americans reversed Comte's priorities, however, and made science the prop for industrial production rather than vice versa. Legitimate rule was then assigned to corporate and political leaders rather than to a scientific priesthood, because such leaders were seen as uniquely capable of organizing society and of augmenting production. In the process, sentiment was deprived of its status *over* reason. And the concern for solidarity was replaced by the Americans with a commitment to administrative fairness. The logic of privatism survived into the age of organization.

This was as far as the Progressives went with the matter. And it is as far as modern liberals have gone—save for the assertion that anyone who cannot deal with the indeterminateness is an "authoritarian."[27] In the new liberalism, progress was God.

For the twentieth-century American, Progress as defined by economic output was supposed to provide legitimacy for rules, purpose for common allegiance, and justification for obligation. It was from this new God that Americans expected to derive their inspiration; for it they were prepared to sacrifice their hopes, by it they would justify their victims, and to it they would address their prayers. For by it, they hoped to be saved. The future was expected to make the crippled whole and the future was therefore worshipped. If in their daily lives people began to tend their own small gardens, it was because they trusted in corporate leaders and political elites to be priests of the larger religion. They could be God's lieutenants.

The new orientation found early and eloquent expression in Frank Norris's powerful novel *The Octopus*. Here, as so often in American life, the important political insights, excluded from formal political analysis, appeared in its literature. Norris's novel gave perfect expression both to the political context of this crisis and to the marked shift in cultural sensibility that occurred between populism and Progressivism. The novel draws to a close after the farmers and settlers of California's Central Valley have been deprived of land promised to them, and gunned down by railroad agents and sheriffs (a fictional rendition of the famous incident at Mussel Slough provoked by the Southern Pacific). It draws to a close, that is, as the politics of populism are being played out to their end. Driven to despair, the protagonist of the novel, Presley, lists the dead and wounded in his journal and then begins to ponder the meaning of what he has seen. "Oh, talk to us now of 'rights of Capital' . . . talk to us of the 'equilibrium between the classes'. . . . *We know*," he writes bitterly. "I can see the outcome. The Railroad will prevail. . . . Here in this corner of a great nation, here, on the edge of the continent . . . the great iron hand crushes life from us, crushes liberty and the pursuit of happiness from us, and our little struggles . . . cause not one jar in the vast, clashing machinery of the nation's life; a fleck of grit in the wheels, perhaps a grain of sand in the cogs." Presley also understands, as the populists came to understand, that corporate capital was at the heart of the problem. ("If it is not a Trust of transportation, it is only another head of the same Hydra.")

Seeking the cause of this misery, Presley enters the office of the president of the railroad, only to receive the following admonition: "Believe this, young man . . . *railroads build themselves*. . . . What do I count for? . . . You are dealing with forces, when you speak of Wheat and the Railroads, not with men. . . . The Wheat is one force, the Railroad is another, and there is the law that governs them—supply and demand. . . . Blame conditions not men."[28] The travail, the deaths, the ruined hopes—the modern, social expression of the ancient dilemma of innocent suffering—was thus explained. The suffering was the price, and the impersonal price, of industrial progress. There were "no enemies," only forces.

Having heard the argument, Presley began to believe. "Nature was, then, a gigantic engine, a vast Cyclopean power . . . a leviathan with a heart of steel." A spectre, withal, not unlike the railroad. The talk about classes, about power, and about winners and losers ceases. It leaves the volume as quickly as it left the dominant sectors of American society. For it is a hard thing to live with defeat, especially in America. And it was not the first time that men wound up worshipping what had destroyed their world. Norris's conclusion rises to an epiphany: "What then was left? Was there no hope?" "What was the larger view, which contributed the greatest good to the greatest numbers?" Yes, he sees, good would issue from the crisis, "untouched, unassailable, undefiled. . . . Falseness dies; injustice and oppression in the end . . . fade away . . . the individual suffers, but the race goes on."[29] Having learned that progress caused the savage reversals of fortune, Presley (and Norris) turned and began to worship it. America followed down the tracks.

The idea of religion—the essential idea of which, from the Latin, is re-ligare, to be bound back—was thus inverted.[30] American commonality, rather than being seen as flowing from a common past, was bound over to the future. The idea of "progress" came to fulfill for moderns the same function the State had fulfilled for classical liberals: it provided a vision of abstract wholeness to a people denied community and condemned to stunting conditions in their daily experiences. It played the same double function Marx identified with traditional Christianity. On one hand it was "the soul of soulless conditions" and provided hope; on the other, it ratified people's debilities. For it helped sustain conditions which required the illusion that the source of people's efficacy was a mythic force beyond their own powers.[31]

Norris's novel, in clearly portraying the historical roots of this theoretical reorientation, revealed the large part that politics played in it. The twentieth-century liberal moved to a faith in the "force" of industrial development after the defeat of the nineteenth-century democratic struggle and in an attempt to reorient himself after the crushing victory of corporate powers. For all the subsequent talk about science, this reveals that faith *preceded* fact. The faith in technological progress that clothed and soon hid the workings of capital followed not from any actual reconciliation of social strife, nor from any demonstration of industry's ability to provide for security and integrity, but from a decision to cut loose from a promise which had been betrayed and to entrust one's life to the unknown future.

THE GOD THAT FAILS

This doctrine of progress made a virtue of necessity. Despite its elegance and the apparent authority of its science, however, it contained flaws, both predictive and conceptual, that prevented it from accomplishing what the Progressives expected. First, the fulfillment of its promise of prosperity and abundance was dependent on a number of conditions the presence of which, in corporate capitalism, could not always be guaranteed. Second, its implicit theory of citizenship was, from a democratic point of view, deficient. Third, its standards of entitlement for leadership and rule were ill-defined. Finally, its basic strategy embodied a fundamentally hollow concept of authority. These flaws deprived the notion of "progress" of its putative power and revealed a root failing of twentieth-century American political theory.

The first problem with the appeal to "consequences" was that, despite some decades of impressive economic advance, modern capitalism was incapable of delivering consistently and dependably on the promise of abundance. For this "promise," as Henry George wrote and Croly admitted, had entailed more than just an assurance of a plethora of unevenly distributed commodities. It was also a promise, extending beyond the middle classes, of abilities to enjoy material wealth dependably, securely, and in conditions permitting dignity. The Progressives' indifference to matters of economic structure and their middle-class faith that corporations, as neutral institutions, could do all things for all people, prevented them from seeing the long-term obstructions to the fulfillment of this promise.

Given the prevailing structures of economic organization—given businessmen's need to control ever-expanding blocks of productive wealth and their sustained power to shape patterns of distribution—the widespread dissemination of consumer wealth in America would be an evanescent thing, susceptible to revocation by wage-cuts, capital strikes, employment of capital-intensive (rather than labor-intensive) machinery, and inflation. Abundance could be guaranteed for a time by implementing the efficiency measures discussed in Chapter Six, or by the government temporarily putting buying power in the hands of consumers (a "crisis of under-consumption" being the sole way modern liberals acknowledged the effects of exploitation and domination). Or new abundance might be provided by super-profits from new areas of commodification or new lands for investment.

But the heart of the promise of "abundance" was the promise of an improved *quality* of life in American society. And as long as even the fleeting enjoyment of consumer goods occurred within a system in which private interests defined the forms of abundance, in which there were incentives for the short-run neglect of the social bases and industrial grounds of productivity, and in which periodic instabilities forced private interests to perfect ever-newer means of capital accumulation, the improvement of people's lives would be a doubtful occurrence. Indeed, such advance might easily presume the *destruction* of the prevailing quality of life.[32]

When corporate capital was beset by its periodic instabilities, furthermore, rather than reducing prices and improving production as required by the market model, it would be tempted to use the newly perfected positive state to help rationalize operations, stifle competition, and pacify its social milieu. And the effect of this would be to compromise the state's claim to neutrality. As a practical matter, then, corporate capital could not guarantee an improved quality of life to all sectors of the population; and the attempt simply to keep itself healthy would force the state to compromise its legitimating mask of impartiality.[33]

Even if it had been possible to deliver on the promise of abundance and preserve this mask, however, there were serious *theoretical* problems with the Progressive approach to authority. Its second weakness was that the idea of citizenship that it embodied amounted to a model of consumership. The consumer in a monopolistic economy occupies a passive role regarding the creation of goods or policies. He is neither an originator nor really a consentor; his role is limited to affirming or denying options defined by others. (And choosing to affirm or deny is far more difficult in politics than in economics, because the "product" one accepts or rejects may be nothing less than the entire milieu in which he or she lives and moves). Most importantly, however, political consumership is not even capable of sustaining itself, at least as an intelligent activity.

The exercise of an electoral veto power, limited though it is, still requires certain skills of political analysis and action. But the consumer model fails to specify how such skills are to be developed and augmented. The guarantee of an occasional right to vote is hardly sufficient for that task. A vote is a *post facto* event, premised on a prior framing of alternatives. Someone whose political experience was limited to the vote, however, would be unable to acquire the information to know when he or she was being provided with the real range of alternatives. Nor would he or she be able to develop the ability to choose between such alternatives well. Tocqueville was surely right here. He found it difficult "to conceive how men who have entirely given up the habit of self-government should succeed in making a proper choice of those by whom they are to be governed."[34] In fact he concluded that voting, that "rare and brief exercise of their free choice . . . will not prevent [a people] from gradually losing the faculty of thinking, feeling and acting for themselves." The citizen as efficient worker and surfeited consumer is really no citizen at all.

Third, the Progressive approach offered an unsatisfying answer to the question of how the acts of officials were to be authorized. Questions about title (about whether an official was doing something by *right*) had been answered in classical liberalism by referring back to an act of consent, by looking to the process of representation from which law-making derived. In practice, of course, many sectors of the population were excluded from effective representation. The new liberal who was aware of these past limitations had two paths open to him. Either he could attempt (like Follett) to diminish the barriers to democratic consent; or he could redefine what "representation" was all about. The Progressives generally adopted the latter course. Laws began to be seen not as crystallizations of prior consent but as anticipations of popular desire. Whether they were deemed just or unjust depended upon the extent to which they furthered "consequences" as defined by the national government; that is, the enactment of laws *preceded* the situations in which it could be determined whether or not the lawmakers had been properly entitled.

This strategy brings us back to the reversal of consent and obligation mentioned earlier. According to the provisions of this reversal, one could never tell at the time whether an official's actions possessed proper title or not. Nor could one tell who were the "authors" of the authorities' acts.

What Croly and the pragmatists had proposed, in fact, was a species of political narcissism. The authorities were supposed to pursue "progress," but in operational terms they would be the legislators of that progress and the authors of their own actions. Just as the ends of life for Holmes had been "more" life, and just as men's energies for Ward and Dewey were fueled tautologically by the need to satisfy "wants," just as the goal of nationalized conduct for Croly was supposed to be "the nation" itself, so officials in this view were supposed to be the sources of their own activities. The Progressive model was essentially a model of a self-enclosed officialdom. It was a formula for political androgyny, for the Progressives lacked an effective principle of entitlement.

The deepest problem with the Progressive-pragmatist strategy for dealing with authority, however, was a fourth one: it attempted to do the impossible. Authority is quintessentially a thing of origins and beginnings, as the idea of author-ship reminds us. Whether or not Arendt was correct when she concluded that traditional authority is no longer available to us, it remains the case that some generative principle is necessary for genuine action and common social effort.[35] *Before* one can enjoy fruits he or she must know which roots are worth cultivating. Before people can muster the courage to make the Jamesean leap into action—action that will create *new* facts—they must be inspired by something stronger than fleeting personal desires.

It was "in the beginning" that there was the Word. The Romans derived their generative principles from the past. The Greeks (and most modern socialists) derived theirs from the idea of an imminent *telos*. And the medievalists had said that a prince was above the law as a house was above its *foundations*. For all of these, authority flowed from beginnings; if it was not there at the start, it—and the possibility of legitimate rule—would not be there at all. This appreciation of first principles was injected into American political thinking for four generations by the classical liberal teachings that laws should embody the consent of the governed and that a right to be heard was part of a person's dignity and self-respect.

This is not to suggest that officials who ignored "origins" would be prevented from effecting *any* kind of order; it is to say that they could not, through simple social engineering and the periodic delivery of goods, establish a healthy political order or give themselves authoritative status. To do that, they would need legitimating principles—shared moral ends to which appeal could be made in cases of dispute, and by which peoples' abilities to act could be augmented. The instrumentalist approach of the Progressives disposed of all these requirements, and in effect reduced the national polity to an instrumental association. Corporate liberal officialdom would in terms of this approach lack authority quite literally—because although it would have "ends," it would lack origins. It would be *intrinsically* illegitimate. Its illegitimacy would be of the kind Jacob Burckhardt identified as typifying those Renaissance states that were founded on personality and pure act, but in neglect of the "laws and usages" of the Western tradition.[36]

A corporate order without any principle of authority might be stable for a time. But its forms and procedures would grow increasingly hollow, its meaning increasingly obscure to those within its precincts. The political obedience elicited within it would become (as Schaar argues it has in fact become) "a matter of lingering habit, or expediency, or necessity, but not a matter of reason and principle . . . of deepest sentiment and conviction."[37] The sort of order erected around this hollowness could be expected to eventually produce two apparently unrelated phenomena: a pervasive lassitude on one hand, and the active threat of military force on the other. For laws cut loose from consent must, when challenged, gravitate toward command. There was a hole at the center of the corporate liberal scheme—a void in the realm of first principles, an absence at the springs of action. The new approach prepared America for a parade where everyone would see that the clothes had no emperor.

"LEVIATHAN WITH A HEART OF STEEL"

To what can this theory of political order be attributed? Not simply to oversight. The best thinkers of an era do not miss something of this magnitude because of poor eyesight. Nor can it be attributed to any intent to deceive. The sincerity of Croly's hope for a new spiritual order and Dewey's hope for new "meanings" cannot be doubted. This approach, rather, found its source in an actual historical collapse of older values, compounded by an epistemological belief that the realm of origins was unknowable and by the logic of contemporary social organization. "How is it," Dewey asked, referring to the latter, "that the machine age in developing the Great Society has invaded and partially disintegrated the small communities of former times without generating a Great Community?" Dewey provided the answer in the course of the question: because its basic way of disintegrating and then reintegrating human effort was mechanical. "Mechanical forces have operated to unify the nation, and it is no . . . surprise if the effect is more mechanical than vital." [38] It is no surprise if the dominant organizations are concerned more with process than with substance, more with external channels than with internal consent, and more with the means of communication than with something to communicate about.

The form of authority appropriate to a mechanically designed organization Weber defined as rational-legal (formal) authority. But rational-legal authority, though perfectly functional for Norris' "leviathan with a heart of steel," is no authority at all, as we have discussed it. Henry Adams saw this clearly. He saw that the attempt to shun inquiries into origins and meanings, the attempt to employ human intelligence exclusively for utilitarian ends, and the faith in technology as the source of social unity, would produce a hollow cultural order. "As Galileo reversed the action of earth and sun, Bacon reversed that of thought and force." [39] And the ultimate epistemological effect of the Copernican Revolution, as Adams saw it, would be to subordinate human effort to external force, to sacrifice mind's attempt to control matter. For when people were reduced to the status of objects, principles of legitimation and questions of meaning would become irrelevant.

But we must follow the causal chain one link farther. The acceptance of mechanized and technicized organization was not a primary fact. It was not an uncaused cause. It followed from certain historical preconditions. Mechanistic social relations followed from prior acceptance of the need for social institutions that would function *without* a sense of legitimacy, without shared meanings, and without appeals to volition in the first place. They followed from an acceptance of social purpose as it had been defined within the limits of corporate capitalist society. Mechanized, bureaucratic organization was the natural product of the attempt, necessary to modern capital, to monopolize initiative and rationalize domination in large institutions. [40] It was also the natural product of implementing economic organization by compulsion rather than free choice (the case in America even when the compulsion is applied subtly, by the obliteration of alternatives). And standardized, rule-bound relations followed, finally, from the attempt by new corporate directors to stifle collective responses to the new conditions.

Modern organization can be seen, then, as the product of specific desires to *remove* generative principles and capacities for common action from social organization, to *remove* the element of authority from interpersonal relations. The real goal, as Weber feared, was the systematic "disenchantment" not only of external nature but of human nature as well. Most of the Progressives accepted the basic outlines of the system, however, as inescapably modern. Their attempt to make authority a thing of the future followed from the de-authorization of the present. But their attempt to defer meaningfulness until the future also ratified its denial in the present.

Progressive thinking in these matters again revealed a technical character and was itself an expression of the logic of technology in modern society. Henry Adams urged that even those who thought they controlled industry "have nothing to tell, but are forces as dumb as their dynamos." And he felt they would remain that way no matter who managed the power. "The conflict is no longer between the men, but between the motors that drive the men."[41]

Adams was correct about the impersonality of modern social forces and about the social impact of technology—as later attested by the weakness of all modern industrial societies for its charms, and by its expression of a political character *as* technology. But he and others who argued for "the autonomy of process" nevertheless underestimated the role of capital in shaping and unleashing that process.[42] Dewey, for example, who saw clearly that people were joined together, "not because they have voluntarily chosen to be united" but because "vast currents are running which bring men together," failed to appreciate that those currents followed from the reign of the economic class he also occasionally acknowledged.[43] Adams saw that it was after the early nineties—after the American people had abandoned a "simply industrial" principle for one that was industrial and capitalist to boot—that the new forces were "condensed into corporations," "domestic education in politics stopped," and "the rest became a question of gear, of running machinery."[44] Adams did not pursue the point. But he was correct in discerning that despite its often autonomous effects, American technology was rooted in particular institutional arrangements. Its threats could not be dealt with adequately without ultimately putting an axe to those roots.

Henry Adams's ideas on the whole matter emerged from a larger view of history as degradation. And he had a point—even beyond his wry desire to stand the Darwinists on their collective head. Where Darwinists and Comtists saw history as progress, Adams presented it as a running down of matter and mind. Where they saw "coherent heterogeneity" and increasing power arising out of "incoherent homogeneity," Adams saw the threat of entropy and weakness emerging from the same. Modern history appeared to him not as a chronicle of man's use of matter, but of matter's use of man. (He registered this drift in his own vocabulary, as when he said he was personally searching for a principle of "attraction" rather than one of "intention.") The irony was not simply Adams's but the era's: the "dynamic" interpretation of history masked the declining powers of men.[45]

Adams did not mention it, but the capitalist corporation epitomized this devolution. It was an organization necessitated by its members' powerlessness and intended to reinforce that powerlessness; it was a monument to their weakness. Rather than expressing people's energies, it was an artificial mechanism for marshalling and deploying individuals who had been denied the capacity to organize themselves. The corporation was not a condensation of power, then, but a school of anomie. It was the only vehicle available for associated effort once vital sources of action had been starved and the possibilities of political interaction suppressed. The corporation was a product, a medium, and an accelerating agent of the devolution Adams had identified.

Sumner had been right. Capitalist organization was the only fence against chaos. It was the only fence because privately oriented, mechanically organized combinations had imposed obstacles to genuine action, shared purposes, and the development of new authoritative relations.

Were other ways possible? Could industrialization have occurred without such de-authorization? Some deny it.[46] But the point for an understanding of American history is that the attempt to chart a more legitimate and legitimizing course for industrialization *was never tried*. The attempt to initiate it by the populists was crushed, and effective barriers were raised against its being tried again.[47] Any attempt to elaborate new principles of social authority would have to pick up along the route where the populists left off. Any real attempt in this direction would, as Henry George saw, first have to break up the monopoly of social initiative enjoyed by corporation capitalists and then assert common rights over the common grounds of social existence. Those would be the starting points for developing a response to the problem of authority more adequate than the Progressive one.

In sum, corporate liberalism contained a facile and inadequate approach to authority. The collapse of the natural rights tradition and simultaneous ascendance of corporate capitalist social organization created a situation in which the dominant schools of American thought saw only two ways of achieving social order: one that led to manipulation and decisionism; the other which led to appeals for cooperation based on the promise of future abundance. The former, as we saw, lacked a real theory of obligation and implied an arbitrary mode of sovereignty. The latter, while embodying a superficial theory of obligation, turns out to have lacked any real principle of action and authorization. This is not to deny that this appeal, like the pragmatist one, had a therapeutic value. But although devoting oneself to practical chores might be distracting, it could not answer underlying questions about the purpose behind the practice. Nor could pursuit of a changing "national interest" reveal a purpose behind the interest. At subsequent periods when political leaders would feel the need for national unity and common purpose, they would turn to the counterfeit of real authority, the oldest substitute for real authority, the creation of an external, all-powerful enemy.

Fashioning social order without God or king was no easy task. Comte knew this when he remarked, uncharacteristically, that life under the positivist patriciate would require "the braving of spiritual terrors." [48] Sumner sensed it as he tried manfully to transform a sense of crushing burdens into a mere sense of duty. But "history" provides no answer to deeper questions. And a high GNP adds little more than Adams's ganoid fish. The image of a future salvation either fails to provide counsel when choice is necessary, or it removes the space needed for real choice in the first place (as in Comte's and Engels's definition of freedom as lying in the recognition of necessity). "History" proceeds, whatever one does. That is why, to take a final example, Erich Fromm was wrong in his introduction to Bellamy's *Looking Backward* when he compared Bellamy's evolutionary faith to the messianic tradition of the Old Testament. [49] The prophets interpreted historical events in order to discern the path of salvation and to assign moral responsibility. Bellamy and the Comtists counted on salvation *by* history, and dissolved questions of morality into matters of lags and gaps. The difference for action is fundamental.

Adams eventually noticed the effect of that difference in himself: "After so many years of effort to find one's drift, the drift found the seeker. . . . He began to mimic Faraday's trick of seeing lines of force all about him where he had always seen lines of will." [50] Adams originally wanted to become "anything but quiet." The corporate liberal order would prove unable to accommodate his desire.

9

Corporativism, the Highest Stage of Capitalism

The world is a great dodger, and Americans the greatest. Because they dodge their very own selves.

—D. H. LAWRENCE

*A*merica is currently involved in a wager, and not for the first time. The first wager was to see whether natural opportunities and independence could be maintained and a producers' democracy established. She lost that. Nor is it the second effort: to see whether she could at least keep class lines fluid, give individuals control over their jobs, and create a culture of solidarity and mutual care. She lost that too. Nor is it the third wager: to see, once the grounds of opportunity and equality had been enclosed, whether she could pass rights grasped by the corporation on to the state for safe-keeping and give the disadvantaged a compensatory claim on the public purse. That too she lost. Now, having lost the space for Lockean freedom, popular politics, and liberal dignity, she faces a new challenge: to see whether she can elicit good behavior and continuing effort from people who are gathered in associations that lack common purpose and fail to provide meaningful work. It is a wager to see whether would-be democrats, increasingly denied a voice in their own affairs and grounds for personal pride, can be kept industrious and obedient through the provision of bread and circuses.

245

In this effort the theory of corporate liberalism provides a powerful support. It persuades where persuasion is possible, corrects older ideas where correction is necessary, and deflects attention from problems it cannot solve. It provides help for the modern Americans' attempts to dodge themselves, as D. H. Lawrence put it. Above all, it tries to reassure a people whose gambling record, as we saw, is not too good. Sometimes this desire for reassurance takes precedence. The claim that votes have established a counterpoise to the power of property, for example, has been defended by arguing that "If this were not so, then industrialization would by its very nature destroy democracy."[1] Such reasoning preserves peace of mind even if it fails to make the point.

We have identified the ideas of representative Progressives in this book in order to examine the core concepts of this new theoretical outlook and discover the logic of contemporary American political culture. The main landmarks of the world behind that culture should be kept in mind as we now draw the diverse lines of our analysis together.

ORGANIZED INDIVIDUALISM

The modern social landscape is occupied by collectives rather than by individuals. Those collectives are organized, however, in line with the requirements of a capitalist society, according to individualist principles. This means, first, that exclusivist and control-oriented forms of wealth-holding are preserved within an organized world. Private property has not been replaced by cooperation, new forms of knowledge, and new strategies for security and dignity; instead, organizational information and institutional positions have come to be seen *as* private commodities. They are hoarded, fenced off, and exchanged for profit, as people attempt to preserve privacy within association, and to assert control over elements of cooperation.

The ascendance of what Follett called "group particularism" means, secondly, the creation of arrangements of hierarchy, privilege, and dependence which are reminiscent of the worst features of medieval corporatism. American society is increasingly an administered society. In fact, its hierarchical character becomes more pronounced—with command increasingly replacing consent—as it is slowly drained of voluntarist means for producing political unity out of its differences.

The ascendance of this form of organization means, finally, that America becomes a polity in which the enjoyment of public, constitutional rights is dependent upon one's attachment to private, secondary associations. For the new lines of administration have not emerged from any statist or technocratic planning organ. They have arisen, as McConnell and Lowi observed, from a plethora of private associations that possess the power to shape their environs. As the corporations annex the powers of an increasingly executive state to help them in their private efforts, the nation approaches the European corporativism of the twenties. It also begins to fulfill Goldsmith's definition of a republic as "a society in which the laws govern the poor and the rich govern the laws." The product of it all is a drastic alteration of the world in which Americans traditionally imagined themselves. Free competition presumed a context that was not itself competition. But small businessmen and farmers now discover what working people and ethnic minorities found out in the last century: corporate interests can become powerful enough to rig the game and shape the field of common effort.

The first thing that strikes the observer of American society is this high degree of large-scale organization. But this "synchronization" also masks a high degree of *dis*-organization.[2] Economically, the disorganization results from the fact that production is still undertaken by private organizations pursuing selfish ends, blind to the larger grounds and consequences of their activity. Politically, it derives from the fact that the ascendant bureaucracies choke off legitimate conflict, rather than promote its expression and resolution. At the same time we witness the extension of technical rationality and bureaucracy, we therefore also experience greater disorder in our personal lives, and economic instability, along with increasing uses of force in the society. This is to say that the impulse to rational administration is to be understood as both a symptom and a cause of deeper social *ir*rationalities. That impulse is rooted in our primary social institution, and it can be expected to become stronger. Frustrated in its attempt to order realities, it can also be expected, like Taylor's approach, to turn belligerent in an attempt to reconstitute them. Institutions bound together by administrative procedures rather than shared purposes, furthermore, will easily take this belligerence to the point of violence when those procedures are challenged.[3]

Modern American society thus captures the worst of both modern and medieval worlds. Corporatist to its core, it creates mechanistic rather than organic social relations. It forces agglomeration, but without community. It mandates corporatism, but without diversity. It imposes close interdependence, without trust. And it justifies hierarchy without enforcing accountability. The irony is that where medieval society extended the mantle of the common good over obvious heterogeneity, modern society farms out sovereignty over an increasingly homogeneous terrain to private parties.

The mystery is not that our society has developed in these ways; it is that modern liberals have acquiesced so completely in the repudiation of their publicly stated goals. The mystery is that after the collapse of those elements of the Progressive and New Deal program which stressed grassroots activity, pluralism, and experimentalism, liberal ranks should have fractured so easily—one part retreating to private life, another trying to stand on the fast-eroding ground of due-process formalism, and the vast majority leaping aboard Norris's "leviathan with a heart of steel" in order to help steer. In the last four chapters we discovered why things have fallen out this way. We found that the mid-century liberal was not who we had taken him to be. We can restate the key elements of modern liberal identity here.

Following the course of events, corporate liberal theory has proposed that the place in American thought which used to be filled by "the individual" should now be taken over by the group—and the group as a functional unit. Instead of a genuine interest-group theory, it has therefore assumed fundamental industrial harmony. Like classical liberalism, it has also ended by absorbing politics into economics. Having fenced in the space for the liberal project, modern liberalism then offered a trade: "equality of opportunity" for equality; bureaucratic regularity for liberty; and consumer goods for the dignity of important work. In place of a meaningful life it offered a higher standard of living. It came to grips with the bourgeois contradiction between formal equality and substantive inequality by resolving it in favor of the latter. And in place of a security which was always illusory for workers and small farmers, it now offers a security which is illusory for white-collar workers and small businessmen as well.[4]

The terms of this bargain have been sweetened by the redefinition of reason that we traced in Chapter Six. Having accepted the fact that political norms find their bases in practical experience, modern liberalism, instead of pressing for the extension of that experience as Dewey first urged, reduces norms to current activity as officially interpreted. "Rationality," having been hollowed out, is then recast into formal terms and treated as the achievement of objective institutions. Bureaucratic rationality replaces individual reason. Despite the early pragmatists' affinities with Marxism, this rationality resembles Hegel's in that it comes into the world from above. But unlike Hegel's, it regards questions about justice or injustice as irrelevant. Once morality is equated with arbitrary habit, the important consideration is not justice but order.

The positive state is presented as the guardian of this new order. It also emerges more silently as the ethical grounding for that order. And having avoided any new principles of legitimacy, the new liberalism forsakes older liberal attempts to create an absolute sovereign who would refrain from becoming arbitrary as well.

Regarding the private power this state is supposed to monitor, modern liberalism reveals a divided mind. It argues simultaneously that private power is nonexistent and that it is necessary. It is said to be nonexistent because the interest of one group is balanced by that of the others, and because the defeat of the populist concept of monopoly has also obscured the fact that private decisions can have binding public consequences. At the same time the exercise of power is said to be necessary because people need it. The personal qualities it takes to coordinate the factors of modern organizational society are, it is said, regrettably scarce. The way to solve problems—Rousseau and Tocqueville notwithstanding—is not to invite a participatory free-for-all; it is to assign the problems to those with special competence. "The people" of nineteenth-century republicanism thus become "the masses" of twentieth-century liberalism.

Current American liberalism, like European Social Democratic thought or structuralism in sociology, thus jumps quickly over the gap that separates concentrated economic power from the public-interest state. It attempts to mask the gap and reassure the masses by arguing that the elites are restrained by the rules of the game (David Truman), or that they are restrained by a post-Lockean form of competition (the pluralists and early Galbraith); or by the fact that the elites express only functional divisions within an integrated industrial framework (Kerr and the later Galbraith); by "a compensatory reaction [that keeps] property tenure conditioned on the performing of a service" (Harbrecht); or simply by the actions of a regulatory state (the whole chorus).[5] These arguments were invented, of course, before the oil companies multiplied their toll on all who use the highways. Despite their large numbers and massive funding, the political scientists who voice these claims have so far failed to discover the law that was so obvious to James Harrington, John Taylor, and Henry George. This was the law that power always followed property.

In all of these ways industrial hierarchy has been squared with equality, and monopoly made to lie down with popular sovereignty. But not all of the elements of the classical theory find adequate expression in this synthesis, and not all modern problems find resolution in it. We have discussed the failure of the new political theory to offer an adequate principle of authority.

The problem of representation posed by corporatism has also been ignored. The liberal strategy of representation, unlike medieval constitutionalism, made no place for corporate entities. The classical liberal saw no justification for giving a few people a political voice equal to that of thousands of their neighbors, for permitting a few well-organized groups to define the public interest, or for officially predetermining "the interests that individuals ought to endorse."[6] Nor is it presently clear how such things would be defended. Perhaps this is why the debates about different forms of representation (functional, proportional, and geographical) that agitated the twenties have been absent from more recent political literature.

Nor has there been any legitimation for the power that corporations actually wield.[7] Nor, finally, has there been a modern translation of the central concern of the classical liberals with providing means for the expression of individual initiative. This is partly because corporate organization has a stake in preventing such initiative, and partly because the modern silence on authority means that many Americans are not sure what they have lost.

The more democratic, grassroots gropings of Progressive thought have been confounded, sidetracked, and defeated. The challenge of the sociological jurists to make bourgeois rights more effective has been dropped. The attempt to define a positive liberty has been abandoned. The realization that purposive interests stand behind law and knowledge has not stimulated empirical inquiry into the structure of contemporary interests. The will to strip the veils from private power and the willingness to accept the responsibilities of political choice have both collapsed.

The liberalism whose evolution we have charted in these pages trusts in the good intentions of the powerful. Blinded by their systems utopia, its practitioners have blamed endemic irrationalities on outside sources and on those who don't fit in. By the last quarter of the twentieth century, it is not surprising that corporate liberals turn out to have more in common with the conservatives they initially fought than with those who cling to the older promises of consent, equality, and the rights of individual reason. Modern administrators turn out to have more in common with corporate businessmen than with the ordinary citizens in their domains. Woodrow Wilson had in fact always been closer to William Graham Sumner than to Tom Watson; Herbert Croly had always been closer to Auguste Comte than to Henry George.

That the inadequacies of the new theory have not been more unsettling is due to the implicit doctrine of inevitability, the dark underside of the religion of progress. Inevitability is the last refuge of the corporate liberal. For when "nothing is any longer good or bad, but only either premature or out of date" (in Camus's words), the place for politics, for choice, for approval or disapproval, disappears. The way things are is accepted as the only way they could be. With this assumption the painful secret of the entire era is revealed: a people that claims to possess unrivaled instruments of power knows itself to be abjectly powerless. In fact, however, a choice exists today about how modern collectives are going to be organized. We know that the modern age is one of combination. The critical question is how our combinations are going to be organized. Will it be as democratic publics, as functional groups, or as crystallizations of that hierarchy and privilege that Americans first spurned as a species of Toryism (and then of "Prussianism," and more recently of Russian-ism)? The assumption of a linear course of progress, however, also obscures this central choice.

The irony is that this doctrine of inevitability has emerged in a world that promised the fulfillment of free will. The Ishmaels of corporate America may want to rethink the free-market model at this point.

MODERN THEORY APPLIED

Corporate liberal assumptions have become so widely accepted that they are often confused with reality itself. It would be impossible to escape them, however, without first recognizing them—impossible to escape them by proposing only partial reconceptualizations or minor practical reforms. To understand the costs of failing to acknowledge the larger theory, it is helpful in conclusion to look more closely at three powerful works of recent political analysis on which we have often depended in this study: Grant McConnell's *Private Power and American Democracy*, Theodore Lowi's *The End of Liberalism*, and Michael Reagan's *The Managed Economy*. To reflect on the conclusions offered by these books is to acquire an education in the unexpected effects of hidden assumptions.

Grant McConnell addressed the place of private associations in American society. Such "small constituencies" had originally been valued because they were private, autonomous, voluntary, and had limited goals. But McConnell demonstrated how, over the course of the nation's history, they had extended their claims until they eventually captured formal segments of state power and metamorphized into private governments themselves. In the process they not only succeeded in building their own power, but also in fragmenting political authority, and in losing the qualities that once made them legitimate.[8] McConnell's proposal to control them and to unify and revitalize American politics was to strengthen the "national constituency". He proposed that "The party system, the Presidency and the national government as a whole represent . . . tendencies" opposed to fragmentation; "to a very great degree, policies serving the values of equality and liberty are the achievement of these [national] institutions."[9]

Lowi, for his part, saw interest groups at the heart of modern American politics. Primary social coordination had shifted from "self-regulation through economics to self-regulation through politics"; the only thing that now distinguished the two political parties from each other was their commitment to different sets of interests. The systematic infiltration of interest groups into the interior processes of government had produced the corporativist polity we observed in Chapter One. And Lowi sharpened familiar criticisms by challenging modern liberals in their central pretensions. They had fashioned a state which could not plan, could not really administer, could not discipline itself to democratic forms, and could not prevent "alienation of the public domain—the gift of sovereignty to private satrapies."[10]

Like McConnell, Lowi also recommended improved coordination and organization at the federal level. His program of "juridical democracy" consisted of restoring the rule of law by preventing improper delegations of legislative authority, strengthening and clarifying rules, and creating a "truly independent" administrative class. In the last paragraph of his book he looked to the Supreme Court to point the way toward a more adequate political theory.[11]

The Managed Economy took its bearings from the modern social commitment to planning. Michael Reagan saw that commitment emerging clearly in the Full Employment Act of 1946, which he described on his first page. For Reagan writing in 1963, however, the triumph of *public* planning was not a foregone conclusion. We have seen that he regarded modern "private enterprise" as "a politico-economic system in which each private group seeks to direct public policy to the improvement of its competitive position, share of national income, or bargaining power. . . . The private elements in the system lie in the insistence by business that in return for public benefits, no limitations be placed upon resultant profits or managerial discretion."[12]

Looking beyond the New Frontier, Reagan saw three possible roads for America. The first was one along which corporations would extend their influence and the public controls on them would weaken. Reagan saw fascism at the end of this course. He defined fascism as domination by a single institution of all areas of social life; or, more specifically, as "rule by an industrial elite exercising paternal control . . . over govern-

ment and people, but lacking reciprocal controls."[13] The second road
was one on which corporations would be restricted to purely economic
functions and public controls on them could be diminished. That route,
though consistent with the traditional theory of the firm, would be "dis-
cordant" with present-day managerial practices and thought.

The third option was that the corporations' social and political
power would continue to grow and that means of public accountability
would also be increased. Reagan preferred the second of these options
but predicted that the third would be chosen. He warned, however, that
a drift toward the first was not wholly fanciful, for it already had strong
roots in practice and ideology: "Notions of a 'better business climate,' of
corporate trusteeship and the corporate conscience . . . of, in short, private enterprise as the end of social action rather than a means of supply-
ing goods—these are all indications of the trend."[14]

The question before American society for Reagan was a variant of
the populists' question. It was whether "ways can be found by which a
new base for personal independence and popular power can be created"
in the new conditions. Reagan thought he saw such a base at the con-
vergence of three phenomena: the creation of new forms of property
("property in one's job"), the increase of voting, and the new allocation
of public resources.[15] But he admitted that this base was still weak, and
he looked more immediately—and in a more Progressive vein—toward
better government organization and coordination in order to implement
reforms. Like McConnell he concluded that "the keys to improved popular control of the government lie in the party system and the use we
make of the presidency."[16]

The three analyses agreed, then, that modern American government was fragmented, accountability obscured, overview diffused, and
politics itself often debased and corrupted. All three went beyond the
narrow-gauge concerns of mainstream political science to address questions of structure and culture. Thus McConnell and Reagan raised questions about the enjoyment of constitutional rights *within* corporations,
even acknowledging that "economic democracy would be incomplete if
we were to achieve popular control over the society-wide effects of corporate decisions, while the internal government of each industrial unit
remained autocratic."[17] And Lowi's insistence on the distinction between law and policy, and his concern for justice, restored classical
themes to American political discourse.

And yet, powerful as these analyses were, the conclusions to which
they led were strangely muted and familiar. Indeed, they expressed that
social formalism whose origins we described. Looking primarily to a

strengthened federal system and a stronger presidency, they failed to examine the structures of private power and the larger social formations in which federal institutions are rooted. Looking to implement rational plans at the federal level, they failed to appreciate the effects of the structured irrationalities they themselves identified. Indeed, none of the proposals really moved beyond the terms Wilson pioneered in his *Constitutional Government* of 1908 and Croly in his *Promise of American Life* of a year later.

Faced with the depredations of powerful interests, Wilson and Croly had also turned their guns on improper delegations of legislative authority, the lack of strong leadership, and poor institutional coordination. They, too, had identified the federal government as the agent of national recovery (the Hamiltonian means needed for Jeffersonian ends). As for them, the presidency appears to contemporary analysts as the unique representative of the whole nation, the parties appear as proper means for binding interests together, and the Court appears as the tool for preventing Congress from farming out the commons.[18] Nor have the revelations of the Vietnam era, the events of Watergate, or the advent of several second-rate presidents in any way dimmed the commitment to this paradigm in the years since McConnell and Lowi offered their prescriptions.

The best of modern analysts thus reveal the influence of the new political theory when they turn from diagnosis to remedy. They become silent on the issue of power. They assume that the capitalist organization of collective effort is unalterable. They ignore the *quality* of our collective goals. And the whole twentieth-century strategy of evading substantive judgments is captured in a continuing preference for formalistic categories—big units versus small, formal procedures versus informal, authorized delegations versus unauthorized.

But would tighter regulation of a society constituted and directed by private collectivisms take us where we want to go? And would sharper statutory definitions of "public interest" enable our regulatory agencies to regulate? No one who reads the newspapers could believe it.[19] To acknowledge these questions, however, would be to admit that private powers strong enough to. penetrate congressional committees are also strong enough to penetrate a better-organized Executive edifice—a truth known to the nineteenth century but ignored by the twentieth-century consensus. (The fate of the Full Employment Act of 1946 itself illustrates the cost of that exclusion.)[20]

Even if it were possible to claim that General Motors and the military-industrial complex are small units (which they are not), it would remain the case that these associations and others like them arose historically not because people confused them with other pluralist bodies, like units of local government or of agrarian democracy, as McConnell suggests. They emerged only after bitter and prolonged struggle *against* such bodies. And their aggrandizing power followed not from their smallness, nor from their privateness per se, but from the substantive character of their power—its business character. But part of the modern refusal to engage in a systematic discussion of power is a refusal to acknowledge the sustained presence and effect of capitalist institutions.

In order to combat the perfectly logical effects of these organizational units it would not be enough, as Reagan suggests, to "balance new forms of power with new forms of accountability."[21] It would be necessary to balance them with new forms of *power*. To get away from the administrative informality that Lowi laments, it would be necessary to prevent private interests from exercising an influence over public offices. And to inject a cogent "public interest" into weak regulatory laws it would be necessary to develop institutions that enabled people to participate actively in politics and thereby *create* a public interest in the first place.

To deal with the threats to democracy that McConnell, Lowi, and Reagan identify, in other words, it would be necessary to *constitute* a power that could stand against the interests which have created those problems. But to consider this is to move beyond current perspectives and confront the need for other ways for thinking about liberty, reason, and national purpose. It is to raise questions avoided by modern analyses—questions about power, membership, obligation, and the character of political action in a democracy.

CORPORATE LIBERALISM OR LIBERAL CORPORATISM?

Let us return to the question posed at the beginning. Is the theory whose evolution we have followed a corporate species of liberalism or a liberal species of corporatism?

It is tempting to see modern American political thought as a variant of the corporatism that emerged in Europe during the twenties. But despite the increasingly group character of life, Americans have developed no explicit justifications of corporatist relations. There is nothing similar to the German view of the thirties in which the corporation was seen as a "social institution"—the central locus of identity, loyalty, and community.[22] Nor has there been any overt acceptance of corporatist principles of representation, nor of a command economy. "Decisionism" has thrived only in flashes of crisis management or in the dark of nonrecognition. A lingering concern for "the rule of law" and the remnants of constitutionalism have so far also prevented the emergence of a leader or movement that would sweep the laws aside. Men like Walter Lippmann or Woodrow Wilson (or later, General MacArthur) might occasionally call for a leader who could embody a translegal national will; but such calls enjoyed only brief vogue.

More deeply, the elaboration of a new outlook in America has involved little of the hostility toward liberal values that was so prominent with European corporatism. There has been no striving for an ethic of mutuality and no rejection of bourgeois egotism, few critiques of the contract model for social relations, and fewer admissions that property is communal in origins, depending ultimately on reciprocal relations rather than fences for its security. "That the life of the individual acquired significance not by 'the self-governing resistance of the ego to the world' but by participation in the collective endeavor of mankind . . . which Europe knew by tragic experience, had not become part of the American tradition," Henry Bamford Parkes wrote at mid-century.[23]

Our managers wish us to avoid the pleasures of direct interaction in our organizations, preferring impersonality and bureaucratic indirection. Croly's hope that familiarity would breed community has proven groundless as American social engineers, following Sumner and Taylor, have sought a positivism far stricter than Comte's. Modern social thought thus finds its central problem in the attempt to explain a reality paradoxically constituted of objective organizations but experienced by isolated subjects. This theoretical puzzle concedes the practical truth, already noted, that the organizations in which we find ourselves are shot through with the logic of privatism. They succeed in preserving not only scarcity within abundance but also selfishness within association.

But to acknowledge this balked corporatism is not to sign a clean bill of health for the liberal element of the mix. That element is diminished and weakened, both in practice and in theory. In practice, those arrangements which underlie a functioning individualism but were never acknowledged by classical liberal theory—a stable community, free opportunities, dependable social relations, a sense of limits—have now begun to be destroyed by the workings of corporate capitalism. A political culture which had always reasoned as if community, tradition, family, and morality made no difference, now finds them disappearing in fact. The result, as the evidence of random violence, mental disorientation, and family instability attest, turns out not to be individualism at all, but an aimless, often wrathful search for identity.

Theoretically, as we have seen, we have ceased to hold a clear concept of individualism even as we cling to an individualist mode of thought. We lack an intellectual defense for individual rights.[24] We lack a theory of autonomous will in an organized world. And we lack a substitute for the older idea of consent—at least since the brief call in the sixties for participatory democracy. This failure to develop a new theory of individualism, to translate what was valuable in classical liberalism into modern terms, is attributable not simply to the hold of old ideas but to the fact that the organizations in which Americans find themselves prevent an understanding that freedom may exist in participation (indeed, Tocqueville said, *only* in participation), and that strength may be nurtured by particular forms of membership.

Our current intellectual commitment remains, then, on balance "liberal." But the fact that deserves attention is the degree to which that commitment has been compromised.

Up to this point we have looked at this compromise as a response to the pressure of the corporation. But it is also instructive to see the theoretical shift as part of the internal evolution of our political theory. For twentieth-century American thought is a chapter not only in the unfolding story of corporatism but also in the continuing story of liberalism. It is a chapter in which liberalism, forced to acknowledge its shortcomings, tries to do so without giving up its basic approach to the world.

The evolution of modern property has forced hidden elements of the classic bourgeois outlook into the open. An implicit commitment to inegalitarian institutions was one of those things. A defense of private power was another. An obfuscation of political choice was a third. More positively, finally, the demise of Enlightenment beliefs in natural rights led some Progressives to recognize the need for political education.

At the risk of personifying a complex historical process, it is as if liberalism decided to meet these challenges halfway. Forced to acknowledge the inescapability of political power, it declined to set priorities for choice and to fashion new institutions, and instead fell back on a group model of competition. Forced to acknowledge human interdependence, it moved only so far as to admit the impersonal coordination of administrative relations. Compelled to confess the political immaturity of natural man, it retreated from a theory of political education to accept the image of the passive consumer in a mass society. It accepted the positive state, but doubted the possibility of a public interest. It accepted association but retained an individualist ethics. It accepted the civil bases of law, but remained complacent about the distribution of power in civil society.

What we see is a political outlook attempting to deal with fundamental challenges without giving up its central assumptions—a collectivist outlook that remains markedly liberal in the way it perceives the world and frames its choices. This outlook still sees social existence as divided between subjective desires and objective order, between the needs for free expression and possessory control. There has been no transcendence of the characteristic polarities of the liberal problematic. Rather, a changed reality has led modern thinkers to emphasize the opposite pole from that of their predecessors. Modern administrators may therefore be expected to become increasingly rigid in their attempts to achieve, through complex engineering, the social coordination necessary for the interaction of large conglomerates. Having no respect for participation, refusing to alter their basic view of social order, and having lost their faith in "the standpoint of the subject," they can be expected to become increasingly objectivist, decisionist, and impositional in their programs.

For those on the receiving end of these programs, corporate liberalism seems to produce a divided mind. They sense that the new view is not complete, so they cling to elements from the past. For the individual citizen the cost of this double vision is a certain loss of honesty. His individualism becomes a thing of style, an act of will. Crowded cheek by jowl with neighbors and co-workers, the would-be loner refuses to acknowledge the webs of cooperation on which he is dependent and declines to take responsibility for them. He lives in bad faith with himself and appears an ingrate to others.

For the society at large, the cost of this split personality is the loss of a chance to make the corporation into an organization responsible to those who work for it and accountable to those whose lives are affected by it, a loss of the chance to make collective enterprise into an expression of people's wills rather than a barrier to them.

Though acceptance of this new political theory is widespread, we can see that different parts of the population therefore subscribe to it in different ways. Those at the corporate and administrative heights see it as most natural and consistent; they are the least troubled by its costs; the ruling ideas of the age are their ideas. Those in the middle have become masters of cognitive dissonance; they use bits and pieces of the old vocabulary to manipulate others even while subscribing to the new outlook themselves. Those at the bottom and at the margins, defeated in past attempts to chart a different course, confused by rapid change, hopeful that official promises will reward their pains, usually express not a consistent attitude but a fitful migration between different outlooks. For all of these groups the contradictions seem negotiable—until crises arise. Then, while some try belatedly to develop a new synthesis and others retire into resentful confusion, those at the top reach for their premises. The real character of modern political thought is revealed at this point.

The past twenty years have thus seen an entire generation of avowed liberals become "the true conservatives of our time." [25] Men respected for their previous stands on civil liberties and civil rights have suddenly revealed the intolerance, the lack of compassion, and the reliance on force as a substitute for authority that were always associated with conservatism. In important areas of public policy during the last twenty years, we have seen very little of the flexibility and experimentalism normally attributed to liberalism.

If it was a one-time college radical who first called troops onto an American campus to quash an eminently liberal struggle for free speech, if it was an influential body of advisers to the Democratic Party that doubted the suitability of democracy for advanced industrial nations, it was not, then, because the blood had slowly cooled in their and their supporters' veins. It was not because their minds had hardened in unconscious obedience to Clemenceau's maxim that he who was not a radical in his youth had no heart, and he who failed to become a conservative in his old age had no head. It was because they were playing out their *kind* of liberalism to its end. There was no apostasy here—only a practical education in the ramifications of inarticulate major premises.

The charge, in other words, is not that our official spokesmen have failed to be real liberals. The point is not to deny their membership in a historical movement that sought to check the anarchy of entrepreneurial capitalism, eliminate social irrationalities, clear the way for merit, establish procedural fairness, increase the industrial product, and extend the bureaucratic regime. Nor is it to deny that these leaders and social scientists have been perfectly liberal toward those who agreed with them, and toward the younger instrumentalists in their train.

But if one lacked the faith that profit-oriented production which violates social needs in the short run would fulfill them in the long run, if one's notion of rationality was not defined by functionality, if one had difficulty trimming social relations to administrative rules, and if one's grievances were prompted by the injustices rather than the inefficiencies of modern society, then something other than tolerance turned out to be in order. The classical liberal did not want to deal with fundamental questions in the first place. The corporate liberal can afford the exercise even less. He has no tools for the job. He suspects that his claims lack the universality of the older values. He lacks the confidence of the classical bourgeois and the faith of the utilitarian. *He* is doing well enough, he tells himself; his benefits have been earned. Boxed in by his premises, confused by the challenges to his conclusions, the corporate liberal turns against the world. His reason becomes a weapon. No longer a means for clarifying ideas and reorganizing procedures, empiricism becomes aggressive. Critics must be silenced not because answers have been found, but because premises must be established. Occam's Razor must do some trimming. Hence the impulse to deny politics in the corporate era. Hence liberalism also winds up repudiating its own values: free opportunities are replaced by "socializing conditions," laws by executive orders, rights by duties, morality by police, and citizens, finally, by subjects. For "form is nothing when substance is gone," as the populists saw clearly a century ago.

BEYOND LIBERALISM

This was not the only way things could have developed. No matter how comforting the claim of inevitability may be for decision-makers, it remains nothing more than a claim. Other grammars were possible in the vocabulary of American politics, other alternatives linked to other commitments in the world. The populists groped toward the more democratic of these alternatives. In their cooperatives and local activities, they struggled to preserve the classical liberal commitments to voluntarism, consent, and equality, though now translated for use in a world of organization. They sustained the older animosity toward "practical Toryism" and preserved the sense that democracy, in the first instance, was a quality of social relations rather than of formal institutions. The attempt to hold fast to these elements of liberalism forced them paradoxically to alter their ideas about individualism, liberty, and ownership, and to begin a hesitant rediscovery of pre-liberal concerns for the commons, for mutual cooperation, and for the place of politics in society.

Even after these populist roots were cut back, new democratic tendrils continued to reach out during Progressivism. The various revolts against formalism that we have mentioned, the struggles for labor and free speech, the recognition of positive forms of political action—all these revealed concerns continuous with the democratic part of American traditions.

Any effort to move beyond classical liberalism without following the corporate liberal course would require a rediscovery of these roots. The current problem is not, as some have suggested, to make the present corporation legitimate; it is to refashion the corporation into a kind of association that can earn people's democratic loyalties. Nor is the problem to create a "new property" and zone of privacy, to redraw the "boundary between public and private power," as Charles Reich urged. While it is true that America must find new ways of assuring a person's "rightful share in the commonwealth," and establish a new economic basis for personal liberty, the mechanism of property is too closely tied to principles of privacy and exclusivity to accomplish these things adequately in modern conditions.[26] We need a new, cooperative status, different from the one which was traditionally approximated by private property.

The choice at present is not between an inevitable twentieth-century corporatism and a renewed nineteenth-century individualism. It is a choice between different *forms* of association. The practical problem is to find a way to make our dominant organizations into vehicles (in Henry George's words) of liberty and union. The deeper cultural problem is to forge a strategy for freedom and dignity fundamentally different from that which distinguished the bourgeois era. For the attempt to acquire a place in the world through private, physical control of the environment and of other people is an expression of profound hubris; it is also ultimately an exercise in futility. Liberal freedom is not only often negligent of the freedom of others; it is now clear that it is also incapable over the long run of sustaining itself. The flight from the commons, in escaping the responsibility for maintaining the grounds of liberty, has turned out to be a flight from liberty itself. The twentieth century offers many proofs of this. The history of modern totalitarianism, for example, is also the history of failed liberal attempts to find freedom by forsaking the public and retreating to a zone of privacy. Good fences have *not*, in fact, made good neighbors.

Any alternative to the outlook we have described in this book will require a reshaping of our institutions. But that reshaping will require a change in the ways we think about politics; indeed, the institutional reforms could not be enacted on a lasting basis without such a theoretical reorientation. The bases for a democratic reorientation are clear from the furtive beginnings and errant insights we have also noted in these pages.

At the heart of a new political theory must be a concept of positive freedom like the one suggested by the populists and some Progressives—a concept that reverses the trend of liberal thought over the last three centuries, and directs attention back toward participation and mutual interdependence as the stable and fertile grounds of personal identity. We might do well to rediscover the old truth that what we are free to do depends on what we share with others.[27]

Following from this is also the need for a notion of consent ("union") that goes beyond a consumer's right to choose between preformed options and recognizes the importance of people's participation in the original shaping of options.[28] A third element of any new democratic theory would be a new concept of equality. This would have to avoid the identification of equality with mathematical equivalence, as Dewey warned and modern businessmen continually remind us. But it would also have to avoid the deceptive attractions of "equality of opportunity" in order to shape an egalitarianism that took its bearings from the need for social reciprocity.

Once American political culture grasps the fact that it lacks not only the guidance of a mythic natural law but also of a mythic technological "progress," it will be necessary to resuscitate the early pragmatist emphasis on "action"—on a constitutive, innovative form of activity. And as preparation for this action, finally, a modern democratic theory would have to rediscover the fleeting Progressive insight that democratic citizens are made, not born. It would have to recognize the necessity of providing a political education, and of an active sort. In fact, a modern democrat would evaluate participation (*or* representation) by considering the political education it provides, not by pointing to the accountability it affords or the efficient decision-making it helps or hinders.

More deeply, the achievement of these theoretical reformulations will require decisive breaks with fundamental casts of the liberal mind. It will require the development of a vision of the world as something other than objective field populated by private individuals or private groups (as we discovered in Chapter Five). It will also require the making of judgments about the substance and the ends of power, the setting of ethical standards, the making of qualitative distinctions. It will require, that is, a departure from the formalistic impulse that has characterized liberalism from the beginning, whether it was expressed in the proceduralism of Madison, the positivism of the Progressives, or the reliance on reformed national institutions by modern reformers.

I argued in the discussion of pragmatism that the modern epistemological dependence on laboratory controls followed only after the acceptance of certain prior assumptions, and that those assumptions run parallel to the logic of the contemporary social order. It is intriguing that the work of Charles Saunders Peirce actually presented two different concepts of objectivity. A comparison of them helps clarify the social implications of the choice that was ultimately made between them.

The first idea was of objectivity as a quality of a pre-existing, external order—or at least as a quality of results obtained from a pre-existing, external set of verifying techniques. The second idea of objectivity saw it as the ultimate *achievement* of inter-subjective reason. ("The opinion which is fated to be ultimately agreed to by all who investigate is what we mean by the truth.")[29] The first view saw objectivity as something ultimately imposed, something to which individual consciousness had to adjust itself. The second view saw objectivity as the evolving product of a consensus among different consciousnesses. The contrast between the two is identical to the contrast Follett made between a social harmony that resulted from "absorption" and one that resulted from "the law of interpenetration." It was the first view that triumphed in Peirce's work and in Progressivism as a whole, and that led Holmes and the others to seek order through "social control," strategies of domination, and—as the modern world reveals—a bootless chase after control at ever-higher levels of disorder.

The adoption of the second idea requires a fundamentally different attitude than that adopted during Progressivism. It requires a recognition that reliability and dependability in knowledge—as well as reliability, dependability, and freedom in social relations—arise only from particular forms of social cooperation, from continuing interdependence. That is to say that if a democratic kind of "objectivity" were to be created, it could only be because a great deal of care were taken to preserve the grounds for continuing interdependence. It could not be because bits of wealth or terrain were successfully controlled. Neither could it be because hollow administrative procedure had been successfully imposed. Any authoritative standards in the ongoing struggle for democracy and any standards from which a democratic form of obligation could be derived, would have to be standards worthy of people's shared commitments, and helpful in the pursuit of the objects of those commitments. Social order is something that beckons, not something that can be owned or imposed.

The political institution capable of sustaining this shared pursuit and of promoting a "collective *self*-control" has been called by such diverse thinkers as Tocqueville, Dewey, Hannah Arendt, and C. Wright Mills a "public."[30] Such association, like Tocqueville's township, invites participation, provides education, grants power over matters that affect its members' lives, and promotes accountability. It is an agency of shared voluntarism. How a society could ever talk about a public interest without having first established such a body as a functioning organization is hard to imagine.

But in pursuing this line of thought we again encounter another association, one that opposes the public and pre-empts the grounds for its existence. This is the corporation, our own *imperio in imperium*—a private state which has grown, as the founders feared, until it finally dwarfs the public state in which it was nurtured. To successfully establish real publics it would be necessary not merely to redistribute income, and not merely to "regulate" corporations which had assumed the right to speak in the name of the people. It would be necessary to remold this organization in order to create a way of constituting social life that would enable people to speak in their own name.

American thought was always said to be Lockean. But Locke provides no answers to the sorts of questions that have been raised in this century. If we insist on addressing those questions without leaving the framework of liberalism, we must be remanded to a prior court. And behind Locke stands Thomas Hobbes, a man prepared to deal with fundamental questions. Behind William James and John Dewey similarly stand Oliver Wendell Holmes, Jr., and Frederick Winslow Taylor. "Our system's sole claim to virtue is that it exists." "In the past the man was first; in the future the system will be first." These are the dicta of corporate liberalism.

So far, this thought has stopped short of an explicit embrace of corporativism. Can that theoretical embrace be expected to follow? If we can predict the future as Henry Adams did, by triangulating from points in the past, and if we take practical developments seriously, then we can answer with an undoubting "yes"—at least for those parts of the society with a stake in corporate capitalism.

But if for classical liberalism the phrases went beyond deeds, for corporate liberalism these deeds still go beyond phrases. And the prospect of an explicit renunciation of democratic principles poses the task for the rest of the society, in addition to challenging the corporation, of moving intellectually beyond "organized individualism" and a scientistic view of social reason. It requires that we develop a political theory which helps us to understand power in our society, helps us see that freedom is a product of cooperation, and helps us to create an alternative to the corporativist state as the guarantor of popular sovereignty.

Notes

Complete author's names, titles, and publication data are given in the Selected Bibliography, pp. 337–346. Works not listed in the Bibliography are cited in full when they first occur in the Notes.

CHAPTER ONE

Epigraph: Charles Reich, "The New Property," *Yale Law Review*, LXXIII, No. 3 (April 1964), p. 771.

1. F. W. Taylor, *The Principles of Scientific Management*, p. 7.

2. Holmes, in *Abrams v. U.S.* 250 U.S. 616 (1919): "The ultimate good desired is better reached by free trade in ideas. . . . The best test of truth is the power of the thought to get itself accepted in the competition of the market." Sheldon Wolin discusses the sublimation of politics into economics in the last chapter of *Politics and Vision.*

3. Christopher Lasch, *The New Radicalism in America, 1889–1963*, p. 147.

4. "The mark of the liberal [is] his assumption that the instruments of government provide the means for conscious inducement of social change, and that without the capacity for such change no experimentation with new institutional forms would be possible" (Theodore Lowi, *The End of Liberalism*, p. 56).

5. Arthur Schlesinger, Jr., *The Age of Jackson* (Boston: Little, Brown and Co., 1945), p. 505. Eric Goldman, *Rendezvous with Destiny*, pp. 5, 19–22, 325–344. Having noted the confusion surrounding the term, Goldman himself chose simply to refer to "the liberalism of the seventies," "of the twenties," and so on.

6. M. Fainsod, L. Gordon, and J. Palamountain, *Government and the American Economy*, 3rd ed. (New York: W. W. Norton and Co., 1959), p. xi.

7. Walter Lippmann, *Drift and Mastery*, p. 126.

8. Richard Hofstadter, *The Age of Reform*, pp. 14–15.

9. Nathan Glazer, *Remembering the Answers* (New York: Basic Books, 1970), p. 3.

10. Louis Hartz, *The Liberal Tradition in America*, p. 8.

11. John Kirby, in Robert Wiebe, *Businessmen and Reform*, p. 18.

12. Adolph Berle, "Economic Power and the Free Society," in Andrew Hacker, *The Corporation Take-Over*, p. 100. Lowi, "How the Farmers Get What They Want."

13. Charles Reich, "The New Property," p. 771. Huey Newton, *The Black Panther*, Vol. V, No. 30 (January 30, 1971).

14. The growth of an unexpected "informalism" in administration is a major theme in Lowi, *The End of Liberalism*, Ch. 5.

15. "Private enterprise is ceasing to be free enterprise and is becoming a cluster of private collectivisms." FDR as cited in Hofstadter, *The Age of Reform*, p. 341; Anthony Jay, *Management and Machiavelli*, p. 225.

16. Henry Adams, *The Education*, pp. 421, 499. Adams himself placed causal emphasis on the "force" rather than the corporation.

17. Alexis de Tocqueville, *Democracy in America*, I, p. 6.

18. Peter Drucker, *The Concept of the Corporation*, pp. 19, 21.

19. Andrew Hacker, *The Corporation Take-Over*, p. 268. Robert Presthus, *The Organizational Society* (New York: Random House, 1962), pp. 16, 136–137, 164.

20. Garry Wills, *Nixon Agonistes*, p. 176.

21. Walton Bean, *California: An Interpretive History* (New York, McGraw-Hill Book Co., 1973), 2nd ed., p. 240.

22. Miller is cited in Howard Jay Graham, "An Innocent Abroad: The Constitutional Corporate Person," p. 158. Judge A. P. McCormick of Texas and Everett Wheeler are cited in John Noonan, *Persons and Masks of the Law* (New York: Farrar, Strauss and Giroux, 1976), pp. 77, 79.

23. Martin Mayer, *Wall Street: Men and Money* (New York: Harper and Bros., 1955), pp. 33–34.

24. Jay, *Management and Machiavelli*, pp. 17, 10.

25. "The man who picks pockets with a railway rebate, murders with an adulterant instead of a bludgeon . . . and scuttles his town instead of a ship, does not feel on his brow the brand of a malefactor" (E. A. Ross, *Sin and Society*, pp. 7–11). "The essence of the wrongs that infest our articulated society is betrayal rather than aggression" (p. 6). Many commentators have located the ultimate source of this logic of impersonality in market relations themselves, from Thomas Hobbes (*Leviathan*, Ch. 10) to Marx (see especially *Capital*, I, pp. 74–75 on commodity fetishism).

26. C. Wright Mills, *White Collar*, pp. xvii and 226. People who remain unattached to organizations begin to be seen by social scientists, conversely, as irrational and unstable. For an excellent discussion of the group basis of modern "reason," see Michael Rogin, *The Intellectuals and McCarthy*, pp. 18–19.

27. Lowi, *The End of Liberalism*, p. 40. See Presthus, *The Organizational Society*, p. 8, for remarks on the "displacement of value." John Kenneth Galbraith caught a sense of the political significance of this when he spoke about "the revised sequence" between consent and social policy. He declined, however, to trace the weighty implications of the phrase. Galbraith, *The New Industrial State*, Ch. 19.

28. Clark Kerr, *The Uses of the University* (New York: Harvard University Press, 1963), pp. 87–88.

29. Karl Renner, *The Institutions of the Private Law and Their Social Function*, pp. 110 and 87.

30. These terms lack widely accepted meanings. My usage has been suggested by the 1972 *Supplement* to the *Oxford English Dictionary*. In order to preserve important distinctions I have also employed the word "corporativist" to describe the system Philippe Schmitter simply called corporatist ("Modes of Interest Interemediation and Models of Societal Change in Western Europe)." For further definitional remarks, see Brady, *Business as a System of Power*, pp. 45–47 and 56ff; Neumann, *Behemoth*, pp. 228–230; Barker, *Principles of Social and Political Theory*, pp. 39–40; and the essays in *Comparative Political Studies*, X, 1 (April 1977).

31. Berle and Means, *The Modern Corporation and Private Property*, pp. 32–33. Berle, "Economic Power and the Free Society," in Andrew Hacker, *The Corporation Take-Over*, p. 102. Forty-nine banks, acting as primary lenders and trustees, control enough stock to control 150 of these corporations and have representatives on 300 of their boards of directors (Richard Barber, as cited in James O'Conner, *The Corporations and the State*, p. 56). The 1962 statistics are from E. Epstein, *The Corporation in American Politics* (Englewood Cliffs: Prentice Hall), p. 196. Epstein also reported that the Big Three auto makers alone at this time held 8.5 percent of the assets of all the corporations listed in the *Fortune* 500. The 1967 official (and understated) figures showed that about 1000 of the million and a half corporations in the country (.06 percent) owned formally 53 percent of the total assets (*Statistical Abstract of the United States*, 1970, Table 719).

32. "If the firm will sacrifice 'profits' . . . for anything else, whether prestige, good will or labor relations, or a quiet life, or liquidity, or security, or what have you, then it is clearly not maximizing utility" (Kenneth Boulding, in Boulding and Spivey, eds., *Linear Programming and the Theory of the Firm*, New York: Macmillan and Co., 1960, p. 4). See also Galbraith, *The New Industrial State*, pp. 128–136.

33. Berle and Means, *The Modern Corporation*, pp. 347, 355–377; see also pp. 67 and 221.

34. Thurman Arnold quipped that the Baltimore and Ohio Railroad Company no more owned the B. and O. than the U.S. Marine Corps "owned" the U.S. Marines (*The Folklore of Capitalism*, New Haven: Yale University Press, 1961, orig. pub. 1937, pp. 118, 122, 202, 353). In modern conditions people struggle "for rank and power—not property" (p. 304). See also pp. 201–202.

35. Paul Harbrecht, *Pension Funds and Economic Power*, pp. 4 and 285. See also Ben Seligman's "American Corporation: Ideology and Reality," *Dissent* (Summer 1964). The Mills quotations are from *White Collar*, pp. 58, 64–65, 71. Mills asserted that modern America had gone beyond both Marxism and liberalism because "labor is everywhere alienated and small property is no longer an anchor of freedom" (p. xix). The prediction about the rise of a society of "posi-

tion" is firmly rooted in the European Social Democratic tradition. Thus Renner wrote in 1904, in *Private Law*, a person's "rights and duties are closely circumscribed and the 'position' has become a legal [public] institution . . . much like the fee of feudal times." He saw the private contract of employment, for instance, developing into a "position of work and service." He added in 1929: "Even now, more prestige attaches to a position than to property" (pp. 121, 209).

36. Marx, *Capital*, III, Ch. 27. Marx called it "social property" because he felt that capital was ceasing to exist "as the private property of individual producers" and was becoming the "property of the associated producers." He predicted the vast pyramiding of credit arrangements that would envelop real, productive property, and saw in it the precursor of larger social transformations (pp. 427–430).

37. Adam Smith, *The Wealth of Nations*, pp. 134, 137. "People of the same trade rarely meet together . . . but the conversation ends in a conspiracy against the public, or in some contrivance to raise prices. . . . The law . . . ought to do nothing to facilitate such assemblies. . . . [but] a law of incorporation . . . renders them necessary" (p. 137).

38. A foremost student of modern health institutions concludes, "A study of underlying causes shows that hierarchy was already there and that technology strengthened it, not vice versa" (Vicente Navarro, *Medicine Under Capitalism*, Reseda, California: Watson Publishing, 1977, p. 206). A business historian has written: "The initial motives for expansion or combination and vertical integration had not been specifically to lower unit costs or to assure a larger output . . . by efficient administration . . . [but] from the desire to assure more desirable marketing facilities or to have a more certain supply of stocks. . . . Managers continued to think of control of competition as [combination's] primary purpose" (Alfred D. Chandler, cited in David F. Noble, *America by Design*, p. 261; and see Noble's further discussion of the point). A recent study of California agriculture concludes, similarly, that "in contrast to the midwest, farms did not grow larger in order to accommodate bigger machines. In fact the reverse may be true; machines became larger to support the large farm" (Philip LeVeen, "The Prospects for Small-Scale Farming in an Industrial Society," Berkeley, unpublished ms., 1977, p. 10).

On the complex relationship between capitalism and technology, see also Karl Polanyi, *The Great Transformation*, p. 119; Andre Gorz's important "Technical Intelligence and the Capitalist Division of Labor," *Telos*, No. 12 (Summer 1972), pp. 27–41. Andrew Hacker argues that the modern corporation is essentially motiveless in his *The End of the American Era* (New York: Atheneum, 1973), Ch. 3 ("Corporate America"), and his articles in *The New York Review of Books*: "Is There a Ruling Class?" May 1, 1975; and "Cutting Classes," March 4, 1976. Jacques Ellul argued the primacy of technology in *The Technological Society*.

39. Income patterns have remained glacially resistant to change for the last half-century. See Gabriel Kolko, *Wealth and Power in America*, p. 14; and Robert Lekachman, "Redistributing Income: What Works, What Doesn't," *The Nation*,

May 11, 1974. The patterns of wealth, by contrast, reveal a tendency toward increasing concentration. Lester Thurow reports that the top fifth of the population owns three-quarters of the nation's wealth, while the entire bottom *quarter* owns a neglible .2 percent (*New York Times Magazine*, April 11, 1976). In the period of greatest labor activity, furthermore, labor's share of the national income barely changed—from 59 percent in 1929 to 61.5 percent in 1954 (Clark Kerr, in *New Concepts in Wage Determination*, F. Pierson and G. Taylor, eds., New York: McGraw-Hill, 1957, p. 280).

Labor's power has always been defensive (employers having the power to initiate and unions only to respond); and it is now on the decline. Michael Reagan discerned its structural weakness twenty years ago, in *The Managed Economy*, p. 17. Furthermore, far from "constitutionalizing industry," as was claimed at mid-century, labor regulations have never attempted to guarantee First, Fifth, or Sixth Amendment rights (the latter to a speedy and public "trial," e.g., before the NLRB) within the factory, let alone to work out an industrial analogue to Article IV's guarantee to all citizens of a "republican form of government."

40. Franz Neumann, *Behemoth*, pp. 312, 361. Behind all the claims about administered pricing, one suspects Saint-Simon's nineteenth-century vision of a rationalized society.

41. Thus Michael Reagan wrote: "In the twentieth century, business promotion has been the direct goal of many measures usually thought of as 'regulatory.' The Transportation Act of 1920, the subsidies of the Civil Aeronautics Act," as well as railroad, oil, and sugar legislation evidence this. "Each of these measures, while ostensibly protecting or enhancing the public's interests, has the effect of promoting and enhancing the financial interests of the producers" (*The Managed Economy*, pp. 169–170). The most authoritative recent corroboration of this was the unanimous report of the Senate Governmental Affairs Committee on over a dozen regulatory agencies, August 1977 (Washington, D.C.).

42. Reagan, *The Managed Economy*, p. 42. Robert Brady saw in 1943 that the powers of the property-holder were no longer constrained by his legal and organizational base; "all the old ownership frontiers are being abandoned, and power flows from the inner sancta like water through a shattered system of dykes" (*Business as a System of Power*, p. 230).

43. Central to Berle's and Means's argument was the recognition that "the explosion of the atom of property destroys the basis of the old assumption that the quest for profits will spur the owner of industrial capital to its effective use." (*The Modern Corporation*, p. 9).

44. Neumann, *Behemoth*, p. 227, and Neumann's preceding section. Also p. 291.

45. *Business as a System of Power*, p. 247. Both Harbrecht's and Mills's historical analyses—as opposed to their conclusions—support this view. Harbrecht, for example, acknowledged that, "power really attaches to him who controls the use of property" (*Pension Funds*, pp. 5, 278, and 282.) The meaning of this transformation of property was grasped by Neumann in the thirties: "Property

changes from a subjective right . . . to an institution, a reified social relation. The contract is not only excluded in practice, it even loses its role in legal ideology. . . . The status of man . . . becomes decisive" (*Behemoth*, p. 449).

46. "To be free and to be secure is to have an effective control over that upon which one is dependent"; in the modern world that would be control over "the job within the centralized enterprise" (Mills, *White Collar*, p. 59). Secure control over one's job, that is, would be the modern correlate to the older institution of property ownership. Concerning the claim about "socialization," see Berle, in A. Hacker, *The Corporation Take-Over*, pp. 99–100. Harbrecht also held "that capitalism's children, the banks, the insurance companies and the mutual funds, are now rapidly socializing the wealth in the . . . corporations." *Pension Funds*, p. 281. And Peter Drucker makes the point about pension funds, ignoring the fact that workers do not "own" their funds in any meaningful sense of the term, lack vested interests in them, and even lack due process rights against their being taken away (*The Unseen Revolution: How Pension Fund Socialism Came to America*, New York: Harper and Row, 1976).

47. Berle saw the possibility of this (Hacker, *The Corporation Take-Over*, p. 107), as did Harbrecht (*Pension Funds*, p. 286). Neither took that possibility seriously enough. Despite widespread announcements of workers' new "property rights in their jobs" it was clear, for example in the Court's ruling in *Flemming v. Nestor* 363 U.S. 603 (1960), that the status was something less than ownership. The Court held in *Flemming* that compulsory payments to a government trust fund, paid over a nineteen-year career, were not an "accrued property right." The worker's interest in them was "noncontractual" and could not be "analogized to that of the holder of an annuity." The worker could therefore be denied payments without violations of due process—in Nestor's case because of unpopular political beliefs (Reich, "The New Property," pp. 768–769).

48. J. A. C. Grant, "The Guild Returns to America," pp. 303–336, 458–477. Goetz Briefs's phrase, a "new estate of the realm," is from *Unionism Reappraised: From Classical Unionism to Union Establishment* (Washington: American Enterprise Association, 1960), the basic argument of which was that America was being transformed into a labor-based corporativism.

49. W. J. Ghent, *Our Benevolent Feudalism*, p. 9. Ghent's title may well have been suggested by Richard Ely's noted article of 1885 on Pullman's company town in Illinois: "Pullman, A Social Study," *Harper's New Monthly*, LXX.

50. Ghent, *Our Benevolent Feudalism*, pp. 8, 57, 184.

51. Polanyi, "Primitive Feudalism and the Feudalism of Decay," pp. 141–147.

52. Mills, *White Collar*, p. xii. Harbrecht and Reich are most prescient on this theme. The truth of Mills's remarks about the feudal situation of small businessmen was borne out by gas station "owners" in the seventies as they faced the oil companies, and by small farmers, beset by bankers on one side and processors on the other.

53. Reich, "The New Property," pp. 767–770 and 785.

54. The personal element of feudalism is obviously lacking in a society, as

Ghent wrote, where "the ceremony of homage may take place in whole regiments by a single rite" (*Our Benevolent Feudalism*, pp. 59–60). Brady's warning about the corporate capitalists' attempt to export their internal modes of organization to the rest of the society was given in "The Fascist Threat to Demcoracy," pp. 148–165.

55. Cited in Leo Panitch, "The Development of Corporatism in Liberal Democracies," p. 62. Panitch's is the best of the recent studies of the topic.

56. Brady, *Business as a System of Power*, pp. 230, 258.

57. Regarding the market order as a corporation, see Renner, *Institutions of the Private Law*, pp. 130–131. Illustrative of this dependence on the State was Madison's early defense of centralized government in America because it would help the individual states quash challenges, like that of Shays, for "paper money, an abolition of debts, an unequal division of property, or any other improper or wicked project" (*The Federalist Papers*, Number Ten, p. 84).

58. Reagan, *The Managed Economy*, p. 8.

59. Lowi, *The End of Liberalism*, pp. 70–85. And McConnell discusses the delegation of authority, in addition to power, in *Private Power*, pp. 210–211.

60. Charles W. Anderson, "Political Design and the Representation of Interests," p. 131. J. A. C. Grant made the same point concerning professional associations that had been granted licensing powers: "It is doubtful if many medieval guilds enjoyed a greater degree of independence than that conferred by these modern statutes. They have virtually erected these supposedly regulated callings into miniature governments. . . . Through their boards, they may issue regulations having the status of laws" ("The Guild Returns to America," p. 324).

61. See Mark Nadel's excellent "Hidden Dimension of Public Policy: Private Governments and the Policy-Making Process," pp. 25–27. As Nadel notes, "When we say that a member of the school board in Sheboygan, Wisconsin, is part of 'the authorities,' but the president of General Motors is not, we cannot go very far in understanding political behavior or public policy" (p. 19). The example in the text refers to General Motors' purchase and dismantling of the Pacific Electric trolley system in Los Angeles after World War II in order to boost the use of cars and buses.

62. McConnell, *Private Power*, p. 163. McConnell notes that if the pre-emption of the public domain characterized the last century, the pre-emption of public policy characterizes this one (p. 200). Reich discusses the same point ("The New Property," pp. 764–767), as does Lowi (*The Ends of Liberalism*, p. 83). An appreciation of the different modes of corporatism has received a strong impetus from the publication of Alan Wolfe's *Limits of Legitimacy*. Wolfe argues that truly corporatist programs, having failed to resolve the contradiction between a formal repudiation of the state and an actual dependence on it, were superseded in Europe and America at the end of the twenties by "the franchise state." In the franchise state, as Wolfe defines it, the government delegates power to private organizations and actively intervenes to help them organize their activities. How much the change of terms is justifiable, however, is doubtful. A statist element is

not as foreign to corporatism as Wolfe suggests. And historically, corporatism always used franchises as one way of achieving its mixed jurisdictions.

63. Grosvenor Clarkson, cited in McConnell, *Private Power*, p. 63. Previous remark by Murray Rothbard, "War Collectivism in World War I," *A New History of Leviathan, Essays on . . . the American Corporate State*, R. Radosh and M. Rothbard, eds. (New York: Dutton and Co., 1972).

64. Though there were only a handful of trade associations at the beginning of the twenties, there were more than two thousand by the end. Goldman, *Rendezvouz with Destiny*, p. 239. Goldman and others present the NRA as having combined the New Nationalist emphasis on public authority with the trade association principle of voluntary cooperation. But General Hugh Johnson, the NRA's director, explained to the NAM more simply that the NRA was "exactly what industry organized in trade associations makes it" (Arthur Schlesinger, Jr., *The Coming of the New Deal*, Boston: Houghton Mifflin Co., 1965, p. 110). Clarence Darrow's later Committee on Industrial Analysis confirmed that the code authorities could be "characterized as the creatures of . . . trade associations." Of the 700 codes that existed by 1935, only three provided for voting members speaking for consumers, and only thirty-seven allowed representatives from labor—not always with the right to vote (Broadus Mitchell, *Depression Decade*, New York: Harper and Row, 1969, p. 243). See also Schlesinger, *The Coming of the New Deal*, pp. 125–126.

65. Brady, *Business as a System of Power*, p. 247, and "The Fascist Threat to Democracy." Brady defined fascism essentially as monopoly capitalism plus the interventionist state. Neumann agreed: "The German economy of today . . . is a monopolistic economy *and* a command economy. It is a private capitalist economy, regimented by the totalitarian state" (*Behemoth*, p. 261). John Chamberlain thought that what Ghent had foreseen was essentially the rise of a fascist society (*Farewell to Reform*, p. 85).

66. McConnell, *Private Power*, pp. 211, 243–244. Though the existence of business associations was often denied by midcentury social scientists (see, for example, Daniel Bell's *End of Ideology*, p. 63), more recent reports have found them alive and well. A newspaper report of July 6, 1975 even found Advisory Councils ascending to the status of a "shadow government" reflecting the "narrow concerns of business or other special interests" (*The San Francisco Examiner-Chronicle*, Knight News Service).

67. For a lucid and early discussion of these inter-industry complexes, see William D. Phelan, "The Complex Society Marches On," *The Ripon Society Forum*, Vol. II, 1969. Such arrangements as the military-industrial complex or the agricultural-oil-food processing complexes function internally as post-market institutions. Prices are set independently of the market; sellers produce to specification rather than for inventory; and profit is separated from risk-taking or efficient resource allocation. Seymour Melman's concept of "state-management" is similar to this; see his *Pentagon Capitalism* (New York: McGraw Hill, 1970). See also Tony Quinn, "Political Action Committees, the New Campaign Bankrollers," *California Journal* (March 1979), pp. 96–98.

68. Moise Ostrogorski, *Democracy and the Organization of Political Parties*, S. M. Lipset, ed. (New York: Doubleday Anchor Books, 1964), cited on p. xxv. Evocative of the classical definition was Dan Nimmo's question: "How far can we go in permitting candidacy for elective office to be treated as an unregulated industry?" (*The Political Persuaders*, Englewood Cliffs: Prentice Hall, 1970, p. 198).

69. Lowi, *The End of Liberalism*, p. 311.

70. Neumann, *Behemoth*, pp. 259–260 and 358. The term "auxiliary guarantee" is suggestive of Karl Renner's "complementary institution" and probably a translation of it (see, for example, *Private Law*, pp. 196 and 290). Galbraith also saw that "the mature corporation so far from being organically separated from the state, exists . . . only in intimate association with it" (*The New Industrial State*, p. 180). But he again failed to trace the implications of this fact. The claim that the involvement of the state will become more pronounced given the structural instabilities of advanced, corporate capitalism is argued persuasively by current Marxist analyses, especially Claus Offe's "The Abolition of Market Control and the Problem of Legitimacy," and "The Theory of the Capitalist State and the Problem of Policy Formation."

71. Richard B. Stewart, "The Reformation of American Administrative Law," pp. 1712 and 1805–1813. Lowi (*The End of Liberalism*) anticipated this point in his question "What constitutes due process in an age of positive government?" (p. 70). He noted that "modern law has become a series of instructions to administrators rather than a series of commands to citizens" (p. 144).

72. Neumann noted this element of response to working-class organization in his "Change in the Function of Law in Modern Society" (now Ch. 2 of *The Democratic and Authoritarian State*, New York, Free Press, 1957). Panitch makes the same point ("The Development of Corporatism," pp. 62–64). And James Petras observed identical tendencies with Latin American corporatism (*Politics and Social Forces in Chilean Development*, p. 199).

73. Reagan, *The Managed Economy*, p. 208.

74. Neumann, "Change in the Function of Law," p. 48.

75. Petras, *Chilean Development*, p. 199.

76. Philippe Schmitter's remarks are also suggestive on the differences between pluralism and corporatism ("Modes of Interest Intermediation," pp. 7–37).

77. See Schmitter, "Interest Intermediation," p. 9; and Charles Anderson, "Political Design and the Representation of Interests," p. 143. That American labor relations are coming to approximate this model rather than the pluralist one is evident from the briefest glance at current labor law. By combining Section 301 of the Taft-Hartley Act (permitting suits against unions) with the "implied no-strike clause" created by the courts, employers have developed a means of disciplining workers and "the law of the collective agreement has been turned around" (Harry T. Wellington, *Labor and the Legal Process*, New Haven: Yale University Press, 1968, pp. 97–98; 113–115; see the *Lucas Four* cases, 369 U.S. 95 (1962). Examples of the denial of group standing are provided by the Court's recent discouragement of class-action suits by broad ranges of consumers, and its

denial of the standing of "suspect class" to parents interested in preserving their children's rights to a public education, in *San Antonio School District et al. v. Rodrigues*, 411 U.S. 1 (1973).

78. The Court held in *First National Bank of Boston v. Bellotti*, 98 U.S. 1407 (1978), that a federal law regulating campaign contributions by corporations was unconstitutional. The capacity of speech to inform the public did not depend, the Court said, "on the identity of its source, whether corporation, association, union or individual."

79. John McDermott, "Knowledge is Power." This situation is a fundamental inversion of Lester Ward's and John Dewey's hopes for "the method of intelligence" (see Chapter Six).

80. Woodrow Wilson, "The Liberation of a People's Vital Energies," in W. E. Leuchtenberg, ed., *Woodrow Wilson*, p. 163. Concerning the distinction between big business and "trusts," see pp. 109, 119.

81. The words of Eduardo Frei, from 1958, are cited in Petras, *Chilean Development*, p. 202. The argument here is not that Roosevelt's and Wilson's positions were identical but rather that they shared the same frame of reference—and that this led ultimately to the same conclusions. Felix Frankfurter noticed this in the thirties, and suggested that Croly's work was seminal for both Roosevelt and Wilson. See Sidney Kaplan, "Social Engineers as Saviors," footnote 13. For a recent defense of the opposing view, see Alan Seltzer's "Woodrow Wilson as 'Corporate Liberal.'"

82. Panitch, "The Development of Corporatism," p. 68. Lowi provides a summary of these justifications, *The End of Liberalism*, pp. 72ff.

83. McConnell, *Private Power*, p. 312; Lowi, *The End of Liberalism*, p. 29.

84. Though Lowi began by rejecting "corporativism" as a useful term, he ended by using it (*The End of Liberalism*, pp. 70–71, 80–81). And he explains late in the book that one of his intentions was to "discredit . . . the pluralist component of interest-group liberalism" (p. 294). The familiar source of the term "corporate liberal" is J. Weinstein's *Corporate Ideal in the Liberal State* (Boston: Beacon Press, 1968). But its real roots lie with two earlier sources. The first is Martin Sklar's incisive "Woodrow Wilson and the Political Economy of Modern United States Liberalism." For example: "Corporate-liberalism . . . is the fundamental element that makes modern United States liberalism the bourgeois Yankee cousin of modern European and English social-democracy" (p. 41). The second was then-President of SDS Carl Oglesby's famous speech of October 27, 1965, to the anti-war march on Washington. Having identified the "illiberal liberalism" that defended neo-colonialism and opposed revolutionary change, Oglesby added: "This is the action of *corporate liberalism*. It performs for the corporate state a function quite like what the Church once performed for the feudal state. It seeks to justify its burdens and protect it from change" (Massimo Teodari, *The New Left: A Documentary History*, New York: Bobbs-Merrill Co., 1969, p. 187).

85. Hofstadter, *The Age of Reform*, p. 133.

86. E. S. Mason, *The Corporation in Modern Society*, p. 4. Charles Anderson writes that pluralism "is a theory of group power, not of group authority. [It has]

no representative theory, no way of saying that this particular configuration of interests was *entitled* to participate in the formulation of this particular policy" ("Political Design," p. 140).

87. James, "The Sentiment of Rationality," in *Essays on Faith and Morals,* p. 83.

88. Norris, *The Octopus,* pp. 385–386, 425–426.

89. Ronald Radosh, "Corporatism, Liberal and Fascist, as Seen by Samuel Gompers," p. 67.

90. See E. K. Hunt, "A Neglected Aspect of the Economic Ideology of the New Deal."

91. Clark Kerr's *Industrialism and Industrial Man* can serve as a perfect example of a work which expresses these different themes.

92. Even the proposals for "constitutionalizing" industry and adopting "the rule of law" accept the dominant frame of reference. See Richard Eels, *The Government of Corporations;* and Seligman, "The American Corporation," for a critique of Eells. See also Earl Latham's "Body Politic of the Corporation," in Mason, *The Corporation in Modern Society.*

93. "What is the nature of the large corporation? What is its relationship to the economy and the larger society? . . . Embedded in the answer[s] is most of our economic activity and a substantial part of our political and social life. Yet these questions have never entered the mainstream of modern economic analysis." Lee E. Preston, "Corporations and Society: The Search for a Paradigm," p. 434. When attention has been given to the world within the corporation, furthermore, it has not been workers' problems that interested modern writers, but the workers *as* problems.

94. Kant and Mill did try to push liberal individualism in ethical and political directions; but, institutionally speaking, they are still waiting for a hearing.

CHAPTER TWO

Epigraph: John Taylor, early Carolina political leader, cited in C. Wright Mills, *White Collar,* p. 13.

1. Charles Francis Adams, Jr., *The Railroads: Their Origin and Problems,* p. 146. Parrington argued that "with the passing out of the frontiers of space and time, [occurred] the discovery of a vast impersonal cosmos that annihilated the petty egocentric world of good and evil." "As physics encroached upon the interest in biology," Americans found not "unity, growth, purpose" but "disunity, flux, chance" (*The Beginnings of Critical Realism,* pp. 191, 202–203).

2. Henry Steele Commager, *The American Mind,* p. 360.

3. John D. Hicks, *The Populist Revolt,* p. 237. C. Vann Woodward used the same terms to characterize the era: "In 1896 agrarian provincialism made its last aggressive stand against capitalistic industrialism" (*Tom Watson: Agrarian Rebel,* p. 330). See also Parrington, *Critical Realism,* pp. 259–266.

4. "Populism was the expression of a transitional stage in the development of our agrarian politics. While it reasserted for the last time some old ways of

thought, it was also a harbinger of the new" (this and the above characterizations are from Richard Hofstadter, *The Age of Reform*, pp. 5–12, 59, and 95; see also pp. 108–109, 133). Eric Goldman's *Rendezvous with Destiny* proposed an interpretation different from the conventional one when it argued that there was a real cleavage between populism and Progressivism. Lawrence Goodwyn's exceptional *Democratic Promise: The Populist Movement in America* also comes down on the side of the original interpretations, as does Norman Pollack's *The Populist Response to Industrial America* (for example, see p. 4).

5. W. D. Burnham, "The Changing Shape of the American Political Universe." Burnham finds that the mean turnout for presidential elections from 1848 to 1896 to 78.8 percent of the eligible electorate. From 1900 to 1916 that dropped to 65.8 percent—the drop occurring in the North as well as the South. See also E. E. Schattschneider, *The Semi-Sovereign People*, Chaps. 5 and 6.

6. Henry Adams, *The Education*, p. 227.

7. Cited in Harold U. Faulkner, *American Economic History* (New York: Harper Bros., 1949), p. 367.

8. Hofstadter, *Age of Reform*, pp. 70–71. Ignatius Donnelly *did*, after all, allege before the Populist Convention of 1891 in St. Louis that "A vast conspiracy has been organized on two continents and is taking possession of the world." Hicks, *Populist Revolt*, p. 436.

9. In Jacksonian parlance, a "monopoly" usually indicated a corporation especially flagrant in its neglect of the public trust. One Jacksonian publicist thus explained: "Business corporations, excluding banks . . . when suitably regulated, seem to me generally beneficial. . . . But if they be placed beyond legislative control and are thus to become monopolies and perpetuities, they assume an aspect the reverse of this and become excrescences upon the body politic" (David Henshaw, "The Dartmouth College Case," in Blau, *Social Theories of Jacksonian Democracy*, p. 163).

10. The banks under the National Bank System were private institutions empowered to issue money within broad guidelines on the basis of government bonds they held. Hicks, *Populist Revolt*, pp. 92–94. The bankers' policies on the retirement of the Civil War debt and the return to specie payments, when adopted by government, resulted in nearly doubling the liability of debtors (measured in terms of commodity values). Following the bankers' advice, in other words, the government interfered with contractual obligations by changing the standard of deferred payments (Parrington, *Critical Realism*, p. 272). One dramatic measure of what the resulting deflation meant was that despite increased manpower and production (wheat trebled, corn doubled, cotton went up 25 percent), farmers' revenues in 1890 were identical to what they had been twenty-five years earlier (Solon Buck, *The Granger Movement*, p. 33). The old charges that farmers merely desired "repudiation" and wanted more money are spurious. The farmers protested an engineered deflation that threatened to ruin them while it favored others.

Worldwide conditions no doubt contributed to the three decades-long price deflation, as populists acknowledged. But humanly fashioned institutions determined how the natural disasters and events played themselves out in the lives of men. "The raw fact—a bad harvest—may seem to be beyond human election. But the way that fact worked its way out was in terms of a particular complex of human relationships: law, ownership, power. When we encounter some sonorous phrase such as 'the strong ebb and flow of the trade cycle' we must be put on our guard. For behind this trade cycle there is a structure of social relations" (E. P. Thompson, *The Making of the English Working Class*, p. 205).

11. Between 1865 and 1895 the railroads acquired four times the amount of acreage staked out by settlers under the Homestead Act: 200,000,000 acres for the railroads, compared to 48,250,000 for the homesteaders (Louis Hacker, *The Triumph of American Capitalism*, p. 393). Harold U. Faulkner added that this was "much of the best land," and considering how few claims were proved, he doubted the significance of the Homestead Act (*American Economic History*, p. 367). Hofstadter concurred (*Age of Reform*, p. 54).

12. One out of every two or three farms in the states of the Middle Border were mortgaged during the 1870s (Buck, *The Granger Movement*, p. 19; Hicks, *Populist Revolt*, p. 84). Regarding the practices of the furnishing merchants, see Goodwyn, *Democratic Promise*, Chaps. 2 and 4. The concentration of ownership in California is legendary. Southern Pacific wound up holding 11 percent of the state's total acreage, most of it in the most productive regions (P. W. Gates, "Public Land Disposal in California," *Agricultural History*, January 1975). One eloquent autobiographical reminiscence of a California farm woman from the seventies recalls: "Land agents sometimes showed their clients a favorable location and had the settler pay his fee. Later, when his papers came back, they would show a different piece of land of less value, and occasionally of no agricultural worth at all. The 'sucker' lived out his time in a confused, tangled manner of extensive correspondence, dispelled hopes and more fees. Others moved back . . . 'burnt out,' they said. This simply meant that the combination of heat, little rain, poor land and no title had stripped them of all their drive and of the resources necessary to keep going" (Fannie Tracy, *The Tracy Saga*, Bakersfield: Cardon House, 1962, p. ii).

13. E. S. Mason, "Corporation," *International Encyclopedia of the Social Sciences*, p. 399.

14. Hofstadter cited the statistics of Charles Francis Adams, Jr., to argue that the high freight rates were not a major cause of farmers' struggles (*Age of Reform*, p. 58). But these figures failed to relate the falling rates to farmers' incomes, to address the questions of seasonal fluctuation and unfair rate structures (such as long-haul and short-haul provisions), and to acknowledge the underlying fact that farmers were put at the mercy of the roads in an essential aspect of their free market activity.

15. Henry George, *Progress and Poverty*, p. 327. The entire first section of this volume was a lyric celebration of industrial progress. Pollack agrees that the populists, while opposing monopoly, "were not bent on eradicating . . . bigness" (*Populist Response*, p. 4). Populism, he concluded, "made the important distinction between technology and social context, holding that society per-

verted its productive forces" (p. 10). Pollack does not, however, discern precisely what "monopoly" meant to the populists; and I believe he erred in suggesting that it was primarily *distributions* of wealth with which they were concerned (p. 10).

16. President Walker of the Pennsylvania Railroad, "Unregulated Competition, Self-Destructive," *Forum*, 1891, cited in Gabriel Kolko, *Railroads and Rate Regulation, 1887–1916*, p. 74.

17. *The Intellectuals and McCarthy.* Rogin's Chap. 6 is excellent on the populists.

18. W. S. Morgan, *The History of the Wheel and Alliance, and the Impending Revolution* (1889). After listing the ways "the agricultural masses" had been "plundered, imposed upon and fleeced," Morgan identified monopolies as the cause of the plunder. He then concluded that monopolies were "against the interests of the people and the welfare of the public. . . . Monopolies exist by law, are chartered by law, and should be controlled by law." Cited in M. Fainsod, L. Gordon, and J. Palamountain, *Government and the American Economy*, 3rd ed. (New York: W. W. Norton and Co., 1959), p. 439.

19. Judge Judson, St. Louis, quoted in Arnold Paul, *Conservative Crisis and the Rule of Law, 1887–1895*, p. 69 and Chap. 4 *passim.*

20. Woodward, *Tom Watson*, p. 178.

21. Thompson's remarks are cited in Paul, *Conservative Crisis*, p. 55. The Alliance newspaper words are cited in both Hicks, *Populist Revolt*, p. 79, and Pollack, *Populist Response*, p. 19. Woodward quotes the words of the Southern politician Robert Toombs (in 1877) to the same effect: "The great question is, Shall Georgia govern the corporations or the corporations govern Georgia? Choose ye this day whom ye shall serve!" (*Tom Watson*, p. 55).

22. Hofstadter, again, can be taken as representative of this school. For him populism arose during a "stage in which the commercial farmer was beginning to cast off habits of thought and action" created by "myth as much as by the realities," and when he "had not yet learned much from business" about market devices, strategies of combination, or pressure politics (*Age of Reform*, pp. 58–59). This formulation reveals the assumption that the farm *had to* wind up looking like the modern American business. It conveniently overlooks the fact that farmers of the eighties had to die so that commercial farmers like those Hofstadter portrays might live. Hofstadter also obscures the role of political choice and of political policies in his account of the causes of protest (pp. 50–57). For further comments on the denial of human agency by this mode of historiography, see Thompson, *English Working Class*, pp. 204–206.

23. Albert Camus, *The Rebel*, p. 209.

24. Henry Adams, *The Education*, pp. 500, 344–345.

25. C. C. Bosland, *Corporate Finance and Regulation* (New York: The Ronald Press, 1949), Chap. 2. And John P. Davis, *Corporations* (New York: Capricorn Books, 1961, orig. pub. 1905).

26. Louis Hartz, *Economic Policy and Democratic Thought in Pennsylvania, 1776–1860*, p. 289. The inadequacy of laissez-faire interpretations of even this era

is indicated by Hartz's further comment that "far from being limited, the objectives of the state . . . were usually so broad" they could not be achieved (p. 292).

27. A. A. Berle, "Economic Power and the Free Society," in Andrew Hacker, *The Corporation Take-Over*, p. 92. The prevailing view on political parties was given in Washington's farewell address as President, cited in V. O. Key, Jr., *Politics, Parties and Pressure Groups*, 5th ed. (New York: Thomas C. Crowell Co., 1964), p. 203. Hamilton extended the fear of internal *imperiums* to the states themselves, to the extent that they legislated "in their corporate capacities" rather than for the "individuals of which they consist" (*The Federalist Papers*, p. 108).

28. Alexis de Tocqueville, *Democracy in America*, Vol. 2, Book II, Chaps. 5 and 7, and Book IV, Chaps. 6 and 7. Also see W. H. George, "Montesquieu, Tocqueville, and Corporative Individualism."

29. "In this state, the legislature transcends its constitutional power if it attempts to farm out the rights of the community and of succeeding generations by means of corporate perpetuities" (David Henshaw, "The Dartmouth College Case" (1837), in Blau, *Social Theories of Jacksonian Democracy*, p. 164). See also Stephan Simpson's "Political Economy and the Workers" (1831), in *ibid.*, pp. 137–162, for an eloquent statement of this theme. See also Hartz, *Economic Policy*, p. 73.

30. *Leviathan*, Chaps. 26 and 29.

31. C. H. McIlwain, *The Growth of Political Thought in the West*, pp. 181, 163.

32. If a lord granted land to a vassal, the lord's right was not extinguished but "a new interest or right in the land had been carved out of the original one . . . and that new interest involved a continuing relationship, reciprocal in character" (McIlwain, *Political Thought in the West*, pp. 176 and 181). The medieval view was the "opposite of that of Locke, that private property is an institution of natural law, and arises out of labor. To the [Church] Fathers the only natural condition is that of common ownership and individual use. The world was made for the common benefit of mankind, that all should receive from it what they require." Admitting that man lived in a fallen state, the medieval view did permit the State to create and limit rights of property ownership. Practically speaking, therefore, "private property . . . [was] the creation of the state" (*ibid.*, p. 162, quoted from Dr. A. J. Carlyle's "Theory of Property in Mediaeval Theology").

33. Charles Reich, "The New Property," p. 787.

34. Randolph, to the Virginia Constitutional Convention, 1829, in *Free Government in the Making*, A. T. Mason, ed. (New York: Oxford University Press, 1949), p. 423. And see Adams, in *ibid.*, p. 6. Daniel Webster wrote that, "In my judgement . . . a republican form of government rests not more on political Constitution than on these laws which regulate the descent and transmission of property." He felt that the pattern of property distribution "fixed the . . . frame and form of government" so markedly that not even universal suffrage could offset its effects of an unequal property distribution. (Massachusetts Constitutional Convention speech, 1820, cited in *ibid.*, pp. 394–397).

35. Noah Webster, cited in Mills, *White Collar*, p. 8.

36. See Simpson, "Political Economy and the Workers," in Blau, *Social Theories*, pp. 141 and 156.

37. "The sphere of contract is made up of this mediation whereby I hold property not merely by means of a thing and my subjective will, but by means of another person's will as well, and so hold it in virtue of my participation in a common will" (Hegel, *Philosophy of Right*, Section 71, p. 57).

38. Locke was explicit about this equation of property and personality. "Man . . . has by nature a power . . . to preserve . . . his property—that is, his life, liberty and estate." (*The Second Treatise of Government*, New York: Bobbs Merrill Co., 1952, Section 87, p. 48.) In Section 44 he speaks of man as the "proprietor of his own person."

39. The seminal inquiry into the relationship between the market order and the psychology of control was Weber's *Protestant Ethic and the Spirit of Capitalism* (New York, Scribner's Sons, 1958, orig. pub. 1904). See also John R. Wikse's *About Possession: The Self as Private Property* (University Park: Pennsylvania State University Press, 1977).

40. John Locke, *Second Treatise*, Section 50, p. 29; Section 34, p. 20. C. B. MacPherson, *The Political Theory of Possessive Individualism*, p. 247.

41. Quotation from John W. Vethake, "The Doctrine of Anti-Monopoly," *New York Evening Post* (October 31, 1835), in Blau, *Social Theories*, p. 216.

42. *Ibid.*, p. 212. The statement about the genius of our institutions is by Theodore Sedgewick, Jr., "What Is Monopoly," in Blau, *Social Theories*, p. 222. Henry Bamford Parkes distinguished "the republic of small property holders" that flourished during this era from "the capitalist people" that were to follow (*The American Experience*, New York: Random House, 1959, p. 121).

43. The political (artificial) character of the corporation was accepted equally at this time by those seeking charters, those opposing them, and those granting them. See, for example, Hartz, *Economic Policy*, pp. 80, 122, and 159.

44. *Munn v. Illinois*, 94 U.S. 125, 113 (1876). Waite did not deny *all* limits to legislative sovereignty. But where physical circumstances permitted railroads and grain elevators to "take toll from all who pass," they made most businesses "virtual monopolies," and supervisable as such. John R. Commons alluded to a similar distinction between a franchise and property by noting that a "franchise proceeded from the common law since it was only the common law that took the ordinary practices of unprivileged persons and erected them into a system of legal rights, duties and liberties" (*The Legal Foundations of Capitalism*, p. 185).

45. *Dartmouth College v. Woodward*, 4 Wheaton 518 (1819). This reasoning was anticipated four years earlier in *Terret v. Taylor* when Justice Story ruled that unless a corporation had been created for public purposes, which he construed narrowly to mean "towns, cities, parishes and counties," it was private and protected against the repeal of its charter or land grant (1815). 9 Cranch 42, 3 L. Ed. 650.

46. Otto Gierke, *Political Theories of the Middle Age*, Introduction by F. W. Maitland, pp. xxiv–xxv.

47. David Henshaw, "The Dartmouth College Case," in Blau, *Social Theories*, p. 172. William A. Williams argues that Marshall made this ruling on the narrow facts of the case and intended no general precedent (*The Contours of American History*, p. 213). The typical formula of American textbooks would eventually mix the two elements of compact and concession. A corporation is thus "a voluntary *autonomous* association formed for the private advantage of its members, which acts with compulsory unity, and is *authorized* by the state for the accomplishing of some public good" (from Lewis Hanley's *Business Organization and Combination*, 1922, cited in Bosland, *Corporate Finance and Regulation*, p. 16, emphasis added). See also Abram Chayes's chapter in Mason, *The Corporation in Modern Society*, p. 35.

48. "Having moved into an era of long-range planning," they sought "an increasingly stable legal and political environment," something that transcended the "meddlesome and restrictive" rulings of the different states (Hartz, *Economic Policy*, p. 252, also pp. 297, 316). These comments refer to the railroads, which by the late 1840s were already the dominant form of incorporated enterprise.

49. Mason, "Corporation."

50. Hartz, *Economic Policy*, pp. 251, 315.

51. A plutocracy, for Sumner, claimed exclusive privileges, mixed political and economic energies, and upset the workings of the beneficent laws of nature. "I regard plutocracy as the most sordid and debasing form of political energy known to us. In its motives, its process, its code and its sanctions, it is infinitely corrupting to all the institutions which ought to preserve and protect society" ("Democracy and Plutocracy," in Persons, *Social Darwinism*, p. 145).

52. Quoted in Ralph Gabriel, *The Course of American Democratic Thought*, p. 152.

53. *The Railroads*, pp. 117, 179, 215.

54. Holmes, *The Common Law* (1881), end of Lecture 1.

CHAPTER THREE

Epigraph: Isaiah, quoted in Henry George, *Progress and Poverty*, p. 432.

1. "What the Railroad Will Bring Us" (1868).

2. The speech at Berkeley is discussed in V. L. Parrington, *The Beginnings of Critical Realism*, p. 132. George's writing had a notable effect not only in America, on Dewey, Henry Demarest Lloyd, and Progressives like Tom Johnson (later mayor of Cleveland), but also in England, on George Bernard Shaw (who "never minimized his debt to Henry George"), Sidney Webb, and H. G. Wells (Daniel Aaron, *Men of Good Hope: A Study of American Progressives*, New York: Oxford University Press, 1951, pp. 78, 80–91).

3. *Progress and Poverty*, p. 7.

4. This was already evident in his early article, "What the Railroad Will Bring Us" (1868), written on the eve of the completion of the transcontinental railroad: "Let us not imagine ourselves in a fool's paradise where the golden ap-

ples will drop into our mouths. . . . Our modern civilization strikes broad and deep and looks high. So did the tower which men once built almost to heaven."

5. Edward Bellamy, *Looking Backward*, p. 208.

6. *Progress and Poverty*, p. 421.

7. George, *Progress and Poverty*, pp. 28, 26, 163. E. P. Thompson cites the testimony of an English silk-weaver in 1834 to a Parliamentary commission to the same effect: "Capital I can make out to be nothing else but an accumulation of the products of labor." The weaver then explained that, "Labor is always carried to market by those who have nothing else to keep or to sell. . . . The labor which I . . . might perform this week, if I, in imitation of the capitalist, refuse to part with it . . . because an inadequate price is offered me for it, can I bottle it? Can I lay it up in salt?" He concluded, unlike George, that "labor and capital can never with justice be subjected to the same laws" (*The Making of the English Working Class*, p. 297).

8. *Progress and Poverty*, p. 72. "Capital is only required when . . . produce is stored up, or . . . placed in the general currency of exchanges without being at once drawn against—that is, sold on credit. . . . It is never as an employer of labor that any producer needs capital . . . it is because he is a merchant or speculator in, or accumulator of, the products of labor" (p. 70). "It is not capital which employs labor, but labor which employs capital" (p. 195, see also p. 162).

9. *Progress and Poverty*, p. 75; see also pp. 148, 149, 74.

10. *Ibid.*, p. 187. The matter of interest rates on capital raises an important point. George's approval of that element of "profit" made up by "wages of superintendence" was consistent with the labor theory of value (p. 163), as was his rejection of that part that accrued only to speculators and monopolizers of labor opportunities. But in justifying a return to mere lenders, he endowed capital with a remunerative power *independent* of its source in labor. The ambiguities thus revealed had been apparent in agrarian thought as far back as with Thomas Paine. George and the others drew back from a strict labor theory of value—at the precise point where it would begin to limit the entrepreneurial ambitions of upwardly mobile workers.

11. *Ibid.*, p. 38.

12. *Ibid.*, pp. 334–336. Note that rights of use apply to "nature," whereas rights of possession attach to the *products* of labor.

13. Adam Smith had written: "The property which every man has in his own labor, as it is the original foundation of all other property, so it is the most sacred and inviolable. The patrimony of a poor man lies in the strength and dexterity of his hands; and to hinder him from employing this strength and dexterity . . . is a plain violation of this most sacred property" (*The Wealth of Nations*, Chap. 10, Part 2, p. 129).

14. Concerning the benefits of companionship and society, and the differences between man as animal and man as citizen, see *Progress and Poverty*, pp. 237–238. George explained nature's impartiality in her exactions in part by noting that "if a king and a common man be thrown overboard, neither can keep his head above water except by swimming" (see pp. 28, 335–336).

15. The normative element of this empiricism was apparent, for example, when George remarked: "Smith and Ricardo use the term 'natural wages' to express the minimum upon which laborers can sustain life; whereas, unless injustice is natural, all that the laborer produces should rather be held as his natural wages." *Progress and Poverty*, p. 163.

16. *Ibid.*, pp. 532–533, 537. The platform is in J. D. Hicks, *The Populist Revolt*, p. 436.

17. *Progress and Poverty*, pp. 530–531, and Book III, Chap. 4, *passim*. "The reaction must come. The tower leans upon its foundations, and every new story but hastens the final collapse. . . . To base on a state of most glaring social inequality, political institutions under which men are theoretically equal, is to stand a pyramid on its apex" (p. 10). George's sophistication in these matters can also be seen in his appreciation of the fact that popular sovereignty did not dispose of the problem of despotism. Where "despotism advances in the name and with the might of the people," there exists "no unenfranchised class" to whom appeals can be made, no middle class like that which had broken the Stuarts. And "a mere aristocracy of wealth will never struggle while it can hope to bribe a tyrant" (pp. 530–531).

18. *Ibid.*, Book III, Chap. 4.

19. "When the Pacific roads form a combination with the Pacific Mail Steamship Company . . . toll gates are virtually established on land and ocean" (*Progress and Poverty*, p. 193).

20. Locke, *Second Treatise of Government*, Chap. V, Sections 36 and 31.

21. *Progress and Poverty* (emphasis added), 166–167, 170, 186, and 342–344.

22. *Ibid.*, p. 342.

23. *Ibid.*, pp. 10, 294, 393, and 549.

24. George proposed something like an iron law of wages applied to labor *and* capital. He argued that rent would rise until it drove wages and interest down to the minimum—as determined by what they could get on the least productive land. The effect would be "to make the lowest reward for which labor and capital will engage in production, the highest they can claim" (*Progress and Poverty*, pp. 166–169). For a prescient prediction why economic "improvements" would *not* ultimately lower prices, and why they would only be a short-term "bribe to . . . propitiate the public" and would be canceled once trusts controlled lines of trade, see Populist Presidential candidate General J. B. Weaver's speech of 1892 in Curti, Thorpe, and Baker, *American Issues: The Social Record*, 4th ed. (Chicago: J. B. Lippincott Co., 1960), p. 696.

25. *Progress and Poverty*, p. 9. The Lewelling circular is discussed in Pollack, *The Populist Response to Industrial America*, p. 89. Marx's insights were similar: "Hence, the economic paradox, that the most powerful instrument for shortening labour-time becomes the most unfailing means for placing every moment of the labourer's time and that of his family, at the disposal of the capitalist for the purpose of expanding the value of his capital" (*Capital*, Vol. I., pp. 395, 409). And in Russia Tolstoy also saw in 1898 that "if the arrangement of society is bad (as ours is), and a small number of people have power over the majority and

oppress it, every victory over Nature will inevitably serve only to increase that power and that oppression. That is what is actually happening" (*Recollections and Essays*, Oxford, 1937, p. 185).

26. To speak of inflation here is not inconsistent with the reality of the deflation of the seventies, eighties, and nineties. Because the prices farmers paid for supplies never fell as far, during these decades, as the prices they received for their crops, any cost-saving effects of deflation were canceled and reversed. The practical effect was the same as during inflation: a progressive deterioration of the farmers' buying power and real wealth.

27. Parrington, *The Beginnings of Critical Realism*, p. 272.

28. Henry Demarest Lloyd explicitly stated that the critical question about any monopoly was not whether it prevented competition: "The question in the end is, does it inevitably tend to public injury?" (*Wealth Against Commonwealth*, p. 11).

29. Karl Polanyi, *The Great Transformation*. "All transactions must be turned into money transactions"; that "requires that the medium of exchange be introduced into every articulation of industrial life" (p. 41). "There must be markets for every element of industry" (pp. 72, 75, and Chap. 10).

30. *Ibid.*, pp. 127, 179, and 57.

31. *Ibid.*, pp. 71–75, and 129.

32. *Ibid.*, p. 193.

33. Robert Brady, *Business as a System of Power*, p. 296. President Cleveland's Attorney General, Richard Olney, grasped the same point. He would refuse to enforce the Sherman Antitrust Act vigorously, he explained, because "*all* ownership is a monopoly." Literal application of the provisions of the statute was "out of the question" (in Lloyd, *Wealth Against Commonwealth*, p. 12).

34. *Progress and Poverty*, p. 384; and Book VII, Chap. 1, *passim*, especially p. 337. George's contemporary, Laurence Gronlund, disapproving of the "communistic" goal of dividing all property equally, proposed the industrial analogue of George's plan—to place "only the instruments of production—land, machinery, raw materials, etc.—under collective control" and to leave the remaining property ("improvements") in private hands. "Instead of taking property from everybody, [socialism] will *enable everybody to acquire property.*" Showing the deep theoretical reformulations of which this thought was capable, Gronlund also recommended to readers that they "get rid of . . . the absolute idea of ownership" and follow the older principle by which people might have an "estate in wealth" but never exclusive possession of it (*The Cooperative Commonwealth*, pp. 75, 94–95).

35. Feudalism had thrown over ownership a mantle of "superior right, and the process of infeudation consisted of bringing individual dominion into subordination to the . . . larger community or nation" (*Progress and Poverty*, p. 377).

36. C. Vann Woodward, *Tom Watson*, p. 55. George's comment about the lack of choice is in *Progress and Poverty*, p. 56. Lloyd drew the same conclusion from his recognition of the fact that "Liberty produces wealth, and wealth destroys liberty" (*Wealth Against Commonwealth*, p. 1).

37. *Progress and Poverty*, p. 341; and further: "The great primary wrong" was "the appropriation as the exclusive property of some men, of the land on which and from which all must live" (p. 340).

38. *Ibid.*, p. 386, and *passim*. Regarding ownership as a trust, see pp. 349 and 344–345: "Has the first comer at a banquet the right to turn back all the chairs . . . ? We arrive and we depart, guests at a banquet continually spread—our rights to take and possess cannot be exclusive; they must be bounded everywhere by the equal rights of others."

39. James Fenimore Cooper, *The Prairie* (New York: Rinehart and Co., 1950), p. 82.

40. *Progress and Poverty*, pp. 390–391. George's cadences and even his formulations are unmistakable in Turner's speech of 1891. But Turner altered the argument in two important ways. He attributed the problem to geography rather than to social organization; and he subsequently looked to the corporation itself and a new capacity for "social control" to provide what had once been provided by the moving frontier (*Frontier and Section: Selected Essays of Frederick Jackson Turner*, Ray A. Billington, ed., Englewood Cliffs, N.J.: Prentice-Hall, 1961, pp. 37–38, 61–62, and 95–97).

41. Cooper, *The Prairie*, p. 82.

42. George refers to "the feeling of Ishmael and the spirit of Cain" (*Progress and Poverty*, p. 510); Watson wrote in his diary that he was "an Ishmael of modern times" (Woodward, *Tom Watson*, p. 37); and Bellamy referred to the existing "land of Ishmael" (*Looking Backward*, p. 212).

43. Such formulations are legion. Parrington refers to the assertion "of the rights of the common man against the encroachments of a class" (*Critical Realism*, p. 286). The Kansas People's Party of 1892 spoke of "vicious legislation in the interests of the favored classes and adverse to the masses of American citizens." Hicks, *Populist Revolt*, p. 211. And see Pollack, *Populist Response, passim*.

44. Hofstadter, *Age of Reform*, pp. 46, 58, and 73. For a hard-hitting response, see Michael Rogin, *The Intellectuals and McCarthy*, pp. 168–169, 182–185.

45. Theodore Draper, *The Roots of American Communism* (New York: Viking Press, 1957), pp. 37–38.

46. For accounts of the fraud and violence perpetrated against third party efforts, see Hicks, *Populist Revolt*; Buck, *The Granger Movement*; and Woodward, *Tom Watson*, Chaps. 13–15.

47. Woodward, *Tom Watson*, p. 135.

48. *Ibid.*, pp. 178 and 182. This is not to argue that these comments were yet informed by a precise class theory. The transitional character of the usage is indicated by Watson's essentially utilitarian defense, and by the fact that the struggle he referred to here was between agrarians and manufacturers—not, strictly speaking, a class conflict at all. The unsettled state of class terminology in these matters was still evident twenty-five years later in Solon Buck's *The Granger Movement* (1913), pp. 310–311.

49. The Weaver comment is from "A Call to Action," excerpted in Curti et al., *American Issues*, p. 697. Similar sentiments were voiced by Mary Elizabeth

Lease; see Hicks, *Populist Revolt*, p. 160. The Waite comment is in Leon W. Fuller, "Colorado's Revolt Against Capitalism," *Mississippi Valley Historical Review*, XXI, No. 3 (December 1934), p. 354. *The Farmer's Light*, a populist paper, explained in October 1892: "There is no wiping out the fact that this is a revolution, and it depends upon the enemy whether it shall be a peaceful or a bloody one. To be candid about the matter, we believe it will be the latter" (Woodward, *Tom Watson*, p. 239). Pollack cites similar utterances, *Populist Response*, pp. 77–79.

50. Woodward, *Tom Watson*, p. 406.

51. Thus in 1894 Watson defended nationalization where a "business is so clearly of a public nature that the individual can only get fair treatment by having the government act for all" (*ibid.*, p. 260). Gronlund urged: "Freedom is something substantial. A man who is ignorant is not free. . . . Freedom is something the individual unaided can never achieve. . . . It is something to be conferred on him by a well-organized body politic" (*Cooperative Commonwealth*, pp. 85–86).

52. Hicks, *Populist Revolt*, p. 437. Pollack also gives some details of farmer-labor cooperation (*Populist Response*, pp. 44, 62–63).

53. The contemporary laborer, this agrarian spokesman observed, was becoming a "mere link in an enormous chain" of producers and consumers, "helpless to move except as they move." He was becoming "a slave, a machine, a commodity—a thing, in some respects lower than an animal" (*Progress and Poverty*, pp. 284–285). George's union affiliation is noted on p. 315.

54. For similar conclusions regarding the change of anti-Semitism, see Rogin, *The Intellectuals and McCarthy*, pp. 493–495, and Herbert Gutman's "The Knights of Labor and Patrician Anti-Semitism: 1891," pp. 63–67. No matter how opportunist were some of the motives, the examples of black-white alliances in the South before 1900, when viewed against the heritage, prevailing standards, and immediate Civil War legacy, are impressive. See Lawrence Goodwyn, *Democratic Promise*, Part II, Chap. 10.

55. He went on to announce that the Chinese "moral standard is as low as their standard of comfort, and though honest in their payment of debts to each other . . . they practice all the unnameable vices of the East, and are as cruel as they are cowardly" ("The Chinese on the Pacific Coast," *New York Tribune*, May 1, 1869). Scurrilous as was this language, the thrust of George's article was economic. It was to attack the West Coast monopolies that imported the Chinese to depress wages and break workingmen's unions. Aside from its racism, the argument's economics were sophisticated enough to impress John Stuart Mill. On the larger issues here, see Alexander Saxton's excellent *Indispensable Enemy*. Saxton suggests that it may have been Mill's response which caused George to change his racial attitudes (pp. 103 and 155).

56. *Progress and Poverty*, Book X, Chap. 2, pp. 503–504, and pp. 498–499.

57. This vision persisted for some beyond the First World War. John Dos Passos wrote in 1932: "However much we may cavil at the Communists, they mean it when they say they are fighting for socialism—i.e., the cooperative com-

monwealth" (John P. Diggins, *Up From Communism*, New York: Harper and Row, 1975, p. 8). Though Dos Passos glossed over them in this remark, there were of course important differences between the vision of the indigenous American radicals and that of the later Communists.

58. *Progress and Poverty*, pp. 327, 508–509, 524.

59. Leon Fuller, "Colorado's Revolt Against Capitalism."

60. The charge of primitiveness, laxity, and essential stupidity occurs, for example, in Turner's famous speech, "The Significance of the Frontier," in Billington, ed., *Frontier and Section*, p. 58. Woodrow Wilson agreed with the other Gold Bugs in characterizing "the means of reform proposed" as the product of "crude and ignorant minds" (Marjorie L. Daniel, "Woodrow Wilson—Historian," *Mississippi Valley Historical Review*, XXI, No. 3, December 1934, p. 37). The view of populism adopted by modern liberals is thus essentially that of the late nineteenth century conservatives.

61. Pollack acknowledged that "Populism was certainly not Marxism," but then clouded the issue by suggesting that the populists *were* class surrogates (*Populist Response*, pp. 68, 83, and Chap. 4, *passim*). See also Rogin, *The Intellectuals and McCarthy*, pp. 182–191.

62. *Progress and Poverty*, p. 404.

63. *Ibid.*, p. 524 (on the characteristics of association). In *Social Problems*, George wrote that, "The concentration that is going on in all branches of industry . . . is not itself an evil. If in anything its results are evil, it is simply because of our bad social adjustments." The whole question hinged on "whether the relation in which men are . . . compelled to act together shall be the natural relation of interdependence in equality, or the unnatural relation of dependence upon a master" (cited in Aaron, *Men of Good Hope*, pp. 84–85). In George's regard for cooperation, his doubts about the inevitability of progress, and his explicit repudiation of the survival instinct as the master motive of human life, he had already moved into conscious opposition to the Social Darwinists (*Progress and Poverty*, pp. 462–463 and *passim*).

64. The contradictions of that final position were expressed lucidly forty years later in Clarence Darrow's report on the NRA, when he urged strict enforcement of the antitrust laws and also called for "something like a socialist system" (Goldman, *Rendezvous with Destiny*, pp. 270–273).

65. While Watson's vote in the Presidential election of 1904 dropped to 117,000 votes (from 217,000 in 1896 and a Populist Party vote of nearly two million in the local elections of 1894), Debs's vote as a Socialist rose to 400,000 (from 90,000 in 1900). A year later an organizer for the Georgia Populists echoed others when he wrote that, "Most of the leading Populists of this section are Socialists. They are my friends; but in no way enthusiastic in the work of keeping Populist papers alive" (Woodward, *Tom Watson*, pp. 329, 362, 404). Henry Demarest Lloyd (with Debs) was in the vanguard of this leftward movement. Indeed, he sought an American form of socialism as early as 1890.

66. George, *Progress and Poverty*, pp. 507, 560, and see p. 470.

67. Though the socialist ideal was "grand and noble," George allowed, it would prove eventually to be stifling because it substituted "governmental direction for the play of individual action" (*ibid.*, pp. 310–320).

68. Hicks, *Populist Revolt*, pp. 110, 147, and 206; as late as 1889 one wing of the Alliance still insisted on the non-political stance. This contradiction was also apparent with Gronlund, an explicit socialist. One could not minimize the importance of "the state," he argued; because the state *was* society, "including with the people, the land and all that the land produces. . . . The 'Government'—the punishing and restraining authority—may be dispensed with at some future time. But the State—never." Gronlund suggested, then, that an organic society could function without *creating* a public interest and without implementing political choice. As such, his was a curious reassertion of the basic liberal faith in natural harmony—a faith replicated in yet another way by the syndicalists. Gronlund, *The Cooperative Commonwealth*, Chapter 4, *passim*.

69. See George, *Progress and Poverty*, pp. 437 and 404. It was unclear, for example, how most working people would be able to buy the land priced according to local rates of productivity, or once they had bought it, how they would compete with producers already using expensive machinery—such machinery being part of "improvements" and thus exempt from the tax. George's program, if implemented, would have been fated to a replay of the Jacksonian drama. Henry Demarest Lloyd saw very early that the effect of George's scheme would "be infallibly to shift its possession to those who had the money to pay the taxes" (in Pollack, *Populist Response*, p. 96).

70. John Chamberlain, *Farewell to Reform*, p. 47.

71. Carey McWilliams's term, used often in *California: The Great Exception* (New York: A. A. Wynn, 1949).

72. Cooper, *The Prairie*, p. 79. Strictly speaking, the trapper here would have indicted Henry George as well as Ishmael Bush. But his fears and George's were occasioned by the same thing—America's exhaustion of the space for the liberal project.

73. Woodrow Wilson, "Democracy and Efficiency," *The Atlantic Monthly*, LXXXVII (March 1901), pp. 289–299. "There has been a singular unity in our national history" demonstrating the laws of expansion and of the extension of free institutions. "Our almost accidental possession of the Philippines" will "make [that unity] complete." It is "our present and immediate task to extend self-government to Porto Rico and the Philippines, if they be fit to receive it, so soon as they can be made fit." The same ideas were repeated in "The Ideals of America," *The Atlantic Monthly*, XC, December 1902, pp. 721–734. "They [the Filipinos] can have liberty no cheaper than we got it. . . . We are old in this learning and must be their tutors."

74. George, *Progress and Poverty*, p. 406.

CHAPTER FOUR

Epigraph: Lamont's response to charges by journalists that the House of Morgan was organizing a power trust. Quoted in Claude Cockburn, *The Devil's Decade* (London: Sedgewick and Johnson, Ltd., 1973), p. 117.

1. Adams, *The Education*, pp. 225–226.

2. Sumner, "Socialism," in Persons, *Social Darwinism*, p. 75.

3. Sumner, "The Absurd Effort to Make the World," *ibid.*, pp. 160, 171; and *What Social Classes Owe to Each Other*, pp. 13; 58–66; and 137.

4. Sumner, *Social Classes*, p. 94.

5. "The state" was "only a little group of men chosen in a very haphazard way by the majority of us to perform some service for all of us." Usually it amounted to "some obscure clerk hidden in the recesses of a government bureau" (*ibid.*, p. 9).

6. "Sociology," in Persons, *Social Darwinism*, p. 17. The effect of reformers' "so-called progress" was only to make "evil alter its forms" ("Socialism," *ibid.*, p. 95).

7. Sidney Fine, *Laissez-Faire and the General-Welfare State*, p. 84. And Sumner: The men competent to "run great enterprises . . . are found by natural selection, not political election" (*Social Classes*, p. 103).

8. Sumner, *Social Classes*, pp. 92–93. Rather than looking to economic institutions, as George had done, Sumner focused on the threat being posed by extra-constitutional *political* agencies: "the party organizations, the primary, the convention, etc. All this apparatus is well-adapted to the purposes of plutocracy: it has to do with the *formative stage* of political activity." Its operations "are irresponsible, yet they reach out to, and control, the public and civil functions." He also acknowledged the "tendency of all civilized governments toward plutocracy" ("Democracy and Plutocracy," in Persons, *Social Darwinism*, pp. 144–145, 148). Sumner defined a plutocrat as a man who "instead of employing laborers, enlists lobbyists" (p. 146). "A plutocracy would be a civil organization in which the power resides in wealth, in which a man might have whatever he could buy, in which the rights, interests and feelings of those who could not pay would be overridden." He believed that a society erected on plutocratic principles could easily become worse than the regime against which the modern democracies had originally rebelled (*Social Classes*, pp. 89–95).

9. Ralph Gabriel, *The Course of American Democratic Thought*, pp. 236–237.

10. T. C. Cochran, "Entrepreneurship," p. 88.

11. Sumner, "The Concentration of Wealth," in Persons, *Social Darwinism*, p. 157.

12. Sumner, *Social Classes*, p. 48.

13. "The Concentration of Wealth," in Persons, *Social Darwinism*, pp. 150–154. "Combinations of capital are indispensable because we have purposes to accomplish which can be attained in no other way; *monopolies exist in nature*." "Democracy and Plutocracy" (*ibid.*, p. 147, emphasis added).

14. Herbert Spencer, *First Principles*, 4th American ed. (New York: 1900), p. 407.

15. "The Concentration of Wealth," in Persons, *Social Darwinism*, p. 151.

16. See Morton J. Horwitz, *The Transformation of American Law* (Cambridge: Harvard University Press, 1977). And concerning the changing institution of property in George's California, see H. Scheiber and C. W. McCurdy, "Eminent-Domain Law and Western Agriculture, 1849–1900," *Agricultural History*, I (January 1975), pp. 112–130.

17. Concerning this theory of value, see Cochran, "Entrepreneurship," p. 89, discussing the work of the economist Francis A. Walker.

18. Charles Francis Adams, Jr., *Autobiography, 1835–1915*, p. 179.

19. Henry Adams, *The Education*, p. 225.

20. Comte, *Positive Philosophy*, Vol. I, pp. 1–3; also, *A General View of Positivism*, Chapter I.

21. The implications of this have not been taken seriously enough by students of social thought. Galileo was a close student of the neo-Platonists in sixteenth-century Italy, and Platonic assumptions inform the idea of science that was modeled on Galileo's approach. Not the least important of these assumptions was the idea that mathematics caught the essential structure of the universe. Americans who have perceived Platonic ideas quickly enough in foreign political systems have been unaware of the subtle Platonic influence on their own thought. See E. A. Burtt, *The Metaphysical Foundations of Modern Science*, and the introduction to Morris Cohen's book on C. S. Peirce: *Chance, Love and Logic*.

22. When Tocqueville wrote that "a new science of politics is needed for a new world" (*Democracy in America*, Intro. to Vol. I), he did not mean a new methodology; he meant an improved knowledge of substantive political phenomena.

23. Comte, *Positivism*, p. 50.

24. Quoted in Fine, *Laissez-Faire*, p. 84; and Sumner, "The New Social Issue," in Persons, *Social Darwinism*, p. 167.

25. The quotation is from Henry Steele Commager, *The American Mind*, p. 360. See also Justice Brewer's statement of the property doctrine in terms of the instincts for acquisition and possession, cited in Paul, *Conservative Crisis and the Rule of Law*, p. 70. Dreiser did not, of course, celebrate this new naturalism as did Sumner and Fields.

26. Sumner, *Social Classes*, pp. 68, 98, 104.

27. Sumner, "The Concentration of Wealth," in Persons, *Social Darwinism*, p. 151. "What law of nature, religion, ethics or the state is violated by inequalities of fortune? The inequalities prove nothing." And see Comte, *Positivism*, pp. 181, 398, 448. Also Fine, *Laissez-Faire*, p. 82.

28. Sumner, *Social Classes*, pp. 51ff.

29. "Democracy and Plutocracy," in Persons, *Social Darwinism*, p. 137. Also see *Social Classes*, pp. 58–59.

30. "Social War in Democracy," in Persons, *Social Darwinism*, p. 62. See also "The Absurd Effort to Make the World Over," *ibid.*

31. Sumner, "The Forgotten Man," in Persons, *Social Darwinism*, p. 120. "If

no man can be held to serve another man's happiness, it follows that no man can call on another to serve his happiness" (*ibid.*, p. 103). Also see *Social Classes*, p. 34.

32. Sumner, *Social Classes*, pp. 82ff. regarding trade unions, and p. 96 regarding the value of association for "the independent action of self-governing freemen."

33. This was in an early appearance before a Congressional committee. Fine, *Laissez-Faire*, p. 83.

34. Sumner was convinced that capital would seek to defend itself and that it could probably "not defend itself without resorting to all the vices of plutocracy. . . . Thus the issue of democracy and plutocracy, numbers against capital, is made up" ("Democracy and Plutocracy," in Persons, *Social Darwinism*, p. 140). Sumner made the intriguing claim that "so surely as democracy yields to socialism, socialism will prove a middle stage toward plutocracy" ("The New Social Issue," in Persons, *Social Darwinism*, p. 167).

35. "Democracy and Plutocracy," in Persons, *Social Darwinism*, p. 145; and *Social Classes*, p. 58.

36. *Social Classes*, pp. 58–59.

37. Richard Hofstadter, *Social Darwinism in American Thought*, p. 66.

38. Herbert Gutman, "An Iron Workers' Strike in the Ohio Valley"; "Trouble on the Railroads in 1873–74," and "Two Lockouts in Pennsylvania, 1873–74."

39. From "Interview with a Miner," *Chicago Tribune*, June 30, 1874, cited in "Reconstruction in Ohio . . . 1873–74," *Labor History*, III, No. 3, (Fall 1962). The origins of the idea went back forty years: "The notion developed [in the Pennsylvania mines of the 1830s] that a worker had a vested right in his job and hence an equal claim with the employer upon profits accruing from new machinery" (Hartz, *Economic Policy and Democratic Thought*, p. 198). The idea also emerged across the country. Alexander Saxton writes that "in California, miners had learned to regard the opportunity of finding and exploiting gold deposits as a kind of property right, inherent in Anglo-Saxon descent." On the Comstock Lode, where "placer mining was of only slight importance [however,] the miners' community became a community of wage earners; and the concept of property right was transferred from entrepreneurial opportunity to job opportunity" (*Indispensable Enemy*, p. 57).

40. Jacobus TenBroek, *The Anti-slavery Origins of the Fourteenth Amendment*, pp. 219, 224. L. Frantz, "Congressional Power to Enforce the Fourteenth Amendment Against Private Acts," p. 1366.

41. Demonstrating that traditional sentiments regarding monopoly were as strong with some conservative lawyers as with the agrarians, Campbell in defense quoted one classic authority who styled monopolies "a nest of wasps—a swarm of vermin that have overcrept the land. Like the frogs of Egypt they have gotten possession of our dwellings . . . they sup in our cup; they dip in our dish; they sit by our fire" (*Slaughterhouse Cases*, 16 Wall. 36, 1873). For another reference to the attempt to create a property right in one's job, see *In re: Jacobs*, 98 N.Y. 98 (1885).

42. *Civil Rights Cases*, 109 U.S. 3 (1883). This point was made eloquently by Justice Harlan in dissent.

43. *Sta. Clara County v. Southern Pacific Railway*, 118 U.S. 394 (1886). This elevation of status then became doctrine and "oblivious to its˚lack of authority, it began presently to assert its claim as a holding" (Walton Hamilton, "The Path of Due Process of Law," p. 146). See also Howard J. Graham's excellent "An Innocent Abroad: The Constitutional Corporate Person."

44. *The Railroad Commission Cases*, 116 U.S. 307 (1886). "The power to regulate is not the power to destroy," Waite added in a thenceforth widely quoted phrase. For discussion of the increasing confusion between legislative questions of due process and judicial ones of eminent domain, see E. S. Corwin, *American Constitutional History: Essays by E. S. Corwin*, A. T. Mason and Gerald Garvey, eds., Chap. 4.

45. Dissent in *Munn v. Illinois*.

46. *Chicago, Milwaukee and St. Paul Ry. Co. v. Minn.*, 134 U.S. 418 (1890). Brewer's statement is in Arnold Paul, *Conservative Crisis*, pp. 71–72; the others are in *ibid.*, pp. 42–43. Paul discovers the reference to Dred Scott by an ex-President of the Tennessee Bar Association (*ibid.*, p. 222) as well as in a number of other places. In the next forty years state regulatory attempts were struck down a total of 401 times, more than half of them under these precedents. Leonard Levy, in *American Constitutional Law*, p. 130, notes: "In the entire history of the Court before 1898 there had only been 171 cases, involving all parts of the Constitution, in which state legislation had been judicially vetoed."

47. During the 1870s, for example, the Southern Pacific contested its valuation for tax purposes at $16,500 a mile while it was actually capitalized at, and was basing its rate charges on, the figure of $43,500 a mile. By invalidating commission attempts to enforce rates on commission-found valuations, the Court prevented California from protecting shippers and passengers from arbitrary rates. Graham discusses this in "An Innocent Abroad," pp. 190–191.

48. *Monongahela Navigation Co. v. U.S.*, 148 U.S. 312 (1893). Discussed in J. R. Commons, *The Legal Foundations of Capitalism*, pp. 182–183, and *Reagan v. Farmer's Loan and Trust Co.*, 154 U.S. 362 (1894).

49. *Allgeyer v. La.*, 165 U.S. 578 (1897). Roscoe Pound, "Liberty of Contract," pp. 445, 470.

50. The 6 percent rate was set in the *Consolidated Gas* cases of 1907 (157 Fed. 849). The willingness of some corporate directors to accept regulation as early as the 1840s in return for the 6 percent is recorded in Hartz, *Economic Policy*, p. 259; and those in the 1880s in Gabriel Kolko, *Railroads and Rate Regulation, 1887–1916*, p. 35.

51. The citation here is from *Godcharles v. Wigeman*, 113 Pa. St. 431 (1886). Of the cases turning on freedom of contract in the next six years, two out of three were decided by the Godcharles reasoning (Paul, *Conservative Crisis*, p. 45).

52. "Employment at will" means that in the absence of an agreement about the term of employment, employment can be terminated whenever the employer chooses. The doctrine's acceptance in American law was promoted by a

legal writer, H. G. Wood, in 1877, and was eventually adopted by the Court in the *Adair* case (1908). It differed from the customary legal assumption that where intentions had been unexpressed, the employment was either for one year or could be terminated (in lieu of cause) only after a customary or reasonable notice period (J. Peter Shapiro and James F. Tune, "Implied Contract Rights to Job Security," *Stanford Law Review*, XXVI, 2, January 1974).

53. Receivership was essentially a device to permit railroads, putatively bankrupt, to continue business as usual—and even to cut wages—secure in the knowledge that recalcitrant workers would be disobeying "officers of the Court." For an excellent discussion, see Gerald Eggert's *Railroad Labor Disputes*, (for example, pp. 23, 35, and 231). The significance of the judge-made law of receivership during these years cannot be overestimated. In 1893–1894 the Courts took over companies holding one-fifth of the total railroad lineage in the country (p. 109). The corporatist mix that would later become familiar was already evident in these policies. For purposes of investing in plant, rewarding or punishing locales, raising rates, or paying workers, railroad corporations were private agencies. But for purposes of restraining workers from striking, they were common carriers once again, clothed with a public function.

54. That the purpose of the new injunction was to crush Debs and the American Railway Union is generally acknowledged. It was successful in this purpose, and in the larger purpose of quashing big strikes. Railroad tie-ups like those that had been common before 1894 ceased for thirty years. And when the strike of 1922 occurred, it was met again with a new blanket injunction—which labor obeyed (Eggert, *Railroad Labor Disputes*, pp. 2, 239).

55. Paul, *Conservative Crisis*, p. 143.

56. See John Roche, "Entrepreneurial Liberty and the Commerce Power," p. 686. The Commission fulfilled Olney's expectations. When it tried to legalize pooling and create virtual cartels, however, the Court pre-empted some of its functions. The Court had been warned that if loose combinations were banned, close ones would be formed; and this in fact happened in the intensive merger wave of 1897–1903 (Kolko, *Railroads*, pp. 30–31, 74–83).

57. Paul, *Conservative Crisis*, p. 189. The Act was gutted in the famous sugar case, *U.S. v. E. C. Knight*, 156 U.S. 1 (1895). Merle Fainsod *et al.* note that the Act was invoked only once during a period when combinations were being formed "at a rate never equalled before or since," and they suggest that the Act was *intended* to be weak. They conclude that the manner in which it was enforced also promoted trustification (Fainsod, Gordon, and Palamountain, *Government and the American Economy*, New York: W. W. Norton, 1959, pp. 439–452 and 472).

58. "The triumph of conservatism" is Arnold Paul's phrase, though he notes that the ascendant conservatism was not of a traditional variety. Paul also observes that though more moderate regulatory decisions emerged after the turn of the century, "the doctrines of judicial supremacy . . . were not abandoned; even the much-publicized Brandeis brief effected no more than the concession that in the determination of 'reasonableness,' economic and social data were admissable" (Paul, *Conservative Crisis*, p. 228). John Roche develops the

idea of "entrepreneurial liberty" in three discerning articles: "Entrepreneurial Liberty and the Commerce Power," "Entrepreneurial Liberty and the Fourteenth Amendment," and "Civil Liberty in the Age of Enterprise."

59. Thomas Hobbes, *Leviathan*, Chap. 26.

60. Abram Chayes, "The Rule of Law," in E. S. Mason, *The Corporation in Modern Society*, p. 37.

61. Marx, *Capital*, I, p. 584.

62. J. R. Commons, *The Legal Foundations of Capitalism*, pp. 163–165 (emphasis added).

63. *U.S. v. Cassidy* (1895). Eggert, *Railroad Labor Disputes*, pp. 130–132 and 67.

64. William A. Williams, *The Contours of American History*, pp. 320–321.

65. Samuel Hays sees the political parties as having adopted a corporate form of organization during these years. "While the party rested on geography, and the interest group on function, the corporate system rested upon the integration of different functional groups, often located in different geographical areas, into single systems of activity, and under centralized control." Hays, "Political Parties and the Community-Society Continuum," in W. D. Burnham and W. N. Chambers, *The American Party Systems*, p. 168.

66. Solon Buck, *The Granger Movement*, pp. 215 and 206.

67. C. Vann Woodward, *Tom Watson*, p. 260.

68. Rousseau, *The Social Contract*, Chap. 3.

69. Michael Reagan, *The Managed Economy*, p. 18.

70. Sumner, *Social Classes*, p. 141.

71. Cited in E. Kirkland, *Charles Francis Adams, Jr.: Patrician at Bay*, p. 168.

72. Adams, *Railroads*, pp. 85 (emphasis added), 186, 193, and 202.

73. *Ibid.*, p. 193.

74. Smith wrote: "The proposal of any new law or regulation of commerce which comes from this order [merchants and master manufacturers] ought always to be . . . examined . . . with the most scrupulous [and] suspicious attention. It comes from an order of men whose interest is never exactly the same with that of the public, and who have generally an interest to deceive and even to oppress the public" (*Wealth of Nations*, Book I, Chap. 11, pp. 219–220).

75. Adams, *Railroads*, p. 138.

76. *Ibid.*, p. 187.

77. *Ibid.*, p. 15.

78. Such programs were implemented at the time at Rockefeller's Fuel and Iron Company, the Baltimore and Ohio, the Pennsylvania and Reading Railroads, and Pullman's model city. The plans are described in W. J. Ghent, *Our Benevolent Feudalism*, p. 64 and *passim*, and Kirkland, *Charles Francis Adams*, pp. 55, 96–97. Lest their class character be considered accidental, a passage from Adams's *Autobiography* is instructive. "I don't associate with the laborers on my place," he explained, "nor would the association be agreeable to either of us. Their customs, language, habits and conventionalities differ from mine as do

those of their children. . . . I believe in the equality of men before the laws; but social equality whether for man or child is altogether another thing" (pp. 15–16).

79. "Nobody regards Pullman as a real home. . . . Whether the power of George Pullman be exercised rightfully or wrongfully, it is there all the same. . . . The idea of Pullman is un-American" (R. T. Ely, "Pullman: A Social Study," *Harper's New Monthly Magazine*, 1885, excerpted in John A. Garraty, *The Transformation of American Society, 1870–1890*, New York: Harper Torchbooks, 1968, pp. 176–177). Regarding the new villeinage, see Ghent, *Our Benevolent Feudalism*, pp. 64, 184.

80. Andrew Carnegie, "The Gospel of Wealth," p. 655.

81. *Ibid.*, pp. 653, 660–661. Interestingly enough, Carnegie never admitted the failure of the self-regulating market regarding production. Despite the new concentration of power, the rising entry costs to business, and the emergence of an American caste system, he still insisted that new businesses would arise whenever shoddy goods were produced or excessive prices charged. A few men meeting in a room could never "change the great laws which govern . . . the business world." "Capital wisely managed yields its legitimate profit," Carnegie insisted in a tone reserved for successful millionaires ("The Bugaboo of Trusts," pp. 149, 145).

82. Carnegie, "The Gospel of Wealth," pp. 660–661.

83. Walton Bean, *California: An Interpretive History* (New York: McGraw-Hill, 1968), p. 275.

84. Buck, *The Granger Movement*, Chaps. 4 and 5.

85. Kolko, *Railroads*, pp. 76 and 28 (emphasis in original).

86. Though unsuccessful in their immediate goal of legalizing pooling, the corporation spokesmen were able to get a bill that failed to outlaw pooling, left the bases for rate valuations vague, and located the new agency in the Executive branch where it could be sheltered from—and act as Olney's "barrier" against— popular pressures (Kolko, *Railroads*, pp. 42–43). W. J. Ghent, for one, was aware of the importance of this latter provision. "A marked tendency of recent legislation . . . is that toward the creation of boards charged with administrative, executive, semi-judicial, and even police powers. The institution of these boards means simply a further removal from the people of the conduct of public affairs" (*Our Benevolent Feudalism*, p. 84). This interpretation of the origins of the ICC is now widely accepted. See, for example, even the brief *The Wall Street Journal* article by Lindley Clark, January 9, 1973. Kolko notes that as far back as the railroad strikes of 1877 the owners' magazine, *The Railway World*, had urged that railway lines "no longer . . . be considered merely state organizations . . . but national in their character" (*Railroads*, p. 14).

87. Marver Bernstein, *Regulating Business by Independent Commission* (Princeton: Princeton University Press, 1955). McConnell's and Lowi's remarks on modern regulatory agencies were discussed in Chapter One. See also Reagan, *The Managed Economy*, pp. 169–170.

88. Kolko, *Railroads*, pp. 44–45, 61.

89. *Ibid.*, pp. 36–37. The bill he helped author, the Rice Bill, was the one over which Perkins had waxed enthusiastic.

90. A key holder in the companies that combined to form the American Refining and Smelting Co. in 1897, Adams admitted that the new company was a "trust," and hoped "it is a monopoly; out of that monopoly I trust to make much money." He also approved of the Court's striking down of a Kansas tax on a stockyard in which he had a large interest as confiscatory and discriminatory; he noted that "Justice Brewer argued our case for us" (cited in Kirkland, *Charles Francis Adams*, pp. 181–182). Regarding the bribes, see *ibid.*, pp. 107–111.

CHAPTER FIVE

"The United States Incorporated" is the title of Chapter 3 of John Dewey's *Individualism, Old and New* (1929). Epigraph: Garry Wills, speaking of the baroque funeral preparations for Ralph Waldo Emerson, in *Nixon Agonistes* (New York: Signet Books, New American Library, 1971), p. 172.

1. And this, despite the fact that Senator Sherman declared in 1890 that unions attempting to reduce hours of labor or increase wages could "not possibly be included in the words or intent of the bill as now reported" (G. Eggert, *Railroad Labor Disputes*, p. 115).

2. Robert Wiebe, *Businessmen and Reform*, p. 18.

3. A. F. Bentley, *The Process of Government*, pp. 204, 209.

4. Oliver Wendell Holmes, Jr., in *Vegelahn v. Guntner*, 167 Mass. 92, 104 (1896).

5. Otto Gierke, *Political Theories of the Middle Age*, pp. 67–69, 87.

6. Regarding the idea of a "harmoniously articulated community," see Gierke, *The Middle Age*, pp. 72–74, 94–98. Laski's phrase is from W. Y. Elliott, *The Pragmatic Revolt in Politics*, p. 158.

7. These different dimensions of the pluralist impulse are treated in K. C. Hsiao, *Political Pluralism*, for example, pp. 49, 141.

8. In 1900 there were 185 industrial combinations in the country, making up less than .5 percent of the businesses but owning 15 percent of the capital; within four years their number had doubled and they controlled 40 percent of the nation's manufacturing capital (Joseph Rayback, *A History of American Labor*, p. 191). By 1904 Moody listed 318 corporations, 234 (75 percent) of which had been organized since 1898. These held six-sevenths of the total capitalization (Hofstadter, *The Age of Reform*, p. 169). To take only one example of what "combination" meant, the Santa Fe Railway System of 1899 consisted of what had been over one hundred smaller companies.*

9. "*Political capitalism* is the utilization of political outlets to attain conditions of stability, predictability and security—to attain rationalization—in the economy. . . . By *security* I mean protection from the political attacks latent in any formally democratic political structure" (Kolko, *The Triumph of Conservatism*, p. 3; see also William A. Williams, *The Contours of American History*, p. 351).

J. Weinstein discusses the NCF in *The Corporate Ideal in the Liberal State*. By

1903 there were representatives in the NCF of one-third of the 367 corporations with a capitalization of more than ten million dollars, and representatives of 16 of the 67 largest railroads. Members included Marcus Hanna, Samuel Insull, Charles Francis Adams, Jr., Andrew Carnegie, several partners of J. P. Morgan, and—in the Connecticut organization—Louis Brandeis. The NCF is also discussed in Milton Derber, "The Idea of Industrial Democracy in America, 1898–1915."

10. Despite the NCF's inability to get labor exempted from the provisions of the Sherman Anti-Trust Act, J. David Greenstone writes that it nevertheless proceeded with "sophisticated or enlightened methods . . . [to pull] the teeth of aggressive unionism. . . . It was concerned with settling strikes—and often settlements it applauded were disastrous to unionism" (*Labor in American Politics*, p. 27).

11. Weinstein, *The Corporate Ideal*, p. 87. And to a House Committee, Low explained that "regulation, not prohibition should be our watchword" (*ibid.*, p. 80).

12. Kolko, *Triumph of Conservatism*, pp. 75, 77.

13. *Ibid.*, p. 163. Judge Gary repeated a belief he shared with Mellen and Carnegie, when he said to a House Committee of 1911 that "we must come to enforced publicity and government control . . . even as to prices" (Weinstein, p. 84). Perkins, still active, reported to the Industrial Commission: "I have long believed that cooperation through large industrial units properly supervised and regulated by the Federal Government is the only method of eliminating the abuses from which labor has suffered under the competitive method" (Derber, "Idea of Industrial Democracy," p. 273). For statements of similar opinions by Cyrus McCormick and Samuel Insull, see Weinstein, *The Corporate Ideal*, pp. 33, 85, 87.

14. Weinstein, *The Corporate Ideal*, pp. 20, 7. So committed were these industrialists to the group perspective that they were outraged more by the individualists in the NAM than by the workers in the AFL. "Our enemies," said Low in 1909, "are the socialists among the labor people and the anarchists among the capitalists" (*ibid.*, p. 11).

15. Cited in Weinstein, *The Corporate Ideal*, p. 10.

16. Grosvenor Clarkson, *Industrial America in the World War* (1932), cited in Grant McConnell, *Private Power and American Democracy*, pp. 373, n. 18; see also p. 63.

17. Roosevelt's administration brought only 54 anti-trust prosecutions in seven years, and far fewer convictions; Taft's administration brought nearly 90 in four years. The averages were Roosevelt less than 9 per year and Taft over 22 per year (Hofstadter, *Age of Reform*, p. 228).

18. Cited in Kolko, *Triumph of Conservatism*, p. 162.

19. Eggert, *Railroad Labor Disputes*, pp. 224–225.

20. *Vegelahn v. Guntner*, 167 Mass. 92, 104 (1896); also *Plant v. Woods*, 176 Mass. 492 (1900).

21. *Northern Securities Co. v. U.S.*, 193 U.S. 197, 400 (1904). It was in *Dr. Miles*

Medical Co. v. Park and Sons Co., 220 U.S. 373 (1911) that Holmes delivered his curious economic theory. A. J. Eddy cited Holmes's dissent in *Dr. Miles* with approval in his appeal for open price arrangements in *The New Competition* of 1912 (New York: D. Appleton and Co., p. 6). Eddy's motives, however, were less those of a business corporatist than those of a proponent of cooperative social arrangements, like Dewey or Croly.

22. *American Column and Lumber Co. v. U.S.*, 257 U.S. 377 (1921). See also *Liggett Co. v. Baldridge*, 271 U.S. 105 (1928). Holmes's private view about the Sherman Act was identical to Olney's. It was "a humbug based on economic ignorance and incompetence" (letter to Sir Frederick Pollack, July 23, 1916, *Holmes-Pollack Letters*, Mark de Wolfe Howe, ed., I, p. 163).

23. *Lochner v. N.Y.* 198 U.S. 45, 74 (1905). Oliver Wendell Holmes, Jr., *The Common Law*, p. 100.

24. *Truax v. Corrigan*, 257 U.S. 343 (1921).

25. Holmes, "Law and the Court" (1913), in Max Lerner, ed., *The Mind and Faith of Justice Holmes*, p. 389. See Walter Lippmann, *Drift and Mastery*, pp. 42–43.

26. The critique of Spencer was delivered in a commentary on the gas-stokers' strike of London in 1873, cited Lerner, *Justice Holmes*, p. 50. Holmes concluded from the inevitability of conflict simply that great legislative reforms were impossible, and that the most one could expect was that "legislation might [slowly] . . . modify itself in accordance with the will of the *de facto* supreme power in the community" (*ibid.*; see also Howe, *Holmes-Pollock Letters*, Letter to Pollock, June 20, 1928; also letter to Wu, June 21, 1928, cited in Lerner, *Justice Holmes*, p. 435). Generally, Holmes rejected the idea that there were class issues at stake and attributed workers' demands to wrong-headed individualist selfishness.

27. In the *Vegelahn* case he had presented "society" as "disguised under the name of capital," thus equating the two entities. On *Loewe*, see Philip Taft, *The AFL in the Time of Gompers*, p. 266.

28. *Schenck v. U.S.*, 249 U.S. 47 (1919).

29. Max Lerner argues that Holmes steered a middle path between an "objective" test on one hand and the "known tendencies" doctrine on the other (*Justice Holmes*, pp. 292–294). But that is a misleading distinction. In fact, Holmes's test amounted in practice to an "objective test"—though it turned on an objective determination of "circumstances" rather than (as with Learned Hand) of intent. Both the *Debs* and *Whitney* cases—249 U.S. 211 (1919), and 274 U.S. 357 (1927)—illustrated the non-libertarian ends for which this test could easily be used.

30. *Abrams v. U.S.*, 250 U.S. 616, 624 (1919).

31. Holmes's opinions in *Gitlow v. N.Y.* (268 U.S. 672, 1925) and *U.S. v. Schwimmer* (279 U.S. 653, 1928) might make a better case for his libertarianism. But their oft-quoted phrases (notably "every idea is an incitement") are usually taken out of context. What protected Gitlow, for Holmes, was that he had proposed overthrow of the government "at some indefinite time in the future" and

there was no present danger of it. Nor could Holmes refrain from characterizing Gitlow's utterance as "the redundant discourse before us" and as "futile." These cases revealed Holmes's willingness to rule on the *content* of the defendants' ideas—to judge individual rights by prevailing group mores—a practice far from libertarian in its implications. Similarly, it was important for Holmes that Rosika Schwimmer was a woman of "superior character and intelligence" and that her pacifist ideas would probably not lead to activities "such as were dealt with in Schenck. . . . Her position and motives are wholly different from those of Schenck."

32. Holmes, *The Common Law*, p. 49.

33. Tocqueville, *Democracy in America*, II, p. 171. See also Reinhard Bendix's remarks in *Work and Authority in Industry*, p. viii–ix.

34. Bentley, *Process of Government*, p. 90 (emphasis added).

35. *Ibid.*, pp. 200–202. "That which takes us farthest along the road to quantitative estimates will inevitably be the best statement" (*ibid.*).

36. "The phenomena of government are from start to finish phenomena of force"—or, because he wanted to avoid the bad connotations of that word, of "pressure" (*ibid.*, pp. 258–259).

37. *Ibid.*, p. 171.

38. *Ibid.*, pp. 372 and 226; and regarding groups and interests, p. 211.

39. See Mary Parker Follett, *The New State*, pp. 3 and 85. Dewey also proposed that "society means association" (*Reconstruction in Philosophy*, p. 205). In Dewey's case I shall depart from my practice in this book and include works written in the twenties and thirties. This is because his formulations captured Progressive thought in its classic form, and because the germs of his later ideas were already evident in his articles during the earlier period.

40. Follett, *The New State*, p. 310.

41. John Dewey, *The Public and Its Problems*, pp. 21, 98. Concerning the lack of human content in modern industrial organization, see Dewey, *Individualism*, p. 39.

42. Cited in Follett, *The New State*, p. 305.

43. Dewey, "Austin's Theory of Sovereignty," pp. 31–52.

44. Dewey, *The Public and Its Problems*, pp. 152–153.

45. Dewey, *Individualism*, pp. 61 and 87–88. "Our sociability is largely an effort to find substitutes for that normal consciousness of connection and union that proceeds from being a sustained and sustaining member of a social whole" (*ibid.*).

46. Dewey, *The Public and Its Problems*, pp. 109 and 203; *Individualism*, pp. 30, 49 and 59; and *Liberalism and Social Action*, p. 82. Dewey did recognize, however, that the state's "exercise of power is pale in contrast with that exercised by concentrated and organized property interests" (*ibid.*, p. 64).

47. Herbert Croly, *The Promise of American Life*, pp. 11, 13, 23, 62, 189, and 358. The "promise" for Croly included the promise of meaningful work, the "test" of "responding to a fair chance," and security in the fruits of one's labor—as it had for the Jacksonians and the populists.

48. Dewey, *Liberalism*, pp. 61, 76.

49. Dewey, *The Public and Its Problems*, pp. 3–5.

50. Dewey, concerning "integration," *Individualism*, pp. 48, 53, 57, 148, and 167. The remark about technology is from *Individualism*, p. 30.

51. Follett, *The New State*, pp. 22, 49, and 160.

52. Croly, *The Promise*, pp. 207, 285. Edmund Wilson later wrote that Croly's real concern was not with political activity itself but with a deeper "democratic spirit" that might or might not avail itself of political means ("An Appeal to Progressives," from January 14, 1931, issue of *The New Republic*, reprinted in *The Shores of Light*, New York: Vintage Books, 1961, p. 521).

53. Croly, *The Promise*, p. 124. "The solution of the social problem demands the substitution of a conscious social ideal for the earlier instinctive homogeneity of the American nation" (*ibid.*, p. 139).

54. Dewey, *The Public and Its Problems*, pp. 158 and 176–177. See also *Liberalism*, pp. 67–68; Dewey gave appropriate reference to Henry George on this point.

55. Dewey, *Individualism*, pp. 33–34.

56. Dewey, *The Public and its Problems*, pp. 152–153, 146. Also: "Personality must be educated. . . . Full education comes only when there is a responsible share on the part of each person . . . in shaping the aims and policies of the social groups to which he belongs" (*Reconstruction*, p. 209).

57. Follett, *The New State*, pp. 62 and 115.

58. Cited in Mancur Olson, *The Logic of Collective Action*, p. 115. Cole's quotation about representation is from Elliott, *Pragmatic Revolt*, p. 95; Follett's point about republicanism is on p. 178, *ibid.*

59. Follett, *The New State*, pp. 142, 168, 173; concerning her opposition to functional representation, see pp. 76–77 and 293.

60. Croly, *The Promise*, pp. 408, 359–368.

61. *Ibid.*, p. 124.

62. For the development of this conclusion, see *ibid.*, pp. 359–368; on the effects of private property, pp. 181–183.

63. *Ibid.*, pp. 365–368.

64. Walter Lippmann, *A Preface to Politics*, pp. 22, 25.

65. He added: "Combinations in industry are the result of an imperative economic law which cannot be repealed by political legislation." Roosevelt on this occasion agreed with Croly—and disagreed with Sumner—that "the true conservative is he who insists that property shall be the servant and not the master of the commonwealth" (Theodore Roosevelt, "The New Nationalism," August 31, 1910, in William E. Leuchtenberg, ed., *Theodore Roosevelt: The New Nationalism*, pp. 27, 29).

66. Quoted in Morton White, *Social Thought in America: The Revolt Against Formalism*, pp. 101–102. Thus Dewey: "The notion that men may be free in their thought even when they are not in its expression and dissemination had been sedulously propagated. . . . [But] such a consciousness presents the spectacle . . . of mind deprived of its normal functioning . . . baffled by actualities . . .

and driven back into secluded and impotent revery" (*The Public and Its Problems*, p. 167, and Chap. 5 *passim*). This notion of "positive freedom" was clearly anticipated by the populists.

67. Michael Rogin, "Non-Partisanship and the Group Interest," p. 114.

68. Follett, *The New State*, p. 69. Croly, *The Promise*.

69. Croly, *The Promise*, pp. 359 and 387.

70. Dewey, *The Public and Its Problems*, p. 154. "To learn to be human is to develop through the give-and-take of communication an effective sense of being an individually distinctive member of a community." And see note 56 above.

71. McConnell, *Private Power and American Democracy*, p. 142.

72. Dewey, *Reconstruction*, p. 186, also pp. 208–209. See *Liberalism*, p. 56, for identical formulations almost two decades later.

73. Alexis de Tocqueville, *Democracy in America*, Vol. II, Book IV, Chap. 5 *passim*. Tocqueville's political vision and theory of local government cannot be understood apart from the tradition of European commentary on—and critique of—monistic forms of sovereignty. I am not aware of any studies which have acknowledged this, but the point is apparent in the chapter cited.

74. *Ibid.*, Vol. I, p. 71, and Chapter 5 *passim*; Vol. II, pp. 7 and 125.

75. *Ibid.*, Vol. I, p. 69.

76. Real freedom consisted for Follett in "obedience to the law of one's nature"; and the law of human nature was said to be "the capacity for union." In a curious image for a Jamesean vitalist, but one reminiscent of Wilson's liberty of the piston, Follett likened the situation of people vis-à-vis each other to that of "the nut and the screw [which] form a perfect combination not because they are different, but because they exactly fit into each other and together can perform a function neither could perform alone" (*The New State*, pp. 55, 64–70).

77. Dewey, *The Public and Its Problems*, p. 148. To talk about individuals separate from society was like talking about letters apart from an alphabet, he wrote (*ibid.*, p. 69). But he ignored the fact that society is made up of several alphabets, and that individuals are often faced with the task of choosing between them.

78. Croly, *The Promise*, p. 414.

79. McConnell, *Private Power*, p. 142. "The interests of a superior reality held up in contrast to the abstract 'public interest' were not mere self-interests, but *group* self-interests" (p. 160). Similarly, Elliott wrote that though Laski "banished authority in the name of the individual so far as legal sovereignty was concerned, he reintroduced the subordination of the individual in the name of the group" in a manner identical to Leon Duguit's. "The authority he has taken from law he has given to pseudo-individuals whom he calls corporate persons" (Elliott, *Pragmatic Revolt*, pp. 146, 151).

80. As Charles Anderson puts it: "When an organization becomes the official representative of a particular interest it becomes, in effect, part of the political system. Furthermore, it becomes in some significant sense, an involuntary organization. For both of these reasons, to be compatible with democratic theory, the internal government of the interest organization must itself be democratic" ("Political Design and the Representation of Interests," p. 145).

81. This educational function had been central for Tocqueville. He felt that it was "vain to summon a people" who had lost the habits of participation to periodic elections; "this rare and brief exercise of their free choice . . . will not prevent them from gradually losing the faculties of thinking, feeling and acting for themselves" (*Democracy in America*, Vol. II, p. 339).

82. Bentley, *The Process of Government*, p. 186.

83. Gierke's call to grant authority to "real" groups thus wound up, ironically, justifying the grant of authority to groups which embodied the standardized, mechanical, and anti-organic forms of association he lamented.

84. Dewey, *Liberalism*, p. 81. And see *The Public and Its Problems*, pp. 70–71.

85. A regime in which the "individuals" who challenged the state were corporations, W. Y. Elliott remarked in 1928, took us back to the world of Hobbes. For "if life under it not be solitary . . . it is nasty, brutish and short enough to spare" (*The Pragmatic Revolt*, p. 109).

86. Bentley, *The Process of Government*, pp. 442–445.

87. Follett, *The New State*, p. 117.

88. "The pressure system . . . gets results by being selective and biased; *if everyone got into the act the unique advantages of this form of organization would be destroyed*" (E. E. Schattschneider, *The Semi-Sovereign People*, pp. 32–35, emphasis in original).

89. Lippmann, *Drift and Mastery*, p. 155.

90. The "temporary parallelogram of forces" is in Harold Laski, *Introduction to Politics* (London, Unwin Books, 1930), p. 17; also see pp. 39–42. Dewey, *Reconstruction*, pp. 202–204. But Dewey soon abjured all anticipatory prescriptions regarding the state and advised judgment by case-by-case "consequences." This was in the book in which, having set out to dispose of negative definitions, he reduced the state to a mutual insurance agent for the unexpected social costs of private transactions (*The Public and Its Problems*, pp. 17, 27, 73–74). Follett's program for the state was to base it on "multiple group organization," but she said nothing about which groups should be represented, or how (*The New State*, pp. 259, 310).

91. George Mowry, *The California Progressives*, p. 100; Older's comments are from issues of *The San Francisco Bulletin* of 1909 and 1911. And concerning the corporation's breeding of authoritarian character traits, see Robert Presthus, *The Organizational Society*, pp. 122–134. Follett sometimes even praised the corporation as the harbinger of the new order, despite the fact that it would be hard to conceive of an organization, short of the army, more devoted to top-down principles (her criticism of Hegel), more crowd-oriented, and more devoted to the "absorption" of individuals than the corporation (*The New State*, pp. 8, 322; see pp. 105–107, and 363–365 for other examples).

92. Bentley, *The Process of Government*, pp. 314, 358. Illustrative of the debilitating effects for political analysis of Bentley's process-orientation and of his faith in automatic balancing was his interpretation of Roosevelt's mediation in the coal strike of 1902. He interpreted this act, which was undertaken from motives similar to Olney's and Holmes's, as following from the President's respon-

siveness not to "the system" but "on a deeper-lying level . . . [to] the great interest groups not effectively represented in the existing government"—by which
he meant labor and the consumers (p. 346). Bentley's method did not permit him
to weigh the data before him with reference to the context from which they
derived.

93. Dewey, *The Public and Its Problems*, pp. 203, 174. Louis Brandeis, *The
Curse of Bigness*; esp. two chapters, "Industrial Democracy and Efficiency," and
"The Curse of Bigness."

94. E. H. Carr, *The New Society* (Boston: Beacon Press, 1957), p. 65.

95. Dewey, *Individualism*, p. 171; Follett, *The New State*, p. 105; Croly, *The
Process of Government*, p. 284.

96. This functionalism was more explicit with some of the European philosophers. Comte proposed explicitly that security in the new era would follow
from a recognition of function and duty; it would be guaranteed by "the general acknowledgement of reciprocal obligations" (*A General View of Positivism*,
p. 400). At the same time the Progressives were writing, Leon Duguit in France
was comparing individuals in society to cells in a living body, the element of will
being reduced to a capacity for accepting what had been determined as "the law
of the group." As with Engels, freedom from such a view lay in the recognition
of necessity. Duguit also argued that modern public law should become "objective" because it was "no longer concerned with deciding conflicts between the
subjective rights of the individual and the subjective rights of a personified state,
but simply with regulating the performance of the social functions of the government" ("Law in the Modern State," in Margaret Spahr, *Readings in Recent Political Philosophy*, p. 492; and see Elliott, *The Pragmatic Revolt*, p. 234).

97. Follett, *The New State*, p. 131; Bentley, *The Process of Government*, pp. 157,
272; Dewey, *The Public and Its Problems*, pp. 54–56. The criminal law was thus
said to be merely a system that specified conditions "in reference to consequences which may be incurred if [those conditions] are . . . transgressed."
Dewey went so far as to hold that "habit is the mainspring of human action." He
also proposed that "thinking is secreted in the interstices of habits." But when he
went on to say that the idea that men are moved by an intelligent and calculated
regard for their own good is pure mythology," he threw out his intentionalist
baby with the utilitarian bathwater (*ibid.*, pp. 159–160).

98. Andrew Fraser, "The Legal Theory We Need Now," pp. 171 and 172.

99. See, for example, Dewey, *Liberalism*, p. 80.

100. Bentley, *The Process of Government*, pp. 260–261. And see Norman
Jacobson's excellent "Causality and Time in Political Process: A Speculation,"
American Political Science Review, LVIII (March 1964), pp. 15–22.

101. The failure of American political thought to move beyond this impasse
is nowhere better illustrated than in the historical interpretations of Progressivism itself. The consensus school of historiography, which dominated the scene
at mid-century, concentrated on individual events, personalities, and court
holdings, and tended to ignore power. It ignored the question of power, for example, in explaining why American labor failed to become socialist, and why

American capital was able to postpone throughout Progressivism and until the New Deal social legislation that had been granted in Germany, France, and England by 1900. See, for example, Hofstadter's *Age of Reform*, pp. 242–256.

The more recent school of interpretation has attempted a broader view of the social system and addressed itself directly to power. (See, for example, Weinstein's *Corporate Ideal in the Liberal State* and Kolko's *Triumph of Conservatism*.) It has been accused by exponents of the former view of holding a mechanistic, conspiracy view of history; and its response has not always been persuasive. Weinstein, for example, though explaining that his book "is not based on a conspiracy theory," went on to add that "it posit[s] a conscious and successful effort to guide and control the economic and social policies of . . . government . . . by the most sophisticated leaders of America's largest corporations and financial institutions" (*The Corporate Ideal*, pp. ix, xii).

The essential truth of Kolko's and Weinstein's thesis, however, is not in its attribution of motives (speaking of the Progressive movement as a whole), but in its identification of *effects*. As Robert Wiebe states the case: "The more prosperous businessmen so conditioned the debates over economic legislation [that their] programs continued to set legislative limits well after 1912. . . . They set boundaries even when they did not dictate legislation" (*Businessmen and Reform*, pp. 212, 214). The point is not that big businessmen originated everything themselves, but that class institutions were able to set outer limits on what could succeed.

With this larger picture in mind, it becomes clear that the middle class was not a neutral pivot or "makeweight for compromise," as George Mowry suggested in *California Progressives*. The Hiram Johnsons and new urban professionals, indeed the group theorists themselves, functioned rather as a vanguard for corporate capitalist *social* arrangements—smoothing the way, resolving disruptions, and refashioning political institutions and thought.

102. Cited in Elliott, *Pragmatic Revolt*, pp. 211–212.

103. Faced by increasing attacks by employers' associations, the AFL was finally prosecuted successfully under the Sherman Act in the celebrated Danbury Hatters' case (1908). Union members then found themselves, unlike corporate directors, individually liable for the actions of their associations. Concerning the capitalists' growing powers in national markets, see Commons et al., *The History of Labor in the United States*, Vol. I, Chap. 1; and Gerald Grob, *Workers and Utopia: Ideological Conflict in the American Labor Movement, 1865–1900*, Chaps. 5 and 6.

104. These forced mergers usually worked to the benefit of the stronger union, even when the weaker one had been the original affiliate. Thirty-five such unions were created from above between 1896 and 1901. See Philip Taft, *The AFL in the Time of Gompers*, p. 210; Grob, *Workers and Utopia*, pp. 140 and 158; and Rogin, "Voluntarism: The Political Functions of an Anti-Political Doctrine," in McLaughlin and Rehmus, eds., *Labor and American Politics*, pp. 103–106. Joseph Raybeck also writes: the "nationals . . . gradually increas[ed] control over locals and funds, destroying some aspects of local autonomy, and building the princi-

ple of trade solidarity. . . . The principle of craft autonomy sometimes surrendered to the principle of might" (*A History of American Labor*, pp. 207–208).

105. Commons *et al.*, *History of Labor in the United States*, I, p. 575.

106. Michael Rogin, "Voluntarism," p. 117. For the different stages of the voluntarist doctrine, see also Marc Karson's *American Labor Unions and Politics, 1900–1918.*

107. J. R. Commons, in McLaughlin and Rehmus, *Labor and American Politics*, pp. 91–92. For an account of the socialists within the AFL, see Grob, *Workers and Utopia*, pp. 176–186.

108. John Spargo, *Syndicalism, Industrial Unionism and Socialism* (New York: Huebsch, 1913), p. 30. On the IWW, also see Karson, *American Labor Unions*, pp. 159–209.

109. The dialogue with Hillquit is in Leon Litwack's *The American Labor Movement* (Englewood Cliffs, N.J.: Prentice-Hall, 1962), pp. 40–41. The quotation from Gompers is in McLaughlin and Rehmus, *Labor and American Politics*, pp. 103–106. This rejection of a conscious theoretical point of view left the AFL with a weak basis for social criticism, as indicated in its inadequate response to the threats of scientific management. See M. Nadworny, *Scientific Management and the Unions, 1900–1932*, pp. 26, 43, 51.

Gompers did actually hold to one "ideological" tenet during his life—often taking it to "doctrinaire" extremes, in the words of his noted biographer, Philip Taft. This was his opposition to social legislation, such as laws regulating wages and hours. See also Karson, *American Labor Unions*, p. 134. Also expressive of "ideology" was Gompers's rejection of the offer of alliance from the populists because, as farmers, they were presumably an employing class. See Grob, *Workers and Utopia*, p. 167, and Pollack, *The Populist Response*, pp. 62–64.

110. In Grob, *Workers and Utopia*, p. 181.

111. Ronald Radosh, "The Corporate Ideology of American Labor Leaders from Gompers to Hillman," p. 71.

112. Ronald Radosh, "Corporatism, Liberal and Fascist, as Seen by Samuel Gompers," p. 67. Mancur Olson cites John R. Commons's somewhat similar views. In his last book, Commons suggested that the economic pressure groups, concentrating in Washington, D.C., were more representative of the nation than a Congress elected by territorial divisions. They constituted "an occupational parliament of the American people. . . . They are the informal counterparts of Mussolini's 'corporate state'" (cited in Olson, *The Logic of Collective Action*, p. 116; see also Laski, *Introduction to Politics*, p. 42). Grant McConnell noted that a group is not truly voluntary unless its members have alternatives to membership in it. As AFL nationals have become successful and increasingly integrated into corporate and federal benefit structures, however, the alternatives to membership in them have, in effect, disappeared.

113. Ralph Gabriel, on the spread of Comte's influence in the United States, in *The Course of American Democratic Thought*, p. 478, note 21.

114. Dewey, *The Public and Its Problems*, pp. 134–135. The passages from *Human Nature and Conduct* are cited in Elliott, *Pragmatic Revolt*, pp. 225–228. See

also Dewey, *Individualism*, pp. 49–50, concerning Dewey's lack of concern for the distinctive characteristics of corporate organization. For Follett's similar remarks, see *The New State*, pp. 62–63.

CHAPTER SIX

Epigraph: Walton Hamilton, "Property, According to Locke," p. 871.

1. The agreement permitted coal companies to increase prices by the 10 percent it had increased wages, and permitted the companies to ignore the provisions of the Sherman Anti-Trust Act.

2. This independence was questionable. The labor representative had to be smuggled onto the commission as a sociologist. That Roosevelt's intervention was not a neutral act, as many (including Arthur Bentley), thought, was obvious to the more populist-leaning Henry Demarest Lloyd at the time. "On the Eve of the Anthracite Coal Strike Arbitration: Lloyd at UMW Headquarters," C. M. Destler, *Labor History* XIII, No. 2 (Spring 1972). Also see Bentley, *The Process of Government*, p. 351.

3. John Garraty, *The American Nation* (New York: Harper and Row, 1966), p. 658. For an interesting contemporary account of the mine conditions and a view of the unions as a nationalizing vehicle for immigrants, see Frank J. Warne, *The Slav Invasion and the Mine Workers* (Philadelphia, 1904).

4. Lincoln Steffens, *The Shame of the Cities*, pp. 181, 185, 201–202.

5. See David F. Noble's *America by Design: Science, Technology and the Rise of Corporate Capitalism*.

6. Samuel Haber, *Efficiency and Uplift: Scientific Management in the Progressive Era, 1890–1920*, p. 61.

7. Henry Jones Ford, "Present Trends in American Politics," *American Political Science Review*, XIV, No. 1 (1920), p. 6. And see Woodrow Wilson's "Democracy and Efficiency."

8. Philip Wiener, *Evolution and the Founders of Pragmatism*, pp. 4, 81–83.

9. Haber, *Efficiency and Uplift*, p. 11.

10. Noble, *America By Design*, p. xxi.

11. E. Kirkland, *Charles Francis Adams, Jr.: Patrician at Bay*, p. 160.

12. Auguste Comte, *A General View of Positivism*, trans. J. H. Bridges, pp. 65, 110, 172.

13. John Locke, *An Essay Concerning Human Understanding*, ed. G. W. Ewing (Chicago: Henry Regnery Co., 1960), p. 13.

14. *Ibid.*, as cited in Morton White, *Science and Sentiment in America*, pp. 13, 19–20. "I doubt not but from self-evident propositions by necessary consequences, as incontestable as those in mathematics, the measures of right and wrong might be made out to anyone that will apply himself with the same indifferency and attention. . . . Where there is no property, there is no injustice, is a proposition as certain as any demonstration in Euclid." *An Essay Concerning Human Understanding*, Book IV, Ch. III, Sect. 18 (p. 254).

15. "Though marching with the people, the progressive reformers clearly

marched at their head" (Haber, *Efficiency and Uplift*, p. 101). And more pointedly: "'Let the people rule' is a historical phrase. The Progressives who greeted efficiency with enthusiasm were often those who proposed to let the people rule through a process in which the bulk of the people most of the time ruled hardly at all" (*ibid.*, p. xii). Rogin has characterized populism as a mass uprising but Progressivism as "primarily an elite phenomenon" (*The Intellectuals and McCarthy*, p. 179).

16. K. C. Hsiao, *Political Pluralism*, p. 193.

17. Christopher Lasch, *The New Radicalism in America*, p. 176. Lasch's Chapter 5, "Politics as Social Control," is excellent on this contradiction.

18. Cited in "Action, Conduct, and Self-Control," by Richard Bernstein, in Bernstein, ed., *Perspectives on Peirce*, p. 67.

19. Cited in Dewey, *Essays in Experimental Logic*, p. 306.

20. Oliver Wendell Holmes, Jr., *The Common Law*, pp. 5, 32.

21. "How to Make Our Ideas Clear," in Wiener, *Values in a Universe of Chance*, p. 124. Previous sentence from James, "What Pragmatism Means," *Pragmatism*, p. 45.

22. Pound, "Liberty of Contract," p. 455.

23. Holmes, *The Common Law*, p. 5; and "The Path of the Law," in Max Lerner, ed., *The Mind and Faith of Justice Holmes*, p. 80.

24. Dewey, *The Pubic and Its Problems*, p. 199.

25. David W. Noble, *The Paradox of Progressive Thought*. Charles Beard, a half-century later, decried this as "the relativism that will ruin liberalism" (quoted in Eric Goldman, *Rendezvous with Destiny*, p. 280).

26. Henry George, *Progress and Poverty*, p. 507; see also p. 468.

27. Ward argued that nature's story was not one of efficiency but of waste, and pointed to such things as natural disasters and the vast numbers of unhatched eggs and seeds. Natural competition also worked, he argued, to prevent biological forms from "attaining [their] maximal development." His central point, however, "as all biologists perfectly understand" was that "those who survive simply prove their fitness to survive." That was something "wholly different from real superiority" in human terms. Lester Ward, "Psychic Factors of Civilization" (1893), in Commager, ed., *Lester Ward and the Welfare State*, p. 156; and Ward, "The Laissez-Faire Doctrine Is Suicidal" (1884), *ibid.*, p. 66. Ward was called the prophet of the New Deal by Perry Miller, *American Thought: the Civil War to World War I* (New York: Holt, Rinehart and Winston, 1954), p. xxix.

28. Ward, "Psychic Factors of Civilization," in Commager, *Lester Ward*, pp. 132, 148.

29. *Ibid.*, p. 156; and "Art Is the Antithesis of Nature" (1884), in Commager, *Lester Ward*, p. 84.

30. Goldman, *Rendezvous With Destiny*, pp. 72–78.

31. Cited in Morton White's *Science and Sentiment*, p. 133.

32. This essay, "Evolution of Self-Consciousness," is included in Perry Miller, *American Thought*. Wright also anticipated the pragmatists in viewing scientific principles as "finders" rather than "summaries" of truth—that is, in an

open-ended view of science (see E. H. Madden, *Chauncey Wright and the Foundations of Pragmatism*, p. 76).

33. From "A Neglected Argument for the Reality of God," in Wiener, *Values in a Universe of Chance*, p. 378.

34. William James, "The Sentiment of Rationality," in *Essays on Faith and Morals*, pp. 98–99.

35. *Ibid.*, p. 83.

36. William James, "The Will to Believe," in *Essays on Faith and Morals*, pp. 57, 59. This theme was also developed in "The Sentiment of Rationality": "belief [as measured by action] not only does and must continually outstrip scientific evidence, but . . . there is a certain class of truths of whose reality belief is a factor as well as a confessor." (pp. 96–97).

37. One of Wright's biographers argues that it was with Wright in mind that James, in "The Will to Believe," reminded readers that *not* acting also implied serious choices (Madden, *Chauncey Wright*, pp. 30, 43–50, 143ff).

38. From "Notes on Positivism," in Wiener, *Values in a Universe of Chance*, p. 141.

39. "The Dilemma of Determinism," *ibid.*, p. 161. A few pages later James asks, like an American Ivan Karamazov, "If God be good, how came he to create—or . . . to permit—the devil?" (p. 167); see also p. 177.

40. William James, *The Pluralistic Universe*, p. 193.

41. Ralph Barton Perry, *The Thought and Character of William James*, p. 128. James also referred to this in "Is Life Worth Living?" in *Essays on Faith and Morals*, p. 21. He criticized Mill's and Bentham's associationist psychology from the same perspective because of its "mind-dust" view of reality. Perry, *William James*, p. 27.

42. Dewey, *The Public and Its Problems*, pp. 7 and 195–199. The statement about judgment is from *Essays in Experimental Logic*, p. 1. This approach also led James and Dewey to criticize stimulus-response psychology. Psychologists could never speak accurately as external observers about human stimuli, they held; they had to know what the stimulus *meant* for the human being that was being affected (Madden, *Chauncey Wright*, p. 140).

43. William James, "What Pragmatism Means," *Pragmatism*, pp. 47 and 59.

44. Peirce, "What Pragmatism Is," in Wiener, *Values in a Universe of Chance*, p. 182. James had already criticized this approach in "The Will to Believe": "Science has fallen so deeply in love with the method that one may say she has ceased to care for truth by herself at all. It is only truth as technically verified that interests her" (*Essays on Faith and Morals*, p. 52).

45. Peirce, "How to Make Our Ideas Clear," in Wiener, *Values in a Universe of Chance*, p. 133. For an account of Peirce's critique of Darwin's evolutionary biologism, see Wiener, *Evolution and the Founders of Pragmatism*, pp. 77, 86. The focus of Peirce's inquiry, as he put it, was "the living inferential metaboly of symbols whose purport lies in conditional generals to act" (in Richard Bernstein, *Praxis and Action*, p. 186, to which much of this summary of Peirce is indebted).

46. C. S. Peirce, "The Place of Our Age in the History of Civilization," in

Bernstein, *Praxis and Action*, p. 11. The remark on the connection between cognition and purpose is in "What Pragmatism Is," *ibid.*, p. 184.

47. Bernstein, *Praxis and Action*, p. 199.

48. Wiener, *Evolution and the Founders of Pragmatism*. "*Every* great institution is perforce a means of corruption. . . . Only in the free personal relation is . . . full ideality to be found" (p. 127). Also see the important passage in Hofstadter, *Social Darwinism*, p. 135; and for an expression of some deeper confusions on this score, James, "The Moral Philosopher," in *Essays on Faith and Morals*, pp. 203–204.

49. Peirce tried often to distinguish his philosophy from James's, which he saw as reducing pragmatism to a simple practicalism, if not opportunism. To someone "who still thought in Kantian terms most readily," Peirce wrote, "*practisch* and *pragmatisch* were as far apart as two poles." Only the latter was purposive and open to ethical counsel and the lessons of experiment. Peirce claimed to be interested in utility, not sensation, and in lines of conduct, not single deeds. He also opposed overly utilitarian standards for judging the legitimacy of particular inquiries. Peirce finally even coined a new word, "pragmaticism," to protect his product. ("What Pragmatism Is," in Wiener, *Values in a Universe of Chance*, p. 183; and "How to Make Our Ideas Clear"—"What a thing means is . . . the *habits* it involves.")

That Peirce was on to something despite James's denials is clear from James's own words in "What Pragmatism Means." Pragmatism, James wrote, "agrees with *nominalism* in always appealing to particulars; with *utilitarianism* in emphasizing practical aspects; with *positivism* in its disdain for verbal solutions, useless questions and metaphysical abstractions" (in James, *Pragmatism*, p. 47, emphasis added).

50. Dewey, *Reconstruction in Philosophy*, pp. 156–157. Also "Authority and Social Change," in Joseph Ratner, *Intelligence in the Modern World* (New York: The Modern Library, 1939), p. 358. Dewey intended his approach to be "quite free from dependence upon a voluntarist psychology" and from appeals to "emotional satisfaction or the play of desires." From *Essays in Experimental Logic*, cited in Charles Morris, *The Pragmatic Movement in American Philosophy* (New York: Braziller, 1970), p. 37. Also see Bertrand Russell's criticism cited in Wiener, *Evolution and the Founders of Pragmatism*, p. 112.

51. Dewey became aware of the similarities between his and Peirce's view on this only late in life; earlier he attributed the idea to Henry George (*The Public and Its Problems*, p. 158).

52. James, "The Dilemma of Determinism," *Essays on Faith and Morals*, p. 154. Of course James and Dewey really criticized not idealism but a caricature of idealism. Idealist philosophy does not deny plurality but, strictly speaking, only that plurality which is irreducible. K. C. Hsiao's discussion of this point is important; see his *Political Pluralism*, pp. 176–182. Concerning one's "right" to supplement the empirical order with what one wants to believe, see James, "Is Life Worth Living?" *Essays on Faith and Morals*, pp. 21, 28; and "The Will to Believe," *ibid.*, p. 61.

53. "The task of the democratic school is to produce people with an experimental habit of mind and with the moral character which can cooperate with other people in associated action consonant with the democratic ideal." Dewey, cited in Morris, *The Pragmatic Movement*, p. 162. Previous remark about "intelligence" from Dewey, *Liberalism and Social Action*, p. 93.

54. Dewey, *Liberalism and Social Action*, pp. 31, 49, 92, 85.

55. *Ibid.*, p. 70.

56. Madden, *Chauncey Wright*, p. 70. The argument here, that there was a constitutive problem in pragmatism, is at odds with most interpretations. For a different view, see Charles Morris, *The Pragmatic Movement*, and Morton White's *Science and Sentiment in America*.

57. Interestingly enough, Dewey was sometimes quite precise about the difference between lived experience and experience-as-rationally-expressed. The distinction between "the two types of experience is evident to anyone who will . . . recall what he does most of the time when not engaged in meditation or inquiry" (*Essays in Experimental Logic*, p. 2; also see pp. 1–8).

58. Peirce's "conception of truth and reality makes everything depend upon . . . the methods of inquiry," as Dewey saw and admired (Morris Cohen, ed., *Chance, Love and Logic: Philosophic Essays of C. S. Peirce*, p. 306). Max Fisch argued that the young pragmatists had accepted Bain's definition of "belief" as "that upon which one is prepared to act"—not because of a substantive analysis of the concept but because the definition lent itself to empirical verification ("Justice Holmes, The Prediction Theory of Law and Pragmatism," p. 92).

59. Ward, "Dynamic Sociology," in Commager, *Lester Ward*, pp. 41ff. Ward, like Comte, also assumed that social facts could be "studied by man in the same way [as] physical phenomena . . . by the scientific method" (in Sidney Fine, *Laissez-Faire and the General Welfare State*, p. 257).

60. Cited in White, *Science and Sentiment*, p. 289, and *Social Thought in America: The Revolt Against Formalism*, p. 195. Holmes's remark is from "The Path of the Law," in Max Lerner, *Justice Holmes*, p. 81. Dewey also repeated the contemporary refrain that science only progressed when people abandoned the search for "essences" and turned to "what is going on and how it goes on." If social science would turn from the why to the how, he said, it would demonstrate the same cumulative and progressive advance as the physical sciences. See, for example, "Authority and Social Change" in L. Lancaster, *Masters of Political Thought* (New York: Houghton Mifflin Co., 1959), Vol. III, p. 338.

61. Comte, *A General View of Positivism*, pp. 28–29, 59, 62, 396.

62. Comte, *Positive Philosophy*, pp. 1–3. In Comte's society of the future, sociologists would serve as priests, financial experts as a Patriciate, and a feminine Ministry as moral advisors. Comte's God would be Humanity itself, and science would point the way for "incorporat[ion] into this Great Being" (*A General View of Positivism*, pp. 384, 390, 101). Thomas Huxley wrote that Comte had succeeded in presenting "Catholicism without the Christianity" (Rene König, "Comte," *International Encyclopedia of the Social Sciences*).

63. "Psychic Factors" in Commager, *Lester Ward*, p. 146. Science, Ward

wrote, mandated the opposite approach to moral problems from the traditional one, which put forth fruitless "prohibitions." Rather than trying to "curb" dangerous motives, the point was rather to "remove the conditions under which [the motives] arise" ("Ethical Aspects," *ibid.*, pp. 143, 247). In his social ideas, Ward also neglected the capitalist character of the corporation, and assumed (like Sumner) that it was primarily the product of natural evolution. (See Hofstadter's *Social Darwinism in American Thought*, p. 73; and Ward, "Ethical Aspects," in Commager, *Lester Ward*, p. 253; see "Psychic Factors of Civilization," *ibid.*, p. 147, concerning the manipulative potential). Ward's "psychic factor" has to be understood as having entailed a defense of social, not individual, purposiveness; it entailed a defense of "collective telesis." There was a pathos in this, for Ward more than the others retained from his rural youth a real respect for common people, and he frequently proposed radical reforms (*ibid.*, pp. 99–105). Along with E. A. Ross, he supported Bryan in 1896, and endorsed much of the populist program.

64. *Ibid.*, p. 184. See Wiener, *Values in a Universe of Chance*, pp. 107–108. Peirce defined retroduction, also called abduction, as proceeding by "the spontaneous conjectures of instinctive reason" to hypothesize explanations for phenomena newly observed or to infer antecedents from consequences. (See "A Neglected Argument for God," in *ibid.*, pp. 368–371, and W. B. Gallie's discussion in *Peirce and Pragmatism*, New York: Dover Publications, 1966, pp. 97ff.) The remark about Boole and DeMorgan is in Wiener, *Values*, p. 263.

65. Dewey, *Liberalism*, p. 81; also see p. 74. For a discussion of the corporation as primarily a vehicle of technology, see Dewey, *Individualism*, pp. 30, 36. The destructive aspects of modern technology Dewey attributed solely to "the pecuniary order in which science is employed" (*ibid.*, p. 134).

66. Dewey, *The Public and Its Problems*, pp. 197, 199. As late as 1938 Dewey believed that although the conditions of social inquiry were more complicated than those of the laboratory scientist, this "is not a fact which constitutes an inherent logical or theoretical difference between the two kinds of inquiry" (*Logic: The Theory of Inquiry*, in Lancaster, *Masters of Political Thought*, p. 347). Also Morton White, *Science and Sentiment*, pp. 272–273; and W. Y. Elliott, *Pragmatic Revolt*, p. 42.

67. "In studying this subject [political science] we must be content if we attain as high a degree of certainty as the matter of it admits. The same accuracy . . . is not to be looked for in all discussions any more than in all the productions of the studio and the workshop. . . . It is a mark of the educated man . . . that in every subject he looks for only so much precision as its nature permits" (Aristotle, *The Nicomachean Ethics*, J. A. K. Thomson, translator, Penguin Books: London, 1953, Book 1, chap. 3, p. 27).

68. "The fundamental problem in philosophy is the problem of scientific method . . . of the method of experimentation, of controlled inquiry" (Joseph Ratner, a main expostulator of Dewey's philosophy, in *Intelligence in the Modern World*, pp. 240–241). Morris Cohen, in his volume of Peirce's essays, noted that modern philosophy is "entirely dominated by the assumption that one must

study the process of knowing before one can find out the nature of things known (*Chance, Love and Logic,* p. xxxii).

69. He also wrote that the study of method is "about what Morals comes down to" (Wiener, *Values in a Universe of Chance,* p. xx). The statement on metaphysics is from "How to Make Our Ideas Clear," *ibid.,* p. 135. The definition of real questions is from "Peirce as an American," by Rulon Wells, in Bernstein, *Perspectives on Peirce,* p. 26. For a lucid expression of Peirce's ambiguities on this topic, see his "Notes on Positivism," in Wiener, *Values,* pp. 139–140.

70. John Schaar, "Legitimacy in the Modern State," p. 284.

71. E. A. Burtt, *The Metaphysical Foundations of Modern Science* (Garden City, New York: Doubleday and Co., 1932), p. 229.

72. What differences arose were attributed to different levels of information or different proposals for means to agreed-upon ends. Ward, "Psychic Factors," in Commager, *Lester Ward,* p. 174; and see pp. 15–17.

73. Dewey, *Liberalism,* p. 79; and *Individualism,* p. 147.

74. Lester Ward, "Scientific Lawmaking" (1877), in Commager, *Lester Ward,* p. 18. These conclusions followed from his earlier premises. If social problems were caused by "friction" and could not be solved by "exhortation"—that is, by education and persuasion attempted by actors within a situation—then it could only be engineered from outside the situation. In this way social science came to be seen as mandating the external manipulation of moral situations, the "control" of social "forces." Regarding the anti-moral epistemology of Progressivism more generally, consider Fremont Older's later thoughts about his exposing of municipal graft in San Francisco: "It never occurred to me in those days that these men . . . were not especially evil men. They were just doing evil things. We made the mistake then in assuming that it was a moral question" (Lasch, *The New Radicalism,* p. 151).

75. See W. B. Gallie's comments on the unsuitability of the scientific community as a model for society, in *Peirce and Pragmatism,* pp. 160 and 177; and Rulon Wells' extremely pertinent comments in Bernstein, *Perspectives on Peirce,* pp. 22–27 and 37–41. None of this is even to raise the important question about the possibility of scientific "reversibility" or corrigibility once experimentation is transposed from the laboratory to the realm of full-scale social institutions.

76. "The Economic Basis of the New Society" (1939), in Ratner, *Intelligence in the Modern World,* p. 431. Dewey, *Individualism,* pp. 34, 83–88; and *The Public and Its Problems,* pp. 150–155.

77. Dewey, *Logic,* pp. 104–105. And previous judgment about discussion and dialectic, *Liberalism,* pp. 70–71.

78. Normally Dewey ignored these questions, though sometimes he simply expressed indifference about how they were resolved. Thus: "There is no question of false or true, or real and seeming, but only of stronger and weaker. The question of which one *should* be stronger or weaker is as meaningless as it would be in a cockfight" (from *Experience and Nature,* 1926, cited in Lancaster, *Masters of Political Thought,* p. 357).

79. The anti-moralistic stance we have identified in Ward and Peirce was sometimes evident in Dewey as well. "There is a peculiar inconsistency in the current idea that morals *ought* to be social," Dewey wrote. Imposing an "ought" implies an "assertion that morals depend upon something apart from social relations. . . . [but] morals *are* social" (from *Human Nature and Conduct*, 1922, in Elliott, *Pragmatic Revolt*, p. 225). Morals, that is, were already contained *in* realities. But this argument was deceptive. Because morals were contained *in* society, it in no way followed that they were unified, that choice was unnecessary, nor that people could dispense with "oughts." As Morton White noted, Dewey often failed to make the critical distinction between things desired and things desir*able*, between questions of fact and questions of value (*Revolt Against Formalism*, pp. 212–219).

80. Ward, in Commager, *Lester Ward*, p. 84.

81. The phrase "bureaucratic epistemology" is from Schaar, "Legitimacy." C. Wright Mills also describes it in *The Sociological Imagination*, (Chaps. 4 and 6). A bureaucratic epistemology is one which accepts as legitimate knowledge only that which can be operationalized by bureaucracies and validated by their procedures. It is the "expropriated rationality" of which Mills spoke in *White Collar*, pp. xvii and 226.

82. Peirce, quoted in Bernstein, *Praxis and Action*, p. 198. "Psychological insight·shows that there is nothing which distinguishes my personal identity except my faults and limitations—or, if you please, my blind will, which it is my highest endeavor to annihilate." Peirce defined one of the purposes of science as disposing of arbitrariness; science would thereby purify itself "more and more . . . [of] the dross of subjectivity" (Gallie, *Peirce and Pragmatism*, p. 88). The comment about "dominant energies" is from Dewey, *Individualism*, p. 65. See also *ibid.*, p. 162.

83. He concluded *Pragmatism*, for example, urging that the way to "escape evil" was not by getting it "aufgehoben. . . . It is by dropping it out altogether, throwing it overboard" (*Pragmatism*, p. 191). In *Essays in Radical Empiricism* he invoked the "active sense of living" that was presumably "self luminous and suggest[ed] no paradoxes" before reflection "shattered the instinctive world" (p. 92). His argument was that reality had no "inner duplicity" and that duplicity was the product simply of the observer's perspective (p. 9). He evaded the problem of evil most clearly in *The Pluralistic Universe*, when he claimed that "the immediate experience of life solves the problems which so baffle our conceptual intelligence" (p. 260).

84. Reason for him, it was said, was "either a blind leap in the dark or an autopsy performed on the corpse of dead acts" (Elliott, *The Pragmatic Revolt*, p. 63). James's view of free will may have been flawed from the start by the naturalist origins of his psychology (see Wiener, *Evolution and the Founders of Pragmatism*, pp. 108–109, 116–117).

85. A perfect example was his conclusion to "The Moral Philosopher and the Moral Life": "The highest life consists at all times in the breaking of rules

which have grown too narrow for the actual case. There is but one unconditional commandment, which is that we should seek incessantly, with fear and trembling so to vote as to bring about the largest total universe of good which we can see" (*Essays on Faith and Morals*, p. 209).

86. C. W. Mills presents this scientism as "the methodological inhibition," in *Sociological Imagination* (p. 72 and Chap. 6, *passim*). An extended comment by K. C. Hsiao on this point bears repetition. "The metaphor of reality as a ship" in *Pragmatism* was suggestive, Hsiao wrote, "but no one would be willing to sacrifice his time and risk his life in some *aimless* drifting in a ship full of holes and loose joints, and with a pilot who neither knows its destination nor cares to know it. . . . Suppose Columbus had gone to Isabella and said: I do not know anything about the shape of the earth . . . nor do I have any idea where I intend to go; I shall not even bring with me a compass or a map of the seas, because my trip being an adventure, I shall leave everything unfixed; as to my competence as a sailor, well that will be amply proved by my ability to keep the ship *always sailing* . . . ; as to the soundness of my voyage-idea, let us defer its consideration and leave [it] to the test of subsequent events" (Hsiao, *Political Pluralism*, pp. 191–192). Such an attitude, Hsiao noted, would not only have failed to impress the Queen, it would also have proven incapable of keeping the crew sailing, and indeed of inspiring Columbus in the first place.

87. Randolph S. Bourne, *War and the Intellectuals*, p. 60.

88. Jean-Jacques Rousseau, *The Social Contract* (New York: Washington Square Press, 1967), Book I, Chap. 2, p. 8. Dewey's question is from *Human Nature and Conduct* (1922), and cited in Elliott, *Pragmatic Revolt*, pp. 225–226.

89. Holmes, *The Common Law*, pp. 31–33.

90. A few years later, seeming to relent by admitting that "no doubt behind . . . legal rights is the fighting will of the subject to maintain them," he nevertheless added that "even a dog will fight for his bone" (from "Natural Law," 1918, in Lerner, *Justice Holmes*, p. 397).

91. Holmes, *The Common Law*, pp. 32, 89.

92. The prediction theory, *ibid.*, p. 169. The proposal to delete moral terms, from "The Path of the Law" in Lerner, *Justice Holmes*, p. 72. Anticipations of most of Holmes's later doctrines were in *The Common Law*: the belief that "public policy sacrifices the individual to the general good" (41); the idea that "moral predilections must not be allowed to influence . . . legal distinctions" (118, 129); and the roots of the clear and present danger test (pp. 54, 61).

93. Lerner, *Justice Holmes*, pp. 73, 76.

94. *The Common Law*, pp. 43, 54, 61–62, 129.

95. *Ibid.*, p. 89.

96. Lerner, *Justice Holmes*, p. 71.

97. John Dewey, "Justice Holmes and the Liberal Mind," pp. 210–212. Jerome Frank, cited in W. Friedmann, *Legal Theory*, p. 258. Friedmann also offers a good discussion of legal realism, pp. 308 and 402–404. Frankfurter is cited in Yosal Rogat's "The Judge as Spectator," p. 253.

98. Lerner, *Justice Holmes*, pp. 45, 201–202.

99. *Buck v. Bell,* 274 U.S. 200 (1927). Holmes, "Natural Law," in Lerner, *Justice Holmes,* p. 397. Also see *Buck v. Bell.* And in *The Common Law:* "No society has ever admitted that it could not sacrifice individual welfare to its own existence" (pp. 36–37). See also *U.S. Zinc v. Britt,* 258 U.S. 268 (1922). And Holmes's defense of Nebraska's right to ban the teaching of German in primary schools for political reasons was inconsistent with a commitment to free speech. *Meyer v. Nebraska,* 262 U.S. 390 (1923).

100. Holmes upheld the legality of racial legal classifications even where conservatives like Charles Evans Hughes refused. Yosal Rogat, "The Judge as Spectator," p. 216. The figures on his votes to overrule state laws are in John Roche, "Entrepreneurial Liberty and the Fourteenth Amendment," p. 29.

101. A tremendous amount has been written about this difference, but for a succinct expression of this position, see S. I. Benn and R. S. Peters, *The Principles of Political Thought* (New York: The Free Press, 1965), Chap. 1, pp. 24–31, and Chap. 3.

102. Rogat, "The Judge as Spectator," p. 225.

103. *Ibid.,* pp. 248–249.

104. John T. Noonan, Jr., *Persons and Masks of the Law* (New York: Farrar, Strauss, and Giroux, 1976), pp. 12–13. Noonan's and Rogat's works, along with Peter J. Riga, "Prudence and Jurisprudence: Authority . . . [for] Thomas Aquinas," in *The Jurist,* 1977 (Vols. 3–4), pp. 287–312, stand outside the mainstream of Holmes scholarship and present interpretations consistent with the one presented here.

105. Holmes, "The Path of the Law," in Lerner, *Justice Holmes,* pp. 76–77.

106. After talking about the influence of his father, Emerson, and Ruskin on his life, he added, "I think science was at the bottom." And again: it was "the scientific way of looking at the world that made the difference" (Wiener, *Evolution and the Founders of Pragmatism,* p. 173). The equation of intellectual advance with the advance of quantitative methodology is from "Law in Science; Science in Law," *Collected Legal Papers,* pp. 226, 231, 242. It was also a scientistic assumption in *The Common Law* which led Holmes to assume that the multitude of legal rules could be reduced to a few principles grouped around a master principle. And what was Holmes's prudent man standard but an investigative device that would do for him what Maxwell's or Darwin's instruments had done for them— provide a means for making diverse phenomena commensurable and subject to common manipulation? See also "Path of the Law," in Lerner, *Justice Holmes,* p. 79.

107. Holmes, "Law in Science," *Collected Legal Papers,* p. 226. He added that he began "with one or two instances of the help of history in clearing away rubbish."

108. Jacques Ellul, *The Technological Society,* p. 293. Rogat notes pointedly that "preferring [exact] rules would not necessarily indicate an unusual lack of concern for other goals . . . [just for] the unjust consequences of externality" ("The Judge as Spectator," pp. 221–222).

109. As he wrote to his friend Pollack: "In a civilized state it is not the will of

the sovereign that makes lawyer's law, even when that is its source, but what a body of subjects, namely the judges by whom it is enforced, say is his will" (in Fisch, "Justice Holmes," p. 93). Juries are of pivotal importance because they articulate standards of "reasonable care" in civil cases and "reasonable doubt" in criminal ones. Holmes's passage on juries is from "Law in Science," *Collected Legal Papers*, pp. 237–238. "I confess that in my experience I have not found juries specially inspired for the discovery of truth" (*ibid.*). The relevant passage from Tocqueville is *Democracy in America*, I, pp. 295–296.

110. The Brandeis invitations were to the Lawrence textile mills. Holmes later failed to see why the Sacco-Vanzetti case "left such deep prejudices." He dismissed talk about exploitation because it "indicates emotional attitudes . . . which always rather gets my hair up" (Rogat, "The Judge as Spectator," pp. 246–247 and 253; and see letter to John Wu, in Lerner, *Justice Holmes*, p. 435). The Sherman Act he condemned as "based on . . . ignorance and incompetence" because of his faith in the automatic benefits of monopoly (Noonan, *Persons and Masks of the Law*, p. 102, and Rogat, "The Judge as Spectator," p. 246). Holmes mentioned the Brandeis invitation both in letters to Lewis Einstein (July 6, 1919) and to Pollack (May 26, 1919); in both he quipped: "I hate facts." He also disapproved of Beard's thesis about the Constitution because it was "ignoble" (letter to Wu, in Lerner, *Justice Holmes*, p. 435).

The examples of his haphazard economics are numerous. The wages-fund theory of workers' pay underlay his disdain for union wage demands, mentioned in Chapter Five. In a famous resale price maintenance agreements case, he defended the accused company because he felt people "exaggerate[d] the . . . importance of competition." Proposing something on the order of a demand side economics, he claimed that "what really fixes price is the competition of competing desire." The highest profits were coincident with "the fair price." *Dr. Miles Co. vs. Park and Sons* (220 U.S. 373, 409), 1911.

111. Holmes, *The Common Law*, pp. 61–62. See also p. 43 and on 49: "The law may . . . throw the actor on his peril, not only of the consequences foreseen by him, but also of the consequences which, although not predicted by common experience, the legislator apprehends."

112. Holmes, *The Common Law*, pp. 38 and 42, "Notes on the Gas-Stokers' Strike" in Lerner, *Justice Holmes*, p. 50.

113. Thomas Hobbes, *Leviathan*, Chap. 6, p. 48 (emphasis added). "There [is] nothing in the world universal but names"; "*true* and *false* are attributes of speech, not of things" (Chap. 4, pp. 35–36).

114. *The Holmes-Pollack Letters*, Mark de Wolfe Howe, ed., Letter of December 20, 1918, Vol. I, p. 274; and see Pollack to Holmes, June 13, 1927, II, p. 200. The Holmes-Otto correspondence is in *The Journal of Philosophy*, XXXVIII (1941), pp. 389–392. In it Holmes noted that many of his "can't helps are shared either by all my fellow men or by such of them as I think worth considering." To James he explained complacently that he meant by "truth" what he "can't help thinking. . . . I can't help preferring champagne to ditch water—I doubt if the universe does." Letter of March 24, 1907, in Lerner, *Justice Holmes*, p. 415.

115. "Metaphors, and senseless and ambiguous words, are like *ignes fatui*; and reasoning upon them is wandering amongst innumerable absurdities; and their end, contention and sedition." Therefore people must set up "some arbitrator, or judge, to whose sentence they will both stand." Hobbes's reasoning here, at the beginning of his discourse, underlay his later political argument for the Leviathan (*Leviathan*, Chap. 5, pp. 46, 42; see also Chap. 15). Concerning the substitution of order for justice, see also Ellul, *The Technological Society*, p. 295.

116. Holmes, *Collected Legal Papers*, p. 339. "Deep-seated preferences cannot be argued about. . . . [I]t is true that deep-seated beliefs have a transcendental basis in the sense that their foundation is arbitrary. You cannot help entertaining and feeling them and there is the end of it" ("Natural Law," *ibid.*, p. 396).

117. Franz Neumann, "The Change in the Function of Law in Modern Society," in *The Democratic and the Authoritarian State*. During the Middle Ages, for example, Neumann explained, "Not every measure of the sovereign and not only measures of the sovereign [were] law;" law also embodied *ratio* (pp. 26–28).

118. Stanley Aronowitz, "Law, the Breakdown of Order and Revolution," in R. Lefcourt, *Law Against the People* (New York: Vintage Books, 1971), p. 177. Previous references from Neumann: in *Authoritarian State*, pp. 61, 64. Stressing the technical aspect of this outlook, Ellul adds: "Application of law no longer arises from popular adhesion to it but from the complex of mechanisms which, by means of artifice and reason, adjust behavior to rule." "The law and the police become identical" (*The Technological Society*, pp. 294–295). Lowi also refers to this change in the *form* of law: "Obviously modern law has become a series of instructions to administrators rather than a series of commands to citizens" (*End of Liberalism*, p. 144).

119. The claim that Holmes merely wanted to find out what "law was" is Friedmann's, in *Legal Theory*, p. 249. Concerning "isness" and "oughtness," see Rogat, "Judge as Spectator," p. 236. Holmes remarked that his epitaph ought to read, "Here lies the supple tool of power" (*ibid.*, p. 249).

120. Dewey's hopes about Holmes's commitment to the method of intelligence notwithstanding, Holmes was partial to the military virtues. He thought the faith "true and adorable" which led the "soldier to throw away his life in obedience to a blindly accepted duty, in a cause which he little understands" (Lerner, *Justice Holmes*, p. 20; also "Natural Law," *Collected Legal Papers*, p. 398). Morton White chides Lerner for his approval of this, and judges Holmes's "fighting faith" "neither profound nor interesting. . . . Wars may bring visions of unimaginable wholes, but postwar periods mean hangovers and delirium" (*Social Thought in America*, p. 173).

121. Ellul, *The Technological Society*, p. 296.

122. L. L. Bernard, "The Transition to an Objective Standard of Control," pp. 519–537.

123. *Ibid.*, p. 531; and see p. 527.

124. "Individuals have no liberties in opposition to a scientifically controlled society but find all their legitimate freedom in . . . furtherance of . . . social func-

tioning" (*ibid.*, p. 536). For previous passage about elites selecting activities, p. 534.

125. Aristotle, *The Nicomachean Ethics*, Book VI, Chaps. 5, 9, and 12. Hobbes, *Leviathan*, Chap. 5. The theory of "action" referred to briefly here is taken from the works of Arendt, Tocqueville, and Nietzsche.

126. Thus Thomas Edison: "Problems in human engineering will receive during the coming years the same genius and attention which the nineteenth century gave to the more material forms of engineering. . . . A great field for industrial experimentation and statesmanship is opening" (Noble, *America by Design*, p. 257).

127. Two excellent studies of Taylor are Haber, *Efficiency and Uplift*, and Judith A. Merkle, *Management and Ideology: The Legacy of the International Scientific Management Movement* (Berkeley: University of California Press, 1980). The scientific management movement emerged, interestingly enough, from the engineering profession (see Noble, *America by Design*, Chaps. 2 and 10).

128. F. W. Taylor, *The Principles of Scientific Management*, pp. 100, 114. The phrase "mental revolution" is from his testimony before R. Hoxie's Commission on Industrial Relations (1912), given in Taylor's other book, *Scientific Management*, p. 29.

129. Dewey had referred to the same discipline when he talked about "incorporating the dominant energies" of the day. And a subsequent exponent of the school would speak of the necessity of a scientific form of "mental hygiene" (George Lundberg, *Can Science Save Us?*, New York: Longmans, Green and Co., 1947, 1961, Chap 1).

130. Judith Merkle, "The Taylor Strategy: Organizational Innovation and Class Structure," p. 61. "Rationality as an ordering device became a weapon to be used against the natural instincts and combinations of man." Also see Clark Kerr and Lloyd Fisher, "Plant Sociology: The Elite and the Aborigines" (Berkeley: The Institute of Industrial Relations, 1958).

131. Taylor, *Scientific Management*, p. 25. Taylor promised individualism, but in "a diminished" form. "The worker was granted an individuality of incentive but not of discretion" (Haber, *Efficiency and Uplift*, p. 24). The phrase about "exact knowledge" is from Nadworny, *Scientific Management and the Unions*, p. 90. Taylor's personal system never enjoyed great commercial success. Industrial psychology eventually turned away from his focus on individual motivation to a manipulative concern for the dynamics of the work group. But the larger movement eventually enlisted support from both business and the AFL (Nadworny, *Scientific Management and the Unions*, pp. 114–141). And more broadly, " 'Efficiency' regarded as inherent in a systematic subdivision of tasks interrelated in mechanical fashion according to precise standards recorded at every step on paper, passed into industrial culture as . . . a synonym for rationality" (Merkle, "The Taylor Strategy," p. 61).

132. Stephen S. Cohen, *Modern Capitalist Planning: The French Model* (Berkeley: University of California Press, 1977), p. xv.

133. From the point of view of the scientific manager, workers lacked the

capacity for intelligent participation anyway. As Georg Lukács saw, Taylor's analytic redaction of the production process necessarily entailed "the fragmentation of its subject. . . . The human qualities of the worker appear increasingly as *mere sources of error* when contrasted with abstract special laws functioning according to rational predictions" (*History and Class Consciousness*, p. 89).

134. These phrases were part of Taylor's anecdote about what occurred after he had been promoted to gang-boss over the lathe workers at Midvale Steel; they referred, that is, to men who had previously been his fellow-workers (*Scientific Management*, pp. 49, 83, 90–95). The degree to which Taylor was willing to make the factory into what Bernard called a "compulsory unity" was revealed in his opinion that "deliberate loafing is almost criminal" (p. 82). Taylor's sentiments about workers were generally reciprocated: "union men did leave every plant where Taylor was employed" (Nadworny, *Scientific Management and the Unions*, pp. 21–26).

135. Regarding this substitution of executive or administrative methods for politics, see James Weinstein, *The Corporate Ideal in the Liberal State*, Chap. 4. That the decline of urban democracy was *not* an inevitable product of the adoption of administrative methods was indicated by the Socialists' realistic proposals to combine the advantages of efficiency with participation and accountability. (See Carl D. Thompson, "The Vital Point of Charter-Making from a Socialist Point of View," *National Municipal Review*, XIII, 1913, pp. 417–426; also earlier, pp. 132–134.)

136. Concerning these ideologies, see Reinhard Bendix, *Work and Authority in Industry*, pp. 202–211, 267–287.

137. For example, Stephen A. Marglin, *What the Bosses Do: The Origins and Functions of Hierarchy in Capitalist Production* (Cambridge, Mass.: Harvard University Research Paper, May 1971).

138. Noble, *America by Design*, p. 262; Mills, *White Collar*, pp. xvii and 226; and Bendix, *Work and Authority in Industry*, pp. 202, 303.

139. Herbert Marcuse, *Reason and Revolution: Hegel and the Rise of Social Theory*, Preface to the 1960 edition, p. xiv. For a slightly different notion of "rationalized domination," which has nevertheless contributed to my own analysis, see Jean Cohen's excellent "Max Weber and the Dynamics of Domination," *Telos*, XIV (Winter 1972).

140. "Modern management issued from the requirements of machine production in the capitalist mode and provided the social basis for technical developments designed to reinforce that mode" (Noble, *America by Design*, p. 263).

The pro-business bias of American social science of this time is obvious. That most of the early sociologists and psychologists assumed that their job was to help adjust workers to the new factories, and help industrialists boost productivity, is apparent from any of the early issues of, say, *The Journal of Applied Psychology*. The first volume (1917) displays articles not only on "Human Engineering," devoted to improving productivity, but also on such things as "Improving Business Correspondence." That the bias was not universal is indicated by A. A. Roback, in the same volume and, for example, E. A. Ross in *The American Journal of Sociology*, Vol. XVI (1911), p. 641. But the main drift was clear, and even the critics failed to articulate premises that would propel social science in a different direction.

141. The most brilliant insight into the essential congeniality of market reason and scientific rationality was probably offered by Frederich Tönnies: The subject of scientific reason "is the man who is objective. . . . Scientific concepts which by their ordinary origin and their real properties are judgments by means of which complexes of feeling are given names, behave within science like commodities in society. They gather together within the system like commodities on the market. The supreme scientific concept which is no longer the name of anything real is like money. E.g., the concept of any atom, or of energy" (Lukács, *History and Class Consciousness*, p. 131; for Weber on the same theme, see p. 96).

142. Marx, "The Eighteenth Brumaire of Louis Bonaparte," *The Marx-Engels Reader*, Robert Tucker, ed., p. 444. Lukács in 1922 saw Kant as a pivotal figure of the bourgeois era because he had simultaneously given expression to its original promise of totality (with his concept of the transcendental ego) and to its actual opacity (with the idea of an unbreachable *ding an sich*); *History and Class Consciousness*, pp. 121, 124–134.

143. Bernstein, *Praxis and Action*, pp. 167, 171. Part of this is from Dewey's account of Hegel's influence on G. S. Morris, but as Bernstein notes, Dewey could as easily have said it of himself.

144. Marx, "Theses on Feuerbach," in Tucker, *Marx-Engels Reader*, pp. 107–109.

145. Galileo, "Two Great Systems," cited in E. A. Burtt, *The Metaphysical Foundations of Modern Science*, pp. 75, 79.

146. It was a kind of reasoning, that is, opposed to disputation about "substances" and "essences." Galileo's opinion was that experiential sense impressions of color, temperature, texture, and taste were "secondary qualities," productive of illusion and lacking in objective reality. Underlying them, however, were what he considered the real "primary qualities" of force, velocity, and magnitude. These revealed that the basic structure of the universe was mathematical (Burtt, *Modern Science*, pp. 89–90; see also Chap. 7). In this neo-Platonism the individual appeared as he would later to Peirce, Holmes, and Taylor: a bundle of mere impressions, a lamentable source of error.

147. "Democracy means the power and the freedom of those controlled by law to change the law . . . ; but more than that, it means some kind of collective self-control over the structural mechanics of history itself" (Mills, *Sociological Imagination*, p. 116 and Chap. 10, *passim*). Such *self*-control would, however, require different epistemological assumptions than those that emerged during Progressivism.

148. "Channeling" Document, Selective Service, July 1, 1965. Reprinted in Skolnick and Currie, *Crisis in American Institutions* (Boston: Little, Brown and Co., 1970), pp. 162–167. National decision-makers had by 1965 clearly learned not only Bernard's lesson but his underlying theory as well: "Feeling can easily

be regulated socially through the control of habit formations, and thus pleasant feeling may be made to correspond to any useful social activity which is supported by . . . organized society" ("The Transition to an Objective Standard of Social Control," p. 531). Such a conclusion was a long way from where the pragmatists began.

CHAPTER SEVEN

Epigraphs: Herbert Croly, *The Promise of American Life*, p. 212; "Interview with Robert Heilbroner," *Psychology Today*, Vol. VIII, No. 9 (February 1975), p. 100.

1. These orientations often overlapped. Though Holmes was a Reform Darwinist, he nevertheless defended war as "a price well-paid for the breeding of a race fit for leadership and command" (quoted in Max Lerner, *The Mind and Faith of Justice Holmes*, p. xliii). He argued that legislative tinkering with property was pointless as long as people "failed to take life in hand and prevent the continuance of the unfit" ("Ideals and Doubts," in Lerner, *Justice Holmes*, p. 393). Also, see his opinion in *Adkins v. Children's Hospital*, 261 U.S. 525, 567 (1923).

2. Croly, *The Promise of American Life*, p. 24. Previous remark, *ibid.*, p. 270.

3. See d'Entreves, *The Notion of the State*, Part II. Previous remark about the rule of law from Clinton Rossiter's Introduction to E. S. Corwin, *The Higher Law Background of American Constitutional Law*, p. v.

4. Harold Laski, "Political Theory in the Later Middle Ages," p. 641. Similarly, C. H. McIlwain cites Aquinas's definition of law as "some ordinance of reason for the common good promulgated by him who has the care of the community," and noted that this reason was regarded as being infused with divine justice (*The Growth of Political Thought in the West*, p. 326).

5. Cited in C. H. McIlwain, *Constitutionalism: Ancient and Modern*, p. 3.

6. *Democracy in America*, ed. Phillips Bradley, Vol. I, p. 272. Tocqueville employed the same concept of tyranny when he spoke of the "tranquil, legal and philanthropic" way in which the Americans exterminated the Indians, succeeding where the more barbaric Spaniards had failed. It was impossible to destroy men, he observed, "with more respect for the laws of humanity" (*ibid.*, p. 369). For a definition of how he saw the "content" of justice, see Vol. I, p. 269.

7. See Corwin, *Higher Law Background*.

8. Statement by Justice Dillon, in Sidney Fine, *Laissez-Faire and the General-Welfare State*, p. 140, emphasis added.

9. 273 U.S. 418, 445 (1927).

10. By June 1890, the Bellamyite Nationalist newspaper reported 127 clubs in 27 cities. They reached their highwater mark in the early months of the following year with 167 clubs; thereafter the number declined (Ralph Gabriel, *The Course of American Democratic Thought*, p. 212).

11. Edward Bellamy, *Looking Backward*, p. 150; previous remark, p. 165. The right to education was grounded in three sources: the first was self-interest; the

second, "the right of his fellow-citizens to have him educated," and the third, "the right of the unborn . . . to an intelligent and refined parentage" (p. 152).

12. "All men who do their best, do the same." *Ibid.*, pp. 75–76. Concerning industrial evolution, see pp. 53–55.

13. Like subsequent technocrats, Bellamy believed that "because the machine is truer than the hand" the largest businesses were better and "more accurate" than smaller concerns (p. 55). This view of work, and the lapse of individualist values in general, limited Bellamy's appeal for the populists. Asked why he disapproved of Bellamy's nationalism, Robert Ingersoll explained in 1892 that "We are believers in individual independence and will be, I hope, forever" (cited in Ralph Gabriel, *The Course of American Democratic Thought*, p. 212). Gabriel actually felt that "as a popular movement, Bellamy's nationalism was a failure" (p. 223).

14. Society as a "national family," Bellamy, *Looking Backward*, p. 171.

15. *Ibid.*, pp. 154, 165. See also pp. 212–213.

16. It is significant that Bellamy's society of the future would be a "paradise" not of liberty, equality, and fraternity, but of "order, equity and felicity" (*ibid.*, p. 179).

17. Cited in Fine, *Laissez-Faire*, pp. 278–279. Woodrow Wilson wrote in *The State*, "The modern idea is this: the state no longer absorbs the individual; it only serves him" (p. 48).

18. For the Reverend Josiah Strong the new approach was "a Christian school of political economy." Twenty-three clergymen, including Washington Gladden and Lyman Abott, were charter members of the American Economic Association (Fine, *Laissez-Faire*, p. 201).

19. Edmund James, a founder of the Academy of Political and Social Science (*ibid.*, p. 208). Simon Patten explained that "The objective laws of a given society are not simply the laws of nature; they are the laws derived from the particular combination of natural forces of which society makes use" (*ibid.*, p. 242).

20. From an early program penned by Edmund James and Patten (*ibid.*, p. 209).

21. This three-part distinction is based on Fine, *ibid.*, p. 251.

22. Concerning the approach to regulation-as-publicity, Wilson believed, "Nothing checks all the bad practices of politics like public exposure. You can't be crooked in the light" (Wilson, "Let There Be Light," in Leuchtenburg, ed., *Woodrow Wilson: The New Freedom*, pp. 76–77). Regarding Wilson's distinction between artificial and natural mergers, see Martin Sklar, "Woodrow Wilson and the Political Economy of Modern United States Liberalism," p. 40. The ex-populist Henry Demarest Lloyd, by contrast, proposed outright government ownership of trusts, because industry like government existed through cooperation, and therefore like government should permit people to share in its direction (Fine, *Laissez-Faire*, pp. 343–344).

23. "It was this mixture of classical nineteenth-century liberalism with conservative-historicism that made Wilson the Progressive he was" (Sklar, "Wood-

row Wilson," p. 21). The confusions involved with this mix did not trouble Wilson. Defending the virtues of individualism, he also, like Sumner, defended the organization of large-scale business as being "normal and inevitable" (*ibid.*, pp. 19, 23).

24. Wilson, *The State*, p. 19. Citing Bagehot's "Physics and Politics" (from which Wilson doubtless derived this idea), Henry George had noted: "Mr. Bagehot does not . . . explain how it is that eighteen hundred years ago civilization did not give the [same] advantage over barbarism that it does now. But there is no use talking about that. . . . To anyone who has seen how the contact of our civilization affects the inferior races, a much readier though less flattering explanation [for success in the competition of customs] will occur" (*Progress and Poverty*, p. 500).

25. Wilson, *The State*, pp. 30–31. Law, he added, like Holmes, "seeks to command the outward character of men. . . . It may be . . . instructed by the ethical judgments of the community, but its own province is not distinctively ethical" (p. 85). Concerning his rejection of contract theory, see pp. 9–13.

26. "Laws have never altered the facts." "What Is Progress?"—address at Richmond, Va., February 1, 1912, cited in Leuchtenburg, *Woodrow Wilson*, p. 36.

27. *Constitutional Government in the United States*, pp. 56–57. A. Lawrence Lowell also expressed this belief that government, rather than being a "machine," was an "organism whose various parts act and react upon one another. . . . In order to understand the organic laws of a political system, it is necessary to examine it as a whole, and seek to discover not only the true functions of each part, but also its influence upon every other part, and its relation to the equilibrium of the complete organism." Cited in Martin Landau, "The Myth of Hyperfactualism in the Study of American Politics," pp. 388–391.

28. "We cannot give them any quittance of the debt ourselves have paid. They can have liberty no cheaper than we got it." "They are children and we are men in these matters of government and justice" ("The Ideals of America," pp. 730–731; also see his "Democracy and Efficiency"). Wilson's entire statement of the idea that government was the executive organ of society, ("the organ through which its habit acts"), is in *The State*, p. 30. The view was identical to Durkheim's.

29. See Sklar, "Woodrow Wilson," pp. 19, 21–22. On the necessity of gradual reform, see the last page of *The State* (p. 639).

30. On the indispensability of corporations, see *ibid.*, p. 22. Also: "In the readjustments that are about to be undertaken in this country not one single legitimate or honest arrangement is going to be disturbed; but every impediment to business is going to be removed" ("The Emancipation of Business," in Leuchtenberg, *Woodrow Wilson*, p. 151; see also Wilson, "The Law and the Fact," p. 9).

31. For Wilson and others this involved going beyond the party system, which had already played "an extraordinary part . . . in making a national life [out of what] might otherwise have been loose and diverse almost to the point of being inorganic" (*Constitutional Government*, p. 218, see also p. 217). Recognizing

that business had ceased to be a private matter, Wilson occasionally spoke of corporations as existing "for the convenience of society," and as "instrumentalities" *of* that society ("The Law and the Fact," pp. 9, 11).

32. Concerning these appointments and the record of the Wilson administration with the Federal Reserve and Clayton Acts, see Robert Wiebe, *Businessmen and Reform*, especially Chap. 9. Regarding his unique view of freedom, see Leuchtenberg, *Woodrow Wilson*, p. 166; and his likening of social cooperation to a "perfected, coordinated bee-hive" (*ibid.*, p. 44). The Hamiltonianism was evident in all of his early work, but he explicitly invoked Hamilton's tradition in "The Ideals of America" (p. 727) and in *Constitutional Government* (pp. 45, 200).

33. For a contrary interpretation and one critical of Sklar's original thesis, see Alan L. Seltzer's "Woodrow Wilson as 'Corporate-Liberal': Toward a Reconsideration of Left Revisionist Historiography." Seltzer argues, with careful adumbration of the anti-trust prosecutions under Wilson's Justice Department, that Wilson "should not be understood to have been a supporter of or spokesman for large corporate interests" (p. 207); he did not "share a community of agreement with Roosevelt." Seltzer's purpose is to disprove the utility of both the ruling-class and the power-elite models for interpreting the politics of the era (p. 212). But his argument turns on precisely how "community of agreements" is defined. If it were defined to indicate the conscious sharing of immediate interests, his argument would be correct. But that would be a narrow and inadequate way of defining the phrase.

Neither the ruling-class nor the power-elite model (and Seltzer notwithstanding, these are different models) proposes conscious agreement about all interests at all times. What both do propose are shared views about the justice of basic structures of power and about legitimate social *questions*, shared ideas about the limits of the possible. Wilson's nationalism, organicism, administrativism, civil law approach, and acceptance of the dominance of the private corporate form all distinguished his approach from a Jeffersonian one. These orientations—along with his desire to use a strengthened federal executive to curb the corporation's worst excesses—located him in the same context as Roosevelt, though his was surely a different spirit from Roosevelt's.

34. For example, the concept of a "latent function," a concept suggesting that unofficial though durable social patterns might fulfill necessary functions for a society. Thus Croly explained the persistence of the boss system as the necessary "extra-legal counterpoise" of an inadequate legalism (from Landau, "The Myth of Hyperfactualism," p. 393). The concept yielded insights not only in the study of bosses but also of congress, the political parties, and eventually the presidency. See, for example, Henry Jones Ford in *The Rise and Growth of American Politics*, pp. 71, 215.

35. Wilson, *Congressional Government*, pp. 76 and 206; see also p. 145. A similar description led to similar conclusions in *Constitutional Government*, p. 41. The previous explanation about why he did not indict trusts is from Sklar, "Woodrow Wilson," p. 19. And further: "No man undertakes to say that the

things that have happened by operation of irresistible forces are immoral things" (*ibid.*, and p. 23).

36. He lamented that "under our system we have isolation *plus* irresponsibility—isolation and *therefore* irresponsibility. . . . Other Executives lead; our Executive obeys" (*The State*, pp. 549–550, the concluding words of the main text).

37. From "The Parliament of the People" and "Let There Be Light," in Leuchtenberg, *Woodrow Wilson*, pp. 71 and 81. The remark about the courts is from *Constitutional Government*, p. 17. Concerning his faith in the existence of an underlying unity and "pattern" behind the fragments, see also "The Law and the Facts," p. 6.

38. A fascinating example of Wilson's acceptance and defense of a social "top" and "bottom" was his argument that renewal came from below, in his campaign speech to a working-class audience, "Life Comes from the Soil," in Leuchtenberg, *Woodrow Wilson*. This line of thought led to the staggering conclusion that "the Catholic Church . . . is a great democracy" (p. 62).

39. Fine, *Laissez-Faire*, p. 209 (from "Fraternalism vs. Paternalism in Government," 1898). Wilson concluded *Constitutional Government* asserting that "we must think less of checks and balances and more of coordinated power, less of separation of functions and more of the synthesis of action" (p. 221). Lowi notes, concerning the paradox noted in the preceding paragraph, that modern "government is unlimited in scope but formless in action" (*The End of Liberalism*, p. x).

40. E. K. Hunt, "A Neglected Aspect of the Economic Ideology of the Early New Deal," p. 187.

41. Paul Baran could still note at mid-century that "in our time . . . faith in the manipulative omnipotence of the State has all but displaced analysis of its social structure and understanding of its political and economic functions" (cited in James O'Connor, *The Corporations and the State*, p. 79).

42. Walter Weyl, *The New Democracy*, pp. 262 and 168. Concerning class arrangements, see Croly, *The Promise of American Life*, pp. 138–140.

43. Lippmann, *Drift and Mastery*, p. 161.

44. *Ibid.*, pp. 42–43.

45. Brandeis's contemporary revelation, in C. Forcey, *The Crossroads of Liberalism*, p. 164.

46. "The American problem is the social problem partly because the social problem is the democratic problem" (Croly, *The Promise of American Life*, pp. 24–25). There were differences between these three men. Lippmann tended to look to science more than the others, and was also more intrigued with psychology. Weyl downplayed the importance of leadership and the spiritual aspects of social problems. Croly gave the need for brotherhood and new cultural ideals a more central place in his work, and also demonstrated a greater interest in and grasp of American history. But these were differences in emphasis occurring within a shared frame of reference.

47. Lippmann, *Drift and Mastery*, p. 71. The Croly passage, *The Promise of American Life*, p. 380.

48. Weyl, *The New Democracy*, p. 144. The view that consumers provided the key to social unity is also in Weyl. Lippmann trusted that "with the consumer awake, neither the worker nor the employer can use politics for his special interest" (*Drift and Mastery*, p. 54).

49. Lippmann, *Drift and Mastery*, p. 118. *Ibid.*, p. 126. See also pp. 116, 136.

50. Cited in Forcey, *Crossroads*, p. 117.

51. Croly, *The Promise of American Life*, p. 434.

52. Lippmann, *Drift and Mastery*, p. 55. "Six grocers in three blocks . . . little retail businesses with the family living in the back room, the odor of cooking . . . and fly-specks on the goods"—all this was what "the village view" conjured up for the young Lippmann.

53. Lippmann, *Drift and Mastery*, p. 150.

54. *Ibid.*, pp. 87, 50. Weyl believed that beneficial federal reforms were finally being worked, "thanks largely to the incentive of businessmen" (*New Democracy*, p. 311).

55. Croly, *The Promise of American Life*, pp. 367–368.

56. Weyl, *New Democracy*, p. 75. "More and more . . . the ruling plutocracy gives up its petty business corruption [and] small cheatings . . . as a man puts away childish things. It finds it does not pay to rob its own cash drawer" (pp. 142–143). Anticipating the adoption of Taylor's methods, he saw industry already dividing up every industrial operation into its constituent parts, subjecting these "to a minute and searching analysis," and reconstructing them "on a more paying basis" (p. 75). Croly wrote that the state "must help those men to win who are most capable of using their winnings for the benefit of society" (*The Promise of American Life*, p. 193, also see pp. 117 and 398).

57. Croly, *Promise*, pp. 387–390; Lippmann, *Drift*, pp. 99, 62. Weyl, *New Democracy*, pp. 292–293. Also see Forcey, *Crossroads*, pp. 157–158, 185, 190.

58. Croly, *Promise*, p. 276. "Only a comparatively small minority are capable at any one time of exercising political, economic and civil liberties in an able, efficient or thoroughly worthy manner" (p. 194).

59. Lippmann, *Drift*, pp. 108, 141–142.

60. Croly, *Promise*, p. 14. "The essential wholeness of the community depends absolutely on the ceaseless creation of a political, economic, and social aristocracy and their equally incessant replacement" (p. 196).

61. Croly, *Promise*, Chap. 7, *passim*. Most Progressives dismissed the need for such inquiry, equating the idea of sovereignty with a metaphysical belief in the subjective personality of the state.

62. *Ibid.*, pp. 81, 88. The flow of Croly's argument has been altered slightly, though not as to change its meaning.

63. *Ibid.*, p. 181.

64. Cited in Robert Nisbet, *The Quest for Community*, p. 102. Lippmann felt that "a State is absolute in the sense which I have in mind when it claims the right to a monopoly of all the force within the community, to make war, to make peace, to conscript life, to tax, to establish and dis-establish property, to define

crime, to punish disobedience, to control education, to supervise the family, to regulate personal habits, to censor opinions." This thinking was pure Hobbes. The argument earlier in the paragraph is from Croly, *The Promise of American Life*, pp. 177–178 and 255.

65. Lippmann, *Drift*, p. 50.

66. Croly, *Promise*, see Chap. 9, section 3.

67. *Ibid.*, p. 285. G. W. F. Hegel, *Philosophy of Right*, trans. Knox; see Section 189, pp. 126, 134; and "Addition" to Section 290, pp. 290–292.

68. Preceding two paragraphs: Croly, *Promise*, pp. 282–284. Croly lamented that, "One may be evangelized for a lifetime. A group of men can only be evangelized for many years. Multitudes of men can only be evangelized for a few hours" (*ibid.*). Though his heart was with Jesus, the laurels went resignedly to Paul. To give him his due, Croly admitted that not every "piece of legislation . . . is national because it is Federal" (p. 274); but he provided little right or protection for those who would challenge the equation of the two in practice (p. 286).

69. The approach was substantially the same as Durkheim's. Having criticized the atomistic and mechanistic approach of the utilitarians, Durkheim urged that beyond material links, it was also "necessary that there be moral links" between people, but he believed that "material continuity by itself produces links of this kind, provided it is durable." Emile Durkheim, *The Division of Labor*, George Simpson, trans. (New York: The Free Press, 1964), p. 277. Also see pp. 278 and 368. Hegel has often been accused of proposing a "statist" or impositional theory of social order. But whatever other criticisms may be lodged against him, he did conceive of an ethical object for people's shared commitment: the ethical mind "manifest and revealed to itself" (meaning substantive rationality), embodied in actual institutions and providing collective guarantees for "genuine individuality and ethical life" (*The Philosophy of Right*, Knox trans., sections 257–258).

70. Lippmann, *Drift and Mastery*, p. 71. The Croly citation from *The Promise of American Life*, p. 278.

71. Starting from the whole, medieval thought also "ascribes an intrinsic value to every Partial Whole down to and including the individual" (Gierke, *Political Theories of the Middle Age*, p. 7). "The Whole only lives and comes to light in the Members. . . . Every Member is of value to the Whole, and . . . even a justifiable amputation of a Member is always a regrettable operation" (p. 27). McIlwain discusses the "antique" element in *Constitutionalism*, pp. 69–71.

72. Gierke, *Political Theories*, p. 74. "The notion that a king or lord [during the Middle Ages] should decide out of his own plenary power and according to his own will was quite foreign at least to the theory of the proceedings" (George Sabine, *A History of Political Theory*, p. 218).

73. "There were the liberties of the church, based on law superior to that of the King; there was the law of nature, graven on the hearts of men . . . and there was the prescription of immemorial local and feudal custom stereotyping a variety of jurisdictions and impeding the operation of a single will. There was no

sovereignty capable of eradicating bondage by royal edict or act of parliament" (Nisbet, *Quest for Community*, p. 110; also see p. 123). This is also fully discussed in Marc Bloch's *Feudal Society*, trans. Manyon, Vol. I, p. 112, for example.

74. Gierke, *Political Theories*, p. 34. "In this there was an aspect of mutuality . . . which has almost entirely vanished from modern political relationships" (Sabine, *Political Theory*, p. 217). Bloch reports the feudal proviso that "a man may resist his king and judge when he acts contrary to law, and may even help to make war on him" if the king has not fulfilled his part of the agreement (*Feudal Society*, Vol. II, pp. 451ff; also p. 224).

75. Bertrand de Jouvenal, *Sovereignty*, p. 209. Previous citations from pp. 204 (from 1576), and 184 (from 1609).

76. *Ibid.*, pp. 201, 209; the distinction between "arbitrary" and "absolute" sovereignty is defined by de Jouvenal in Chapter 12. McIlwain discusses it in *Growth of Political Thought*, pp. 354–355. Locke also employed the distinction in *The Second Treatise of Government*, Chapter 11, section 139: "Even absolute power, where it is necessary, is not arbitrary by being absolute."

77. A. Passerin d'Entreves, *The Notion of the State*, p. 78; de Jouvenal, *Sovereignty*, p. 187. Holmes clearly vindicated their worst fears. Also see the definition of sovereignty discerned by Joseph Tussman, *Obligation and the Body Politic*, p. 64. Bertrand de Jouvenal notes that the Austinian theory implies "that there is no antecedent notion of justice . . . an opinion which was open to Hobbes [and modern liberals] but . . . not to Christian thinkers" (p. 201).

78. K. C. Hsiao, *Political Pluralism*, p. 144.

79. *Ibid.*, p. 139.

80. "Government should not be made an end in itself; it is a means only—a means to be freely adapted to advance the best interests of the social organism. The State exists only for the sake of Society" (Wilson, *The State*, p. 636). The approach again bore great similarities to the Frenchman Léon Duguit's theory of "objective law." See his "The Transformation of the State," in M. Spahr, *Readings in Recent Political Philosophy*, pp. 476, 481.

81. Tussman, *Obligation and the Body Politic*, pp. 5–7. Tussman's discussion of this outlook is primarily philosophic and analytic rather than historical; but his remarks are germane because the model he analyzes is substantially the one adopted by the Progressives.

82. Andrew Fraser, "The Legal Theory We Need Now," pp. 169–171. Fraser's analysis is of contemporary law, but the character of this legality was anticipated during the Progressive era.

83. See J. P. Plamenatz, *Consent, Freedom, and Political Obligation*.

84. Tussman, *Obligation*, pp. 5–7.

85. Hsiao, *Political Pluralism*, pp. 219, 137.

86. Tocqueville denied the equation of positive law with justice: "When I refuse to obey an unjust law, I do not contest the right of the majority to command; I simply appeal from the sovereignty of the people to the sovereignty of mankind" (Vol. I, p. 269). Croly's remark about absolute power is in *The Promise of American Life*, p. 177.

87. Subsequent American liberals would also eschew a close look at the empirical effects of corporate power and simply assume that the bulk of the new federal laws constituted, as Michael Reagan put it, "community-protecting limitations on . . . private property" and provisions for new forms of "property" (*The Managed Economy*, pp. 54–56).

88. Hegel's ideas provide food for thought. He criticized post-revolutionary France because it lacked "corporations and local government, i.e., associations wherein particular and universal meet. It is true that these associations won too great [power] . . . in the Middle Ages, when they were states within states. . . . But we may none the less affirm that the proper strength of a state lies in these associations. In them the executive meets [contending] interests . . . and the individual . . . links his private interest with the maintenance of the whole. . . . It is of the utmost importance that the masses should be organized. . . . Otherwise they are nothing but a heap, an aggregate of atomic units" (Hegel, *Philosophy of Right*, "Addition" to Section 290, pp. 290–291). The corporation also played an important part in Hegel's theory of representation (see Section 311, pp. 202–203). Of course the explicit corporativists in America did propose a representative role for the corporations; but they did so for reasons of logistics and efficiency, not for reasons of education or ethics.

89. Forcey, *Crossroads*, pp. 303, 295. Edmund Wilson, writing on Croly's death in 1931, felt it was no longer possible to believe in "the salvation of our society by the gradual and rational approximation of socialism which [Croly] himself called progressivism. . . . That benevolent and intelligent capitalism on which liberals . . . counted," had not only failed to materialize but capitalism had not even been able to avert major economic disaster. ("An Appeal to Progressives," *The New Republic*, January 14, 1931, in *The Shores of Light*, New York: Random House, 1952, pp. 521–522).

90. Croly did eventually break with the approach and turn to questions of religion, though he still attempted to find a synthesis between religion and science. But Lippmann, doubting the ability of the masses and skeptical of changing property relations, proposed to organize neutral "intelligence bureaus coordinated by a central agency that could discover the facts and provide a bar of judgment for warring interests" (quoted in Forcey, *Crossroads*, pp. 297–305).

91. Wilson, *The State*, pp. 30–31; and see his distinction between natural and political "laws," p. 607.

92. Yosal Rogat, "Mr. Justice Holmes, A Dissenting Opinion," p. 11. Also see Rogat, "The Judge as Spectator," p. 254.

93. From *American Banana Co. v. United Fruit Co.* 213 U.S. 347 (1909), p. 358. See John Noonan, *Persons and Masks of the Law*, pp. 103–109: "The roots of the scheme were theological, disclosed by Holmes's refusal to inquire into the divisible nature of sovereignty. . . . Holmes came from a tradition of monotheists. He would not entertain polytheism when he framed his concept of the sovereign as god. In any place where there was law, there must be but one sovereign. . . . That the sovereign should be subject was 'a contradiction in terms'" (p. 109).

94. *Buck v. Bell* 274 U.S. 200 (1927). And in a letter to John Wu of August

1926: "I don't believe that it is an absolute principle . . . that man always is an end in himself. We march up a conscript with bayonets behind to die for a cause he doesn't believe in, and I feel no scruples about it. Our morality seems to me only a check on the impulse of every pig to put his feet in the trough" (in Lerner, *Justice Holmes*, p. 431). This aspect of Holmes's reasoning is discussed by Rogat, "Mr. Justice Holmes, A Dissenting Opinion," p. 14. It was apparent already in *The Common Law*, pp. 37 and 41.

95. *Moyer v. Peabody*, 212 U.S. 70, 84 (1909). Holmes's approach led easily to making the enjoyment of a government benefit conditional upon the surrender of a constitutional right—as when in *McAuliffe v. New Bedford* he declared that "the petitioner may have a constitutional right to talk politics, but he has no constitutional right to be a policeman"; 155 Mass. 216; 29 N.E. 517 (1892).

96. Lerner, *Justice Holmes*, p. 289.

97. "Those who won our independence believed . . . that public discussion is a political duty; and that this should be a fundamental principle of American government. . . . Believing in the power of reason as applied through public discussion, they eschewed all silence coerced by law. . . . Fear of serious injury alone cannot alone justify suppression of free speech and assembly"; *Whitney v. Calif.*, 274 U.S. 357 (1927).

98. *The Federalist Papers*, Number 84 (Hamilton), p. 514.

99. Tocqueville, *Democracy in America*, Vol. I, p. 269.

100. E. E. Schattschneider, *Party Government*, pp. 52 and 59.

CHAPTER EIGHT

Epigraph: Louis Hartz, *The Liberal Tradition in America*, p. 71.

1. Walter Lippmann, *Drift and Mastery*, p. 116.

2. William James, "The Sentiment of Rationality" in *Essays on Faith and Morals*, p. 83; and *The Pluralist Universe*, p. 193.

3. James's remarks had a marked Nietzschean flavor. Nietzsche often used the image of horizons to speak about authority. "A living thing can only be healthy, strong and productive within a certain horizon"; and "When the lines of [one's] horizon are constantly changing . . . he cannot shake himself free . . . for a downright act of will or desire" (*The Use and Abuse of History*, trans. Adrian Collin, Indianapolis: Bobbs-Merrill, 1949, pp. 7–8). It was also authority that Nietzsche spoke of in his parable of the madman, when he announced the death of God and asked, "Who gave us the sponge to wipe away the entire horizon?" (From "The Gay Science," in Walter Kaufman, ed., *The Portable Nietzsche*, New York: The Viking Press, 1954, p. 95).

4. Parrington, *The Beginnings of Critical Realism*, pp. 189–202, 316–327. Most American writers and political commentators recognized this collapse only after the World War and the Depression. Edmund Wilson spoke of it in his obituary for Croly in 1931.

5. Henry Adams, *The Education*, pp. 344–345, 421. To others "the dynamo . . . was but an ingenious channel for conveying somewhere the heat latent in a

few tons of poor coal hidden in a dirty engine-house carefully kept out of sight; but to Adams the dynamo became a symbol of infinity. . . . Before the end one began to pray to it; inherited instinct taught the natural expression of man before silent and infinite force" (p. 380).

6. Henry George, *Progress and Poverty*, p. 480.

7. *Ibid.*, p. 528. The remark about Christianity is from p. 543.

8. Schaar, "Legitimacy in the Modern State," pp. 278–279.

9. Hannah Arendt, "What Is Authority?" pp. 121–122. See also Peter J. Riga, "Prudence and Jurisprudence: Authority as the Basis of Law According to Thomas Aquinas."

10. Schaar, "Legitimacy in the Modern State," pp. 291–292.

11. *Ibid.* "Force can bring political power into being but cannot maintain it. For that something else is required" (p. 287). Also see A. Passerin d'Entreves, *The Notion of the State*, Part II, Chaps. 2, 3, 10.

12. Arendt, "What is Authority?" p. 106.

13. Comte, *Positive Philosophy*, p. 408.

14. Laski, "Political Theory in the Later Middle Ages," *The Cambridge Medieval History*, Vol. VIII, p. 641.

15. *Democracy in America*, Vol. I, pp. 97, 253–254. "Men are not corrupted by the exercise of power or debased by the habit of obedience, but by the exercise of a power which they believe to be illegitimate, and by obedience to a rule which they consider to be usurped and oppressive" (p. 9). "I confess that I do not rely upon the calculating patriotism which is founded upon interest and which any change in interests may destroy. . . . I will never admit that men constitute a body simply because they obey the same head and the same laws" (p. 408).

16. Henry Adams, *The Education*, p. 225.

17. *Ibid.*, pp. 229–230. "He wished to be shown [where] changes in form caused evolution in force; [where] chemical or mechanical energy had by natural selection and minute changes, under uniform conditions, converted itself into thought" (p. 339). And "the matter of direction seemed vital" (p. 400). (We remember that Henry George and Lester Ward had sought the same "evolution of mind," in reaction against the drift toward materialism.)

18. Lowi, *The End of Liberalism*, p. 58.

19. From "Life as Joy, Duty, End," in Lerner, *Justice Holmes*, pp. 42–43. "Like so many realists," Harold Höffding wrote of another exponent of the approach, "he lost reality because he sought for it on the surface of events" (*A History of Modern Philosophy*, New York: Dover Edition, 1955, p. 24).

20. Gompers's response to the socialist Hillquit, cited in Leon Litwack, ed., *The American Labor Movement* (Englewood Cliffs, N.J.: Spectrum Books, Prentice-Hall, 1962), pp. 40–41.

21. Their legalism was limited first by their appeal to social "will" and habit, as mentioned in Chapter Seven; and second, as Lowi notes, by a hidden belief that in the modern state "all formalisms [should be] effectively set aside, as though formalism were the enemy of democracy" (*The End of Liberalism*, p. x).

22. John Dewey, *The Public and Its Problems*, pp. 98, 155, 151. The specifically human aspect of cognition for Dewey was precisely this ability to understand "consequences" (*ibid.*, pp. 11–12).

23. Lippmann, *Drift and Mastery*, pp. 140, 150–151, emphasis added. The formulation, again, was similar to Peirce's.

24. Herbert Croly, *The Promise of American Life*, p. 139.

25. *Ibid.*, p. 432. The American habit and tradition "estimate[s] excellence almost entirely by results."

26. Comte, *Positive Philosophy*, p. 79.

27. Fred Rodell, responding to criticisms of Holmes: "The single trait that binds together the critics of Mr. Justice Holmes, be they Catholics, Protestants or Jews, is a belief in some sort of Absolute, outside and beyond the minds of men. His critics, authoritarians all, will accept no moral code that does not embody a set of timeless superhuman principles" ("Justice Holmes and His Hecklers," pp. 622–623).

28. *The Octopus*, pp. 386–387; previous passage, pp. 360–361. The ascendance of "force" in the new world-view was evident here, as in Adams's *Education* (see *Octopus*, pp. 425–426). Norris echoes Thomas Carlyle in the pivotal passage of his last chapters. Thus Norris: "Colossal indifference only, a vast trend toward appointed goals. Nature was, then, a gigantic engine, a vast Cyclopean power, huge, terrible, a leviathan with a heart of steel, knowing no compunction, no forgiveness, no tolerance; crushing out the human atom standing in its way" (p. 386). And Carlyle: "To me the universe was void of all Life, of Purpose, of Volitions, even of Hostility; it was one huge, dead, immeasurable Steam-engine, rolling on, in its dead indifference, to grind me limb from limb" (*Sartor Resartus*, Modern Library, 1937, p. 164). I am indebted to Professor David Schuman of Deep Springs College for pointing out this similarity.

29. *Ibid.*, pp. 427–428.

30. The definition of religion is in Arendt, "What is Authority?" p. 21.

31. "The call to abandon illusions . . . is a call to abandon a condition which requires illusions." Marx, "Critique of Hegel's Philosophy of Right," in Robert Tucker, ed., *The Marx-Engels Reader*, p. 12. A major strain of Marxism has also tried to locate authority with the future. Marx wrote that "The social revolution of the nineteenth century cannot draw its poetry from the past but only from the future" ("Eighteenth Brumaire," in *Marx-Engels Reader*, p. 429). As Arendt notes, though, part of the modern impulse to revolution grows out of the attempt to "revolve" back to the authority of foundations (pp. 139–140). Equally important is the fact that Marx himself, in distinction from most Marxists and the scientistically inclined Progressives, was firmly rooted through Hegel and Kant in the authoritative Western concepts of reason and freedom.

32. "It is quite possible for statistical averages and human experiences to run in opposite directions. . . . People may consume more goods and become less happy or less free at the same time" (E. P. Thompson, *The Making of the English Working Class*, p. 211).

33. Concerning the interconnections of the accumulation and legitimation crises, see Alan Wolfe's *Limits of Legitimacy*, James O'Connor's *Fiscal Crisis of the State*, and Claus Offe's "The Abolition of Market Control and the Problem of Legitimacy."

34. Tocqueville, *Democracy in America*, II, p. 339.

35. Arendt's conclusion is in "What is Authority?" pp. 128, 141.

36. Jacob Burckhardt, *The Civilization of the Renaissance in Italy* (London: Phaidon Press, 1965), Chap. 1. The point was captured perfectly for Burckhardt in the actual ascendance to thrones of bastard princes: it was truly an age when "the sons of Popes were founding dynasties" (p. 12).

37. Schaar, "Legitimacy in the Modern State," p. 279.

38. Dewey, *The Public and Its Problems*, pp. 98, 115, 126–127.

39. Henry Adams, *The Education*, p. 484.

40. To say that the mechanization of associations is appropriate to corporate capitalism is not to say it is unique to corporate capitalism. As a matter of historical fact, however, it followed in America from certain prior "decisions."

41. Henry Adams, *The Education*, p. 421.

42. The primary modern writer on "the autonomy of process" is, of course, Jacques Ellul, in *The Technological Society*. John McDermott offered important remarks about the politics of technology *as* technology in "Knowledge Is Power," *The Nation*, April 14, 1969.

43. Dewey, *The Public and Its Problems*, pp. 203, 107.

44. Henry Adams, *The Education*, pp. 344 and 499.

45. Last paragraph of the volume, *ibid.*, p. 505; previous citation, p. 485. Adams's general outlook was summarized in a letter in which he explained that he was "trying to work out the formula of anarchism; the law of expansion from unity, simplicity, morality, to multiplicity, contradiction, police. . . . Law . . . would disappear as theory of a priori principle, and give way to force. Morality would become police. Explosives would reach cosmic violence. Disintegration would overcome integration." Cited in Francis M. Carney's "Zero or One: The Influence of Henry Adams on Mailer and Pynchon" (unpublished manuscript, Riverside, California, 1975), p. 13.

46. Ellul sees the de-authorization of human relations as inevitable: for technological problems people will wind up proposing technological solutions.

47. To speak only of the electoral obstacles to renewed attempts, W. D. Burnham noted that the achievement of the "system of 1896" was to raise "constitutional restraints on democratic political action" ("The Changing Shape of the American Political Universe," p. 26). Burnham also writes: "In most other regions of advanced industrialization the emergence of corporate capitalism was associated with the development of mass political parties;" these permitted the expression of "deep conflicts over the direction of public policy." But in America what occurred was "the elimination of organized partisan combat, an extremely severe decline in electoral participation, the emergence of a Republican 'coalition of the whole' and a highly efficient insulation of the controlling industrial-

financial elite" ("The End of American Party Politics," in J. R. Fiszman and G. Poschman, eds., *The American Political Arena*, 3rd ed., New York: Little, Brown and Co., 1972, pp. 251–252).

48. Comte, *Positive Philosophy*, p. 119.

49. Introd. to Edward Bellamy, *Looking Backward*, pp. vii–viii.

50. Henry Adams, *The Education*, p. 426.

CHAPTER NINE

Epigraph: D. H. Lawrence, *Studies in Classic American Literature* (New York: Viking Compass Books, 1961—originally published 1923), p. 1.

1. Michael Reagan, *The Managed Economy*, p. 31.

2. Robert Brady noted the desire for "synchronization" during the thirties among spokesmen of free enterprise themselves. "The Fascist Threat to Democracy," p. 157.

3. For further remarks on this route to modern violence—a route independent of that historically taken by either the petty tyrant or the capitalist master—see John Schaar and Sheldon Wolin on the University of California's response to the builders of a "people's park": *The Berkeley Rebellion and Beyond* (New York: New York Review of Books, 1970), p. 89.

4. To note these promises of due process and regularity is not to say that such promises can be fulfilled. Indeed, the story that remains to be written about modern organization concerns the ways in which it *prevents* due process, discourages openness, and insulates decision-makers from accountability.

5. The Harbrecht quotation is from *Pension Funds and Economic Power*, p. 279. For an example of the wrongheadedness of this reasoning, see Berle's erroneous conclusions from 1964 about the "planned oil economy," in Andrew Hacker, *The Corporation Take-Over*, p. 101.

6. Charles W. Anderson, "Political Design and the Representation of Interests," pp. 143, 148.

7. "We talk of the power of organized interests. We do not speak of their authority" (*ibid.*, p. 132).

8. Grant McConnell, *Private Power and American Democracy*, pp. 162–163. Adopting a species of pluralism himself, McConnell concluded that "the dominant power . . . lies in different hands," and that businessmen "tend to pursue a policy of noninvolvement in the large issues of statesmanship" (pp. 193 and 339; see also p. 254).

9. McConnell, *Private Power*, p. 8. McConnell assumed that "in general, the liberty of individuals is more secure in a large constituency than in a small" (p. 365 and Chap. 10 *passim*).

10. Theodore Lowi, *The End of Liberalism*, pp. 40, 29, 289, 294, and 310. "Nineteenth-century liberalism was standards without plans. . . . But twentieth-century liberalism turned out to be plans without standards" (p. 288).

11. *Ibid.*, Chap. 10 *passim*.

12. Reagan, *The Managed Economy*, p. 208. Previous arguments on pp. 8 and 42.

13. *Ibid.*, pp. 235, pp. 122 and 123.

14. *Ibid.*, pp. 235–236. "I am not accusing the business community of seeking fascism but of failing to recognize that its demands for a privileged position . . . and its unwillingness to accept public accountability would move us in that direction" (p. 236; also see p. 109). Against this trend Reagan looked to the countervailing weight of American beliefs in egalitarianism, radicalism, "a deep belief in the self-governing capacity of the citizen," and commitment to private enterprise.

15. *Ibid.*, pp. 53–54.

16. *Ibid.*, pp. 228, 231.

17. *Ibid.*, p. 243.

18. Wilson, *Constitutional Government*, pp. 17, 68–69, 127, 207, 217–218. One might argue that Wilson went beyond recent analysts in stressing the necessity of "genuine common counsel," which "can be obtained only by genuine representative institutions" (p. 222). This formal stress was vitiated, however, by the substance of Wilson's outlook.

The current analysts begin to go beyond Progressivism when they admit real conflicts of purposes in current politics, and real choices between different views of the public interest. These fault lines, however, become blurred again when it comes to proposals for reform.

19. A recent example of failed regulation, the Clean Air Act of 1970, is particularly important in this regard because the legislation establishing it attempted precise definitions of goals and powers; the law has been gutted nonetheless. "Most critics of the erosion of the . . . Act ascribe the failure of 'law' to a failure of judicial logic or administrative will-power." But it is "in effect, impossible to simply legislate clean air" (pp. 241, 243). "The regulators do not control the central variables which determine the [patterns of urbanization, transportation and energy-use]. . . . They do not control the key decisions over production, investment, employment and location. They can only try to redirect the decisions of those who do have these basic economic powers" (*ibid.*, pp. 254, 253). R. Walker and M. Storper, "Erosion of the Clean Air Act of 1970: A Study in the Failure of Government Regulation and Planning," *Boston College Environmental Affairs Law Review*, VII, No. 2 (1978).

20. It should be added that the author of the Full Employment Bill, Bertram Gross, has moved on to admit the implications of Reagan's lucid prediction, while Reagan himself, judging by subsequent publications, has not (see Gross, *Friendly Fascism: The New Face of Power in America*, New York: M. Evans and Co., 1980).

21. Reagan, *The Managed Economy*, p. 250.

22. Thus Franz Neumann: "For [legal] positivism the plant [was] a technical unit . . . while the enterprise is an economic unit in which [the property owner] pursues his business policy. Institutionalism [the doctrine developed in the thir-

ties] transforms the plant into a social community. The enterprise becomes a social organization and the joint stock company changes from an association of legal persons . . . into an Anstalt" (*Behemoth*, p. 449).

23. Henry Bamford Parkes, *The American Experience* (New York: Vintage Books, 1959), pp. 193 and 195; see also p. 295).

24. Andrew Fraser: "Rights become socio-historical, rather than ontological phenomena. . . . Consequently, the 'rights of man' must now be understood in terms of their relevance to harmonious ordering of the various . . . [organized] interests within the corporate state" ("The Legal Theory We Need Now," p. 172).

25. Richard Hofstadter, *The Age of Reform*, pp. 14–15. Cited in Chapter One.

26. The preceding passages from Charles Reich are in "The New Property," pp. 771, 785–786. That the perspective of property is inescapably one also of retreat from the commons is revealed by Reich's terms. Thus he seeks "a hiding place from the all-pervasive system of regulation" and "sanctuaries or enclaves" where self-sufficiency can be preserved. Reich did not take seriously enough his own argument that the "self" emerges atop or within social supports, not outside them (*ibid.*). Neumann noted the privatistic impulse in the institution of property when he wrote that "property for Rousseau is only property to the extent it remains an individual and particular right" ("The Change in the Function of Law," p. 51).

27. This is not intended to challenge the values of privacy or autonomous moral consciousness. But privacy itself, as one writer has put it beautifully, "is an aspect of community. . . . Privacy is the communion we hold with other human beings when we are retired from them, physically or spiritually." Privacy "is a form of communion and implies an effective community." He adds that "when the tissue of social trust is forever strained and riven, when a broken promise is the most familiar condition of our lives, then all discussion of privacy is dangerously close to nostalgia" (Emile Capouya, "Bicentennial Reflections," Parts I, II, III, *The Nation*, March 13, April 10, May 5, 1976).

28. "Freedom is not . . . merely the opportunity to choose between set alternatives. Freedom is, first of all, the chance to formulate the available choices, to argue over them—and then, the opportunity to choose" (Mills, *The Sociological Imagination*, p. 174).

29. Peirce, "How to Make Our Ideas Clear," in Wiener, *Values in a Universe of Chance*, p. 133.

30. C. Wright Mills, *The Sociological Imagination*, Chap. 9 *passim*; Hannah Arendt, *The Human Condition* (Garden City, N.Y.: Anchor Books, 1959), Part II; and John Dewey, *The Public and Its Problems*.

Selected Bibliography

Adams, Henry. *The Education*. New York: Houghton Mifflin, 1961.

Adams, Charles Francis, Jr. *Autobiography, 1835–1915*. New York: Houghton Mifflin, 1916.

————. *The Railroads: Their Origin and Problems*. 1878.

Anderson, Charles W. "Political Design and the Representation of Interests." *Comparative Political Studies* X, No. 1 (April 1977).

Arendt, Hannah. "What Is Authority?" Chapter Three of *Between Past and Future*. Cleveland: Meridian Books, 1954.

Bellamy, Edward. *Looking Backward*. New York: New American Library, 1960. Originally published 1888.

Bendix, Reinhard. *Work and Authority in Industry*. New York: Harper and Row, 1965.

Bentley, Arthur F. *The Process of Government*. Evanston, Illinois: Principia Press of Illinois, 1908.

Berle, Adolph A. *Power without Property*. New York: Harcourt, Brace and World, 1959.

————, and Gardner Means. *The Modern Corporation and Private Property*. New York: Macmillan and Co., 1932.

Bernard, Luther Lee. "The Transition to an Objective Standard of Social Control." *The American Journal of Sociology* XVI (January 1911).

Bernstein, Richard J. *Praxis and Action*. Philadelphia: University of Pennsylvania Press, 1971.

————, ed. *Perspectives on Peirce*. New Haven: Yale University Press, 1965.

Blau, Joseph, ed. *Social Theories of Jacksonian Democracy*. New York: Bobbs-Merrill Co., 1954.

Bloch, Marc. *Feudal Society*. Translated by L. A. Manyon. Chicago: University of Chicago Press, 1961.

Bourne, Randolph S. *War and the Intellectuals*. New York: Harper and Row, 1964.

Brady, Robert. *Business as a System of Power*. New York: Columbia University Press, 1943.

————. "The Fascist Threat to Democracy." *Science and Society* II, No. 2 (Spring 1938).

Brandeis, Louis. *The Curse of Bigness.* New York: Viking Press, 1934.

Buck, Solon. *The Granger Movement.* Cambridge, Massachusetts: Harvard University Press, 1913.

Burnham, Walter D. "The Changing Shape of the American Political Universe." *The American Political Science Review* LIX, No. 1 (March 1965).

———, and William N. Chambers. *The American Party System.* New York: Oxford University Press, 1967.

Burtt, Edwin A. *The Metaphysical Foundations of Modern Science.* New York: Doubleday and Co., 1932.

Camus, Albert. *The Rebel.* New York: Vintage Books, 1956.

Carnegie, Andrew. "The Bugaboo of Trusts." *North American Review* CXLVIII, No. 1 (January 1889).

Chamberlain, John. *Farewell to Reform.* Chicago: Quadrangle Books, 1965.

Cochran, Thomas C. "Entrepreneurship." *The International Encyclopedia of the Social Sciences,* David L. Sills, ed. New York: Macmillan Co. and The Free Press, 1968.

Cohen, Jean. "Max Weber and the Dynamics of Domination." *Telos* XIV (Winter 1972).

Commager, Henry Steele. *The American Mind.* New Haven: Yale University Press, 1950.

———, ed. *Lester Ward and the Welfare State.* New York: Bobbs-Merrill Co., 1967.

Commons, John R. *The Legal Foundations of Capitalism.* New York: Macmillan Co., 1924.

——— et al. *History of Labor in the United States,* Vol. I. New York: Macmillan Co., 1918.

Comte, Auguste. *A General View of Positivism.* Translated by J. H. Bridges. Stanford, California: Academic Reprints. Originally published 1848.

———. *The Positive Philosophy of Auguste Comte.* Translated by Harriet Martineau. New York: C. Blanchard, 1858.

Corwin, Edward S. *The Higher Law Background of American Constitutional Law.* Ithaca: Great Seal Books, 1955.

———. "The Basic Doctrine of American Constitutional Law." *American Constitutional History: Essays by E. S. Corwin.* Edited by Alpheus T. Mason and Gerald Garvey. New York: Harper Torchbooks, 1964.

Croly, Herbert. *The Promise of American Life.* New York: E. P. Dutton and Co., 1963. Originally published 1909.

de Jouvenal, Bertrand. *Sovereignty: An Inquiry into the Political Good.* Chicago: University of Chicago Press, 1959.

d'Entreves, A. Passerin. *The Notion of the State.* London: Oxford University Press, 1967.

Derber, Milton. "The Idea of Industrial Democracy in America, 1898–1915." *Labor History* VII, No. 3 (Fall 1966).

Dewey, John. *Essays in Experimental Logic.* Chicago: University of Chicago, 1916.

———. *Individualism Old and New.* New York: Capricorn Books, 1962. Originally published 1929.

———. *Liberalism and Social Action*. New York: Capricorn Books, 1963. Originally published 1935.

———. *Logic: The Theory of Inquiry*. London: Allen and Unwin, 1939.

———. *The Public and Its Problems*. Chicago: Swallow Press, 1954. Originally published 1927.

———. *Reconstruction in Philosophy*. Boston: Beacon Press, 1948. Originally published 1920.

———. "Austin's Theory of Sovereignty." *Political Science Quarterly* IX (March 1894).

———. "Justice Holmes and the Liberal Mind." *The New Republic* XIII (November 1928).

Drucker, Peter. *The Concept of the Corporation*. New York: New American Library, 1946.

Eells, Richard. *The Government of Corporations*. New York: Free Press of Glencoe, 1962.

Eggert, Gerald. *Railroad Labor Disputes: The Beginnings of Federal Strike Policy*. Ann Arbor: University of Michigan Press, 1967.

Elliott, W. Y. *The Pragmatic Revolt in Politics*. New York: Macmillan Co., 1928.

Ellul, Jacques. *The Technological Society*. Translated by J. Wilkinson. New York: Vintage Books, 1964.

Federalist Papers, The. Edited by Clinton Rossiter. New York: New American Library, 1961.

Fine, Sidney. *Laissez-Faire and the General-Welfare State*. Ann Arbor: University of Michigan Press, 1964.

Fisch, M. H. "Justice Holmes, The Prediction Theory of Law and Pragmatism." *Journal of Philosophy* XXXIX (1942).

Follett, Mary Parker. *The New State*. Edited by Peter Smith. Gloucester, Massachusetts, 1965. Originally published 1918.

Forcey, Charles. *The Crossroads of Liberalism*. New York: Oxford University Press, 1961.

Ford, Henry Jones. *The Rise and Growth of American Politics*. New York: Macmillan and Co., 1914.

Frantz, Laurent B. "Congressional Power to Enforce the Fourteenth Amendment Against Private Acts." *Yale Law Journal* LXXIII, No. 8 (July 1964).

Fraser, Andrew. "The Legal Theory We Need Now." *Socialist Review* Nos. 40–41 (July–October 1978).

Friedmann, W. *Legal Theory*. 4th ed. Toronto: Carswell Co., 1960.

Fuller, Leon. "Colorado's Revolt Against Capitalism." *Mississippi Valley Historical Review* XXI, No. 3 (December 1934).

Gabriel, Ralph. *The Course of American Democratic Thought*. 2nd ed. New York: The Ronald Press, 1956.

Galbraith, John K. *The New Industrial State*. New York: Signet Books, 1967.

Gallie, W. B. *Peirce and Pragmatism*. New York: Dover Publications, 1966.

George, Henry. *Progress and Poverty*. New York: Robert Schalkenbach Foundation, 1931.

————. "The Chinese on the Pacific Coast." *New York Tribune*, May 1, 1869.

————. "What the Railroad Will Bring Us." *The Overland Monthly*, October 1868. In *The California Dream*, D. Hale and J. Eisen, eds. New York: Collier Books, 1968.

George, William Henry. "Montesquieu, Tocqueville and Corporative Individualism." *American Political Science Review* XVI (February 1922).

Ghent, William J. *Our Benevolent Feudalism*. New York: Macmillan and Co., 1903.

Gierke, Otto. *Political Theories of the Middle Age*. Translated with an Introduction by F. W. Maitland. Boston: Beacon Press, 1958. Originally published 1900.

Goldman, Eric. *Rendezvous with Destiny*. New York: Vintage Books, 1952.

Goodwyn, Lawrence. *Democratic Promise: The Populist Movement in America*. New York: Oxford University Press, 1976.

Graham, Howard J. "An Innocent Abroad: The Constitutional Corporate Person." *U.C.L.A. Law Review* II, No. 2 (February 1955).

Grant, J. A. C. "The Guild Returns to America." *Journal of Politics* Part 1, IV (August 1942), Part 2, IV (November 1942).

Greenstone, J. David. *Labor in American Politics*. New York: Knopf, 1969.

Grob, Gerald. *Workers and Utopia: Ideological Conflict in the American Labor Movement, 1865–1900*. Chicago: Quadrangle Books, 1961.

Gronlund, Lawrence. *The Cooperative Commonwealth*. Edited by Stow Persons. Cambridge, Massachusetts: Belknap Press, 1965. Originally published 1884.

Gutman, Herbert. "An Iron Workers' Strike in the Ohio Valley." *The Ohio Historical Quarterly* LXVIII (October 1959).

————. "The Knights of Labor and Patrician Anti-Semitism, 1891." *Labor History* XIII, No. 1 (Winter 1972).

————. "Reconstruction in Ohio, Negroes in the Hocking Valley Coal Mines, 1873–1874." *Labor History* III, No. 3 (Fall 1962).

————. "Trouble on the Railroads in 1873–4: Prelude to 1877." *Labor History* II (Spring 1961).

————. "Two Lockouts in Pennsylvania 1873–4." *The Pennsylvania Magazine of History and Biography* LXXXIII (July 1959).

————. "Work, Culture and Society in Industrializing America." *American Historical Review* LXXVIII (June 1973).

Haber, Samuel. *Efficiency and Uplift: Scientific Management in the Progressive Era, 1890–1920*. Chicago: University of Chicago Press, 1964.

Hacker, Louis. *The Triumph of American Capitalism*. New York: Columbia University Press, 1940.

Hacker, Andrew. *The Corporation Take-Over*. New York: Harper and Row, 1964.

Hamilton, Walton. "The Path of Due Process of Law." In *American Constitutional Law: Historical Essays*, Leonard Levy, ed. New York: Harper Torchbooks, 1966.

————. "Property, According to Locke." *Yale Law Journal* XLI, No. 6 (April 1932).

Harbrecht, Paul. *Pension Funds and Economic Power*. New York: Twentieth Century Fund, 1959.

Hartz, Louis. *Economic Policy and Democratic Thought in Pennsylvania, 1776–1860*. Cambridge, Massachusetts: Harvard University Press, 1948.

——. *The Liberal Tradition in America*. New York: Harcourt, Brace and Co., 1955.

Hegel, G. W. F., *Philosophy of Right*. Translated by T. M. Knox. New York: Oxford University Press, 1967.

Hicks, John D. *The Populist Revolt*. Lincoln, Nebraska: Bison Books, 1961.

Hobbes, Thomas. *Leviathan*. Edited by Michael Oakeshott. Introduction by Richard S. Peters. New York: Collier Books, 1962.

Hofstadter, Richard. *The Age of Reform*. New York: Vintage Books, 1955.

——. *The American Political Tradition*. New York: Vintage Books, 1957.

——. *Social Darwinism in American Thought*. Boston: Beacon Press, 1944.

Holmes, Oliver Wendell, Jr. *Collected Legal Papers*. New York: Harcourt, Brace and Co., 1920.

——. *The Common Law*. Boston, Little, Brown and Co., 1881, 1963 ed.

——. *Holmes-Pollack Letters*. Edited by Mark de Wolfe Howe. Cambridge, Massachusetts: Belknap Press, 1961.

Hsiao, Kung-Chuan. *Political Pluralism*. New York: Harcourt, Brace and Co., 1927.

Hunt, E. K. "A Neglected Aspect of the Economic Ideology of the New Deal." *The Review of Social Economy* XXIX, No. 2 (September 1971).

Jacobson, Norman. "Causality and Time in Political Process: A Speculation." *American Political Science Review* LVIII, No. 1 (March 1964).

James, William. *Essays on Faith and Morals*. Cleveland: World Publishing Co., 1962. Essays originally published 1896–1911.

——. *Essays in Radical Empiricism*. New York: Longmans, Green and Co., 1912.

——. *The Pluralistic Universe*. London: Longmans, Green and Co., 1916.

——. *Pragmatism*. New York: Meridian Books, 1955. Originally published 1907.

Jay, Anthony. *Management and Machiavelli: An Inquiry into the Politics of Corporate Life*. New York: Holt, Rinehart and Winston, 1968.

Kaplan, Sidney. "Social Engineers as Saviors." *Journal of the History of Ideas* XVII, No. 3 (June 1956).

Karson, Marc. *American Labor Unions and Politics, 1900–1918*. Carbondale, Illinois: Southern Illinois University Press, 1958.

Kirkland, Edward C. *Charles Francis Adams, Jr.: Patrician at Bay*. Cambridge, Massachusetts: Harvard University Press, 1965.

Kolko, Gabriel. *Railroads and Rate Regulation, 1887–1916*. Princeton: Princeton University Press, 1965.

——. *The Triumph of Conservatism*. Chicago: Quadrangle Books, 1963.

Landau, Martin. "The Myth of Hyperfactualism in the Study of American Politics." *Political Science Quarterly* LXXXIII (September 1968).

Lasch, Christopher. *The New Radicalism in America, 1889–1963*. New York: Vintage Books, 1965.

Laski, Harold. "Political Theory in the Later Middle Ages." *The Cambridge Medieval History*. C. W. Prévite-Orton, ed. Vol. VIII. New York: Macmillan, 1936.

Lerner, Max, ed. *The Mind and Faith of Justice Holmes*. New York: Modern Library, 1943.

Leuchtenburg, William E., ed. *Theodore Roosevelt: The New Nationalism*. Englewood Cliffs, New Jersey: Prentice-Hall, 1961.

———, ed. *Woodrow Wilson: The New Freedom*. Englewood Cliffs: Prentice-Hall, 1961.

Lippmann, Walter. *Drift and Mastery*. Englewood Cliffs, New Jersey: Prentice-Hall, 1961. Originally published 1914.

Lloyd, Henry Demarest. *Wealth Against Commonwealth*. Edited by Thomas Cochran. Englewood Cliffs, New Jersey: Prentice-Hall, 1963. Originally published 1894.

Locke, John. *The Second Treatise of Government*. Edited with an Introduction by T. P. Peardon. New York: Bobbs-Merrill, 1952.

Lowi, Theodore. *The End of Liberalism*. New York: Norton and Co., 1969.

———. "How the Farmers Get What They Want." *The Reporter*, May 21, 1964.

Lukács, George. *History and Class Consciousness*. Translated by Rodney Livingstone. Cambridge, Massachusetts: MIT Press, 1971.

McConnell, Grant. *Private Power and American Democracy*. New York: Vintage Books, 1966.

McDermott, John. "Knowledge Is Power." *The Nation*, April 14, 1969.

McIlwain, Charles H. *Constitutionalism, Ancient and Modern*. Ithaca: Cornell University Press, 1943.

———. *The Growth of Political Thought in the West*. New York: Macmillan, 1932.

MacPherson, C. B. *The Political Theory of Possessive Individualism*. New York: Oxford University Press, 1962.

Madden, Edward. *Chauncey Wright and the Foundations of Pragmatism*. Seattle: University of Washington Press, 1963.

Marcuse, Herbert. *Reason and Revolution: Hegel and the Rise of Social Theory*. New York: Oxford University Press, 1941.

Marx, Karl. *The Marx-Engels Reader*. Edited by Robert Tucker. New York: W. W. Norton and Co., 1972.

———. *Capital*, I. Moscow: Foreign Languages Publishing House, n.d.

———. *Capital*, III. Moscow: Foreign Languages Publishing House, 1962.

Mason, Alpheus T. "Business Organized as Power: The New Imperium in Imperio." *American Political Science Review* XLIV, No. 2 (June 1950).

Mason, Edward S. *The Corporation in Modern Society*. Cambridge, Massachusetts: Harvard University Press, 1959.

———. "Corporation." *International Encyclopedia of the Social Sciences*. David L. Sills, ed. New York: Macmillan Co. and The Free Press, 1968.

Merkle, Judith. "The Taylor Strategy: Organizational Innovation and Class Structure." *Berkeley Journal of Sociology* XIII (1968).

Mills, C. Wright. *The Sociological Imagination*. New York: Oxford University Press, 1959.

———. *White Collar*. New York: Oxford University Press, 1951.

Mowry, George. *The California Progressives*. Chicago: Quadrangle Books, 1963.

Nadel, Mark. "The Hidden Dimensions of Public Policy: Private Governments and the Policy-Making Process." *Journal of Politics* XXXVII, No. 1 (February 1975).

Nadworny, Milton. *Scientific Management and the Unions, 1900–1932*. Cambridge, Massachusetts: Harvard University Press, 1955.

Neumann, Franz. *Behemoth: The Structure and Practice of National Socialism, 1933–1944*. New York: Harper Torchbooks, 1966. Originally published 1942.

———. "The Change in the Function of Law in Modern Society." *The Democratic and the Authoritarian State*. New York: The Free Press, 1957.

Nisbet, Robert. *The Quest for Community*. New York: Oxford University Press, 1953.

Noble, David F. *America by Design*. New York: Alfred A. Knopf, 1977.

Noble, David W. *The Paradox of Progressive Thought*. Minneapolis: University of Minnesota Press, 1958.

Norris, Frank. *The Octopus*. New York: Bantam Books, 1958. Originally published 1901.

O'Connor, James. *The Corporations and the State*. New York: Harper Colophon Books, 1974.

Offe, Claus. "The Abolition of Market Control and the Problem of Legitimacy." *Kapitalistate* No. 1 (1972) and No. 2 (1973). Federal Republic of Germany: Politladen Erlangen.

———. "The Theory of the Capitalist State and the Problem of Policy Formation." In Leon Lindberg *et al.*, *Stress and Contradiction in Modern Capitalism*. London: Lexington Books, 1975.

Olson, Mancur. *The Logic of Collective Action*. Cambridge, Massachusetts: Harvard University Press, 1965.

Panitch, Leo. "The Development of Corporatism in Liberal Democracies." *Comparative Political Studies* X, No. 1 (April 1977).

Parrington, Vernon L. *The Beginnings of Critical Realism*. New York: Harcourt, Brace and World, 1930.

Paul, Arnold. *Conservative Crisis and the Rule of Law, 1887–1895*. New York: Harper Torchbooks, 1960.

Peirce, Charles S. *Chance, Love and Logic: Philosophic Essays of C. S. Peirce*. Edited by Morris Cohen; afterword by John Dewey. London: Kegan, Paul, Trech, Trubner and Co., 1923.

———. *Values in a Universe of Chance: Selected Writings of C. S. Peirce*. Edited by Philip P. Wiener. New York: Doubleday Anchor Books, 1958.

Perry, Ralph Barton. *The Thought and Character of William James*. New York: Harper Torchbooks, 1964.

Petras, James. *Politics and Social Forces in Chilean Development*. Berkeley: University of California Press, 1969.

Plamenatz, John P. *Consent, Freedom and Political Obligation*. 2nd ed. New York: Oxford University Press, 1968.

Polanyi, Karl. *The Great Transformation.* Boston: Beacon Press, 1944.

———. "Primitive Feudalism and the Feudalism of Decay." In George Dalton, ed., *Economic Development and Social Change: The Modernization of Village Communities.* Garden City, New Jersey: Natural History Press, 1971.

Pollack, Norman. *The Populist Response to Industrial America.* New York: W. W. Norton and Co., 1962.

Pound, Roscoe. "Liberty of Contract." *Yale Law Journal* XVIII (1909).

Preston, Lee E. "Corporations and Society: The Search for a Paradigm." *Journal of Economic Literature* XIII, No. 2 (June 1975).

Radosh, Ronald. "The Corporate Ideology of American Labor Leaders from Gompers to Hillman." *Studies on the Left* VI (November 1966).

———. "Corporatism, Liberal and Fascist, as Seen by Samuel Gompers." *Studies on the Left* III (Summer 1963).

Raybeck, Joseph. *A History of American Labor.* New York: Free Press, 1959.

Reagan, Michael. *The Managed Economy.* New York: Oxford University Press, 1963.

Rehmus, Charles M., and Doris B. McLaughlin, eds. *Labor and American Politics.* Ann Arbor: University of Michigan Press, 1967.

Reich, Charles. "The New Property." *Yale Law Journal* LXXIII, No. 3 (April 1964).

Renner, Karl. *The Institutions of the Private Law and Their Social Function.* London: Routledge and Kegan Paul, 1929, revised edition. Originally published 1904.

Riga, Peter J. "Prudence and Jurisprudence: Authority as the Basis of Law According to Thomas Aquinas." *The Jurist, Studies in Church Law and Ministry* III–IV (1977).

Roche, John. "Civil Liberty in the Age of Enterprise." *University of Chicago Law Review* XXXI (1963).

———. "Entrepreneurial Liberty and the Commerce Power." *University of Chicago Law Review* XXX (1963).

———. "Entrepreneurial Liberty and the Fourteenth Amendment." *Labor History* IV (1963).

Rodell, Fred. "Justice Holmes and His Hecklers." *Yale Law Journal* LX (June 1961).

Rogat, Yosal. "The Judge as Spectator." *University of Chicago Law Review* XXXI (Winter 1964).

———. "Mr. Justice Holmes, A Dissenting Opinion." *Stanford Law Review* XV (December 1962).

Rogin, Michael. *The Intellectuals and McCarthy.* Cambridge, Massachusetts: The MIT Press, 1967.

———. "Non-Partisanship and the Group Interest." In *Power and Community: Dissenting Essays in Political Science,* Philip Green and Sanford Levinson, eds. New York: Vintage Books, 1969.

Ross, Edward A. *Sin and Society: An Analysis of Latter-Day Iniquity.* New York: Harper and Row, 1973. Originally published 1907.

Sabine, George. *A History of Political Theory.* 3rd ed. New York: Holt, Rinehart and Winston, 1961.

Saxton, Alexander. *The Indispensable Enemy: Labor and the Anti-Chinese Movement in California*. Berkeley: University of California Press, 1971.

Schaar, John. *Loyalty in America*. Berkeley: University of California Press, 1957.

———. "Legitimacy in the Modern State." In *Power and Community: Dissenting Essays in Political Science*, Philip Green and Sanford Levinson, eds. New York: Vintage Books, 1969.

Schattschneider, Elmer E. *Party Government*. New York: Rinehart and Co., 1942.

———. *The Semi-Sovereign People*. New York: Holt, Rinehart and Winston, 1960.

Schmitter, Philippe. "Modes of Interest Intermediation and Models of Societal Change in Western Europe." *Comparative Political Studies* X, No. 1 (April 1977).

Seligman, Ben. "The American Corporation: Ideology and Reality." *Dissent* (Summer 1964).

Seltzer, Alan. "Woodrow Wilson as 'Corporate-Liberal': Toward a Reconsideration of Left Revisionist Historiography." *The Western Political Quarterly* XXX, No. 2 (June 1977).

Sklar, Martin. "Woodrow Wilson and the Political Economy of Modern United States Liberalism." *Studies on the Left* I (1960).

Smith, Adam. *The Wealth of Nations*. Edited by J. C. Bullock. New York: P. F. Collier and Sons, 1909.

Spahr, Margaret, ed. *Readings in Recent Political Philosophy*. New York: Macmillan Co., 1935.

Steffens, Lincoln. *The Shame of the Cities*. New York: Sagamore Press, 1957. Originally published 1904.

Stewart, Richard B. "The Reformation of American Administrative Law." *Harvard Law Review* No. 8 (June 1975).

Sumner, William Graham. *What Social Classes Owe to Each Other*. New Haven: Yale University Press, 1925.

———. *Social Darwinism: Selected Essays of William Graham Sumner*. Edited by Stow Persons. Englewood Cliffs, New Jersey: Prentice-Hall, 1961.

Taft, Philip. *The AFL in the Time of Gompers*. New York: Harper and Brothers, 1957.

Taylor, Frederick Winslow. *The Principles of Scientific Management*. New York: W. W. Norton and Co., 1967. Originally published 1911.

———. *Scientific Management: Comprising Shop Management, The Principles of Scientific Management, and Testimony Before Special House Committee*. New York: Harper and Row, 1947.

TenBroek, Jacobus. *The Anti-Slavery Origins of the Fourteenth Amendment*. Berkeley: University of California Press, 1954.

Thompson, Carl D. "The Vital Points in Charter Making from a Socialist Point of View." *The National Municipal Review* II (1913).

Thompson, Edward P. *The Making of the English Working Class*. New York: Vintage Books, 1966.

Tocqueville, Alexis de. *Democracy in America*. Edited by Phillips Bradley. 2 vols. New York: Vintage Books, 1945.

Tussman, Joseph. *Obligation and the Body Politic*. New York: Oxford University Press, 1960.

Ulman, Lloyd. *The Rise of the National Union*. Cambridge, Massachusetts: Harvard University Press, 1966.

U.S. Selective Service. "Channeling." Reprinted in Jerome Skolnick and Elliott Currie, eds., *Crisis in American Institutions*. Boston: Little, Brown, 1970.

Weber, Max. "Bureaucracy." In *From Max Weber*, Hans Gerth and C. Wright Mills, eds. New York: Oxford University Press, 1946.

Weinstein, James. *The Corporate Ideal in the Liberal State*. Boston: Beacon Press, 1968.

Weyl, Walter. *The New Democracy*. New York: Harper Torchbooks, 1964. Originally published 1912.

White, Morton. *Social Thought in America: The Revolt Against Formalism*. Boston: Beacon Press, 1964. Originally published 1947.

———. *Science and Sentiment in America*. New York: Oxford University Press, 1972.

Wiebe, Robert. *Businessmen and Reform*. Cambridge, Massachusetts: Harvard University Press, 1962.

Wiener, Philip. *Evolution and the Founders of Pragmatism*. Cambridge, Massachusetts: Harvard University Press, 1949.

Williams, William A. *The Contours of American History*. Chicago: Quadrangle Books, 1961.

Wilson, Woodrow. *Congressional Government*. New York: Meridian Books, 1956.

———. *Constitutional Government in the United States*. New York: Columbia University Press, 1908.

———. *The State*. Boston: D. C. Heath and Co., 1898.

———. "Democracy and Efficiency." *The Atlantic Monthly* LXXXVII (March 1901).

———. "The Ideals of America." *The Atlantic Monthly* XC (December 1902).

———. "The Law and the Fact." *American Political Science Review* V, No. 1 (February 1911).

Wolfe, Alan. *The Limits of Legitimacy: Political Contradictions in Contemporary Capitalism*. New York: The Free Press, 1977.

Wolin, Sheldon. *Politics and Vision*. Boston: Little, Brown and Co., 1960.

Woodward, C. Vann. *Tom Watson: Agrarian Rebel*. New York: Oxford University Press, 1938.

Index

Designer: Rick Chafian
Compositor: G&S Typesetters, Inc.
Printer: Vail-Ballou Press
Binder: Vail-Ballou Press
Text: Linotron 202 Palatino
Display   Phototypositor Palatino Bold